Women Interrupting, Disrupting, and Revolutionizing Educational Policy and Practice

A volume in
Educational Leadership for Social Justice
Jeffrey S. Brooks, *Series Editor*

Women Interrupting, Disrupting, and Revolutionizing Educational Policy and Practice

edited by

Whitney Sherman Newcomb
Virginia Commonwealth University

Katherine Cumings Mansfield
Virginia Commonwealth University

INFORMATION AGE PUBLISHING, INC.
Charlotte, NC • www.infoagepub.com

Library of Congress Cataloging-in-Publication Data

A CIP record for this book is available from the Library of Congress
http://www.loc.gov

ISBN: 978-1-62396-703-1 (Paperback)
978-1-62396-704-8 (Hardcover)
978-1-62396-705-5 (ebook)

CONTENTS

PART I

LOOKING BACK TO UNDERSTAND THE PRESENT

PART II

UNDERSTANDING AND STRENGTHENING STUDENTS' LIVED EXPERIENCES

PART III

UNDERSTANDING AND STRENGTHENING LEADERS' LIVED EXPERIENCES

PART IV

PRESSING FORWARD TO CHANGE THE FUTURE

INTRODUCTION

WHERE HAVE WE BEEN? WHERE ARE WE GOING?

Charol Shakeshaft

ABSTRACT

This chapter explores the roots of the current feminist focus on women's leadership, examining the themes that have been recurrent during the past 40 years. By probing the intent of researchers and the relationship of research to advocacy and equity, the chapter provides a foundation for the chapters that follow. Because some questions continue to beg an answer, much of the research in the field seems to be covering old ground. However, it is from of that ground that new research has struggled to be recognized, in much the same way as earlier work that often had to overcome publication bias. Current research expands the understanding and definition of women's leadership and provides a link between disruption and progress.

In 1970, when I was 21, I learned a word that explained everything that, up to that time, I had no language to describe. That word—feminism—has shaped my life in the 43 years since. Even without a label, I had struggled with trying to understand why my life as a girl, and then a woman, was so different from my brother's life as a boy, and then a man. The results of one of my first negotiations, way back in kindergarten when I kicked Steven Hutchings for looking up my dress at naptime, was the first of many failed

Women Interrupting, Disrupting, and Revolutionizing Educational Policy and Practice, pages ix–xxi
Copyright © 2014 by Information Age Publishing

protests. Our teacher, Ms. Wells, was not enlightened by my explanation that it was not fair that girls had to wear dresses and boys did not or that I thought it was fair for me to kick Steven since he was invading my space. I was punished, he was not. I transgressed, he did not. And the pattern continued. Girls could not be crossing guards. My petition did not help. Girls could not run in the school track meet. My winning race prior to the track meet against the fastest boy in school did not change anyone's mind. Girls could not wear pants, even in the coldest Iowa winters, walking to school in blizzard conditions. And those cancans—they really scratched my frozen skin. Girls couldn't take shop classes. Girls couldn't, couldn't, couldn't.

Discovering the feminist movement gave me a language. Having a language helped me think and act differently. Betty Friedan was born the same year as my mother and both had an ambivalent relationship with expected feminine behavior. The difference between them was that Friedan graduated from Smith and did graduate work with Erik Erickson at Berkeley. My mother didn't finish high school and lived in rural Iowa. Friedan had an education that helped her negotiate her life. My mother had a husband and five children and no access to these ideas. Her isolation was academic, geographic, and social. And yet, she struggled to make sense of her life as a woman.

Fifty years after the *Feminine Mystique* (Friedan, 1964) was published, we have a name for "the problem that has no name." But new problems that need new names keep popping up. This volume addresses many of these equity and development issues within the context of educational policy and practice, moving beyond narrow concepts of women's leadership and influence by broadening our understanding of the pressure points that open our female chakras.

Research on U.S. women administrators in schools began to percolate again[1] in the mid to late 1970s. These studies documented the proportion of administrative jobs held by women and the reasons why those proportions were so out of alignment with the 70 to 80 percent representation of women in teaching. This was practical, useful, and activist research, which might have played some role in the dismissal of its importance. The resistance was contradictory: research on women isn't important because women aren't important and research on women's access to administrative positions is dangerous because it might result in more women in positions of power.

Studies of women's competence soon appeared, comparing female processes, values, and outcomes with those of males in similar positions. That those studies tended to show either no differences or that women outperformed men surprised many of the gatekeepers, most of whom were not women. Interestingly, quantitative studies tended to report no difference between females and males while qualitative studies found differences.

While the findings might be an outgrowth of the methods, they might also represent the types of quantitative measures that were used for comparisons. All of them had been developed by watching or interviewing males and then developing a survey that would "measure" how closely or how well female respondents conformed to this male definition of a leader. What those studies told us was that "anything you can do I can do better" (or at least as well).

Inquiries turned to documenting the ways in which women carry out leadership in schools. This focus gained popularity at about the same time as qualitative researchers were pushing for a new paradigm in educational research methods and the two were well partnered. The qualitative studies examined how and why women behaved and uncovered all types of leadership behavior that had been left out of the male defined surveys.

This trajectory, more or less, describes research from the U.S., Canada, Great Britain, New Zealand, Australia, Hong Kong, and Japan. Research reports from the biennial conference of Women Leading in Education (2013) confirm that, globally, researchers tend to be somewhere on this inquiry developmental path. One large difference is that in most westernized countries, where universal schooling is the law, there is little research related to PreK–12 school attendance by girls. In countries where universal schooling is not required, there is a much greater emphasis on understanding who goes to school and how to increase the number of females who successfully navigate the primary and secondary education systems.

Clearly, this research pattern is not a straight line. In some ways, it resembles the cloverleaves of an interstate highway, with all of the exits and return ramps. An example of this moving forward toward more understanding and circling back to update old notions sometimes feels repetitious and unnecessary. If we know the barriers to women's participation, why examine this question again? If we know that women are underrepresented, why start all over? We do so because having documented the issues once doesn't mean they have gone away. They may have changed form, but almost all barriers that were identified in the 1970s still exist in some configuration.

Researchers examined proportional representation in the 1970s, 80s, 90s, and into the present. What else is new and what do we still need to know? Using representation as an example, I would argue that this inquiry teaches us more than just gains or losses.

One issue that has plagued accurate scorekeeping on the number of women in administrative positions is the lack of reliable and current data. This has not changed in the past 50 years of the study of women's representation in formal school leadership. Historically, one goal of activist research and practice is simply an increase in the number of women in key positions. And yet, if we have no way of documenting numbers, how do we know the outcomes? And if we don't know the outcomes of our work, how do we know what to change? Or, more fundamentally, what works?

Risha Berry, a doctoral student, and I have been trying to determine the most recent proportion of women, and particularly women of color, in the principalship in the United States. The relevant data sets are several years out of date and it is nearly impossible to disaggregate so that race and gender are isolated. This failure isn't surprising; I have been commenting on it every year since 1979. What is surprising to me is that there seems to have been no headway made to secure comprehensive and reliable numbers. The U.S. Department of Education's latest School and Staffing (2011–2012)[2] survey was posted in August 2013 with several tables provided. The number of principals is disaggregated by gender or by race/ethnicity, but not both. In order to be able to disaggregate, a researcher has to be approved for restricted use access, which requires a separate computer used only for analysis. Knowing how far we've come is necessary in the struggle to bring women into school leadership as well as into the academy. It shouldn't be so hard to learn the proportion of Black women high school principals.

In Chapter 1, Margaret Grogan challenges readers to move beyond the theory comfort zone and explore gender perceptions within organizational life. Grogan explores the implications of gendering practices and practicing genders within education workplaces. The former refers to the individual socialized behaviors that were learned from childhood onward, while the latter are the "micro-interactional moments that constitute the gender order." Grogan continues to argue, as do Harding et al. (2013), that three feminist theories may bring further understanding of gendered relations in organizations. Those three lenses—intersectionality, the politics of recognition, and feminist readings of Greek myths and tragedies—will encourage new perspectives for studying educational leadership.

Grogan reminds us that studies of leadership often fail to explain the variance of gender, race, and class. She also reminds us that gender is not just about females. Finally, Grogan challenges us to "expose the harmful effects of the dominant values driving education practice and policy."

Mary Hermann and Miriam David explore, among other things, the question of progress for women in academia and leadership. Hermann reviews the model of male success and its implications and usefulness for women. Her analysis of the "extreme-work model" is useful in analyzing motivation for leadership. Sandberg's (2013) answer to what she sees as stagnation in the momentum to bring more women into leadership positions is for women to be more insistent in the workplace and not let barriers get in the way—or, in Sandberg's words, to lean in to seize more authority in their career lives.

To some degree, this advice ignores what motivates women. The rewards of leaning in, as they are now defined, are more likely to connect to the motivators for males, rather than females. Authority at work is usually associated with more benefits and higher earnings, leading to the hypothesis that more authority might also be related to less stress, particularly because of the autonomy that comes from authority. Studies indicate two differences between women and men who have the same amount of authority in an organization (Schieman, Schafer, & McIvor, 2013). The first is that having authority does not result in the same satisfaction for women as it does for men. Men feel satisfied by authority, job resources, or both. Women feel motivated by a combination of job resources and job authority.

These results suggest that when women "lean in," they may not experience the rewards of authority in the same way as men. As a result, there may not be enough satisfaction or intrinsic reward for women to justify sacrifice of family and friends.

David, in her exploration of feminism in the academy, interviewed women whose experiences have been much like mine, and they report that "My whole adult life is lived as a feminist and it has shaped everything I have studied and written" or "My entire life has been shaped by feminism." The narratives reflected the experiences from three waves of feminist academics: those born before 1950, those born from 1950 to 1965, and those born in the late 1960s and 1970s. Interestingly, many experiences run throughout all three groups of women. For me, an interesting observation by David is that her group—despite traditional socioeconomic status—was mostly first in the family to attend university. This is very different for men, where family university attendance is highly related to family income and prestige with the first in the family more likely coming from working class or minority ethnic backgrounds. This has implications for the way we use socioeconomic status in studies of academics.

Four chapters examine leadership from the perspective of students: Mansfield, Welton, Brock & Perry, Gasman, and Bryant each approach the disruption of educational policy through studies of student leadership practices. Traditionally, the voices of students have been absent in discussions of revolutionizing educational policy and practice. In her study of an all-girls' 6–12 school, Katherine Mansfield explores the concept of safe space as girl-only space. There has been considerable research that supports the benefits of same-sex schools for girls. The literature on same-sex schools for boys is more mixed. For privileged boys or majority race boys, the effects tend to be negative. For boys from racial/ethnic groups that have been oppressed, the research tends toward a positive experience. For both females and males from racially oppressed groups, these arrangements are safe because they prevent the entrance of either males of all races or white males and all females. While the literature on single-sex schools supports the quotation from one parent in Mansfield's chapter—"This is more than a school. They're preparing you for life"—it begs the question of what it would take to provide safe spaces in a school that is not segregated by race or gender. The attributes that Mansfield identifies are all behaviors and pedagogies that could be done in mixed classrooms—but they aren't. Thus the choice to move out, not change within.

Anjalé Welton, Brooke Brock, and Mercedes Perry provide a critical analysis of participation in V.O.I.C.E.S., Verbally Outspoken Individuals Creating Empowering Sistahs. Brock and Perry were high school students in the program, and Welton served as facilitator. These experiences are examined through a variety of lenses that are seldom used in traditional leadership research: youth activism, Black feminist thought, and hip-hop feminism. The authors celebrate a core of their history that is not emphasized in most schools:

> The only storylines from our history that we were exposed to in our K–12 schooling were that of enslavement, segregation, and Dr. Martin Luther King.... Black women beyond Rosa Parks getting on the bus were portrayed as tertiary, not necessarily instrumental to pivotal moments in our history. Now that we are greater architects of our own knowledge and have found epistemologies that better align with our experiences as young Black women, we have come to realize that activism is very much a part of our history and is an innate component of our moral core.

Their hip-hop feminist analysis includes activism and represents the "everyday identify politics that we as young, Black women faced resisted, and acted upon in high school settings." The members of V.O.I.C.E.S. clearly demonstrated that activism can occur anywhere and pushed adults to accept young, Black women as authentic leaders.

What is the place of historically Black colleges and universities (HBCUs) in what many have termed as a post-Civil Rights era? Marybeth Gasman leads the reader through the history of female students in HBCUs , describing the sexism and racism by White missionaries, the hidden role in the 1960s campus and civil rights protests, and a discussion of how women in HBCUs encounter their education and place in the world. Gasman points out that of female Black graduates, 20% of whom attended an HBCU, the HBCU graduates account for a disproportionate number of degrees in STEM areas: "38% in the biological sciences, 41% in chemistry, 40% in computer sciences, 40% in math and 40% in physics." This is a powerful example of an activist feminist agenda—conscious or not—within HBCUs. And, like Mansfield's work, it begs the question: Why doesn't this happen in mixed-race universities?

Cathy Brant reminds us that "simply taking a gender-neutral or sexuality-blind stance not only perpetuates the status quo, but also weakens education reform efforts that claim to strengthen student outcomes." This is particularly relevant in schools, where 75% of teachers are females. In studies of preservice teachers, half condemn homosexuality, and female teachers have been found to have more negative attitudes than male teachers. While these studies are somewhat dated, teacher attitudes about addressing gay and lesbian issues in schools continue to be problematic.

Four chapters examine the experiences of female administrators. Noelle Witherspoon examines the way in which a Black female principal turns labels constructed for her around. The labels of "nice" and "bitch" are used within organizations as a form of gender entrapment. The principal in this study addresses appearances head on, taking pride in her beauty and sexuality. She rejects advice to tone down her beauty and femininity. Rather, she used them to her advantage. Witherspoon reminds us of the tyranny of niceness in conceptions of women's leadership and provides a discourse on how we might expand acceptable professional identities of women leaders.

Cosette Grant addresses the difficulty of transforming turn-around schools, particularly the experiences of African American female principals. Studies indicate that African American principals are more likely to be placed in schools with the most challenges, rather than in high-income and/or high-achieving schools. Grant explores the role of mentoring in helping African American women principals negotiate the complexities of high need urban schools. The women she studied benefitted from mentoring, particularly mentoring that focused on student achievement.

In her research, Kerry Robinson seeks to understand the lived experiences of women superintendents. While she initially began a study of why women leave the superintendency, she also learned about why they chose the position to begin with. Robinson's work reaffirmed the research that women educators choose the work because they want to make a difference. They enter the profession as change-makers, even if they have little understanding of how this occurs. As the women superintendents in her study worked their way up the ladder, they most often took jobs because they saw them as opportunities to increase student learning, particularly for those students who had not been well served by the educational system. Many didn't aspire to be superintendents but entered the position because of their beliefs that the position offered a chance to change what happened in the classroom. Unfortunately, many were disappointed in the limitation of the superintendency in areas of curriculum reform. These women were frustrated by the belief of school boards that curriculum and instruction was not the purview of superintendents. Instead, superintendents were supposed to be about "bigger" things. The traditional male model of what a superintendent does was problematic for many of the women superintendents and, at times, put them in conflict with their boards. This conflict took a heavier toll on these women than has been reported for men in areas of health, family, and economics.

The stories the women superintendents told were often stories of micro-aggression, small annoyances where the whole is much bigger than its parts. They reminded me of the studies that compared Black and White women professionals with similar family, educational, and career backgrounds. Black women experienced more microaggressions than did White women, and their higher stress and poorer health reflect these differences.

Whitney Newcomb challenges us to think about leadership of women through mentoring. She focuses on the relationships between junior and senior professors in university academic departments. She describes an amazing two-year collaboration of five tenured and untenured faculty members and a doctoral student from four institutions in two states. These women ranged from 30 to 70 years old and were either White or Latina/o. These women came together at research meetings and at times outside of professional commitments to share research, to work on their writing, and to plan and carry out publications and presentations. As a colleague in the same department, I know that Whitney, a member of this collaborative, is known not only for her research on mentoring, but also for her outreach to and support of women, helping them make connections and inviting them to collaborate on work that both helps them build their curriculum vitas and offers mentoring experiences. The collaborative described in this chapter is unusual because it consists mostly of junior members who work together to help everyone move forward. It's an important model to consider, particularly for women who reside in institutions where there is no mentor available.

The collaborative network developed by these women offers an alternative to traditional mentoring relationships that often require the mentee to become like the mentor. Those relationships, while powerful, can also be limiting, and studies indicate that they come with their own issues.

It is instructive that many of the obstacles that these women faced in their academic departments are similar to the ones those in my generation faced more than 30 years ago, a finding that is both distressing and unacceptable. When I was a doctoral student, there were no female professors and only two or three women doctoral students. While the male students would spend time in the offices of the professors, talking about research and who knows what else, the women were required to stand in the hall when we had an appointment with a professor, a practice that reduced the interactions between professors and students. I had no mentoring from my professors or from colleagues in my department. My research on women was discounted as irrelevant for many years. While none of the women in Newcomb's study had to stand in the hall, many of them experienced the isolation of not being valued by department members and/or professors in their doctoral programs. Thirty plus years has seen many improvements in the lives of women academics, but the women in Newcomb's collaborative remind us that we aren't there yet.

Newcomb's study also reminds us that we still need to understand more about how women can mentor other women. In her collaborative, many of the members were relatively equal in stature. As a senior woman, I am reminded that what worked for me might not work for these women. What I haven't understood, but am beginning to, is how often my behaviors telegraph messages that I don't wish to send to junior women in the academy. While they do need to make a comfortable space for themselves, I want them to be able to say "No" to unacceptable expectations without harming their reputations. That's a very complicated transaction to pull off successfully. For the most part, I did not do that. Instead, I did the things I didn't want to do rather than the things I did want to do and ended up with the unreasonable workload that Newcomb's collaborative addresses.

Christa Boske provides additional insights into the continuing need for safe space that Mansfield described in her chapter. Boske has turned her attention to preparing women to lead for social justices through the senses. The stories of the marginalization of women's experiences in organizations often focus on the practice of identifying women's truth as emotional and, therefore, irrelevant. Women are all too often commanded to "stick to the facts" as if facts have no emotional context or foundation or as if emotions are not facts. When women disagree, they are often marginalized by describing the disagreement as a "cat fight" or as something personal between the women, instead of accurately acknowledging that there is a disagreement about substance.

Because leaders are often constructed as rational and without emotions, those who are identified as emotional are, by definition, not leaders. While it is true that we often turn to women to build community and tend to the needs of those in the organization, we do not identify these services as leadership. Having lived long in this profession, I have many stories in which I have been marginalized because of my emotions. At one point in my department chair tenure, we had a particularly difficult and challenging meeting, one that caused me, and others, to cry. After the meeting, an old hand and former White male superintendent stopped me in the hallway. He put his hands against the wall, one on each side of me so that I couldn't get away without physical pushback and said, "Let me give you some advice. Never cry. Leaders don't cry. When I'm upset, I turn to my friend Johnny. Johnny Walker." And then he walked off, leaving me with all sorts of emotions—anger, frustration, scorn, and sadness for a man who had to drink instead of feel. It also made me think about the usefulness of tears as a way to cleanse the body of toxins and to further reflect that when women cry in organizational contexts, they are often experiencing anger, not sadness. Male anger, although not encouraged, is not seen as unleader-like. When a man becomes angry and yells, rarely would he be told that "Leaders don't yell." And yet, when a woman cries, her emotions are trivialized. Moreover, if she were to exhibit anger in a traditional male format, she would be equally at risk for negative descriptions.

My recent experience in building community among department members was not identified as leadership, but rather something that took us away from our real work at the university. Departments don't need to be communities, I'm told. Rather, they should be organizations for individuals to pursue their work, which does not include community building. Again, the message is that real leadership is rational and product driven, not the fuzzy stuff of emotions or process.

Many of us who have been socialized in these "rational" institutions suffer from something like the Stockholm syndrome. We begin to accept the institutional definition of what counts as leadership, what counts as "real work." We lose our capacity to connect to our emotions. For us to reconnect, Boske argues, we need approaches that disrupt our paradigms and expectations. Her chapter examines how artmaking can be used to prepare women "to lead for social justice through the senses—ways in which school leaders perceive their lived experiences and relation to others."

Boske explains that "women are traditionally prepared to understand their roles as managers of systems rather than deepening their empathic responses and connections with school communities." Artmaking can lead to the release of creativity and understanding that other forms of reflective practice might miss. The women in Boske's study report that their experiences in artmaking allowed them to get in touch with what they feel and then to connect what they feel with what they think, a process that often led to the realization that what the women really believed was something different after the experience of artmaking than it was before. Boske reports:

> The reflective process invited the cultivation of an internal dialectic. It became a call to examine personal responses to interactions, scholarly readings, colleagues, and community at large. Their sensibility exhibited their new sense of self as a vital position to understanding and realizing the need to be firm, unyielding, and strong. The examination of their histories and origin of life, they formulated new understandings of self, which led to discovering the nature of intellectual development and the need to actively engage in imaginative possibilities. The reflective process utilized audio/video tools, which encouraged them to venture toward uncharted territory in an effort to better understand the impact of their lived experiences.

Katherine Mansfield, Anjalé Welton, and Margaret Grogan argue that policy and organizational studies have too long been embedded within research methods that claim neutrality, thus positioning studies that are cultural and race responsive outside the bounds of science. They offer alternative ways of framing policy problems from a feminist perspective, noting that a critical perspective is more likely to result in methodologies and questions that "disrupt the status quo and revolutionize the field."

In another chapter, Rachel McNae asks the reader to think about ways in which organizations can help young women develop as global citizens and to provide spaces where women are active contributors to change. While giving voice to female students is an approach that might bring them into these spaces, McNae argues that such an approach has the potential to essentialize young women's voices. She reminds the reader that adults and students must continue to ask such questions such as: Whose voices are heard? Who listens to what voices? What voices are ignored? What happens when young women say things that we don't want to hear? and What action comes from such dialogue?

There is relatively little research on ways to create student–adult partnerships in making organizational decisions in schools. McNae describes such a partnership, named Revolution by the students, and the complexities that arise if it is to be authentic. All too often, leadership programs for youth are developed and then youth are invited to participate in what has been decided by adults as appropriate. In this case, the program was co-constructed by McNae and the young women who elected to participate. Unlike many "ready-made" programs, this one resulted in the young women feeling rewarded and valued in the process of co-constructing the program. However, co-construction is complex and difficult, which is only one of the reasons why most adults don't attempt it. Very few writers have accurately documented the process of co-construction, instead leaving the impression of linearity and camaraderie. McNae is not one of those researchers. She helps us understand the process, not only for her but also for students who, as much as they might want co-construction, have been socialized into a traditional teacher–student paradigm. The majority of students in any PreK–12 classroom, whether in New Zealand or the United States, are not prepared to take ownership and leadership of their own learning. We often fail to understand that scaffolding is necessary to move from one paradigm to another.

McNae writes about the delicate balance of student voice, particularly when some voices are louder than others and some voices aren't easily heard. Moreover, McNae concludes that "I learned that simply having a voice might not be enough to create change. When those sharing voices are not in a position to make decisions, it is difficult for change to happen."

Co-creation takes considerable teacher time and student commitment. While we voice democratic processes in schools, the reality is that these types of initiatives often take too much time and their value is questioned. We talk about the importance of content, as if democratic process is not content. This observation holds true in universities as well as PreK–12 schools.

I'm always dismayed when I hear a chairperson or a dean assure the faculty that the faculty won't be troubled with meetings or decision-making that takes them away from their "real" work of teaching and research. I'm even more dismayed when colleagues accept this division of power that does not count creating and sustaining a democratic organization as the work of academics, even academics whose research is social justice. McNae's conclusion that "there is an obligation for school leaders and students to critique the traditional leadership structures of our schools...and to model democratic practices within these structures" is equally important for academic departments.

In closing, Autumn Cyprès tackles the nexus of politics and identity called "fit" and the relationship to leadership, career politics, and change. One of my first battles with fit came in a superintendent's search in the high-income White district in which I lived and my daughter went to school. One of the candidates that I nominated was an outstanding Black male. The search committee chair thanked me for my suggestion, but noted that my candidate wouldn't "fit" in our district. Although I knew what he meant, I pushed him, asking why? I pointed out that, with a PhD, he was of the same educational and professional background of the community. I also shared that his class background was probably somewhat higher than many in our community, since he had been born into a prestigious and upper-class family. The search consultant nodded but repeated that he just wouldn't fit in and that the community would never accept him. I asked the consultant how he knew that, to which he replied, "I just know." Case closed. Fit is not just about how we see our own identity, but how that identity is framed by others.

Cyprès illustrates how the convergence of identity, hegemony, and social construction plays out in the politics of an organization as well as the effects on individual leadership. If fit were a perfect construct, then fit within an organization or group would not result in disruption, unless, of course, the nature of the group is to disrupt. As academic players, we often portray ourselves as disruptors who ask questions, shoot down theories, and offer new paradigms of discourse. And yet, it has been my experience that academic workplaces are often very traditional when it comes to who fits and who doesn't. Autumn provides examples of this incongruity and the tipping points that move organizational members forward.

This book reminds us that much has changed for women and girls but that we still have not achieved equality. The authors of the chapters in this volume explore ways in which women and girls disrupt organizations to move toward equality while exploring just how difficult disruption is. Leadership is always a form of disruption and is always risky. Flowing through all of these chapters is a continuous message: disruption is dangerous, disruption is necessary, and disruption is the only way forward.

NOTES

1. There were quite a few articles written about women teachers and principals between 1900 and 1930.
2 The survey is administered every four years. The last survey provided data from 2007–2008.

REFERENCES

Friedan, B. (1964). *The feminine mystique.* New York, NY: Dell.

Harding, N., Ford, J., & Fotaki, M. (2013). Is the 'F'-word still dirty? A past, present and future of/for feminist and gender studies in Organization. *Organization, 20*(1), 51–65.

Sandberg, S. (2013) *Lean in: Women, work, and the will to lead.* New York, NY: Knopf

Schieman, S., Schafer, M., & McIvor, M. (2013). The rewards of authority in the workplace: Do gender and age matter? *Sociological Perspectives, 56*(1), 75–96.

PROLOGUE

APPLYING TORQUE TO THE FLYWHEEL

Whitney Sherman Newcomb and Katherine Cumings Mansfield

The idea for this book was born from discussions at several recent academic events including the Women Leading Education (WLE) International Conference in Volos, Greece (2012) and the University Council for Educational Administration (UCEA) Conference in Pittsburgh, Pennsylvania (2011) as well as from informal dialogue amongst ourselves and various colleagues, both new and veteran to the field of educational leadership and, in particular, dedicated to the study of women in leadership. At both the WLE conference and the UCEA conference, we heard frustration from veteran women in the field that the study of women in leadership is stagnant and has not moved forward in several years; with scholars new to the field continuing to write and publish work about barriers to aspiring and practicing women leaders (the same types of reports that began the "formal" inquiry into women's lives as leaders back in the 1980s) without being able to push forward with "new" information or ideas for change. In essence, the concerns and questions that were posed from some veteran women were: Why are we continuing to report the same things that we reported 30 years ago? Why are we still talking about barriers to women in leadership? and Why haven't we moved past gender binaries in regard to leadership ideas and practice?

Women Interrupting, Disrupting, and Revolutionizing Educational Policy and Practice, pages xxiii–xxv
Copyright © 2014 by Information Age Publishing

Considering these questions, some women new to the field countered with their own set of responses and questions that included: Is it not significant to report that some women are still experiencing the same types of barriers in leadership that were highlighted 30 years ago? Is it accurate to report that all women's voices have now been heard/represented? and How can we report something different if it hasn't happened?

Furthermore, some pointed out that while 30 years ago, the field was opened up to women, the reality was that most of these women were of White, European descent and mostly straight in sexual orientation. And, the advent of critical theory in education has helped scholars articulate that girls and women come to the educational setting with other identity intersectionalities such as race/ethnicity, social class, religious affiliation (or not), nationality, language, and other social complexities. So, on the one hand, some things had changed and some women were ready to move on. On the other hand, other women were taken aback by the readiness of some to declare that we needed to move on to bigger and better things in terms of research studies (content and methodologies). The contrary voices insisted that some women (even White, straight women) still encountered difficulties in K–12 and higher education, and that we, as a field, had only begun to tease out this whole notion of identity intersectionalities and what that meant for what our research questions should be, who we should study, how we should study them, what we should report on, and how we should move forward if, indeed, it was actually time to do so.

As faculty who encourage our leadership students to utilize metaphors in their personal sense-making, we, too, envisioned a metaphor developing as we witnessed the above conversation occur both literally (in person) and figuratively (as we left the conversation and grappled with our own internal meaning-making of the conversation). A flywheel is a rotating mechanical device that stores rotational energy. While a flywheel has continuing energy, it naturally resists changes in rotational speed. However, applying torque (or a twist of force) to it can increase the rotational speed by using its stored energy. What veteran women have managed to do for the field of educational leadership is to create a flywheel of the study of women. They demanded and created a space for the study of women and have provided continuous energy to a topic that was traditionally underserved and without energy. Veteran women created continuous energy for an energy source that was nonexistent or, at best, discontinuous. However, a flywheel can be used to create pulses of energy that exceed the abilities of the original energy source. In other words, stored energy can be released at a much higher rate. We think this is what veteran women are calling for—pulses of energy from women new to the field that advance the study of women in new directions. So, the question becomes, How do we apply torque to the study of women in educational leadership while also honoring the fact that, in some instances, change has not occurred? Or, How do we best reveal stagnation while also moving forward?

The discussions that have ensued between veteran women and those new to the field inspired us to develop a book that situates women in leadership exactly where we are today (and reports the status of girls who are positioned to continue the "good fight" that began many years ago) and that both highlights the changes that have occurred and reports any stagnancy that continues to threaten women's positionality in educational leadership literature, practice, and policy. It forefronts the voices of women educational scholars who have been (and are) interrupting, disrupting, and revolutionizing educational policy and practice. Our book reports women's leadership activities and knowledge in both the K–12 and university settings and concludes with chapters ripe with ideas for pushing for change through policy, advocacy, and activism. The final chapter presents themes that emerged from the individual chapters and sets forth an agenda to torque the flywheel and move forward with the study of women in leadership.

ACKNOWLEDGMENTS

We have been friends and colleagues for several years, but this was our first collaborative book venture. It was both challenging and inspiring as we faced working with multiple authors, varying schedules, and competing demands. As with all enterprises of this nature, contributions to the fulfillment of this book extend both to the individual authors and to those who have provided significant support to the writers and to the project itself. First, we would like to extend our sincere gratitude to the women authors who contributed chapters to this book. Their insight and contributions to the field of educational leadership, policy, and practice are meaningful and will inevitably torque the flywheel forward. Second, we would like to acknowledge the study participants highlighted in various chapters who were willing to share their time, experiences, and voices to contribute to the growing depository of knowledge on how women are interrupting, disrupting, and revolutionizing education and leadership. Third, we would like to thank the Information Age team and the *Educational Leadership for Social Justice* series for giving us the space to leave literary footprints in the field. Finally, we would like to thank our families for their support and love.

Whitney would like to thank: her parents (Pam and Jeff Sherman), who inspired in her independence, strength, compassion, and the will to achieve (special thanks to Jeff Sherman for some of the photos used in the cover of the book); her brother (Micah Sherman), who reminds her to live every day with courage, intention, and happiness; and her husband (Jason Newcomb), who encourages her to dance to the beat of a different drum and that it's never too late to achieve a dream.

Women Interrupting, Disrupting, and Revolutionizing Educational Policy and Practice, pages xxvii–xxviii
Copyright © 2014 by Information Age Publishing

Katherine would like to thank: her late mother (Diane Barry) for the memories of Chopin, Johnny Cash, and Johnny Mathis on the phonograph and trips to the library every Saturday; her father (Jon Cumings) for modeling a strong work ethic and creative spirit; her husband (David Mansfield) for being her champion and the love of her life for almost three decades; her son (Ian Mansfield) and her daughter (Kate Mansfield) for their patience and the gut-busting laughter.

PART I

LOOKING BACK TO UNDERSTAND THE PRESENT

CHAPTER 1

RE(CONSIDERING) GENDER SCHOLARSHIP IN EDUCATIONAL LEADERSHIP

Margaret Grogan

ABSTRACT

Gender, gender roles, and gender identity, as well as femininities and masculinities, have continued to be studied and theorized in sociology, philosophy, psychology, and other disciplines. But in education research, particularly in the educational leadership discourse, the nexus between gender and leadership appears to be less interesting than it was previously—not surprisingly, since the prevailing attitudes among many women and men is that gender is irrelevant. How might a gender frame help us to understand leadership inequality better and, more to the point, how might gender theories allow us to transform education? This chapter argues for the reinvigorated use of robust feminist theories and gender theories that shed light on current constructions of gender in education and the intersectionalities of gender, race, class, ethnicities, religion, sexuality, and so on within educational leadership. In addition to furthering our knowledge of how women are positioned in the educational leadership discourse, a better grasp of gender allows us to contemplate how men are being shaped by various masculinities as well.

INTRODUCTION

As we settle into the 21st century and take stock of where women have made inroads into the leadership arena, we begin to understand more about how leadership has been (and is) gendered. Despite an increase in women demonstrating leadership in public roles such as running for political office, taking on high-profile public positions, serving as CEO of Fortune 500 companies, and leading universities and school districts, attention is always given to the fact that they are women (see Australian Prime Minister Julia Gillard's speech on misogyny, 2012). And they are often criticized for using stereotypically female leadership approaches (see the press about President of UVA, Teresa Sullivan, who was initially charged with spending too much time getting consensus and building faculty support for her ideas, Stripling, 2012.) One mustn't forget the amount of press Hilary Clinton got when she cried on the campaign trail.

Women are still underrepresented in educational leadership in the United States. The most encouraging figures available for the superintendency suggest that women hold about 24 percent of the top jobs (Kowalski, McCord, Petersen, Young, & Ellerson, 2011). According to the 2007/8 Schools and Staffing Survey, women hold slightly more elementary principalships than men (58.9%), but less than a third of secondary principalships (28.5%). The same survey reveals that nearly 85% of elementary teachers are women and women account for close to 80% of all teachers in this country. Therefore, women should be far better represented in leadership positions at all levels. Even at the elementary level, the fact is that men, who comprise 15% of the elementary teaching positions, hold over 40% of the administrative jobs. This persistent discrepancy cannot be explained away as unrelated to gender. As Marshall and Wynn (2012) observe, "That women continue to be underrepresented, undervalued, and underutilized as leaders gets little attention" (p. 884).

There is a body of scholarship on educational leadership informed by feminist theories or attention to gender constructs. The majority of this work is more than a decade old (for example, see Addi-Raccah, 2006; Bell & Chase, 1995, 1996; Blackmore, 1999; Blackmore & Sachs, 2007; Blount, 1995, 1998; Brunner, 2000, 2005; Brunner & Schumaker, 1998; Chase, 1995; Christman & McClellan, 2008; Coleman, 2002; Court, 2005; Dillard 2003; Eagly, Karau, & Johnson, 1992; Gardiner, Enomoto, & Grogan, 2000; Grogan, 1996, 1999a, 1999b, 2000, 2002; Hertz-Lazarowitz & Oplatka, 2006; Jones, 1990; Lugg, 2003; Mahitivanichcha & Rorrer, 2006; Marshall, 1985; Mendez-Morse, 2003; Ortiz & Ortiz, 1995; Rusch, 2004; Rusch & Marshall, 2006; Scott, 2003; Shakeshaft, 1990; Sherman, 2005; Sherman & Beaty, 2010; Skrla, 1999, 2000; Skrla, Reyes, & Scheurich, 2000; Smulyan, 2000; Strachan, 1999, 2000; Tallerico, 2000; Tallerico & Blount, 2004; Young & Skrla, 2003a & 2003b). However, some of these studies use gender as a variable and not as an analytical framework. And there has been even less discussion of gender and leadership of late—particularly from a theoretical perspective. A recent exception is Arar, Shapira, Azaiza, and Hertz-Lazarowitz' (2013) research on Arab women in Israel. Interestingly, Harding, Ford, and Fotaki (2013), writing about research and theory in the world of management and organization, share similar beliefs.

Some of the markers used to distinguish the genders in the past have changed. For instance, early sociological studies of gender concentrated on male and female roles in the so-called "separate spheres" of home and outside the home. "Widely accepted by the late nineteenth century in the United States, this doctrine stated that males and females should dominate in different kinds of social activities because of purportedly essential differences in the biological and psychological natures of men and women" (Kramer, 1991, p. 15). The 20th century saw remarkable changes in this belief. Writing of the Women's Liberation Movement in the 1960s, Collins (2009) documents the steady rise in the percentage of married women working outside the home. Now, with the ongoing economic crisis here in the United States as well as elsewhere, we have seen the lines separating these spheres blur even further. Women are participating much more fully in the global economy. "In 2009, in the United States, women held 49 percent of all nonfarm jobs. The number of women earning $100,000 or more tripled between 1991 and 2001. Between 2000 and 2008 women's average weekly wages grew steadily, while men's didn't grow at all" (Dychtwald, 2010, p. 5). Many men lost their jobs in sectors like manufacturing and construction. And it is not clear the extent to which such employment will return. On the other hand, although women also lost jobs through cutbacks in civil service positions, healthcare, and teaching, more women than men are employed part time. Mothers in particular are doing this work in the home as they juggle their family responsibilities. Regardless of employment status, more women than men do unpaid household labor (Miller & Sassler, 2012). Rampell (2012) quotes from the OECD report *Closing the Gender Gap: Act Now* (2012):

> [M]others generally make much wider use than fathers of parental leave options, part-time employment opportunities, and other flexible working time arrangements like teleworking.... [E]ven when policies allow or encourage women to change the nature of their participation in employment or their hours of work, inequalities at home and in contributions to home life have a tendency to remain. (http://economix.blogs.nytimes.com/2012/12/19/in-most-rich-countries-women-work-more-than-men/)

Thus, to mention a marker that has been relevant in the discussion of gender and work, the home is now the site of both paid and unpaid labor for many women and some men.

Gender, gender roles, and gender identity, as well as femininities and masculinities, have continued to be studied and theorized in sociology, philosophy, psychology, and other disciplines. But in education research, particularly in the educational leadership discourse, the nexus between gender and leadership appears to be less interesting than it was previously—not surprisingly since the prevailing attitudes among many women and men is that gender is irrelevant. Yet, as Gillard's and others' stories reveal, gender seems to matter just as much today as it always has. While it is not uncommon to see a news headline mentioning the appointment of a "first" woman superintendent in such-and-such a district or a "first" woman college president, more often one hears statements like: "Vote for someone because of their plumbing? No. I don't care about a candidate's sex, sex partners or the color of his or her skin" (Kerr, 2013). This is from a letter to the editor about the possibility of a woman mayor in Los Angeles. According to contemporary rhetoric, neither gender nor race/ethnicity matters in the suitability for or practice of leadership.

Research in educational leadership has documented (and continues to) women's experiences of being principal and superintendent (White women's experiences and, less often, women of color's). For example, studies focus on preparation and development of leaders, career paths, leadership styles, barriers to accessing the position, leadership behaviors and purpose, mentoring and sponsorship, and overt discrimination among other topics. For a comprehensive review of such scholarship see Shakeshaft, Brown, Irby, Grogan, and Ballenger (2007). Also, there continues to be quite a large number of educational leadership dissertations written about women's issues. But, by and large, new knowledge about leadership inequalities in education is lacking. Perhaps revisiting gender scholarship and scholarship on intersectionality will yield further insights.

How might a gender frame help us to understand leadership inequality better and, more to the point, how might gender theories allow us to transform education? This chapter argues for the reinvigorated use of robust feminist theories and gender theories that shed light on current constructions of gender in education and the intersectionalities of gender, race, class, ethnicities, religion, sexuality, and so on within educational leadership. In addition to furthering our knowledge of how women are positioned in the educational leadership discourse, a better grasp of gender allows us to contemplate how men are being shaped by various masculinities as well. "Gender issues are about men, quite as much as they are about women" (Connell, 2009, p. x).

To assist with this project, in this chapter I briefly discuss a selection of research on ways to understand gender, including gender theories that might be useful to apply to educational leadership. The ideas and works referenced are by no means exhaustive. My aim is to offer enough food for thought to encourage new and seasoned scholars to problematize the prevailing belief that gender is not a leadership issue. I also encourage research in our field that develops and tests new gender-related theories. "[T]he most important question a critical scholar must ask is, What mechanisms are currently constructing inequality, and how can these be transformed to create a more just world?" (quoting Risman, 2003, in Risman 2004, p. 445).

CONTEMPORARY GENDER THEORIZING

Leading gender scholar, Raewyn Connell (2009), summarizes the various approaches to the study of gender in both the "majority world" (developing world) and "the metropole" (Western world). In so doing, she also highlights effects of race, class, sexuality, religion, colonialism, and postcolonialism on gender constructs. By drawing on a wide spectrum of research in several languages, and cultural settings, her work presents deep and broad, contemporary views of gender. She argues that theories of gender "must address: the institution of the family, gender divisions of labour [sic], ideologies of womanhood, and strategies of change in gender relations" (Connell, 2009, p. 32). Of major interest to us in the educational leadership context is the way gender is perceived in organizational life. Gender relations in organizations attract many gender researchers and theorists (see, for example, Acker, 2006; Brescoli, 2012; Burton, 1987; Connell, 2006; de la Rey, 2005; Foldy, 2012; Harding et al., 2013; Kanter, 1977; Martin, 2003, 2006; Mills & Tancred, 1992; Ridgeway & Correll, 2004; Risman, 2004).

Gender is seen as deeply embedded in cultural beliefs. "The process that links gender beliefs and social relational contexts is automatic sex categorization" (Ridgeway & Correll, 2004, p. 514). Human beings are thought to follow a sociocognitive process that prompts us to label individuals as male or female and to sex categorize ourselves as either similar to or different from each (Ridgeway & Correll, 2004). The problem with this automatic process is that the widely held cultural beliefs about gender privilege men (and, most often, White, middle-class, heterosexual men). Ridgeway and Correll (2004) report on studies that document the stereotypical man as having more agency than women, more instrumental rationality and more competence at highly valued things: "Women are seen as less competent in general but "nicer" and better at communal tasks" (p. 513, quotation marks in the original). The authors argue that sex categorization is based on individual appearance and behavior. Gender is a background identity in the context of social interaction, but it becomes more important in situations where individuals of both genders are present. Even in nonhierarchical settings, there is evidence that deeply embedded presumptions informed by gender affect workers' performances and evaluation. Even men's and women's voluntary choices of gendered (or neutral) expression are shaped and constrained by existing gender structures. Martin (2006) contends that much practicing of gender occurs unintentionally and unreflexively, particularly in the workplace. But she also warns of the damage to women of the collective practicing of certain masculinities by men at work—those that exclude or disparage others. In short, many gender researchers using contemporary analytical tools integrate cognitive schemas, individual behaviors and practices, and the notion of a socially constructed stratification system (Risman, 2004).

Connell (2009) contends that organizations have gender regimes that describe who does what kind of work, the social arrangements within them, how emotional relations are developed, and how the organization relates to families and other social institutions. Such regimes are not fixed and do change but they are part of the wider gender order of a society. "Gender relations are always being made and remade in everyday life" (Connell, 2009, p. 73). Although we construct our own gender, we are not free to make it as we might wish. We are always constrained by the gender order within which we live. The workplace is a reflection of these broader gender relations (and race relations). This gender structure is created every day by human behavior. According to Martin (2003), "men and women socially construct each other at work by means of a two-sided dynamic of *gendering practices* and *practicing gender*" (p. 343, emphasis added). Martin further argues that this dynamic influences men's and women's work experiences and that women workers are often negatively impacted by gendering practices. *Gendering practices* refers to those expressions of gender we learn and enact in childhood, schools, intimate relationships, families, workplaces, places of worship, and so on. They are done together with others and/or as a result of interaction with others. She argues that over time they become almost automatic. The second dynamic, *practicing gender,* describes the activities, words and actions of gender in an organization—the microinteractional moments that constitute the gender order. A good example would be when a community member asks a woman principal if he or she can speak to the "real" principal. Such practices are often hard to detect since they happen quickly and often subtly. To fully understand gender relations in the workplace, it is necessary to capture the dynamics as they occur. Martin's advice to researchers is to pay more attention to issues of individual agency, intention, awareness, reflexivity, position, power, experience, choice, accountability, and audience. "These issues are ignored or addressed only implicitly in many studies of gendering dynamics at work" (2003, p. 355).

Another approach is to utilize a multistructured model for seeing gender relations (Connell, 2009). While the dimensions and structures apply to gender relations in wider social contexts, they are useful for analyzing organizational life. The four dimensions Connell identifies are *power relations; gendered accumulation; emotional relations;* and *symbolism, culture and discourse* as signifiers of gender meanings. She calls these dimensions "tools for thinking" about how the gender order is maintained—that is, how one gender benefits from arrangements more than the other. For instance, in organizations, managers have a larger share of power than others. Principals and superintendents have the power to make rules and decisions that advantage or constrain others in the organization. Managers are often men and others are mostly women in educational institutions. The dimension of gendered accumulation follows from power in that the largest share of resources in organizations often flows to middle class, White men through wage structures, benefits packages, and sometimes flexible time. The dimension of emotional relations in the workplace refers to the importance of producing a particular emotional relationship with clients/stakeholders. This relationship is fundamental to the work itself. In education, the nurturance of students and connections with families is expected more of teachers than leaders. But it is valued less than the strategic planning and organizational direction-setting of leaders. Finally, the dimension of symbolism, culture, and discourse provides insights into how particular organizations reference gender. In schools, gender symbolism is reinforced through the importance attached to boys' sports teams compared to girls' teams and to nonsports activities for instance. In addition, the discourse of education still often includes the gender modifier to signify a woman in the leadership role. We never refer to a man superintendent! Connell believes that researching the gender order in an organization is helpful in the quest to reach gender equality. The reshaping of gender relations is necessary to arrive at gender democratization. She does not argue for de-gendering families, workplaces, or politics. "[D]emocratic action in the world gender order must be what democracy always means: moving towards equality of participation, power, and respect" (Connell, 2009, p. 151).

More broadly speaking, inequality in organizations can be defined as "systematic disparities between participants in power and control over goals, resources, and outcomes; workplace decisions such as how to organize work; opportunities for promotion and interesting work; security in employment and benefits; pay and other monetary rewards; respect; and pleasures in work and work relations" (Acker, 2006, p. 443). Acker suggests the term "inequality regimes" to help conceptualize the patterns of organizational inequality, which must be studied with attention to the intersecting structures of race/ethnicity, gender, and class. Inequality regimes are in flux all the time. Although they are connected to societal inequalities, it is in the local and particular organizational practices and sensemaking that we can best understand their effects. Research on sensemaking, in particular, has yielded nuanced understanding of gender regimes. "When we make sense of something, we are a force in its creation, maintenance and modification" (Foldy, 2006, p. 354). Acker adds that studying efforts to change inequalities in organizations offers a particularly rich opportunity to understand "frequently invisible aspects of the *reproduction* of inequalities" (2006, p. 441, my emphasis). To make these aspects visible, like Martin (2003), Ridgeway and Correll (2004) advocate the collection of detailed data on social relational processes, in addition to stated policies and procedures in formal organizations as well as in more innovative work settings. Risman (2004) includes the important recommendation that we provide evidence of change and equality instead of studying only inequality.

To inform such research, theoretical constructs include Martin's (2003, 2006) twin dynamics of practicing gender and gender practices, Connell's (2009) gender dimensions and structures, Risman's (2004) gender structure theory, Acker's (2006) notion of inequality regimes and Foldy's (2006) dialectical sense-making of gender. In addition, Harding et al. (2013) advocate three theories informed by feminist thought as highly useful in studying organizations. These are first, intersectionality; second, the politics of recognition; and third, feminist readings of Greek myths and tragedies. These theoretical frames can surely stimulate new research studies of gender in educational leadership. It is exciting to know that gender scholars in other disciplines are currently developing and refining ways to interrogate gender in organizational life. Thus, I offer these contemporary analytical constructs to help reinvigorate gender scholarship in educational administration, building on the tradition of gender scholarship in this field that already exists. In the next section, I raise the issue of reconsidering this gender scholarship in the context of building on what we already know.

A CALL FOR MORE ROBUST RESEARCH INTO GENDER AND EDUCATIONAL LEADERSHIP

Like Shakeshaft (1987) and Marshall (1984), Skrla (2003) points out that research on women leaders of education has remained marginalized. For change to occur, she makes a strong argument for "thorough examination of underlying normalizations that structure discourses and practices in educational administration" (p. 252). Marshall and Wynn (2012) ask "how has women's scholarship infused educational administration with scholarly challenges?" (p. 886). They assert that women scholars produce scholarship that documents gender inequalities but often lack the courage to name all the "confounding effects of race, sexuality, and gender" (p. 885). Indeed, there is much missing from our narratives, but I wonder if painful truth-telling would have the desired affect? Nevertheless, at least there is a body of scholarship to build upon even if women's scholarship and scholarship about women leading education has had little impact on setting research agendas in the field. Shakeshaft et al.'s (2007) extensive review of the research on gender equity in leadership since 1985 establishes a baseline for what we know about the subject. All the published empirical research and dissertations on women in educational leadership were reviewed. It was found that the majority of the studies (nearly 900) were unpublished dissertation studies. "Therefore, many studies on gender and leadership reach a limited audience and do not add to the theoretical or practice foundation of the discipline" (p. 107). Yet the review offers a wealth of knowledge. For instance, among other things, we learn that most of the barriers to women in educational leadership that were documented earlier still exist. Gender stereotyping and discrimination continues. Women's career patterns are still affected by home and family responsibilities. Gender gaps in administrative salaries persist. Hostile work environments discourage women from participating in educational leadership. However, "[w]omen no longer lack confidence, aspiration, or motivation" (Shakeshaft et al., 2007, p. 114).

Shakeshaft et al. (2007) offer 12 recommendations for research "[t]o address the striking imbalance in the numbers of women and men in the highest position of educational leadership, as well as to address successful administrative approaches" (p. 119). Suggestions are given to investigate recurring problems that were identified in the review, such as examining curriculum in educational leadership programs for infusion of gender equity and social justice issues, studying how women have engaged the legal system to fight discrimination in hiring, investigating gender aspects of organizational decisions, conducting equity audits of school district policies and practices, and profiling the careers of successful women and minority leaders. All are excellent avenues to explore in efforts to reach gender equality.

In addition, the review addressed the relevance of traditional theories of educational leadership. Much of the gender scholarship was critical of the value and usefulness of most theories that were taught in educational leadership preparation programs. Concerns identified in the gender scholarship included the lack of relevance of theories embedded in men's lives and experiences to women leaders, the fear that such theories actually contributed to gender discrimination and stereotyping, and the belief that they were a hindrance to men's and women's working together effectively in educational settings. The teaching of traditional theories in preparation programs was seen to legitimize men's behaviors and views and delegitimize those of women. The hope was expressed that research and scholarship emanating from women's experiences of leadership would influence all leadership practice and thus lead to new theories of educational leadership. So the issue is twofold: To reach equality in educational leadership, on the one hand, we need more research on women's and men's experiences of educational leadership informed by gender frameworks, and on the other, we need new gender-related theories that provide greater explanatory power. I am not arguing for the creation of new theory for theory's sake, especially not in an applied field like educational leadership. I think there is practical worth in critiquing the existing gender order using analytical tools that allow new insights into women's and some men's inferior position in educational leadership. Our task will be to translate our new knowledge into useful learning.

In addition to research that interrogates new questions, scholarship that builds on extant research in this arena lends greater credibility to future findings, especially when studies are well designed and methodologically sound. An open question is whether gender issues are changing or have changed since the bulk of this research was conducted. Is there a collective effect of the increase in women principals and/or superintendents? Has the presence of more women professionals and women serving in public leadership roles influenced the work of women educational leaders? What are young women experiencing in school and district leadership today? What do their prospects for entering leadership positions look like? What leadership theories and practices hold meaning for women? What effects has their leadership had on student learning? on the lives of their students, families and communities? How are women leaders influencing education policy and politics? How can a gender lens help to critique education policy? Echoing Marshall (1997) and Young (2003), feminist and gender theories provide powerful insights into how meta-narratives in education frame issues as gender-neutral when there are significant gender implications embedded within such frames. As Young (2003) found, "Unless the leadership shortage is treated as a gendered issue, the solutions that grow out of task force analyses will not only fail to adequately address the predicted shortage but will continue to perpetuate the gendered leadership crisis in educational administration" (p. 293).

GENDERED ORGANIZATIONS

One advantage of reaching gender equality in leadership is that it will confirm for girls that women lead organizations and that women have power and agency. More persuasive than any family or teacher encouragement is the presence of women in these positions—whether they are good or bad at their jobs. We have plenty of examples of men who have been bad leaders, but that has never discouraged any boys from aspiring to and preparing for leadership. For the next generation of women, as girls learn how to be women, their experiences of school are either going to continue to limit their imaginations or expand them.

And what of boys as they learn how to be men? And men as they learn how to be leaders of education? Research that examines the effects of the strong masculine culture still prevalent in educational settings would add much to the knowledge base. Raewyn Connell's (2005) discussion of men, masculinities and gender equality provides us with a global view of the research on men's gender identities and practices. Growing out of increasing recognition of the negative effects of traditional male behaviors such as violence and those associated with patriarchy, there have been widespread public debates, conferences and seminars. Research reports have multiplied and crossed national boundaries. There has been recognition in 2001 by the UN General Assembly that men and women must work together to advance gender equality. The value of such attention is that "the emergence of new arenas of social relationship on a world scale creates new patterns of gender relations" (p. 1804). But Connell reminds us that despite the worldwide acceptance of the need to problematize men and masculinities, the privileged position of men has not changed much. Yet there are embedded disadvantages to men's gendered lives, which also may or may not be changing.

Connell (2005) mentions the fact that men are employed in more dangerous occupations and pay more taxes. They are more often targets of criminal assault and more often incarcerated and executed. In two other areas, men's relative disadvantage compared to women is not as certain as it has been in the past. Now that women are beginning to join the ranks of combat troops, they too will find themselves targets of military violence—though perhaps not in numbers equal to men for some time to come. The second disadvantage that has begun to shape women's lives more than in the past is the "social pressure to remain employed" (p. 1809). I would argue that the widespread unemployment, at least in the United States at present, calls into question whether men are under more pressure than women to remain employed. In all these examples, though, education, socioeconomic status and race/ethnicity play a significant role. Like women's, even when disadvantageous, men's gendered experiences are not all equally disadvantageous.

For reasons that have to do with family, philosophy, ethics, and politics, men are engaged in the promotion of gender equality. Many men are particularly concerned that their daughters, nieces, and other family members get equal opportunities. Family structures are changing. But, in the organizational workplace, there is possibly less recognition of the way masculine cultures damage women and some men and hinder the progress towards equality. For example, it is not clear the extent to which men are aware of the effects of their collective work behaviors. Martin (2001) identifies two categories of masculinities, *affiliating* and *contesting*, that emerge in organizations. She describes these as mobilizing masculinities: "Men mobilize contesting masculinities when they act in concert to distance—differentiate, separate—themselves from others by showing superior rank or status, obtaining control over others, or obtaining benefits from work that others do" (p. 603). Practices that contribute to contesting masculinities include peacocking, self-promoting, dominating, and expropriating others' labor. In many instances, the primary audience for such behaviors is other men, except for dominating and expropriating others' labor. Affiliating masculinities were detected when men "aligned—connected, linked—with others in ways that benefited self" (p. 604). Practices that define affiliating masculinities include visiting, "sucking up," protecting, supporting, deciding based on liking or disliking, and expressing fondness. Again, the primary audience for these behaviors is men.

Martin (2001) argues that women, and some men, are harmed by these behaviors because of their collective nature. They may be the primary source of damage to women in organizations rather than acts by an individual man. Moreover, since most of the behaviors are targeted at other men, an important recognition is that women and some men are harmed by a sense of exclusion. Indeed, such practices likely have negative effects on the organization as a whole. Raising awareness of the effects of masculinities in the workplace is a major factor in advancing gender equality.

POTENTIAL FOR TRANSFORMING THE FIELD

As Harding et al. (2013) assert, "there remains a largely unexplored treasurehouse of feminist ideas that offer much potential for developing sophisticated, innovative, highly informed analyses of organizations and working lives" (p. 60). This chapter makes the case that to tap into such a store, we need more reflexive, theoretically informed critiques of how gender is being done and undone in school and district organizations. Echoing Eacott (2010) and Waite (1998), who put out general calls for moving beyond what is known in educational leadership, I would like to challenge those who study this field to generate deeper, theory-driven, and derived understandings of gender and leadership. In 1998, Duncan Waite believed that educational leadership had a very conservative reputation. Fortunately, there have been recent studies of educational leadership informed by critical race theory, and broader theories of social justice, including intersectionality, though I think it is fair to say that in the last decade or so, only a few well-designed and executed empirical studies grounded in or illuminated by gender/feminist theories have been published. I have done very little myself.

However, the time appears right for revisiting the potential in these theories and for generating new theory. Marshall and Wynn (2012) challenge us to "demand that women's issues and feminist scholars' insights be incorporated into the educational administration canon.... [Such work] will hopefully provide educational administrators with models that are more useful than the competitive discourse that threatens public education today" (p. 891). As we respond to this call, our work needs to expose the harmful effects of the dominant values driving education practice and policy. Both women and men leading educational institutions have been shaped by the rhetoric that glorifies standardized testing and disregards the social and emotional well-being of students and their families. This is happening globally. Access to local narratives of gender relations and gendered practices in educational settings across the world will aid in new forms of theorizing leadership. Reinvigorated gender scholarship in our field must critique the normative accounts of leading schools and districts in which large numbers of students struggle to learn. The purportedly gender- and race-neutral rhetoric supporting policies that harm students, families, teachers, and their communities must be unmasked. Feminist and gender theories offer multiple avenues to pursue new knowledge. The lively debates in journals such as *Signs* and *Gender and Society*, where research is grounded in these theories reveal that there is as much variety of analytical frames, approaches, and methods among those researchers as there is among researchers utilizing more traditional epistemologies. In the very best case, if we produce a more robust body of research informed by gender and feminist theories and the intersectionalities, perhaps we will begin to engage others in the field in a genuine dialogue.

REFERENCES

Acker, J. (2006). Inequality regimes: Gender, class and race in organizations. *Gender and Society, 20*(4), 441–464.

Addi-Raccah, A. (2006). Accessing internal leadership positions at school: Testing the similarity-attraction approach regarding gender in three educational systems in Israel. *Educational Administration Quarterly, 42*(3), 291–323.

Arar, K., Shapira, T., Azaiza, F., & Hertz-Lazarowitz, R. (2013). *Arab women in management and leadership. Stories from Israel.* New York, NY: Palgrave Macmillan.

Bell, C., & Chase, S. (1995). Gender in the theory and practice and of education leadership. *Journal for a Just and Caring Education, 1*(2), 200–223.

Bell, C., & Chase, S. (1996). The gendered character of women superintendents' professional relationships. In K. Arnold, K. Noble, & R. Subotnick (Eds.), *Remarkable women: Perspectives on female talent development* (pp. 117–131). Cresskill, NJ: Hampton.

Blackmore, J. (1999). *Troubling women.* Philadelphia, PA: Open University Press.

Blackmore J., & Sachs, J. (2007). *Performing and reforming leaders: Gender, educational restructuring and organizational change.* Albany, NY: SUNY Press.

Blount, J. (1995). The politics of sex as a category of analysis in the history of educational administration. In B. Irby & G. Brown (Eds.), *Women as school executives: Voices and visions* (pp. 1–5). Huntsville, TX: Sam Houston Press.

Blount, J. (1998). *Destined to rule the schools.* Albany, NY: State University of New York Press.

Brescoli, V. L. (2012). Who takes the floor and why: Gender, power and volubility in organizations. *Administrative Science Quarterly, 56*(4), 622–641.

Brunner, C. C. (2000). Unsettled moments in settled discourse: Women superintendents experiences of inequality. *Educational Administration Quarterly, 36*(1), 76–116.

Brunner, C. C. (2005). Women performing the superintendency: Problematizing the normative alignment of conceptions of power and constructions of gender. In J. Collard & C. Reynolds (Eds.), *Leadership, gender and culture: Male and female perspectives* (pp. 121–135). New York, NY: Open University Press.

Brunner, C. C., & Schumaker, P. (1998). Power and gender in the "new view" public schools. *Policy Studies Journal, 26*(1), 30–45.

Burton, C. (1987). Merit and gender: Organisations and the mobilisation of masculine bias. *Australian Journal of Social Issues, 22,* 424–435.

Chase, S. (1995). *Ambiguous empowerment: The work narratives of women school superintendents.* Amherst, MA: University of Massachusetts Press.

Christman, D., & McLellan, R. (2008). "Living on barbed wire": Resilient women administrators in educational leadership programs. *Educational Administration Quarterly, 44*(3), 3–29.

Coleman, M. (2002). *Women as headteachers striking the balance.* Sterling, VA: Trentham Books.

Collins, G. (2009). *When everything changed. The amazing journey of American women from 1960 to the present.* New York, NY: Little, Brown and Company.

Connell, R. (2005). Change among the gatekeepers: Men, masculinities, and gender equality in the global arena. *Signs, 30,* 1801–1825.

Connell, R. (2006). Glass ceilings or gendered institutions? Mapping the gender regimes of public sector worksites. *Public Administration Review, 66,* 837–849.

Connell, R. (2009). *Gender.* Malden, MA: Polity Press.

Court, M. (2005). Negotiating and reconstructing gendered leadership discourses. In J. Collard & C. Reynolds (Eds.), *Leadership, gender and culture: Male and female perspectives* (pp. 3–17). New York, NY: Open University Press.

de la Rey, C. (2005). Gender, women and leadership. *Agenda, 65,* 4–11.

Dillard, C. (2003). The substance of things hoped for, the evidence of things not seen: Examining an endarkened feminist epistemology in educational research and leadership. In M. D. Young & L. Skrla (Eds.), *Reconsidering feminist research in educational leadership* (pp. 131–160). Albany, NY: State University of New York Press.

Dychtwald, M. (2010). *Influence.* New York, NY: Voice.

Eacott, S. (2010). Bourdieu's strategies and the challenge for educational leadership. *International Journal of Leadership in Education: Theory and Practice, 13*(3), 265–281.

Eagly, A. H., Karau, S. J., & Johnson, B. T. (1992). Gender and leadership style among school principals: A meta-analysis. *Educational Administration Quarterly, 28,* 76–102.

Foldy, E. G. (2012). Something of collaborative manufacture: The construction of race and gender identities in organizations. *Journal of Applied Behavioral* Science, 48(4) 495–524.

Gardiner, M., Enomoto, E., & Grogan, M. (2000). *Coloring outside the lines: Mentoring women into school leadership.* Albany, NY: State University of New York Press.

Gillard, J. (October, 2012). Misogyny. Retrieved February 2, 2013, from http://www.youtube.com/watch?feature=player_embedded&v=ihd7ofrwQX0

Grogan, M. (1996). Voices of women aspiring to the superintendency. Albany: State University of New York Press.

Grogan, M. (1999a). Equity/equality issues of gender, race and class. *Educational Administration Quarterly, 35*(4), 518–536.

Grogan, M. (1999b). A feminist poststructuralist account of collaboration: A model for the superintendency. In C. Brunner (Ed.), *Sacred dreams: Women and the superintendency* (pp.199–216). Albany, NY: State University of New York Press.

Grogan, M. (2000). Laying the groundwork for a reconception of the superintendency from feminist/postmodern perspectives. *Educational Administration Quarterly, 36*(1) 117–142. (Reprinted in M. Young & L. Skrla (Eds.). (2003). *Reconsidering feminist research in educational leadership* (pp. 9–34). Albany, NY: State University of New York Press).

Grogan, M. (2002). Influences of the discourse of globalisation on mentoring for gender equity and social justice in educational leadership. *Leading and Managing, 8*(2), 124–135. (Reprinted in *Leadership, gender and culture*, pp. 90–102, by John Collard and Cecilia Reynolds, Eds. 2004, New York: Open University Press.)

Harding, N., Ford, J., & Fotaki, M. (2013). Is the 'F'-word still dirty? A past, present and future of/for feminist and gender studies in Organization. *Organization, 20*(1), 51–65.

Hertz-Lazarowitz, R., & Oplatka, I. (2006). Epilogue: Feminist pedagogy; an alternative look at female leadership. In I. Oplatka & R. Hertz-Lazarowitz (Eds.), *Women principals in a multicultural society: New insights into feminist educational leadership* (pp. 193–204). Rotterdam: Sense Publishers.

Jones, B. K. (1990). The gender difference hypothesis: A synthesis of research findings. *Educational Administration Quarterly, 26*(1), 5–37.

Kanter, R. (1997). *Men and women of the corporation.* New York, NY: Basic Books

Kerr, J. (2013, January). Letters: If the next mayor is a woman. Retrieved from http://www.latimes.com/news/opinion/letters/la-le-0201-friday-mayor-woman-20130201,0,4802412.story

Kowalski, T., McCord, R., Petersen, G., Young, I. P., & Ellerson, N. (2011). *The American school superintendent 2010 decennial study.* Lanham, MD: Rowman & Littlefield.

Kramer, L. (Ed.). (1991). *The sociology of gender.* New York, NY: St. Martins Press.

Lugg, C. (2003). Sissies, faggots, lezzies and dykes: Gender, sexual orientation and a new politics of education. *Educational Administration Quarterly, 39*(1), 95–134.

Mahitivanichcha, K., & Rorrer, A. M. (2006). Women's choices within market constraints: Re-visioning access to and participation in the superintendency. *Educational Administration Quarterly, 42*(4), 483–517.

Marshall, C. (1984). The crisis in excellence and equity. *Educational Horizons, 63,* 24–30.

Marshall, C. (1985). The stigmatized woman: The professional woman in a male sex-typed career. *Journal of Educational Administration, 13*(2), 131–152.

Marshall, C. (1997). Dismantling and reconstructing policy analysis. In C. Marshall (Ed.), *Feminist critical policy analysis: A perspective from primary and secondary schooling* (pp. 1–40). Washington DC: Falmer Press.

Marshall, C., & Wynn, S. (2012). Expanding the conversation: Collaboration, complexities and the missing pieces. *Educational Administration Quarterly, 48*(5), 883–892.

Martin, P. Y. (2001). Mobilizing masculinities: Women's experiences of men at work. *Organization, 8*(4), 587–618.

Martin, P. Y. (2003). "Said and done" versus "saying and doing": Gendering practices, practicing gender at work. *Gender and Society, 17*(3), 342–366.

Martin, P. Y. (2006). Practicing gender at work: Further thoughts on reflexivity. *Gender, Work and Organization, 13*(3) 254–276.

Méndez-Morse, S. (2003). Chicana feminism and educational leadership. In M. D. Young & L. Skrla (Eds.), *Reconsidering feminist research in educational leadership* (pp. 161–178). Albany, NY: State University of New York Press.

Miller, A. J., & Sassler, S. (2012). The construction of gender among working-class cohabiting couples. *Qualitative Sociology, 35,* 427–446.

Mills, A. J., & Tancred, P. (Eds.). (1992). *Gendering organizational analysis.* Newbury Park, CA: Sage.

OECD (2012). *Closing the gender gap: Act now.* OECD Publishing. doi: 10.1787/978 9264179370-en

Ortiz, F. I., & Ortiz, D. J. (1995). How gender and ethnicity interact in the practice of educational administration: The case of Hispanic female superintendents. In R. Donmoyer, M. Imber, & J. Scheurich (Eds.), *The knowledge base in educational administration: Multiple perspectives* (pp. 158–173). Albany, NY: State University of New York Press.

Rampell, C. (2012, December). *In most rich countries, women work more than men.* Retrieved from http://economix.blogs.nytimes.com/2012/12/19/in-most-rich-countries-women-work-more-than-men/

Ridgeway, C. L., & Correll, S. J. (2004). Unpacking the gender system: A theoretical perspective on gender beliefs and social relations. *Gender and Society, 18*(4), 510–531.

Risman, B. J.(2003). Valuing all flavors of feminist sociology. *Gender and Society, 17,* 659–663.

Risman, B. J. (2004). Gender as a social structure. *Gender and Society, 18*(4), 429–450.

Rusch, E. (2004). Gender and race in leadership preparation: A constrained discourse. *Educational Administration Quarterly 40*(1), 14–46.

Rusch, E., & Marshall, C. (2006). Gender filters: Plotting a course to equity. *International Journal of Leadership in Education, 9*(3), 229–250.

Scott, J. (2003). The linguistic production of genderlessness in the superintendency. In M. D. Young & L. Skrla (Eds.), *Reconsidering feminist research in educational leadership* (pp. 81–102). Albany, NY: State University of New York Press.

Shakeshaft, C. (1987). *Women in educational administration.* Newbury Park, CA: Sage

Shakeshaft, C. (1990). The struggle to create a more gender inclusive profession. In *Handbook of research on educational administration.* San Francisco, CA: Jossey-Bass.

Shakeshaft, C., Brown, G., Irby, B., Grogan, M., & Ballenger, J. (2007). Increasing gender equity in educational leadership, In S. Klein, B. Richardson, D. A. Grayson, L.H. Fox, C. Kramare, D. Pollard, & C. A. Dwyer (Eds.), *Handbook for achieving gender equity through education* (2nd ed., pp. 103–130). Florence KY: Lawrence Erlbaum Associates.

Sherman, W. (2005). Preserving the status quo or renegotiating leadership: Women's experiences with a district-based aspiring leaders program. *Educational Administration Quarterly, 41*(5), 707–740.

Sherman, W. H., & Beaty, D. (2010). Using feminist phase theory to portray women in the principalship across generations. *Journal of Educational Administration and History, 42*(2), 159–180.

Skrla, L. (1999, April). *Femininity/masculinity: Hegemonic normalizations in the public school superintendency.* Paper presented at the annual conference of the American Educational Research Association, Montreal, Canada.

Skrla, L. (2000). The social construction of gender in the superintendency. *Journal of Education Policy, 15*(3), 293–316.

Skrla, L. (2003). Normalized femininity: Reconsidering research on women in the superintendency. In M. D. Young & L. Skrla (Eds.), *Reconsidering feminist research in educational leadership* (pp. 247–264). Albany, NY: State University of New York Press.

Skrla, L., Reyes, P., & Scheurich, J. (2000). Sexism, silence, and solutions: Women superintendents speak up and speak out. *Educational Administration Quarterly, 36*(1), 44–75.

Smulyan, L. (2000). Feminist analysis of nonfeminist subjects: Case studies of women principals. *International Journal of Qualitative Studies in Education, 13*(6), 589–609.

Strachan, J. (1999). Feminist educational leadership: Locating the concepts in practice. *Gender and Education, 11*(3), 309–323.

Strachan, J. (2000). Feminist educational leadership: Not for the fainthearted. In C. Reynolds (Ed.), *Women and school leadership* (pp. 111–126). Albany, NY: State University of New York Press.

Stripling, J. (2012, June). Departing president defends her incremental approach to change at U. of Virginia. Retrieved from http://chronicle.com/article/ Timeline-A-Frenetic-Fortnight/132545/

Tallerico, M. (2000). Gaining access to the superintendency: Headhunting, gender and color. *Educational Administration Quarterly, 36*(1), 18–43.

Tallerico, M., & Blount, J. (2004). Women and the superintendency: Insights from theory and history. *Educational Administration Quarterly, 40*(5), 633–662.

Waite, D. (1998). Editorial: On the occasion of the inaugural issue of the International Journal of Leadership in Education. *International Journal of Leadership in Education: Theory and Practice, 1*(1), 91–93.

Young, M. D. (2003). Troubling policy discourse: Gender, constructions and the leadership crisis. In M. D. Young & L. Skrla (Eds.), *Reconsidering feminist research in educational leadership* (pp. 265–298). Albany, NY: State University of New York Press.

Young, M. D., & Skrla, L. (2003a). *Reconsidering feminist research in educational leadership.* Albany, NY: State University of New York Press.

Young, M. D., & Skrla, L. (2003b). Research on women and administration: A response to Julie Laible's loving epistemology. In M. D. Young & L. Skrla (Eds.), *Reconsidering feminist research in educational leadership* (pp. 201–210). Albany, NY: State University of New York Press.

CHAPTER 2

THE STALLED GENDER REVOLUTION

Implications for Women Leaders

Mary Hermann

ABSTRACT

Women have made significant progress in terms of educational achievement and participation in the workforce in the past five decades, yet men still hold a substantially disproportionate number of leadership positions in almost every industry. This chapter explores factors that have contributed to the dearth of women in leadership positions. These factors include covert and overt gender discrimination, women's socialization, and inhibiting cultural norms. Women struggle to compete with men for leadership positions in a culture in which women are expected to provide more childcare and household management than men. Elevated expectations related to motherhood in American culture and the prevalence of increasingly longer workweeks may impact women's participation in leadership activities as well. This chapter also provides suggestions for both eliminating the obstructions preventing women from achieving leadership roles and creating a more equitable society that supports women reaching their full potential.

Women Interrupting, Disrupting, and Revolutionizing Educational Policy and Practice, pages 21–40

Women have made significant progress in terms of educational achievement and participation in the workforce in the past five decades. In 2011, women comprised 47% of the American workforce and 59% of recent college graduates in the workforce (Spar, 2012). Yet men still hold a substantially disproportionate number of leadership positions in every industry, as exemplified by the 96% of CEO positions and 84% of board seats held by men in Fortune 500 companies (Hymowitz, 2012; Spar, 2012; Taylor, Morin, Cohn, Clark, & Wang, 2008). These statistics are perplexing, as Taylor et al. (2008) revealed that both men and women respondents reported that women have as good or better leadership skills than men. Even more puzzling is that women are often not promoted to senior leadership when they outperform their male colleagues (Draper, 2012). Draper (2012) concluded that if current trends continue, women will not have the same number of leadership positions as men until 2085.

Researchers have posited several theories to explain the dearth of women in leadership positions. Factors impeding women's ascent to top level positions include covert and overt gender discrimination (Collins, 2009; Corbett & Hill, 2012; Hurtado, Eagan, Pryor, Whang, & Tran, 2012; Spar, 2012) as well as women's socialization (Babcock & Laschever, 2007; Corbett & Hill, 2012; Frankel, 2004; Simmons, 2009) and inhibiting cultural norms (Barsh & Cranston, 2011; Frankel, 2004). Women struggle to compete with men for leadership positions in a culture in which women are expected to provide more childcare and household management than men. Arlie Hochschild (2012) asserted that this inequitable division of labor at home, women's "second shift" (p. 7), turned the second wave of the women's rights movement into a "stalled gender revolution" (p. xxiii). Elevated expectations related to motherhood in American culture (Gillespie & Temple, 2011; Warner, 2005) and the prevalence of increasingly longer work weeks (Hewlett & Luce, 2006; Slaughter, 2012) have further stalled the gender revolution. This chapter explores the impact of these factors on women in leadership.

THE GENDER REVOLUTION

Levinson (1996) defined the gender revolution as "a transformation in the meaning of gender, the place of women and men in society, and the relationships between women and men in all aspects of life" (p. 45). Friedan (1963/2001) described this transformation as "revolutionary indeed" (p. 384) and elaborated on the necessity of restructuring marriage, family, education, and psychological theories to support women as they moved into the workforce. Collins (2009) called the progress toward cultural transformation "astonishing" though she acknowledged that the transformation was not complete (p. 8). The lack of gender parity in leadership positions supports the need for further cultural transformation.

Considering the shifts in cultural and work norms in the past 50 years partially explains how the gender revolution stalled. The gender revolution was waged against the backdrop of a society that was less complicated in many ways. Though women have had to break free from the confines of what Friedan (1963/2001) termed the "feminine mystique" of the 1950s, being defined only by the status of wife and mother (p. xv), other cultural norms existed in working women's favor. In the 1950s and 1960s, the forty-hour workweek was a standard work model (Hewlett & Luce, 2006). The pace of life was slower. Relaxation was still highly regarded. Multitasking was not in vogue. Technology didn't perpetuate the intrusion of work into every facet of one's life. And standards of motherhood were less overwhelming.

By the 1980s, motherhood changed from being an expected facet of a woman's life to a chic new lifestyle choice with an increasing time commitment (Howe & Strauss, 2000; Warner, 2005). Howe and Strauss (2000) noted that a 1982 *Time* cover story commented on the trend of thirty-somethings wanting to have children and viewing parenthood differently—"kids were now to be desperately desired, to be in need of endless love and sacrifice and care" (p. 33). Additionally, Warner (2005) recounts the trend of placing a great deal of energy on children's early learning processes as childcare guides taught mothers that children could be smarter and more successful if "they had a mother (it was always a mother then) with the necessary degree of devotion and enlightenment to bring their gifts to light" (p. 35). Balancing career aspirations with new expectations related to motherhood was becoming more challenging.

And though significant numbers of women had moved into the workforce, men were not taking on an equal share of domestic and childcare responsibilities. Thus, women completed the first shift at work and completed the second shift at home. With so much to do and less time to accomplish tasks, Hochschild (2012) found her women research participants in the 1980s were experiencing "a speed-up of work and family life" (p. 10).

Furthermore, stereotypical views of women and gender discrimination persisted. Women were struggling to gain leadership roles. In a *Wall Street Journal* article in 1986, Hymowitz and Shellhardt identified what they called "the glass ceiling," the barriers women encounter as they seek promotions and senior leadership positions in the workforce (Jackson & O'Callaghan, 2009). Levinson's (1996) research participants in the 1980s reported that the glass ceiling was a misnomer—if a woman broke through the glass ceiling, she found herself encountering additional glass ceilings in her next position.

By the 1990s, Ruderman and Ohlott (2002) found that the glass ceiling still impacted women in the workforce. Though these researchers found that in spite of women's lack of presence in top positions, women had made substantial progress in gaining midlevel management positions. Ruderman and Ohlott also noted that the issues encountered by women leaders had evolved from issues related to being a woman in a predominantly male environment to issues related to lifestyle choices, including managing the personal costs associated with leadership roles.

Hewlett (2002) reported on one of these personal costs—the epidemic of childlessness among high-achieving women. The overlap of the years spent building a career and prime childbearing years is partially responsible for women losing the opportunity to become mothers. The compatibility of some careers and motherhood also restricted women's choices, especially as standards of parenting continued to escalate (Warner, 2005).

And the popularity of celebrities encouraging creativity and perfection in cooking and home decor seemed to increase expectations for the second shift. Friedan (1963/2001) commented that "women like Martha Stewart are making megamillions on elaborate do-it-yourself decor and cuisine, selling pretend feminine mystique pursuits as chic new choices" (p. xviii). And these pursuits conflicted with expanding career expectations.

Today women are confronted with excessively long work weeks, technologically induced information overload, an elevated standard of motherhood, and perfectionistic second shift expectations. In describing women's current cultural experiences, Spar (2012) described the "double whammy of impossible expectations—the old-fashioned ones (to be good mothers and wives, impeccable housekeepers and blushing brides) and those wrought more recently (to be athletic, strong, sexually versatile, and wholly independent)" (para. 4). Spar expressed particular concern that women buy into these cultural expectations, attempt to meet these expectations without any assistance, and then regularly criticize themselves for not meeting these impossible standards.

Gillespie and Temple (2011) concluded that "some of the old barriers were falling, but balancing work and family seemed to be getting *harder*" (p. 37, emphasis in original). As a result, current accounts of women's issues (Gillespie & Temple; Spar, 2012; Warner, 2005) are hauntingly reminiscent of the stories of women's experiences as they sought to seek fulfillment beyond the roles of wife, mother, and homemaker in the 1960s (Friedan, 1963/2012), the struggles encountered by women with careers in the 1980s (Levinson, 1996), and the experiences with the second shift reported to Hochschild (2012) in the 1980s. Considering these experiences, Warner (2005) questioned how two generations of feminism have left women with so little progress in so many ways.

CHALLENGES OF WORKING WOMEN
IN THE NEW MILLENNIUM

Extreme Jobs

Sylvia Ann Hewlett, President of the Center for Talent Innovation (formerly known as the Center for Work/Life Policy), investigated the experiences of working women including women in leadership positions and women in academia (Hewlett & Luce, 2006; Hewlett, Forster, Sherbin, Shiller, & Sumberg, 2010). Titles of resulting articles such as "Executive Women and the Myth of Having It All" (Hewlett, 2002) and "The Dangerous Allure of the 70-Hour Workweek" (Hewlett & Luce, 2006) provide a glimpse into an emerging new work culture. Slaughter (2012) refers to the prevalence in many industries of "the culture of 'time macho'—a relentless competition to work harder" (p. 94). Hewlett and Luce (2006) refer to this phenomenon as the "extreme-work model" (p. 4).

The extreme-work model is partially a result of the changing economic landscape (Hewlett & Luce, 2006). As the economy faltered and healthcare premiums increased, companies downsized to decrease overhead expenses (Hewlett & Luce, 2006). With fewer workers, the workers who remain shoulder more responsibility (Hewlett & Luce, 2006). This trend is apparent in most fields, including academia. In academia, budget cuts have increased workloads for professors (Hurtado et al., 2012). Concurrently, promotion expectations have increased with no corresponding additional time to achieve tenure (Hurtado et al., 2012; Philipsen & Bostic, 2010). The result is a workload that is rapidly expanding in academia and other fields.

Competition, technology, and current cultural norms also support the extreme job movement. Cultural views of workers who work an extreme amount of hours have changed from pitying workers with workaholic tendencies to exalting them (Hewlett & Luce, 2006). Competition in American culture is no longer limited to competitive sports. Television provides daily reinforcement of a competitive model infiltrating dancing, singing, designing, cooking, and tots vying for tiaras. Globalization and the resulting competition in the global market have elevated expectations in the business world (Hewlett & Luce, 2006; Rapoport, Bailyn, Fletcher, & Pruitt, 2002). Ironically, the women's movement itself has fueled competition by adding more qualified workers to the workforce. Workers in the United States lead all of those in industrialized nations in the number of hours worked (Rapoport et al., 2002). And technology has facilitated extreme work by shifting expectations, expanding the workday, and interfering with activities outside of the workplace (Hewlett & Luce, 2006). Hewlett and Luce (2006) reflected that "these changes—which include competitive pressures, vastly improved communication technology, and cultural shifts—intersect in powerful ways" (p. 6).

The impact of the current work culture on working women is staggering. In 2002, Hewlett found that a significant number of the professional women in her study reported working 10 to 20 hours more a week than they did in the in the mid to late 1990s. By 2006, the majority of high-achieving workers in a Hewlett and Luce study worked an additional 17 hours per week, 27 to 37 more hours per week than in the mid to late 1990s. Hewlett and Luce (2006) proclaimed that the 40-hour workweek was no longer in existence in many fields, and the 60-hour workweek, once enough to attain leadership positions, was no longer sufficient for the leadership track. The majority of participants in the Hewlett and Luce study reported that they were working at least 70 hours per week. And workers were too busy to take vacation time (Hewlett & Luce, 2006; Ruderman & Ohlott, 2002) or use many of the other work/life benefits that employers provided (Shellenbarger, 2012).

There is a significant negative impact of the extreme-work model to both individuals and society (Hewlett & Luce, 2006; Philipsen & Bostic, 2010; Ruderman & Ohlott, 2002). The Hewlett and Luce (2006) study revealed that the "extreme-work model is wreaking havoc on private lives and taking a toll on health and well-being" (p. 9). Women who work extreme hours often suffer socially because they do not have time to invest in personal relationships (Hewlett & Luce, 2006; Philipsen & Bostic, 2010). Furthermore, Hewlett and Luce found that over two-thirds of their extreme worker participants didn't sleep enough or get enough exercise, and many of the participants overate, drank too much, or needed to use medication to manage their stress. Ruderman and Ohlott (2002) expressed concern about some of the working women in their study who worked so many hours they neglected their health and were diagnosed with chronic, stress-related illnesses. Even after consultation with their doctors, many of these women were not able to follow their doctors' advice because of their commitment to their work.

Hewlett and Luce (2006) reiterated that women are impacted more than men with the extreme-work model. Many women, especially mothers, experiencing an increasingly extreme model of motherhood and the second shift, cannot or choose not to work extreme hours (Halpern, 2008; Hewlett & Luce, 2006). And more men than women have support at home: 25% of men working extreme jobs had a spouse or partner who stayed home, and only 12% of women working these hours had the same luxury. Hewlett and Luce noted that women are well represented in jobs that required less than 60 hours a week, even when these jobs required responding to deadlines and client demands. Yet these researchers concluded that the extreme hour requirement, often a component of leadership positions, disenfranchises women on the leadership track.

Hewlett and Luce (2006) questioned whether the extreme-work model was sustainable, especially for women. Given recent media accounts of high-profile women leaders who left their positions because of the inherent conflict in extreme work and parenting, the lack of sustainability for the extreme-work model for women leaders seems apparent. The July/August 2012 cover of *The Atlantic* magazine displayed the title "Why Women Still Can't Have It All." The article explains why the author, Anne Marie Slaughter, left her job as the first woman director of policy planning at the State Department because of the incompatibility between her job and her parenting obligations. Even single women without children are leaving jobs that demand extreme hours to have better work/life balance (Shellenbarger, 2012).

The Maternal Wall

Researchers consistently report that the baby boomers cracked the glass ceiling (Gillespie & Temple, 2011; Ruderman & Ohlott, 2002; Williams, 2005). Yet recently, researchers have posited that motherhood has created another strong barrier to success in many fields. Williams and Segal (2003) called this intersect of motherhood and employment the "maternal wall" and found that this wall continues to provide a significant challenge and prevents women from gaining senior roles in the workforce (Williams & Segal, p. 77).

One explanation for the maternal wall is that elevated standards of motherhood negatively impact working mothers (Gillespie & Temple, 2011; Hewlett & Luce, 2006). Howe and Strauss (2000) commented that the standards of parenthood were more relaxed in the 1960s and 1970s when baby boomer mothers believed that their "little Gen Xers thrived best when left to their own wits, to grow up tough and self-reliant" (p. 33). Gillespie and Temple (2011) also reported a very different standard than their baby boomer mothers "shooing us into the neighborhood with peanut-butter-and-Fluff sandwiches" with little or no supervision and noted that "standards of maternal success have been elevated to such dizzying levels" (p. 11).

Gillespie and Temple (2011) explored the experiences of today's generation of mothers who were raised to be overachievers in all endeavors, including parenthood. Just as in their professional lives, these women approached motherhood through extensive research and intense effort as they set their goal on "maternal superstardom" (Gillespie & Temple, 2011, p. 16). Gillespie and Temple described a maternal world of "playgroups where the hostess mothers routinely decorated cupcakes (peanut-free of course) with each child's first initial" (p. 16) and "listening to those über-moms from Gymboree, with their whole-wheat pasta and homemade baby food and in utero Spanish lessons" (p. 2). Judith Warner (2005) similarly documented mothers' experiences as a life of "quilt-making at school, carpooling and play dates and mother–daughter book clubs, and getting in to see the *right* dentist and worrying about whether they had the *wrong* pediatrician, and, and, and, layer after layer of trivia and absurdity" (p. 5).

Gillespie and Temple (2011) noted that baby boomer parents taught Generation X that they could do anything they wanted to do, and Generation X women interpreted this freedom as an expectation that they were supposed to have it all. And Gillespie and Temple described the result:

> Perfection became an addiction, motherhood a competitive sport. We raced to make partner at work while playing Mozart to our pregnant bellies... filled our shelves with advice books on sleep schedules and potty training... enrolled our toddlers in Itsy Bitsy Yoga.... We did everything *right*. But, soon, life became a snowballing sprint from wakeup until bedtime. (p. 4)

Warner (2005) found that the more mothers buy into this competiveness, the more their mental health and quality of life suffer. Yet this cultural phenomenon continues to persist and is being fueled by the media, as evidenced by the May 21, 2012 *Time* magazine cover story of a woman breast feeding her three-year-old son with the caption "Are you mom enough?"

In spite of giving the appearance of being fully liberated, Warner (2005) noted parallels between the stories of the mothers in her study and the women interviewed in the book that launched the second wave of the women's movement, Betty Friedan's *The Feminine Mystique* (1963/2001). "The sense of waste. The diffuse dissatisfaction. The angst, hidden behind all the obsession with trivia, the push to be perfect. And the tendency—every bit as pronounced among the mothers I met as it had been for the women Friedan interviewed—to blame themselves for their problems" (Warner, 2005, p. 13). Warner described this as "soul-draining perfectionism" and called it "the *Mommy* Mystique" (p. 13).

Gillespie and Temple (2011) determined that unwavering perfectionism is a serious liability and impediment to a satisfying life. These researchers found that the women in their study fell into two categories: the "good enoughs" and "never enoughs." The good enoughs learned to temper perfectionism and were more satisfied with all aspects of their lives. The never enoughs sought perfection in all aspects of their lives. And participants reported that perfectionism was more detrimental to balancing work and family than all other factors, including inflexible work places, financial pressures, and husbands who didn't contribute enough to parenting and household activities.

Women's struggle with perfectionism is amplified by women not asking for help (Culross, Choate, Erwin, & Yu, 2008; Spar, 2012). The ubiquitous images of superwomen give the impression that this is a realistic standard (Culross et al., 2008). Ruderman and Ohlott (2002) reported on this challenge: "Many of the women in our study internalized the TV model of the conventional family and thus had the cookie-baking mommy embedded in their mental image of a good woman. These societal ideals are hard to fulfill when you are working forty to sixty hours a week" (p. 134). So women compensate by trying to work harder, an approach Gillespie and Temple (2011) found futile. And this work ethic is not tempered by cultural factors, as stereotypical norms provide the perception that a woman's life should be "riddled with sacrifice" (Hewlett, 2002, p. 10). Warner (2005) concluded the culture of motherhood in the United States was "oppressive" and "the pressure to perform, to attain levels of perfect selflessness was insane" (p. 16).

The Second Shift

Compounding women's experiences with extreme parenting and increasing work hours are elevated expectations related to homemaking. The feminine mystique of being perfect wives has reached a new level of expectation. The popularity of Home and Garden Television and the Food Network and celebrities such as Martha Stewart sustain these expectations; the cultural norm of women participating in housework and childcare activities more than men results in these elevated expectations having a more powerful impact on women.

Spar (2012) found that men are doing more domestic work as women have moved into the work world, and Hochschild (2012) reported that the second shift has been cut in half since she first reported on this phenomenon in the 1980s. Yet researchers have confirmed that in almost every occupation, women are working longer hours, still perform more than half of household management, and are primarily responsible for childcare (Hewlett et al., 2010). In academia, women faculty members also report that they are still performing more than 50% of the household duties (Mason & Goulden, 2004; Philipsen & Bostic, 2010; Stinchfield & Trepal, 2010), and Rhoads and Rhoads (2012) found that female tenure-track professors do more childcare than their male counterparts. Spar (2012) found that women spend almost 40 hours per week on household management and childcare, compared to men's 21 hours on those activities. And the second shift exists even when women earn more than their husbands (Hewlett et al, 2010). Hewlett et al. (2010) reported that 39% of women who earn more than their husbands are still performing most of the housework and childcare duties. Furthermore, Spar pointed out that men's activities are often more discretionary as they engage in activities such as mowing the lawn or washing the car or playing with their children. Hochschild concluded that women who work and are responsible for the second shift at home are not able to compete with men who do not have this extra burden.

Inflexible Workplaces

Researchers have also asserted that the reason women have not moved into more leadership roles is because of inflexible workplaces (Hochschild, 2012; Mason & Goulden, 2004). Though women have sought fulfillment beyond the traditional roles of wife, mother, and homemaker for over 50 years (Friedan, 1963/2001), workplaces continue to be inflexible in addressing workers with family obligations (Hochschild, 2012; Hymowitz, 2012; Taylor et al., 2008). In academia, researchers have found that women have substantial responsibilities in their personal lives, but are still expected to function as if they have a stay-at-home spouse or partner who can provide childcare and household management (Halpern, 2008; Mason & Goulden, 2004; Philipsen & Bostic, 2010). One faculty participant in the Philipsen (2008) study compared the early feminist writers' observations with her current experiences and stated "no institutional, cultural, or structural changes have been made that make working mothers' lives easier" (p. 113). In fact, the lives of working mothers in today's culture are made harder by workplace and cultural trends.

Having It All

Slaughter (2012) supports the idea that women can have it all, but not the way our culture is currently structured. Hewlett (2002) found that the women participants in her study were so impacted by this culture that they considered themselves to be selfish for wanting to have it all. Yet researchers have consistently found that there are numerous benefits to having multiple life roles (Culross et al., 2008). Women tend to be happier when they are able to have both a career and a family (Hewlett, 2002). Working mothers have better perspective in the various areas of their lives than women who only had one central life component (Ruderman & Ohlott, 2002). The perspective that comes from activities outside of the office engenders creativity and fosters new ideas (Slaughter, 2012). Ruderman and Ohlott (2002) found that women's performance ratings actually increase as they take on roles outside of work. Ruderman and Ohlott concluded that their research supports the theory that "different facets of life inform and enrich each other, challenging the conventional assumption that the best employees prioritize work above all else. It also suggests that women can and should integrate various life roles, bringing skills from one realm into another" (p. 116).

Ruderman and Ohlott (2002) concluded that working mothers have numerous ways to achieve psychological well-being. Summarizing the interviews with their participants, Ruderman and Ohlott found that these women "believed that well-being was related to a whole life, and they derived self-esteem from many types of activity: raising children, being a friend, being a wife, solving work problems, improving business results, contributing to the community" (p. 114). Yet Slaughter (2012) found that it is simply not possible to manage multiple roles for very long when one of those roles includes extreme hours such as governmental leadership positions.

The challenges of being able to manage a family and career have led a high percentage of career women who are childlessness. When Hewlett started researching her book *Creating a Life: What Every Woman Needs to Know about Having a Baby and a Career* (2004), her plan was to write "a book celebrating women turning 50 at the millennium and to look at what forces had shaped their lives" (Gibbs, 2002, p. 53). What she discovered was that all of the successful women she interviewed sacrificed their plans to have children as they pursued their careers. Hymowitz (2012) similarly found that women leaders in every field are more likely to be childless than other women.

Hewlett (2002) reported that 33% of women professionals such as doctors and lawyers were childless after 40, and 42% of women business leaders in corporate America didn't have children. In academia, women on the tenure track are less likely to have children than men on the tenure track (Philipsen & Bostic, 2010). Mason and Goulden (2002) found that only 62% of tenured women professors in the humanities and social science fields and 50% of women professors in the sciences had children. Hewlett clarified that the majority of the high-achieving women had not chosen to be childless and in fact strongly desired the motherhood role. One of Hewlett's (2002) participants commented that remaining childless was not a choice, it was "a creeping nonchoice" (p. 3). Hewlett concluded that "the brutal demands of ambitious careers, the asymmetries of male–female relationships, and the difficulties of bearing children late in life conspire to crowd out the possibility of having children" (pp. 3–4).

Opting Out and Off-Ramping

Collins (2009) noted that given the challenges of having it all, some young women opt out of working. Others plan to off-ramp for a while

(Hewlett et al., 2010). Hewlett et al. (2010) found that 31% of the professional women in her study left their jobs at some point in their career, usually to care for children. The participants in the Hewlett et al. study revealed that the decision to off ramp was not an easy decision, as they had invested significantly in their careers and defined themselves by their careers. These women also found that on-ramping was much more difficult than they imagined (Hewlett et al., 2010).

Professional women have also taken what Hewlett et al. (2010) described as the scenic route and work part-time or flextime for several years. Hewlett et al. reported that almost 75% of professional women did not follow the "linear lock-step progression of a successful male career" (p. 1). And women suffered from this deviation in both earning power and promotional opportunities.

Discrimination

Researchers have consistently found that in addition to systemic discrimination, overt and subtle gender discrimination disadvantage women in the workforce and prevent women from reaching the top rung of the leadership ladder (Collins, 2009; Corbett & Hill, 2012; Hurtado et al., 2012). Claims filed with the Equal Opportunity Commission and the millions of dollars awarded to women complainants provide evidence of continued gender discrimination (Corbett & Hill, 2012). Researchers conclude that discrimination against working women is demonstrated in the wage gap between men and women (Collins, 2009; Corbett & Hill, 2012; Spar, 2012). In spite of the 50 years that have passed since the promulgation of the Equal Pay Act of 1963, women earn less than men in almost every profession (Corbett & Hill, 2012). Spar (2012) estimated that women still earn only 77% of what men earn. Hewlett (2002) theorized that the wage gap is a result of women interrupting their careers when they have children. Other researchers have found that stereotypes related to occupations appropriate for women and men are also partially responsible for the wage gap (Corbett & Hill, 2012). Corbett and Hill (2012) found that a portion of this wage gap can be explained by choice of college major, occupation, and men's ability to work more hours as they are often not burdened with childcare responsibilities. Yet Corbett and Hill found that even when they controlled for college major, occupation, and number of hours worked, one third of the pay gap could not be explained. And the fact that this wage discrepancy is evident within one year of college graduation speaks to a discriminatory system (Corbett & Hill, 2012).

Corbett and Hill (2012) determined that biases against women still exist, especially in traditionally male occupations. Women in academia report experiencing discrimination twice as often as men (Hurtado et al., 2012).

And cultural gender norms are still in place in the work force, exemplified in academia by women being assigned more service tasks than men, a disservice given that these tasks interfere with the pursuit of a research agenda and are not viewed as favorably in the promotion process (Williams, 2005).

Cultural Conditioning

Another explanation for the lack of women in leadership roles is the socialization women experience. Girls are socialized to be caregivers and nurturers, even at the expense of their own goals and dreams (Pipher, 1994; Simmons, 2009). Furthermore, media glorify an unattainable standard of feminine beauty and women spend a great deal of time and energy trying to attain this unachievable standard. And media reinforce the view of women as "passive, sexualized objects" (Simmons, 2009, p. 11), as opposed to assertive, competent leaders.

Frankel (2004) points out that cultural conditioning is constantly reinforced, not just through the media, but also through sources such as family, friends, and colleagues. In her book, *Nice Girls Don't Get the Corner Office: 101 Unconscious Mistakes Women Make That Sabotage Their Careers,* Frankel notes that the more women have bought into this socialization, the more challenges they may encounter as they seek leadership positions. Women who have accepted cultural limitations may lack critical skills that lead to leadership success (Frankel, 2004; Simmons, 2009). Women may be less likely to promote themselves and assert themselves, which often translates into women being less likely to negotiate promotions and higher salaries (Babcock & Laschever, 2007; Corbett & Hill, 2012; Simmons, 2009). Yet acting in ways inconsistent to these stereotypes leads to negative consequences such as being perceived as difficult or aggressive (Barsh & Cranston, 2011; Frankel, 2004), and learning to manage this negativity is difficult for women as they are socialized to make others happy at the expense of their fulfillment (Frankel, 2004).

Socialization can also work to women leaders' advantage. Behaviors such as listening, collaborating, motivating, and viewing staff as people as well as workers are ingrained in women through a lifetime of socialization and practice (Frankel, 2004). Frankel (2004) explains that when coaching men, she has to help them see that these culturally feminine skills are relevant to leadership. Yet given the cultural conditioning women experience, women have challenges figuring out how to leverage these qualities.

CULTURAL IMPACT ON YOUNG WOMEN

Abeles (2012) reflects on the impact of the extreme work culture on American children. She found that the extreme work phenomenon is becoming the standard for many children and adolescents. Referencing Slaughter's (2012) article in *The Atlantic* illuminating the work on culture's impact on women, Abeles points to the similar experience of our nation's children who are being asked to do well in school, provide leadership in extracurricular activities, participate in sports, and pursue volunteer activities. Abeles' film, *Race to Nowhere* (2010), is a documentary that reports on children experiencing anxiety and stress at alarming rates because of the current culture of overachievement and high-stakes testing. Considering the impact on young women, Cohen-Sandler (2005) concludes that "the pressure to excel is a national phenomenon, and its consequences are wreaking havoc on the lives of teenage girls everywhere" (p. 11). This pressure is also affecting girls as young as elementary school age (Cohen-Sandler, 2005).

Collins (2009) described the many benefits of legislation that opened doors for young women in academics and athletics. But more opportunities seemed to create more pressure for young women (Cohen-Sandler, 2005). "Girls usually see opened doors not as possibilities, but as obligations" (Cohen-Sandler, 2005, p. 32). And Sadker, Sadker, and Zittleman (2009) found that starting in elementary school, girls begin to believe that they need to be "supergirls" (p. 118).

In *Stressed-out Girls: Helping Them Thrive in the Age of Pressure*, Cohen-Sandler (2005) determined that "by the time they enter middle school many girls...face jam-packed schedules, hours of homework, heightened expectations, demanding social lives, and far too little sleep" (p. 3). Girls "worry about completing their assignments well enough to maintain their grades—and also finishing them fast enough to keep up with friendships and hobbies, practice their musical instruments, play sports, participate in school clubs, and look good" (Cohen-Sandler, 2005, p. 4). And in spite of being stressed, overwhelmed, and exhausted, many young women think they should be doing more. These young women are ascribing to the myth of being able to do everything perfectly. "Responding to one of many harmful messages of this culture, they equate being *successful* with being *extraordinary*" (Cohen-Sandler, 2005, p. 4). Just like women in this culture, girls think working harder is the solution, "driving a relentless, unsatisfying, and ultimately self-defeating quest for perfection" (p. 5). As young women see this standard of behavior all around them, they assume that it is normal and do not question it or ask for help (Cohen-Sandler, 2005).

The impact of gender socialization on women's leadership has been explored by Rachel Simmons, founder of the Girls Leadership Institute. Simmons (2009) notes that "our culture is teaching girls to embrace a version of selfhood that sharply curtails their power and potential" (p. 1). The cultural pressure to be nice and modest and selfless "diminishes girls' authenticity and personal authority" (p. 1). Girls are socialized to be perfect and thus they struggle with feedback and perceived failure. As a result they may avoid challenges (Simmons, 2009). Simmons describes "the Curse of the Good Girl," a curse that "erects a psychological glass ceiling that begins its destructive sprawl in girlhood and extends across the female life span, stunting the growth of skills and habits essential to becoming a strong woman" (2009, p. 1).

The messages that impede girls' success are provided by many aspects of society, including the media and schools. Girls are exposed to significant amounts of mass media and are constantly bombarded with degrading messages in plot lines, characterizations, and commercials (Sadker et al., 2009). Furthermore, Sadker et al. (2009) found that girls are not asked as many questions in classes or praised as much as boys; girls learn to smile, be quiet, and defer to boys. Sadker et al. report that "the school curriculum reinforces lessons of female docility with womanless histories, male-oriented science and math classes, and school sports programs that create heroes of male athletes" (p. 21). As a result, girls become less confident and less ambitious, and these consequences persist in their adulthood (Sadker et al., 2009).

The implications of this socialization on leadership aspirations are profound. In high school, girls are significantly more likely to view themselves as leaders and hold more leadership positions than boys (Simmons, 2009). But cultural forces seem to reverse this trend as young women transition to adulthood. By college, women leaders are less prevalent (Simmons, 2009) and in the workforce, the dearth of women leaders is the norm (Hymowitz, 2012; Spar, 2012; Taylor et al., 2008).

CREATING OPPORTUNITIES

Perhaps the most impactful intervention to create better paths to leadership for women is educating the next generation. Abeles (2012) encourages examining the current culture of overachievement and implementing changes to create a culture in which children can flourish. This generation of young women seems to have more exposure to stress-inducing messages and seems more vulnerable to the perpetuation of self-defeating thoughts (Cohen-Sandler, 2005). Yet girls can be taught to critically examine and deflect the media's messages and learn to distinguish healthy messages from unhealthy or unrealistic messages (Cohen-Sandler, 2005; Sadker et al., 2009). Girls can learn to balance the needs of others without sacrificing their own interests and needs (Simmons, 2009). Parents and teachers can be encouraged to help girls set realistic and authentic goals and support girls' success (Cohen-Sandler, 2005). Girls can also learn to reframe failure as opportunity (Simmons, 2009).

Girls can be exposed to media with explanations for cultural norms and empowering messages such as the documentaries *Race to Nowhere* and *Miss Representation*. *Race to Nowhere* challenges the current culture of overachievement. *Miss Representation* provides insight into how the media's portrayal of women contributes to girls' and women's challenges with self-esteem and the underrepresentation of women in leadership positions. The *Miss Representation* website provides activities that support the social action goal of self-actualization for both genders. *Miss Representation* also provides K–12 and university curricula designed to help girls and boys critically examine the media's impact on girls' and women's ability to view themselves as leaders.

Young women need understanding, support, and messages that counteract negative cultural messages (Cohen-Sandler, 2005). Simmons (2009) suggests that leading by example is the most effective tool women can use to help young women become empowered and succeed. Simmons encourages women to assert their authentic selves and live by their own rules, regardless of whether they match cultural stereotypes.

And as women work to change cultural mores, they are wise to involve men (Slaughter, 2012; Spar, 2012). Many men are involved parents and participate in domestic work, and they are seeking a better work/life balance (Philipsen & Bostic, 2010; Slaughter, 2012). Both men and women will benefit from women's ways of working as will clients and other stakeholders (Slaughter, 2012).

Losing talented women leaders has broad social and economic impact on men and women (Slaughter, 2012). Davidson (2012/2013) reported that women board members actually help increase net profits. Similarly, Canning, Haque, and Wang (2012) found a positive correlation between the number of female executives in start-up companies and company success.

If women are going to achieve equity in leadership positions, extreme work hour requirements need to be reconsidered. Efficacy and achievement seem to be suffering rather than increasing by these cultural work trends. And women seeking work/life balance are effectively shut out of many leadership positions when extreme hour requirements are more prized than talent, creativity, and other leadership attributes.

Furthermore, the linear male employment pattern needs to be revisited (Halpern, 2008; Slaughter, 2012). Hewlett (2002) reported that companies with wide-ranging work/life policies were more successful in retaining women. Accordingly, policies that support a variety of employment patterns, including off-ramping for both women and men who have family responsibilities, will need to be implemented or expanded. Telecommuting and flextime, also considered to be effective work/life policies, can be considered (Hewlett et al., 2010; Hymowitz, 2012; Slaughter, 2012). A key component of these policies will be providing mentoring and other support for employees who utilize these policies (Hewlett et al., 2010). And employees need to be able to take advantage of work/life policies without suffering long-term career damage (Hewlett, 2002). Hewlett et al. (2010) notes that it is wise to view these policies not as accommodations, but as "a powerful weapon in the battle to attract and retain key talent" (p. 36).

Changing the attitudes of society will also be necessary if women are going to achieve equity in leadership positions. Our culture needs to reconsider stereotypical views of assertive women, as assertion is a critical leadership skill

(Babcock & Laschever, 2007). Societal comfort with women leaders in general needs to be addressed. Hymowitz (2012) provided information on how the use of quotas requiring women's representation in leadership has helped change the perception of women leaders in other countries. Davidson (2012/2013) advocated for promoting quota-type goals that require legislatures and businesses to include more women and pointed out Title IX as a "shining example of a quota-like goal that proved truly transformative" (p. 74). Davidson notes that when women are on company boards, there are increased numbers of women in top leadership in those companies. Davidson concludes that the ripple effect of quota-type initiatives provides female role models and changes attitudes toward women leaders, which brings more women into leadership positions.

Spar (2012) notes that the lack of women's success in the work force goes beyond lack of supportive policies and discrimination. In addition to changing policies, Spar concludes that women "must instead forge partnerships with those around us, and begin to dismantle the myth of solitary perfection" (para. 9). Similarly, Gillespie, and Temple (2011) found that women found their greatest success when they overcame perfectionism. Spar concludes that if women fail to realize that having it all with perfection is a myth, "we are only condemning ourselves and our daughters to failure" (para. 20).

Frankel (2004) reminds women that they need to revisit the stereotypes that they absorbed in childhood and choose the actions that are authentic and will lead to personal satisfaction and self-actualization. Gillespie and Temple (2011) further clarify that women need to accept that they are not going to have it all by simply working a little harder. The most successful women in these researchers' study made conscious choices and realized they were not going to be able to do everything because it was impossible. They learned to delegate and say no to some requests. And Gillespie and Temple noted that successful women reevaluated their priorities and allocated their time accordingly.

Women also need to view their career path differently. Slaughter (2012) suggests that women view their leadership career path as a vertical slope with the option of plateaus for family care, as opposed to a straight uphill trajectory. And Hewlett et al. (2010) noted that women's networks help nurture ambition through access to women who can serve as mentors and role models.

CONCLUSION

Levinson (1996) cautioned that "a strongly male-centered view of adult life has for centuries been prevalent in our scientific and cultural institutions. It will take time, effort, and sharpened awareness of gender issues to achieve a more balanced view" (p. x). Ruderman and Ohlott (2002) reported that the glass ceiling is cracked and many are poised to dislodge this obstacle. Yet Collins (2009) found that the gender revolution "merely opened doors" for women (p. 371). Statistics on women's lack of parity with men in the work-force and in leadership positions suggest that women may have achieved as much they can without the creation of new solutions to promote women's success (Babcock & Laschever, 2007).

Engaging in dialogues about the social forces that inhibit women's success is critical is this endeavor. Recognizing that the extreme-work model is not sustainable (Hewlett & Luce, 2006; Slaughter, 2012) and redefining the ideal worker by modifying norms, practices, and policies is necessary (Williams & Segal, 2003). Moderating competitiveness with collaboration and support is indicated. Spar (2012) reminds us that feminism was built on communal activities and goals, and women are best served when they work together as opposed to struggling individually. Together, we can remove the obstructions preventing women from achieving leadership roles so that women's voices can be considered in advocating for a more equitable society that supports women reaching their full potential (Friedan, 1963/2001). Only then will the gender revolution envisioned over 50 years ago be complete.

REFERENCES

Abeles, V. (2010). *Race to nowhere* [DVD]. Lafayette, CA: Reel Link Films. Available from http://www.RaceToNowhere.com

Abeles, V. (2012, July 20). *The rat race of childhood: Why we need to balance students' lives* [Web log message]. Retrieved from http://www.washingtonpost.com/blogs/answer-sheet/post/the-rat-race-of-childhood-why-we-need-to-balance-students-lives/2012/07/19/gJQAzvE0wW_blog.html

Babcock, L., & Laschever, S. (2007) *Women don't ask: The high cost of avoiding negotiation—and positive strategies for change.* New York, NY: Bantam Dell.

Barsh, J., & Cranston, S. (2011). *How remarkable women lead: The breakthrough model for work and life.* New York, NY: Crown Business.

Canning, J., Haque, M., & Wang, Y. (2012, September). *Women at the wheel: Do female executives drive start-up success?* Retrieved from www.dowjones.com/collateral/files/womenPE_report_final.pdf

Cohen-Sandler, R. (2005). *Stressed-out girls: Helping them thrive in the age of pressure.* New York, NY: Penguin Group.

Collins, G. (2009). *When everything changed: The amazing journey of American women from 1960 to the present.* New York, NY: Little, Brown and Company.

Corbett, C., & Hill, C. (2010). *Graduating to a pay gap: The earnings of women and men one year after college graduation.* Washington, DC: American Association of University Women.

Culross, R. R., Choate, L. A., Erwin, M. J., & Yu, J. (2008). Finding life balance for women at work. In L. H. Choate (Ed.), *Girls' and women's wellness* (pp. 143–168). Alexandria, VA: American Counseling Association.

Davidson, A. (2012, December/2013, January). Just add women: When quotas require that legislatures and businesses include more women, remarkable things can happen. *MORE, 15*(10), 70–74.

Draper, H. (2012, November 13). Women won't reach leadership parity with men until 2085, DU study finds. *Denver Business Journal.* Retrieved from http://www.bizjournals.com/denver/blog/broadway_17th/2012/11/women-wont-reach-leadership-parity.html

Frankel, L. P. (2004). *Nice girls don't get the corner office: 101 unconscious mistakes women make that sabotage their careers.* New York, NY: Business Plus.

Friedan, B. (2001). *The feminine mystique.* New York, NY: W. W. Norton & Company. (Original work published in 1963)

Gibbs, N. (2002, April 15). Babies vs. career: Which should come first for women who want both? The harsh facts about fertility. *Time,* pp. 49–54.

Gillespie, B. B., & Temple, H. S. (2011). *Good enough is the new perfect: Finding happiness and success in modern motherhood.* North York, Ontario: Harlequin.

Halpern, D. E. (2008). Nurturing careers in psychology: Combining work and family. *Educational Psychology Review, 20,* 57–64.

Hewlett, S. A. (2002). Executive women and the myth of having it all. *Harvard Business Review, 80*(4), 66–73.

Hewlett, S. A. (2004). *Creating a life: What every woman needs to know about having a baby and a career.* New York, NY: Miramax.

Hewlett, S. A., Forster, D., Sherbin, L., Shiller, P., & Sumberg, K. (2010). *Off-ramps and on-ramps revisited.* New York, NY: Center for Work-Life Policy.

Hewlett, S. A., & Luce, C. B. (2006). Extreme jobs: The dangerous allure of the 70-hour workweek. *Harvard Business Review, 84*(12), 49–59.

Hochschild, A. (2012). *The second shift: Working families and the revolution at home.* New York, NY: Penguin Books.

Howe, N., & Strauss, W. (2000). *Millennials rising: The next great generation.* New York, NY: Vintage Books.

Hurtado, S., Eagan, K., Pryor, J. H., Whang, H., & Tran, S. (2012). *Undergraduate teaching faculty: The 2010–2011 HERI Faculty Survey.* Los Angeles, CA: Higher Education Research Institute, UCLA.

Hymowitz, C., & Shellhardt, T. D. (1986, March 24). The corporate woman (A special report): Cover—The glass ceiling: Why women can't seem to break the invisible barrier that blocks them from the top jobs. *Wall Street Journal.* Retrieved from http://proxy.library.vcu.edu/login?url=http://search.proquest.com/docview/397974878?accountid=14780

Hymowitz, K. S. (2012, Autumn). The plight of the alpha female. *City Journal, 22*(4). Retrieved from http://www.city-journal.org/2012/22_4_alpha-female.html

Jackson, J., & O'Callaghan, E. (2009). What do we know about glass ceiling effects? A taxonomy and critical review to inform higher education research. *Research in Higher Education, 50,* 460–482.

Levinson, D. J. (1996). *Seasons of a woman's life.* New York, NY: Ballantine Books.

Mason, M. A., & Goulden, M. (2002). Do babies matter: The effect of family formation on the lifelong careers of academic men and women. *Academe, 88*(6), 21–27.

Mason, M. A., & Goulden, M. (2004). Marriage and baby blues: Redefining gender equity in the academy. *Annals of the American Academy of Political and Social Science, 596,* 86–103.

Newsom, J. S. (Producer). (2011). *Miss Representation* [DVD]. Available from http://www.rocoeducational.com/miss_representation

Philipsen, M. I. (2008). *Challenges of the faculty career for women: Success and sacrifice.* San Francisco: Jossey-Bass.

Philipsen, M. I., & Bostic, T. B. (2010). *Helping faculty find work-life balance: The path toward family-friendly institutions.* San Francisco, CA: Jossey-Bass.

Pickert, K. (2012, May 21). The man who remade motherhood. *Time, 179*(20). Retrieved from http://www.time.com/time/magazine/article/0,9171,2114427,00.html

Pipher, M. (1994). *Reviving Ophelia: Saving the selves of adolescent girls.* New York, NY: Ballentine Books.

Rapoport, R., Bailyn, L., Fletcher, J. K., & Pruitt, B. H. (2002). *Beyond work–family balance: Advancing gender equity and workplace performance.* San Francisco, CA: Jossey-Bass.

Rhoads, S. E., & Rhoads, C. H. (2012). Gender roles and infant/toddler care: Male and female professors on the tenure track. *Journal of Social, Evolutionary, and Cultural Psychology, 6*(1), 13–31.

Ruderman, M. N., & Ohlott, P. J. (2002). *Standing at the crossroads: Next steps for high-achieving women.* San Francisco, CA: Jossey-Bass.

Sadker, D., Sadker, M., & Zittleman, K. R. (2009). *Still failing at fairness: How gender bias cheats girls and boys in school and what we can do about it.* New York, NY: Scribner.

Shellenbarger, S. (2012, May 23). Single and off the fast track. *The Wall Street Journal,* p. D1.

Simmons, R. (2009). *The curse of the good girl: Raising authentic girls with courage and confidence.* New York, NY: Penguin Books.

Slaughter, A. M. (2012, July/August). Why women still can't have it all. *The Atlantic,* pp. 84–102.

Spar, D. (2012, October 1 & 8). Why women should stop trying to be perfect. *Newsweek.* Retrieved from http://www.thedailybeast.com/newsweek/2012/09/23/why-women-should-stop-trying-to-be-perfect.html

Stinchfield, T. A., & Trepal, H. C. (2010). Academic motherhood for counselor educators: Navigating through the pipeline. *International Journal for the Advancement of Counseling, 32,* 91–100. doi:10.1007/s10447-009-9086-0

Taylor, P., Morin, R., Cohn, D., Clark, A., & Wang, W. (2008, August 25). *Men or women: Who's the better leader.* Washington, DC: Pew Research Center.

Warner, J. (2005). *Perfect madness: Motherhood in the age of anxiety.* New York, NY: Penguin Group.

Williams, J. C. (2005). The glass ceiling and the maternal wall in academia. *New Directions for Higher Education, 130,* 91–105.

Williams, J. C., & Segal, N. (2003). Beyond the maternal wall: Relief for family caregivers who are discriminated against on the job. *Harvard Women's Law Journal, 26,* 77–162.

CHAPTER 3

PASSION, PEDAGOGIES, AND POLITICS

Feminists in Academe

Miriam E. David

ABSTRACT

Feminism, as both a political and educational project, is the subject of this chapter. It is based upon interviews and conversations with over 100 international feminists in global academe. In my book *Feminism, Gender, & Universities: Politics, Passion, & Pedagogies* (David, 2014) I developed a life history of feminist activism in academe over the last 50 years, and constructed a collective biography of three cohorts of academic feminists. Illustrations of these three generations of second-wave feminists are provided in this chapter to reveal both the life-changing experience that feminism has been and how important education, and higher education especially, has been to this. While the three generations have different biographies, in that increasing numbers are first generation or first-in-the-family to go to university, all talk with passion about how feminism transformed their lives both in the family and through university. Feminism has enabled them to become the passionate teachers in global academe, and continues to help them to struggle against the changing and constraining conditions of the neoliberal academy. Feminism helps to resist the more overt misogyny that now pervades global academe, despite changes toward gender equality in numbers of undergraduate students.

Women Interrupting, Disrupting, and Revolutionizing Educational Policy and Practice, pages 41–55

41

Fifty years ago, Betty Friedan's *The Feminine Mystique* (1963) became an instant best seller. It was one of several books that launched the women's movement in the United States of America in what has become known as "second-wave" feminism. Friedan's book spoke to what she called "the problem that has no name"—that is, highly educated, middle-class women in the United States feeling dissatisfied with the condition of being housewives and mothers. In the following decades, numerous books and pamphlets were spawned in North America, the United Kingdom (UK), and other parts of Europe and Australia, also known as the "global north."

Titles such as *Of Woman Born: Motherhood as Experience and Institution* (Rich, 1976), *Patriarchal Attitudes* (Figes, 1970), *Sexual Politics* (Millett, 1970), *The Dialectic of Sex* (Firestone, 1970), *The Female Eunuch* (Greer, 1970), and *Women, Resistance and Revolution* (Rowbotham, 1973) spring to mind as key examples of books that inaugurated this phase of the women's movement, along with Adrienne Rich, the American feminist poet and essayist; Eva Figes, the German Jewish refugee to England; Kate Millett, the American artist who wrote her piece as part of her doctorate; Shulamith Firestone, the Canadian orthodox Jewess who sought refuge in New York; Germaine Greer, the Australian émigré to England; and Sheila Rowbotham, the English feminist historian. All of these writers were passionate about women's positions: in the family as daughters, sisters, wives, and mothers; as sexual beings; in education; and in paid and unpaid work or employment. How could women's lives be transformed and made more equal with men's lives in both public and private?

The project of feminism is essentially educational, and indeed pedagogical, while it is also, at its essence, political, aiming to change women's lives in the direction of social equality and social justice, or what has, in the 21st century, become known as gender justice. But questions remain, such as: Just how successful has the feminist project been? What has been accomplished over the last 50 years or so? What remains to be done? What changes have been made that need to be undone in the changing contexts toward neoliberalism? What role has feminism played in academe? and What impact has it had on higher education arenas?

Although there have been innumerable studies of feminism and the women's movement through the years and changing faces and politics, there is comparably less written about how feminism has become a part of academe and contributes (or not) to critiques of traditional disciplines, while also becoming a subject in its own right, as, for instance, women's studies. Many of the women who wrote second-wave feminism books and pamphlets were, indeed, women who had been students in higher education, as had been the American women in Friedan's study. But just how did feminism continue to impact higher education itself? How did feminist knowledge emerge and become a central part of the transformation of higher education? What did feminist academics think and feel about this project, and how did they engage with it?

SWEEPING SOCIAL, ECONOMIC, AND POLITICAL CHANGES

Clearly there have been a multitude of socioeconomic and sociopolitical changes in the last 50 years such that education, generally, and higher education, in particular, are now key parts of the global economy in ways that they had not been in previous decades. We now refer to this phenomenon as the knowledge economy or "academic capitalism," a term coined by the American feminist Sheila Slaughter, with her colleagues, Larry Leslie (1997) and Gary Rhoades (2004). While there are many ways to describe and theorize these manifold and global transformations, a key role has been played by changing forms of education, especially in relation to information and computer technologies (ICT), now known to comprise the knowledge industries.

Questions of gender and sexual relations, violence against women, sexual harassment, and child sexual abuse are now more overtly in the public eye. For instance, it was a young woman medical student whose murder through gang rape in India dominated the global news headlines over the New Year period (2012–2013). Similarly, the Taliban's general political violence in that region of the Indian subcontinent, Afghanistan, and Pakistan, has been perpetrated on young women fighting for girls' education. For example, Malala Yousafzai, a Pakistani schoolgirl fighting for her rights and those of her classmates, was shot in the face, along with other schoolgirls, and left for dead. She was brought to the UK for treatment and, miraculously, able to leave the hospital to recuperate in a temporary place of safety for her family during the same period of time. In the UK, there has been a recent furor over a BBC celebrity, Jimmy Savile, whose sexual harassment and rape of young women over a 50-year period only came to public light recently after his death. These are just a few examples of the violence and sexual harassment of women and girls that are known by the general public via news outlets that may not have been available during the beginning of second-wave feminism.

Why are questions of gender and sexual relations now so visible when they were not even on the public agenda 40 or 50 years ago? Is the way in which they are publicly debated a result of feminist activism? Or does it have more to do with the toxic mix of globalization and changing gender and social relations? What has changed to make these issues visible and open to such intense political debate? And can education be used to try to transform wider social and sexual relations and reduce, if not eliminate, male violence against women?

LOOKING BACK: THE PERSONAL IS POLITICAL

Looking back on my own life as a feminist academic, I remember that Savile was launching his career as a disc jockey on the public stage when I was first a student of sociology at the University of Leeds. Among my friends and acquaintances in Leeds were young women who encountered him. And, around the same time, other women friends were beginning groups as part of the early stirrings of the women's liberation movement that was later to become known as feminism. It was in these consciousness-raising groups that women began to share experiences of intimate sexual relations, while in the relative safety and privacy of groups with like-minded women, reaching out toward some understanding of sexual power relations, with the realization that they were not only individual acts, but also political acts with ramifications. Yet these acts are certainly hidden from the public gaze for the most part.

Thus, the phrase "the personal is political" was coined, leading to discussions about the sexual division of labor, women's rights and women's work, and, more importantly, the rise of intellectual curiosity about how these structured gender relations had come about (David, 2003). Through the women's movement, based, as it tended to be, around young women as students or new graduates, feminists began to develop new "knowledge" and new approaches, including feminist pedagogies grounded in personal experience. At the same time, higher education was expanding, and opportunities for women—not only as students, but also as researchers and academics—were opening up. Women, including feminists, quickly began to enter academia.

GROWING NUMBERS OF EDUCATED WOMEN

Over the last four decades, UNESCO's *World Atlas of Gender Equality in Education* (Fiske, 2012)

> tells the story of enormous growth in educational opportunities and literacy levels throughout the world... especially since the Dakar Forum of 2000. During this period the capacity of the world's education systems more than doubled—from 647 students in 1970 to 1,397 million in 2009. Enrollments increased from... 33 to 164 million in higher education. (p. 9)

Currently, though the headline story is that "Women now account for a majority of students in most countries" (Fiske, 2012, p. 78), "enhanced access to higher education by women has not always translated into enhanced career opportunities, including the opportunity to use their doctorates in fields of research" (p. 75). While these data are presented internationally, there is what is called a "feminization crisis debate" in the UK (Morley, 2011). For example, many policymakers claim that the goals of feminism have been achieved, given the growing numbers of women entering higher education arenas—even blaming women generally, and feminists especially, for gaps in social equality or social mobility between women and men.

Feminism was indeed an educational project to change women's lives in the direction of gender and social equality. However, whether the feminist project has been achieved, or whether it is to blame for increasing gaps between men's and women's progress, remains to be substantiated. As such, my research aims to address the aforementioned questions. The project included talking with a wide range of international feminist educators and academic activists based largely in Anglophone countries of the global north to capture the essence of academic women's pedagogical engagement in higher education aiming for gender and social justice (David, 2014). Additionally, I reviewed the achievements of feminist studies to discover what is left to be accomplished, while also considering obstacles and challenges that hindered the work. I also attempted to understand how changing political and socioeconomic contexts facilitated or blocked educational and pedagogical innovations.

STUDYING WOMEN (FEMINIST) ACADEMICS

Using the now established social and feminist methods of narrative inquiry, I aimed to involve an array of feminist academics from across arts and social science subjects, in diverse higher education settings and across several generations of scholars. Eventually, I approached an opportunity "sample" through a range of international networks that I have been involved with, largely the social sciences, including educational studies, obtaining well over a hundred replies from international women academics across the generations. In particular, I targeted an international network of "education feminists," grouped around the American Educational Research Association (AERA), and a group of women with whom I had worked in the early 1970s, to put together the first UK reader in women's studies—the Bristol Women's Studies Group (1979) who jointly published *Half the Sky: An Introduction to Women's Studies*—and other such colleagues from those early days of the feminist movement in academia. I also included two other networks of feminists, namely the international Gender and Education Association (GEA) and feminists involved in the UK's Society for Research in Higher Education (SRHE). This generated a diverse range of women participants.

My study is, therefore, made up of a diversity of women academics, across multiple generations and ages. Participants are also extremely varied in terms of their social and geographic locations, illustrative of the mobile, transnational academics who are characteristic of the overall academic profession in the 21st century (Kim & Brooks, 2012, in press). While most of the women are now residents in the UK, many come from former British colonies such as Australia, Canada, the Caribbean, India, Pakistan, South Africa, the United States, and other parts of Europe such as France, Greece, Spain. Likewise, all participants who were living in Canada at the time of the study were born in other countries such as Germany, Norway, the UK, and the United States. By contrast, the participants who resided in Australia at the time of the study were born there, although there are several key Australian feminists who are now residents in the UK.

Following the pioneering work of the late feminist sociologist of education, Olive Banks, in her study *Becoming a Feminist: The Social Origins of "First Wave" Feminism* (1986), I decided to divide my participants into three cohorts for the purpose of analysis. The women scholars fell unevenly into three age groups, namely those born before or during the Second World War (1935–1950) and going to university in the late 1950s or 1960s, those born in the heyday of higher educational opportunities of the 1950s to 1965 and going to university in the 1970s, and a younger generation of feminist academics born in the late 1960s and across the 1970s and going to university in the heyday of Reaganism, Thatcherism, and neoliberalism.

The majority of women who responded were from the first cohort, with about half as many in the second cohort, and only about ten percent from the youngest group. Given the increasingly intensive nature of academic work today, I was not surprised that the responses from older and retired women also tended to be more full as they are those who had been fired by feminist passions for political activism and who had eventually become, as I had too, jaundiced by the constant struggles within academia to maintain an emancipatory place and space. Nevertheless, those women of the two younger cohorts were equally passionate about their feminist commitments while leading intensely busy academic lives. Indeed, they had come of academic age during an expansionary, but constrained and constraining, individualized academy, with its metrication of all forms of academic life.

Feminism is Central to Identity

All of the participants felt passionately about how the "new wave" of thinking or the so-called feminist project was vitally important for them in their own learning and their subsequent creation of new knowledge and curricula for their own teaching. Comments such as "it changed my life," and "feminism has been my life project" peppered the interview transcripts. One woman said, "My entire life has been shaped by feminism . . . at university. . . . It was the beginning of the feminist movement, and I joined a women's liberation group. . . . We women were a small minority." Another said that she also became a feminist "at university in the late 1960s . . . My whole adult life is lived as a feminist and has shaped everything I have studied and written. I have been an activist in the WLM and continue to be involved as an activist. As a scholar, I write from a feminist perspective."

One senior education feminist scholar said both passionately and poignantly that:

> I began to self-identify as a feminist when I was a graduate student in 1970. . . . I went into the academy after completing my PhD in Educational Policy Studies. Feminism is woven through every fiber of my being and has been since the early 1970s. . . . My family was not impressed with my move towards radical politics in general nor feminism more specifically. They in fact took issue with who I was becoming both intellectually and personally.

Similarly, a feminist from the second cohort wrote movingly that:

> Feminism has been absolutely central to my life. It allowed me to gradually gain a perspective on Catholicism that eventually allowed me to leave the established church. For a long time I felt that the intellectual, theological knowledge was battling with my intellectual feminism. I would say that through the twists and turns of my life the one intellectual endeavour that I have never doubted is my feminism. I passionately believe in a person's right to equality and especially to have freedom over their bodies. I would say that I still teach from a feminist perspective even if my students would not always recognize this. Feminism informs my personal life profoundly. I have on and off been active in many feminist causes, big and small.

Influential Writers and Texts

Most of the women mentioned feminist literature that had influenced their decisions to become feminists. However, the precise nature of that literature differed across the three cohorts, with the women scholars from the oldest cohort talking about some of the titles and texts mentioned above, such as Betty Friedan or Simone de Beauvoir, whereas the younger two cohorts tended to mention women and feminist literature more specific to their particular fields and from within higher education, rather than the more popular and political tracts of the 1970s, although, the youngest participant did mention many of the early popular texts.

If we turn to the feminists of the first cohort, namely those born between 1935 and 1950, their trajectories into and through universities were very similar. Interestingly, as I talked to these diverse and varied feminists, a number of key texts influenced their budding consciousness and desires to change women's situations. However, none of this generation or cohort of academic women mentioned materials from their courses. It was the materials and texts outside the university, and often part of a wider political project, that first captured their imaginations. For example, Betty Friedan was mentioned several times as a highly influential source by an American living in the UK in the 1970s, and by a British woman who had gone to do a Master's course in the United States. One feminist educator wrote,

> In one sense I was always a feminist. I did not see why my mother, who was so intelligent, was a housewife and devoted to her children (us) without directly using her education. I did not want a future of cooking and cleaning. My parents encouraged all of us to do well in school and go on to higher education and into careers (though we were also to get married). I think my first exposure to feminism per se was reading Betty Friedan's *The Feminine Mystique*, which I loved. However, I can't remember when I read it. I think it must have been when I was at graduate school, not undergraduate. The late 60s were such a time of upheaval, and feminism came along with student protest and civil rights and anti-Vietnam protests. Students formed CR groups and I belonged to one of them. It was exhilarating.

Another put it this way,

> I think I have approached most of my scholarly pursuits through the lens of feminism—both research and teaching. I also have a feminist way of looking at relationships, family, media, and everyday life, but it is not always consistent. Over time, I became less vocal and learned to modulate some of my views in order to have a somewhat easier life. I have never been an activist in the usual sense. Earlier in my career I did quite a lot of organizing of seminars and workshops and so forth on various aspects of gender and education.

Another eminent literary feminist scholar said:

> I went to university in London to University College in the late 1960s, to read English because I loved it and was good at reading and writing. I became a feminist when I went to do an MA at Louisiana State University from 1969 to 1971. I read Betty Friedan's *The Feminine Mystique* and immediately joined the National Organization of Women (NOW) and consciousness-raising and campaign groups.

Yet another of these now senior women academics going to university in the 1960s in England went on to the United States to do a Master's. She wrote that she went to "Oxford in the mid 1960s to do PPE (Politics, Philosophy and Economics) but the reason why is most interesting." She said,

I did Oxbridge entrance in English but got called for interview for PPE as the admissions tutor decided that I would make a good social scientist from reading my entrance exam essay—she was probably right but I have always been somewhere between arts and social science. From Oxford I went to University of Sussex to do a doctorate in the Sociology of Art and Literature but spent a year at Cornell University whilst doing my studies. I was there from 1969–1970 and joined the first ever women's group—we marched, sat in, and campaigned for abortion rights. I returned to the UK and went to Scotland in 1971 but did not really get involved in feminist politics there—made some good friends in the 'Women in Action' group and did march in favour of abortion rights—SPUC off. This was more of a big step for my partner with whom I started living in 1972 as he was raised a Catholic but still joined in the march.

Emergent Feminists From Girlhood

Another one of these now eminent feminist mobile scholars wrote that her education crossed continents, cultures, and subjects, with an initial desire to be an agricultural economist in a developing country, given that she had spent much of her childhood as an Asian living in East Africa, and studying in the United States before coming to the UK for further studies. However, her becoming a feminist predated her university education. She said,

I became a feminist when I was about 12 when I read novels by a Punjabi writer called Nanak Singh. I was also influenced by Amrita Pritam, a Punjabi poet and novelist, and Waris Shah, another renowned Punjabi writer. They all critiqued women's position in Punjabi society. I have been deeply influenced by feminism, and have contributed through activism as well as theory.

By contrast, a now senior feminist sociologist in Canada said her consciousness of feminism was only slowly awakened:

I went to Trinity College, Dublin in the early 1960s, doing Modern History and Political Theory. My choices were limited because of my inadequate schooling and Dublin seemed nicer than the large red bricks. Indeed, it was. I was well taught and I enjoyed myself, though I didn't work in any driven kind of way, and came out with a respectable degree and a husband. There was no feminism around, either in the literature or on the campus, and little radical activity. The Aldermaston marches were happening, but they were a long way away, and I was still too far under my conservative parents' thumb to make the trek. I remember picketing in support of Travellers' camps but not much else. I left university with a wedding weeks away and no idea of what I wanted to do, and with the words of the Dean of Women Students ringing in my ears: that as I was about to marry I should do something easy—like a Dip. Ed. So I did. I did history and then education—which was all prepolitical awakening. What happened then was feminism, and subsequently a transitional diploma in sociology and a PhD in Sociology, which was one of the early explicitly feminist PhDs in the UK. . . . I first became aware of an overt feminist consciousness with an article in the Guardian weekly while I was teaching in Botswana by Jill Tweedie or Mary Stott—I forget which—but it alerted me to the fact that women were meeting and discussing their problems with the way women were treated and located in the world was. As soon as I got back to the UK I tracked down a feminist group in Bristol. I think my early graduate teaching in feminism came in that group and at the feminist conferences and demonstrations of the early 1970s. I was moving rapidly towards a more radical view of the world—both socialist and feminist—and I wanted to root this new awareness in something more systematically intellectual.

Another immigrant to the UK, this time from Australia, read for degree at the University of Melbourne in the mid to late 1950s, studied at Bristol University in the second half of the 1960s, and went on to say:

I wanted to go to University because I had decided when I was about 10 that I wanted to stay on at school and did not want to leave school at 14, get married and have children (which at that time and place meant to be a full time housewife and mother). I was always a voracious reader of just about anything I could get my hands on. This involved first convincing my father to let me go to the High School (6 years possibly leading to matriculation) rather than the Girl's School (5 years, culminating in the school leaving certificate, working in an office or nursing etc.) then getting bursaries in the last 2 years of school and a studentship with the state Department of Education to go to the University before training as a secondary school teacher, the only way it would have been affordable. It also involved a very emotional tussle with my mother, who didn't want me to leave home, or to go to University because of her attitudes to class. . . . I would have done a pure English course except that it was a requirement of the Education Department to have two teaching subjects. I was immersed in Shakespeare, English novelists and English and American poets, but I also loved history—partly from conversations with my parents about local and family history from an early age. These choices were also influenced by one young female English teacher and two older male left wing Irish Australian teachers of History, back from the war. Returned soldiers were also a great influence in the History department at university and the course was influential in my political development, including Marxist historical work, at a time of right wing backlash in the 1950s . . . *I was already a proto-feminist at primary school* [emphasis added]. I identified as a tom-boy, climbing trees—where I would sometimes sit doing embroidery after the example of the heroine of one of my mother's books which was loosely based on a combination of *Twelfth Night* and the *Taming of the Shrew* (Edwardian era girls' novels had some good stuff in them) *Anne of Green Gables*. . . . At university itself, being on the left wing and doing arts subjects we didn't rub up against overt personalized sexism all that much. That came after gradua-tion. And of course that was before we had the reinforcement of *New Wave feminism*, so had to fall back on our own personal resources—though Engels' *The Origins of the Family* helped. The first important new text was a translation of Simone de Beauvoir's *The Second Sex*, which appeared in the early 60s. We did, though, have Communist women's groups. I, and my friends, were per-sonally pretty fiercely independent in our attitudes. Having called myself a Christian Communist—a la Dean Hewlett Johnson while still at school, I had joined the communist party at 18, shortly after Khrushev's denunciation of Stalin.... There was a period in which I went back into school teaching, which was made exciting by the advent of the Women's Liberation Movement. In trying to get to grips with what all this meant, I read across many disciplines, including anthropology as well as literature and history, and the burgeoning writings of the women's liberation movement itself...

"No Permanent Waves"

I started with the assumption that I was developing a collective biography of "second-wave" feminism in the academy, in contrast to the "first-wave'" feminists of Banks' study. For this reason, I did not approach as many wom-en of the youngest cohort, thinking that they saw themselves as an entirely new generation, influenced by different contexts and ideas, and part of yet another new wave of thought, often referred to as "the third wave." But it has become increasingly clear that the wave analogy is a contested notion and is challenged by women from the three cohorts of my study. Indeed, a recent edited collection of essays that tries to recast histories of American feminism is titled *No Permanent Waves*, neatly illustrating another notion of waves, specifically a female one for hairdos. And yet another, is expressed by antipodean feminist who wrote that,

> Women's Lib *hit the air-waves* [my emphasis] during my teachers' college year (1969)....Organized feminism wasn't around me where I lived and worked until my return to full-time study in 1975....I discovered feminist theory and incorporated it into my MA thesis....My mission became one of developing feminist education theory...

The select women of the youngest cohort were equally passionate and had a strong sense of the continuing importance of feminist education: of a vital task yet to be accomplished. For instance, one of the British femi-nists concerned with research on sex and relationships education for young people wrote:

So feminism's woven through my personal journey, which is mirrored by feminist theory journey from liberal to lesbian feminism to socialist feminism to queer theory. Feminist frameworks and politics feel the most central to me although green and anarchist politics (well, activism) is important too. My journey across and between the various social sciences has been through feminist work that didn't respect the disciplinary boundaries and my finding that I could have sexuality as a legitimate research topic is down to this too. Nice finding that the illicit reading on sexuality could be owned and legitimate. Later studies in teaching and learning (PgDip HE) looped back into feminist and queer pedagogies too. Don't think to not be 'out' as a feminist in the academy in research or teaching. Tend to assume it is OK to be a feminist at work and have to be corrected sometimes.

And a colleague of hers, and the youngest participant in my study, wrote, illuminatingly, of the public feminists she read as a teenager:

I became a feminist probably from the age of 10 or 11. By the age of 12, I was writing to the editors of the now defunct *Shocking Pink* magazine asking to contribute. My father [a policeman] intercepted a missive from the radical feminist collective (based in a squat in Brixton) which somewhat thwarted my early dream of feminist journalism. By 15 I was organizing a debating society at my school, on themes such as "Should page 3 be banned" and by 17 I had read Valerie Solanas, Andrea Dworkin, Germaine Greer, Kate Millett, and happily introduced myself to a local feminist library.

In contrast, a young émigré from the United States viewed herself as self-taught and also expressed this rather poignantly:

I became a feminist during university (as a mature student at Middlesex after an Access to HE course) mainly through my own reading...good experiences taught me about inclusive pedagogies. Feminism has been crucial to my learning—indirectly and explicitly—e.g., when I was in a women's aid refuge I first explicitly encountered feminism and this was a life saver in terms of understanding and making sense of my traumatic experiences of domestic violence—and also learning about my rights and my position as a woman—this was strengthened at university when I started to read feminist theories for my coursework—theory has been more directly influential to me than activism...

She is a great contrast with another young feminist who had an elite education and said,

I became a feminist at university. I went to an all girls' school and moved into a mixed environment at Cambridge. In my college I was the only girl of the 14 doing Maths in my year. Some other students and tutors had sexist attitudes. I guess this is what provoked the move....The influence has been huge—most obviously in my work but also in how I dress, what I eat, my friendships....I do not do much in feminist activism . . . more urgent is peace but feminism in daily life e.g., teaching . . . women's studies came gradually.

And a mobile young scholar, moving across the continent of Europe, wrote:

On feminism, interestingly, I never thought of feminism as an identity, until I was much older. I was brought up in a very high aspirational middle class and highly educated family context (and that includes wider family) where women were all in ambitious careers, and gender was never an issue. It was unacceptable (inconceivable) to have low aspirations for either of us girls, or for any of my boy cousins. We were a gender-blind family in that respect . . . Of my 14 cousins, only two women and one man did not study at university and ended up marrying early and having children before 20 (which was considered a scandal in the family circles). I did not come across feminism at university circles either; it was there of course but I never thought it was relevant to me. I became more fully aware of feminist debates once I was in the UK, but I still did not see it as particularly relevant to my life or career. I always saw it as a problem of others. If asked, I would have identified myself as a liberal feminist. This has changed now that I have a more sophisticated understanding of the forms of discrimination and prejudice that people and organizations can exercise, but I still consider myself very lucky and privileged to have had the kind of upbringing where family ambitions [and investment] were not ltd at all by gender. I have never been particularly active in terms of promoting feminism as an ideology. In some ways I feel that I carry this through my life-course and hopefully transmit it to my children as an embodied message! If asked, I would identify myself as a feminist now, but in the circles that I move socially and professionally I do not view it as a big issue.

TENTATIVE CONCLUSIONS

Inevitably, all the women are highly educated and almost invariably have doctorates. This generation of feminists is a dramatic contrast with the first-wave feminists of Banks' study where less than a third had any higher education, but who were political rather than academic activists. Nevertheless, the participants of this study are similar to earlier generations in that they are from a variety of social, ethnic, migrant, and often refugee backgrounds. While they are mainly White, they are not all from middle-class families. The vast majority of the women in my study were "the first in the family" to go to university, whether from upper-class, middle-class, or working-class backgrounds, translating into "first-generation" in the U.S. context.

This is quite contrary to current UK policy thinking about how to use higher education for social mobility where "first in the family" is often assumed to imply people from working class or minority ethnic backgrounds. These women exemplify how university education has expanded and how vital these educational opportunities have been for their working and personal lives, transforming them into passionate academic activists for future generations. All have been researching and teaching for social transformations.

Yet we feminist academics now feel much less sanguine about the future, despite the achievement of gender equality in terms of numbers of students. David Willetts, UK minister for higher education, has yet again expressed a form of political "misogyny," as Julia Gillard put it in the Australian parliament: "He has pitted middle class women against working class men as beneficiaries of university education." In his book, *The Pinch: How Baby Boomers Took Their Children's Future—And Why They Should Give it Back* (2010), Willetts commented that "feminism has trumped egalitarianism." His argument, repeated recently over the Christmas break, suggests that working-class men should be given priority over middle-class women for higher education to right the gender imbalance. But the education he wants working-class men to be given is clearly of a traditional, Conservative kind, not at all transformative of gender and sexual relations.

To paraphrase Morley (2011), this is "misogyny masquerading as metrics," and yet such attitudes are pervasive in policy arenas and prevent the further development of creative thinking for future generations. As the stories of transformation told by the feminist academics in this study indicate, only an emancipatory education can help forge new ways of thinking and begin to develop more appropriate and less violent gender relations. Education, and higher education especially, could be the way to transform the future. For feminists, it feels as if the wave analogy, as expressed so poetically by Stevie Smith, is, after all, apposite: we are "not waving but drowning" in a sea of misogyny. Thus, while higher education played a liberatory role for the women in this study, much remains to be seen on whether feminism will continue to impact the culture at large, especially considering the evolving political context of the past few decades.

REFERENCES

Banks, O. (1986). *Becoming a feminist: The social origins of 'first wave' feminism*. Athens, GA: The University of Georgia Press.

Bristol Women's Studies Group. (1979). *Half the sky: An introduction to women's studies*. London, UK: Virago Press.

David, M. E. (2003). *Personal and political: Feminisms, sociology and family lives*. Stoke-on-Trent, UK: Trentham Books.

David, M. E. (2014). *Feminism, gender and universities: Passion, pedagogies and politics*. London, UK: Ashgate.

Figes, E. (1970). *Patriarchal attitudes*. New York, NY: Stein and Day.

Firestone, S. (1970). *The dialectic of sex*. New York, NY: Farrar, Straus, and Giroux.

Fiske, E. B. (2012). *World atlas of gender equality in education*. Paris, France: UNESCO.

Friedan, B. (1963). *The feminine mystique*. New York, NY: Norton.

Greer, G. (1970). *The female eunuch*. New York, NY: McGraw-Hill.

Hewitt, N. A. (Ed.). (2010). *No permanent waves: Recasting histories of U.S. feminism*. New Brunswick, NJ: Rutgers University Press.

Kim, T., & Brooks, R. (2012). *Internationalisation, mobile academics, and knowledge creation in universities: Comparative analysis*. Unpublished manuscript. SRHE Research Award 2011/12 Final Report.

Millett, K. (1970). *Sexual politics*. London, UK: Granada Publishing.

Morley, L. (2011). Misogyny posing as metrics: Disrupting the feminisation crisis discourse. *Contemporary Social Science, 6*(2), 223–227.

Rich, A. (1976). *Of woman born: Motherhood as experience and institution*. New York, NY: Norton.

Rowbotham, S. (1973) *Women, resistance and revolution*. Harmondsworth, UK: Penguin.

Slaughter, S., & Leslie, L. L. (1997). *Academic capitalism: Politics, policies and the entrepreneurial university*. Baltimore, MD: John Hopkins University Press.

Slaughter, S., & Rhoades, G. (2004). *Academic capitalism and the new economy: Markets, state, and higher education*. Baltimore, MD: John Hopkins University Press.

Smith, S. (1957). *Not waving but drowning*. London, UK: Deutsch.

Willetts, D. (2010). *The pinch: How the baby boomers took their children's future and why they should give it back*. London, UK: Atlantic Books.

PART II

UNDERSTANDING AND STRENGTHENING STUDENTS' LIVED EXPERIENCES

CHAPTER 4

"MORE THAN A SCHOOL"

Providing a Safe Space for Girls to Rewrite, Direct, and Act Their Life Stories

Katherine Cumings Mansfield

ABSTRACT

This chapter shares the story of a group of women educators who created a novel school culture, and the female students who meet them there, to disrupt and transform the dailiness of sexism, racism, and classism. Through a commitment to building robust relationships and forefronting the voices of women, this community of learners is working to confront the past and interrupt the present, and revolutionize their future trajectories. In the words of one parent, "This is more than a school. They're preparing you for life."

As we enter the twenty-first century, girls and women have made great progress in the United States. But large segments of girls, across race and class lines, continue to struggle with issues of identity and the trivialization of their leadership abilities. Most of these girls are in coeducational school systems, and often participate in afterschool or community-based youth programs that fail to recognize their needs and strengths

Women Interrupting, Disrupting, and Revolutionizing Educational Policy and Practice, pages 59–78
Copyright © 2014 by Information Age Publishing

as girls. . . . Programs working with girls must develop new approaches that address girls' needs for support and connection, view girls as assets, help them come to voice, and offer space for critical thinking. (Collaborative Fund for Healthy Girls, Healthy Women [HGHW], 2001, p. 6)

Girls' life stories are often predetermined culturally. It is as if they are reading from scripts, acting how they have been socialized, and following the direction of others in more powerful positions. Around the world, girls play important roles in their families and communities by providing child or elder care and conducting household chores so that adults in their settings may work and earn an income. More often than not, male children are not expected or required to play similar roles. Rather, boys have more freedom to define their personal, familial, and societal roles, which often includes garnering an education and pursuing economic opportunities in the public sphere. While some have begun to recognize this situation as something that might occur in "developing nations," Western society rarely examines its own practices to assess whether girls really do have the self-determination to pursue their full potential. It is easier to see the "other" (as in poor countries or non-Christian nations) as robbing girls of the opportunities to share public space and reach their full potential. In fact, since, in America, we "allow" girls to go to school, we automatically assume that all girls in the United States have access to what it takes to choose their own paths and bring their dreams to fruition.

Thankfully, scholars are bringing to Western society's attention the specific ways schools can be cites of reproduction that continue to perpetuate outdated norms. Some educators now recognize that students, generally, and minorities (Black and Hispanic students as well as females of all ethnicities) in particular, need and should be provided a safe space where the "isms" of society are questioned and/or where their voices are heard (Fielding, 2001, 2004; Greene, Cardinal, & Goldstein-Siegel, 2009; HGHW, 2001; Mansfield, 2011; Mansfield, Welton, & Halx, 2012; Mitra, 2008; Mitra & Gross, 2009; Sands, Guzman, Stevens, & Boggs, 2007; Welton, 2011).

This chapter is the story of a group of women educators who created a novel school culture, and the female students who meet them there, to disrupt and transform the dailiness of sexism, racism, and classism. Through a commitment to building robust relationships and forefronting the voices of women, this community of learners is working to confront the past, interrupt the present, and revolutionize their future trajectories. In the words of one parent, "This is more than a school. They're preparing you for life."

LITERATURE REVIEW ON SAFE SPACE

Safe space is defined as a "girl-only" space where girls have access to a supportive environment; where their physical, psychological, and emotional needs are met; and where they can express themselves without repercussion (Baldwin, 2011; Goal Programme, 2009; Greene et al., 2009; HGHW, 2001; UN Women, 2012). While the concept of safe space takes into consideration physical features and space usage by ensuring that girls feel protected and secure, planning for safe space goes beyond consideration of physical characteristics to evaluation of how certain spaces bolster gender inequality or advance gender equality (UN Women, 2012). For example, how space is used often determines whether and how it becomes gendered: "When certain groups, like women or girls, do not use a space, it is usually an indication that the space feels insecure to members of that group" (UN Women, p. 1). Feelings of security (or lack thereof) can include whether girls have experienced and/or fear sexual violence as well as whether the space is viewed as a place that facilitates social relationships and is specifically designed to support girls and women. Thus, space (schools, homes, city buses, etc.) is not gender-neutral. Rather, space "reflects specific social, economic and historical characteristics that are unique to local women's situations" (UN Women, p. 3). Therefore, to truly activate a "safe space" for girls, concerned groups must purposefully create them.

Schools that create safe spaces for girls should pay attention to five interrelated elements: (a) building robust relationships between and amongst teachers and students, (b) building mentoring and networking programs, (c) engaging critical conversations that address societal norms and entrenched "isms," (d) providing adequate time and space to listening to girls' voices, and (e) creating familial and organizational collaborations (Baldwin, 2011; Greene et al., 2009; HGHW, 2001; Mansfield, 2011, in press-a, in press-b; Mansfield & Jean-Marie, in press).

Building Robust Relationships

For many girls, the arrival of puberty is marked by a decrease of freedom of movement and subsequently, a lack of access to friendship groups and supportive networks (Baldwin, 2011; Greene et al., 2009; UN Women, 2012). This is partially due to the fact that girls, more often than boys, become the caretakers of younger siblings or aging family members, which often hinders their educational and extracurricular activities (Baldwin, 2011; Greene et al., 2009; UN Women, 2012). Even girls who stay in school lack the opportunity to develop robust relationships because they are "torn" between their educational and home responsibilities (Baldwin, 2011; Greene et al., 2009; UN Women, 2012). Also, most schools and community programs fail to pay adequate attention to the specific needs of girls to build the hearty friendship and social networks that girls need to flourish (Baldwin, 2011; Greene et al., 2009; HGHW, 2001; UN Women, 2012). Thus, careful attention to building relationships among peers and teachers is essential to creating a safe space for girls in schools (Mansfield, 2011).

Mentoring and Networking

While building relationships with peers and teachers is essential, it is also important to go beyond the school walls by developing mentoring and networking relationships within and beyond the community. Mentors serve as role models for girls and can include intergenerational efforts to build individual competencies in health behavior education, sexual violence prevention, financial literacy, and tips for negotiating higher education environments (Baldwin, 2011; HGHW, 2001; Mansfield, 2011).

Critical Conversations

Engaging in critical conversations about how youngsters experience gender, race, and class are essential to creating a safe space (HGHW, 2001; Mansfield & Jean-Marie, in press). While critical examination of societal isms is important for all youngsters (Mansfield & Jean-Marie, in press), it is especially important for girls (HGHW, 2001; Mansfield, 2011) because "the gendered nature of how girls experience race, class and culture means that we must pay particular attention to girls' self image and gender stereotyping" (HGHW, 2001, p. 7).

> To understand how to include fully the voices and power of all girls—including poor and disenfranchised girls; lesbian, bisexual and transgender girls; girls of color; and immigrant girls—we must understand the social limitations based on gender; or gender and race; or gender, race, class and sexual oppression...youth programs need to support girls as they negotiate these complex intersections and explicitly address the multiple identities each girl carries with her. (HGHW, 2001, p. 7)

Listening to Students' Voices

Related to facilitating critical conversations is the importance of listening intently to students within this safe space. The process of engaging students in critical conversations and forefronting students' voices is difficult but essential work (Mansfield et al., 2012; Mansfield & Jean-Marie, in press).

While struggle might be inevitable, we believe school leadership practices can act as mediating factors that bridge student voice efforts in challenging contexts. A socially just educational leader must challenge the power structures that silence the voices of students, especially those who are marginalized in a particular educational context. (Mansfield et al., 2012, p. 28)

Leadership practices include examining space to ensure that the environment is conducive to girls' self-expression as well as one that promotes productive conflict resolution (HGHW, 2001). Further, listening to student voice adds moral authority. Students are capable of speaking for themselves and can give adults in their lives important insights into the challenges they face (Greene et al., 2009; Mansfield, et al., 2012). However, understanding girls' unique situations

> requires a fundamentally different starting point: Girls themselves. . . . And integral to that is listening to girls and paying real attention to what they have to say . . . a girl's-eye view of her barriers can point the way to the highest-priority interventions. Girls' opinions reinforce a forbidding reality: they cannot change their lives on their own. Families, teachers, mentors and community attitudes are central to unleashing girls' potential. . . . Girls as a group express the idea that in order to change their lives, we must find ways to open the minds of those around them. (Greene et al., 2009, p. 17)

Familial and Organizational Collaborations

It is essential that schools committed to creating a safe space for girls also reach out to families and community organizations to develop a network of "girl champions" (Greene et al., 2009, p. xxvi) who "prepare the terrain for long-term, sustainable change" to enable a cultural environment that facilitates girls' civic participation and self-expression as well as socioeconomic development. It is difficult for organizations to help girls take advantage of safe space if they do not also work with families and communities to negotiate program responsibilities with family/community obligations (Baldwin, 2011; Green et al., 2009; HGHW, 2001). Attendance and long-term sustainability can be a problem if program developers do not seek to work within the constraints of girls' lives and/or work with families to help them understand the need for altered responsibilities at home (Baldwin, 2011; Green et al., 2009; HGHW, 2001). Further, honoring individual and group culture is complicated further if beliefs and expectations vary between family, culture, and educational programs; making cooperation, conversation, and negotiation all the more essential (Baldwin, 2011; Green et al., 2009; HGHW, 2001).

Taken together, the five interrelated components above represent a way for schools to support girls' social change efforts by creating opportunities for girls to actively represent their communities, engaging girls in critical thinking about issues affecting their lives, and framing social change as a continuum from community service to direct action... particularly true for girls disadvantaged by poverty and other obstacles in their lives. (HBHW, 2001, p. 7)

METHODS

The purpose of the original two-year ethnography was to capture the story of the implementation of one major U.S. city's first and only all-girls public school and the consequent shaping of the school culture according to its unique context (see Mansfield, 2011, for additional details). Presently in its fifth year, the study continues to document the ways safe space is created while also focusing on how this unique school culture might influence students' present location and future trajectories. Specifically, the first graduating class of 2014 is being followed from their seventh-grade year to graduation from high school in 2014 and beyond.

Context

The secondary school, Young Women's Leadership School (YWLS),[1] is located in Southtown Independent School District (SISD) in one of ten largest urban centers in the U.S. and was founded to meet the specific needs of racial and ethnic minority girls living in lower economic circumstances. The grade 6–12 curriculum of YWLS is an advanced program that focuses on three primary areas: (a) Rigorous college preparation, especially coursework in STEM fields; (b) Health and wellness guidance that emphasizes preventing drug abuse, pregnancy, and obesity, and; (c) Training to prepare young women for leadership positions in careers and campus life. The school is the result of a public–private partnership with the Foundation for the Education of Young Women (FEYW), who partially funded and facilitated the development of six public all-girls schools in urban school districts across the state.

Data Collection

Like Wolcott (2008), I believe ethnography is "ideally suited for studying small-scale, isolated, tribal cultures" with an "emphasis on cultural particularism" (p. 28) and local context. Indeed, ethnography was useful for accessing the "black box" of this particular school to answer questions such as, What is going on here? What does it mean to be a member of this group? (Jeffrey, 2008; Walford, 2008). Following the ethnographic tradition, I used three primary means of discovery: *experiencing, enquiring,* and *examining* (Wolcott, 2008). Generally, *experiencing* emphasizes the first-hand familiarity of the researcher by describing what is discovered through the senses while conducting observations in the field, while e*nquiring* entails taking a more active role by asking questions during informal conversations or more formal, if casual, interviews. *Examining* refers to collecting and probing cultural artifacts such as school newsletters and faculty lesson plans at the local site as well as policy documents and newspaper articles available from online and traditional archives.

The primary means of becoming familiar with the school culture has been through participant observation since 2008. The goal has been to experience and describe what the principal, faculty, and staff are doing to craft the school's organizational culture, particularly those aspects that appear to facilitate the creation of safe space for girls. Participant observation has been supplemented regularly by conducting interviews and focus groups with key stakeholders including members of the private foundation, the school board, central office and school administration, teachers, parents, and students. For the purposes of this chapter, findings are focused on data gathering via interviews with the principal, teachers, and parents and focus groups with students, with a particular focus on parents' voices as participants who originally advocated for the placement of their daughters at this particular school.

Data Analysis and Interpretation

It is important to note that description, analysis, and interpretation were not mutually exclusive, nor did they necessarily follow this particular order. Similar to Wolcott (1994), I engaged a fluid process of analysis and interpretation, whereby I constantly collected data, made sense of them, and then revisited analysis of data in light of new experiences. This nonlinear, circular process proceeded akin to a conversation between the researcher and the data.

Following a process outlined by Emerson, Fretz, and Shaw (1995), I conducted "open coding," which entailed reading field notes, interview transcripts, copies of documents, and diaries/journals line-by-line to note consistent themes or story lines. I then enlarged the account beyond description by identifying key concepts and their interrelationships focusing on both culture and context. I then implemented "focused coding" that consisted of additional readings of the data to carefully filter initial impressions. I strived to achieve what Lawrence-Lightfoot and Davis (2002) called "a balanced tension" between having the confidence to observe, name, and verify patterns in the data while remaining grounded in the lived experiences of the participants. Eventually, key ideas were grouped into broader topics, referred to by Lawrence-Lightfoot and Davis (1997) as "repetitive refrains."

FINDINGS

Speaking with the principal, teachers, parents, and students enlightened the various ways Young Women's Leadership School (YWLS) became a safe space for girls to confront the past, interrupt the present, and revolutionize the future. A repetitive refrain among the girls was how YWLS was "weird in a good way" and "opposite of everything else" they had ever experienced before. Teachers remarked how wonderful it was that they *finally* worked with others who were as "committed" as they were to "doing what it takes" to meet the needs of racial/ethnic minority girls living in poverty. Parents recounted the ways their daughters were *finally* given opportunities to "celebrate being a nerd" and grow as leaders. All participants noted YWLS as a place where there was a strong commitment to relationship building and giving special attention to the lived experiences of women.

Attention to Building Relationships

In this particular safe space, building robust relationships meant creating an atmosphere more akin to "familia" and "sisterhood." On numerous occasions, the principals of the school (Ms. Santiago and Mrs. O'Keefe) emphasized the importance of building a school "culture" that "feels like a family" so that girls know they "have a place to go." Across the board, participants believed that it would be impossible to address educational and social issues if students did not feel well cared for.

Parents, like the teachers and principals, seemed to recognize the importance of creating sustaining relationships at the school as well as establishing a rigorous curriculum that addressed the contexts of girls' lives. Parents described profound admiration and appreciation for the principals' and teachers' commitments to their children. When I asked Mr. Peña what he liked the best about YWLS, he remarked: "Sisterhood— I like the fact that they are all considered sisters and take care of each other . . . we are one big family."

Mr. Rios expressed how thankful he was for the relationships his daughter was building with the teachers at YWLS. In addition to receiving "a strong education, they [Mrs. Barnes] in particular, [taught them] values." Mr. Rios explained that, in addition to being teachers, the faculty were strong "role models . . . a father figure . . . like a mother."

Mr. and Mrs. Ortega both talked of their appreciation for "the way they push them and the way they individualize them" at this school. Mr. Ortega remarked,

> And they know their personalities. They know their quirks. They know their *everything*. And to me, that's the ultimate school, you know what I mean? Because the teachers know you. They know what you're capable of. They know when you're down. They know when you're happy. They know how to make you happy, to discipline you because they know how you are . . . they're not a number but a name. They know their background, you know, and to me that's the ultimate thing that I see. . . . They are not just teachers they are like family.

Mrs. Ortega agreed and added,

> The teachers . . . They care more. They really honestly care about these kids. For these kids to be able to have their personal cell numbers or their home numbers to say: "I'm sick" or "I don't know how to do this." And they walk them through on the phone. Or these kids can call them: "I'm having these problems; I don't know what to do. I can't talk to my mom or my dad." They've got an outlet that a lot of times these kids don't have out there. They don't let these girls fail. They push them so that they can succeed. And that's what we need. We need women in the world that can succeed and will succeed.

When students told me this school was "weird in a good way" and "opposite" of other schools they have attended, I asked them to elaborate. The girls offered that it is because of the way the principal and teachers act at the school. For example, the principal and their teachers might become aggravated sometimes, but they are always "calm and nice" and "never go up in our faces." (It became apparent during the study that "getting in your face" was the supreme form of disrespect that angered the girls.) One student described the faculty and principal this way: "[The principal and the teachers] are like little angels floating down." Students also discussed "how you can just be yourself" and "how being smart and being a 'nerd'" was cause for celebration rather than ridicule at this school. While they did complain that a small school often meant an increase in "drama" because "everyone knows your business," students clearly appreciated how the small size of the school enabled them to "know everybody" and helped them feel more like "sisters" or members of a "family."

Hannah Beth described how at prior schools she didn't know her teachers: "But here, I started to create more than just a teacher–student—the way I see it—it's more of a mother–daughter situation." In terms of relationships with peers, the girls shared that there was a lot of fighting at their former schools. Sam and Mercedes described how they felt like they had to do "bad things" in order to protect themselves. I asked the girls how they handled stresses in relationships here at YWLS. Jane answered, "I think here we're more like, close; we're more like, sisters and family. Like, we're more like, relatives and we can have very open conversations." Mixtli added, "Yeah, it's like, we're really close and you actually know almost everybody in the school; whereas, your other middle school, you know this certain group, but you don't know the other groups."

Mercedes spoke of her conviction that despite missing prior friends, YWLS is much better for her and the other students. I asked, "Why do you think it's better for you?" Mercedes answered,

> Because of the way that we're learning and the higher expectations for us, and it's preparing us for college. And the other schools, they're not really. They mostly mess around. . . . And at the other school the teachers, they didn't really care like these ones here. Like, they're willing to sit for tutoring and help you. If you're not passing a class they'll let you retake tests and try to get better grades and help you stay focused on what you're doing.

Attention to Women's Voices and Lived Experiences

Recuperar el Habla (To Find One's Voice)

You cannot have a safe space for girls without providing adequate time and space to develop student voice. Recently, Principal O'Keefe and I were chatting and she brought up the importance of being flexible with class time to meet the needs of students to talk about "real life." She said, "Sometimes the teachers just have to scrap their lesson . . . our math teacher was just talking to me about that. Yesterday, she goes, 'I just want you to know I scrapped my lesson.' I said, 'Sometimes you have to.'"

The teacher, Ms. Fakhoury, would agree, noting that she felt one of her major duties, despite its absence from the formal curriculum, was teaching students how to advocate for themselves as women.

> At our school we give them many workshops . . . about how to present themselves, how to talk to people, how to act in a math class, how to act in a class, period! How to back up what you say with research; with quotations. You know, we do all that and we still throw the curriculum in it. . . . But I think that's what makes our campus so unique . . . the fact that we actually realized that, okay, knowing the plan (in my case knowing the math), getting [good] calculus grades . . . perfect AP scores . . . honor roll classes. It's not going to take them anywhere if they cannot face their professor who says, "You're not doing your job." [I tell the students at YWLS], "You're accepting this guy's answers over [your own]?" If they cannot [advocate for themselves as women], I

don't care how great a student they are: They will not succeed at the university level and that's what I'm preparing them for.

Ms. Fakhoury confessed that sometimes she regretted leaving engineering. She wondered if her path would have been different if she had been taught to advocate for herself. She admitted that she had a difficult time "practicing what she preached."

> I don't *think* I regret it....I thought I would regret leaving engineering. But...it was probably my wake-up call that I needed to go somewhere else. But at the same time, I wonder if I have been taught all those skills that it would have been different....And I went to an all-girls' school! I was taught how to be a lady [but] never really how to sit down and talk to an authority figure and develop that courage to say, "Hey, you suck. Let's talk about this." And you know, to this day, even right now, I mean I have—I know what I am teaching my girls—and it's funny that I can't seem to apply it to myself, you know? It's interesting. But I figured—they are younger, they can still change....And to me, I think that beats any curriculum....If I can teach them how to voice their opinion and how to back up their facts and [insist] to somebody that, "No, I am right." And if they're wrong they're more than happy to say, "Oh, you proved me wrong. Thank you. I'll look for another way now." You know, to me that is more crucial than algebra, calculus, statistics.

Parents also spoke about the importance of their daughters finding their voices and forging their own identities and how the value system at YWLS facilitated that process. For example, while interviewing Mr. and Mrs. Rios, Mr. Rios said,

> They tend to stress that you as an individual are important. And they try and encourage your education. They try and encourage you as an individual and, of course, being a strong woman growing up and where there are your opportunities. These are the things that you can learn. And I think [our daughter] recognized very quickly [these] values that she could appreciate. I think that's what attracted her to [YWLS]...were the things she was missing before.

I then asked Mr. Rios what he thought was missing in his daughter's prior school experiences. He answered,

> I think she wanted an outlet to grow and find herself, her own identity. Because she's very much different from either one of us....So we all are very strong-willed about what we want to do. And I think she wants to create her own identity. And I think being able to participate, being able to do a lot of these classes, art class, gifted and talented, be part of the other clubs. Girl Scouts was another one. Again these are very strong organizations. Very strong things, but she wanted to create her own identity. And I think she's able to do that here.

I went on to ponder aloud, "I wonder why she's able to do that here, but maybe not so much at another place? I wonder what's different?" Mr. Rios said one of the most tangible differences was that at YWLS, they incorporate learning about identity and how to grow into strong women into their regular curriculum and "academic life" during school hours as well as during their afterschool clubs and service opportunities.

Mr. and Mrs. Ortega had similar things to say about their impressions of YWLS. The Ortegas told me that prior to their daughter enrolling at YWLS, they never let her go out for sports. Some of this was due to the Ortegas' distrust of their prior schools, whether their daughter would be properly supervised, and thus, safe. Additionally, with their long work hours, Mr. and Mrs. Ortega lacked much of the support they needed to enable their daughter to stay after school in prior years. However, since coming to YWLS, Mrs. Ortega said her daughter "never played sports but now she wants to play sports...and I let her go full force." While Mrs. Ortega is grateful for her daughter's safety and wellbeing and the emphasis of the school on developing the girls physically and intellectually, she also explained that having her daughter in afterschool activities can be very challenging. She went on to explain that her daughter had to do most of her homework in the car to and from the school. "I would pick her up at 5:30 and I still had errands to run." Her stepfather adds, "She did homework to and from school...all night if she had to...she did not want to have a 'B'—period...she wanted to have her grades be a 96 and up." Her mom adds, "To her, a 90's not good enough." The Ortegas expressed that while challenging, their daughter's new lifestyle was important to support any way they could because she was learning important leadership and responsibility skills that would carry her into the future she was trying to build.

Another parent, Mr. Peña, explained that he really appreciated all the practice his daughter was getting in leadership skills. He said the emphasis on leadership "has made my daughter grow tremendously." He went on to explain that his daughter has "always been very shy and afraid of public speaking." Mr. Pena felt his daughter's experiences at YWLS were helping her to literally find her voice. For example, the day before, she spoke in front of their church. In addition, the school is teaching her how to market her entrepreneurial skills, and she is using that knowledge in her volunteer work in the community. Mr. Peña said,

> [She] was the type of person that would walk in and you'd talk to her and she was very shy...yesterday [at church] they were telling her that they were so proud of her because she got up in front of the congregation to give an announcement...she created this tenny on the converse line and she put the name of the church. It's green because the church is trying to "go green." So they're going to send a pair to the Bishop! And she got up and made this presentation in front of everybody and everybody said she spoke real loud.

Hablar en Contra de (To Speak Against)

Related to developing student voice is providing time and space for more teacher-directed critical conversations that speak against societal norms and entrenched "isms." There was a conscientious effort on the part of the principals and teachers to incorporate what some educational circles refer to as "critical pedagogy." In layperson's terms, there was an honest exchange between faculty and students about some of the barriers students might face either as a person of color, or as a woman (or at the intersection of ethnicity, sex, and socioeconomic status). In addition, the informal curriculum included giving students the tools needed to combat some of the obstacles they might face, from learning how to introduce oneself professionally to learning how to defend oneself if physically attacked. Principal Santiago remarked, "I think that it's a social injustice if you don't let people know what [they're up against], what they need to be aware of in their lives [and how to overcome that]."

Mrs. Barnes spoke often about her quest to integrate feminist ideals and concepts into the formal curriculum. In addition to pushing for variety and balance in the selection of literature, Mrs. Barnes integrated what she called, "a strong women's studies component into all I do." For example, rather than merely have students memorize the definitions and spellings of weekly vocabulary words, Mrs. Barnes also interrogated the origins of words and how and why they have been used throughout history.

> I mean, there's hero-heroine. I said, "Can we think about this for just a second?" I asked the girls, "What's a hero? Who's a hero?" They come up with words like: men, strong, brave, adventurous, and so on. And then I say, "What's a heroine? Who is a heroine?" And they're like, "a female who is a hero?" And I say, "Look it up! Find 'heroine' in the dictionary! Tell me where that word comes from!" And so they did. And you know what they found? (They were pissed!) They found out that "heroine" is the *diminutive* of hero! I mean, what's up with that? Why does the *male* get to be the great big hero and the *female* just a *little bit* of a hero? I mean, sexism is in the words we use every day! We need to learn that and start choosing our words more wisely!

Mrs. Barnes also challenged the girls to understand and interrogate literary concepts traditionally taught in English courses. For example, when studying plot and the variety of roles that are assigned to characters, the students found that—even in the most highly regarded texts—female characters were usually given very stereotypical roles. However, male characters were usually afforded a plethora of complex characteristics and identities.

> So, here again, the girls are pissed! They find out that they only get to be the virgin or the whore or the sexless matron! But the guys get to play all kinds of roles. They are not one-dimensional. They get to be so much more! They

get to be more like real life. But the women: they are relegated to the very few stereotypes that men name for them. That is just wrong and I want them to see it for what it really is!

Ms. Barnes then explained to me how she uses these examples from the curriculum to discuss real-world problems the girls are facing.

> We have had *long* conversations, especially in Prep, about how women are expected to fall into those usual literary roles. We're either the whore or the virgin. I've said, "Listen to the way you talk about each other, ladies: 'so-and-so is a slut, so-and-so is this or that...' We do it, too! We do it to each other!" And we talk about how when they are adults and try to break into new fields of study and so on and so forth that other people will try very hard to place them back into those neat little categories where they think they belong...and how they are going to have to fight tooth and nail to not let that happen.... But the *biggest* thing is: we have to stop doing it to ourselves; to each other. We are sexist with our own language we use! *We've got to start choosing our words more wisely!*

Principal O'Keefe shared the importance of also discussing issues of nationality and language with students. She shared that her father had a first-grade education while her mother had a sixth-grade education before they emigrated from Mexico to the United States. Mrs. O'Keefe told many stories of how her parents may not have been "educated" in the formal sense, but they were very hard workers who appreciated the value of education and pushed her and her siblings to go as far as possible in higher education. She recalled,

> I know when my older siblings—they were about ten to eight years older than me—they went to the East Coast. My brother went to Columbia in the seventies where it was unheard of for minorities to be going to Ivy League schools. And then my sister went to Harvard. So when I was in the ninth grade, I went to see her graduate. They took me to all the Ivy League schools. And I remember my friends in school saying, "Well, why are you visiting *those* schools?" And I said, "Well, *that's* where I want to go!" I said, "Yeah, I'm going to get in!"

Mrs. O'Keefe viewed her older siblings as revolutionary in that they fought an uphill battle as first-generation Americans facing racist and classist attitudes so that she, and others like her, would not have to beat down the doors to opportunity like they did. She explains,

> But it's about teaching kids to believe in themselves because sometimes they go home, unfortunately, and they have people telling them, "What do you doing that for? Why are you staying up late reading? You're not going to college. You're going to work in a restaurant. You're going to do this." And they don't aspire to more so they expect their daughters not to aspire to more. And

that's the battle that we fight. But it's a battle that we're good at fighting...I think also that I've been very blessed to where I had [parents and] educators tell me, "You can do this." And just—I just had a great support system growing up. You know, my older siblings also were great role models when I saw them do it. "Oh, my God, they're getting on a plane and flying all the way to the East Coast." You know, where a lot of my friends never went to college.

Ms. Saaveda's experiences with "isms" were very different from Mrs. O'Keefe's. Her parents viewed education as important. But not for her:

My older brother went off to A&M. I stayed here in [Southtown and attended a local, unrated school], and then my younger brother went to Yale, and then is now in medical school in Chicago....I was the pretty one. I was in pageants. I was like, not very smart and [my parents] kind of let me know that very quickly...not saying like, "You are dumb," but just like..."It's OK. Just stay with us. We will take care of you."

Ms. Saaveda expressed her desire to critique what she saw as traditional roles she was encouraged to take on while growing up and sees her "calling" as helping her girls work through similar cultural prejudices. She shared,

The things that happened have a lot of to do with my paternal grandmother, who just saw fit for me, you know, to crochet, sew, cook, clean. I mean, at the age of 10, I was pretty much running the household....I would take care of my brothers...so a lot of the things that have happened to me growing up, things that I have seen, the prejudices that I faced. Even within my own nuclear family. As a female, as a Latina, as, you know, going to university, what is expected of you, all of the pressures that you constantly have, society-wise, but also family and culturally, and all of this. It falls along the same patterns of the students that I work with.

Escuchar a Otros (To Listen to Others)

Another important component to creating safe space at YWLS included opportunities to listen to women in the community tell their stories of how they learned to find their voice, work against societal prejudices, and reach their full potential. Creating leadership training experiences for girls, such as externships, is important, but should not preclude earlier experiences where girls listen to other women, accompanied by mentoring and networking programs that strengthen familial and organizational collaborations.

Listening to women's stories started with the school's founding principal, Ms. Santiago. She emphasized with me on more than one occasion, how important it was for her to "tell her story" to the teachers, students, and parents so that could "set the tone" and adequately communicate "why I was there and my motivation and why I was going to do whatever it took for the kids to be successful." Principal Santiago explained that she "related to the girls because I grew up in a very similar circumstance. I grew up in poverty and had very little opportunity in terms of school." She also remarked how she saw many of her friends "end up either pregnant or married or just didn't get through school" for a variety of reasons and how sad she felt seeing friends with great potential not meet the dreams they set out to reach at earlier ages. Ms. Santiago also admitted to being a "nerd" growing up and how she shares her lifelong love of learning with the girls and tries to make it "acceptable for them to be different, to be smart." That, along with growing up poor, was something that was "very personal" to her. Ms. Saaveda, the college counselor, also spoke of the importance of "sharing her story" with the girls so that they, indeed, would know she "gets it." She emphasized that her story was not an "act" to get the girls' attention:

> We literally have been like to the same bakeries on Sunday morning, gotten the same things, seen the same lady that is mute and sells candy apples, you know, from time to time, in the hot, hot sun, and how our dads always either bought the candy apple or gave her money. Like, we had the exact same stories. And, they are like, "Wow, you are *me*, Miss. You're *me*." And I said, "That is what I am trying to say. Yes, yes. You're me." And, I said, "Yeah, like I am not kidding when I tell you I get it. I lived there." I showed one of them my house.... "That's literally my room on the other side of that window... you know I used to sleep on the floor, too, because eight houses down, the girl got shot [by a drive-by shooter] and paralyzed from the waist down, when I was in like the fifth grade. And, you know, I could not ride my bike on those two streets there..." They were like, "You are really not kidding." "No, I am *not* kidding you. It is not like this thing that I get up and do, like a little spiel in front of you, kind of thing." So...I think that really makes a difference, when the teachers can really relate to the students.

In addition to the principals and teachers sharing their stories with the girls, there was also a commitment to bringing in women from the community who, like them, may have faced seemingly insurmountable obstacles in their lives in their quest to make their dreams come true. The founding principal emphasized the importance of connecting her students to each other and other women in the community who could act as role models. Ms. Santiago shared:

> One of things that we talked about, actually, with the advisory board early on...is that women helping women is a big important piece that we wanted to stress to the girls. And that sense of giving back, caring for one another...So it was very important that we set the girls up to be good to one another, but also to understand just to be a good woman to other women. So it was a very purposeful thing to consistently push that with them. We had conversations about it in the prep class, made sure that they understood that you treat other people with respect. *You need to treat your sisters well,* you need to do this and then giving them examples of that....So from the very begin-

ning it was very intentional, and we had a lot of our guest speakers that first year talking about that topic as well... women that inspired them and who would help [them], so that the girls could see that it really is about those connections... that those women in your life really are what help propel other women forward, and we wanted the girls to have that understanding. And hopefully, that'll stick strong. I really hope so...

The school's second principal, Mrs. O'Keefe, spoke about how important it was to establish "First Fridays" to give students opportunities to learn from successful businesswomen in the community. During these sessions, guest speakers talk about their struggles with sexism or financial challenges growing up and share advice on how to work within life's constraints and break through barriers. Mrs. O'Keefe noted:

> Today, we have whole bunch of women coming... big wigs from the Chamber of Commerce... and it's just about... that exposure to different careers and different lives that we want to give them.... So many of them have challenges. You know, those financial challenges and then they'll say, "I can do that!" They might not know the world of business or the world of technology and that's why this speaker series is so important to us.

I was present for this particular speaker series session and was astonished at the variety and caliber of well-known women who attended the mentoring sessions: Politicians, business owners, high-ranking military officers, and full-time philanthropists took turns speaking to the student body (grades 6–10 at the time) about their past, present, and future trajectories. After the large-group format, the speakers were assigned small group sessions with the girls for more intimate conversations. I attended the session that included a high-ranking Army officer who leads a well-known military hospital. Students asked more personal questions about how she paid for college, handled the stresses of attending medical school, and now balanced work and family. I was very impressed with the honest exchange between guest and students and the maturity of the questions that students asked. I wrote in my field notes: "Wow. I sure wish I would have had this opportunity when I was a teenager. This woman is amazing!"

DISCUSSION

Creating safe space included a balanced attention to confronting the past, interrupting the present, and revolutionizing the future. Stakeholders' commitment to doing so was evident in their attention to building robust relationships and seeking to listen to the voices of women.

Findings having to do with building relationships all emphasized the importance of creating an atmosphere more akin to a family or sisterhood. Within this culture, respect, trust, love, and openness reigned. It is questionable whether any school could really go to the next step of building student voice without having this foundation of *familia* in the first place.

Findings having to do with voice emerged in three categories that I named: (a) Recuperar el Habla (to find one's voice), (b) Hablar en Contra de (to speak against), and (c) Escuchar a Otros (to listen to others). Finding one's voice meant literally learning to speak out loud one's thoughts and feelings. For some adults and students, it sometimes meant rising above shyness. For others, it meant recognizing how past discrimination or social mores constrained one's voice, then relearning behaviors that were formerly thought of as masculine (such as getting in front of a Catholic congregation and leading a social reform effort).

The next stage, to speak against, was sometimes painful for participants. It meant having to face the fact that, perhaps, one's very own family had held prejudicial attitudes toward women. And, it often meant engaging in difficult conversations at school and at home about cultural expectations. It is doubtful whether just any principal or teacher would have been able to successfully lead and teach in this school. I agree with Saaveda and other participants when they say it really makes a difference that they truly understand what their students are going through because they have literally lived where they live. And it is doubtful whether a comparable safe space could have been created without the commitment of all the teachers (regardless of their personal backgrounds) to purposefully incorporate feminist ideals in the regular curriculum and fearlessly engage in critical conversations about race, sex, class, language, and so on.

As far as Escuchar a Otros (to listen to others), this school chose to bring in speakers and mentors who are women, first of all, and oftentimes women who either have struggled financially or socially or otherwise. While other schools incorporate similar programs, the careful attention to "women helping women" is unique and enhances the characteristics of a girls-only safe space. And in this girls-only safe space, adults and students are able to disrupt and transform the dailiness of sexism, racism, and classism.

Future research includes continuing the present ethnography, now in its fifth year, following the first graduating class of 2014 to college. I hope to find out more about how creating this girls-only, safe space influenced young women's college and career decisions and campus leadership behaviors.

CONCLUSION

Schools are not written for students. They're written for adults: society's directors of culture (Bourdieu, 1984, 1990). It takes brave and loving school leaders to create a culture of resistance, along with critical teaching by knowledgeable teachers to interrupt, disrupt, and rewrite educational policy and practice. For many students, it means purposefully creating a safe space that includes building social networks and cross-generational relationships as well as providing leadership opportunities to develop collective power. And by doing so, girls are able to take ownership as actors of their life stories and become healthy and whole.

NOTE

1. All people and places are pseudonyms.

REFERENCES

Baldwin, W. (2011). Creating 'safe spaces' for adolescent girls. *Promoting healthy, safe, and productive transitions to adulthood* series, brief no. 39. The Population Council. All briefs available at www.popcouncil.org/publications/serials-briefs/TABriefs.asp

Bourdieu, P. (1984). *Distinction: A social critique of the judgment of taste* (R. Nice, Trans.). Cambridge, MA: Harvard University Press.

Bourdieu, P. (1990). *The logic of practice.* Stanford, CA: Stanford University Press.

Emerson, R. M., Fretz, R. I., & Shaw, L. L. (1995). *Writing ethnographic fieldnotes.* Chicago, IL: University of Chicago Press.

Fielding, M. (2001). Students as radical agents of change. *Journal of Educational Change, 2*(2), 123–141.

Fielding, M. (2004). Transformative approaches to student voice: theoretical underpinnings, recalcitrant realities. *British Educational Research Journal, 30*(2), 295–311.

Goal Programme. (2009). *Creating a safe space.* London, England: Standard Chartered Bank. Additional information available at: http://goalprogramme.org/

Greene, M. E., Cardinal, L., & Goldstein-Siegel, E. (2009). *Girls speak: A new voice in global development: A girls count report on adolescent girls.* The International Center for Research on Women (ICRW). Report available at: http://www.icrw.org/files/publications/Girls-Speak-A-New-Voice-In-Global-Development.pdf

HGHW (Collaborative Fund for Healthy Girls, Healthy Women). (2001). *The new girls' movement: Implications for youth programs.* The Ms. Foundation for Women. Report available at: https://www.nttac.org/views/docs/jabg/grpcurriculum/girls_movement.pdf

Jeffrey, B. (2008). "Characterising social settings as the basis for qualitative research in ethnography." In G. Walford (Ed.), *How to do educational ethnography* (pp. 141–164). London, UK: The Tufnell Press.

Lawrence-Lightfoot, S., Davis, J. H. (2002). *The art and science of portraiture.* Jossey-Bass.

Mansfield, K. C. (2013). "I love these girls—I was these girls": Women leading for social justice in a single-sex public school. *Journal of School Leadership, 23*(4), 634–657.

Mansfield, K. C. (online first, October 17, 2013). How listening to student voices can inform and strengthen social justice research and practice. *Educational Administration Quarterly*, DOI: 10.1177/0013161X13505288, Available at: http://eaq.sagepub.com/content/early/2013/10/16/0013161X13505288

Mansfield, K. C. (2011). *Troubling social justice in a single-sex public school: An ethnography of an emerging school culture*. Unpublished doctoral dissertation, The University of Texas at Austin.

Mansfield, K. C., & Jean-Marie, G. (in press). Courageous conversations about race, class, and gender: Voices and lessons from the field. *International Journal of Qualitative Studies in Education*.

Mansfield, K. C., Welton, A., & Halx, M. D. (2012). Listening to student voice: Toward a more inclusive theory for research and practice. In C. Boske & S. Diem (Eds.), *Global leadership for social justice: Taking it from field to practice* (pp. 21–41). Bingley, UK: Emerald Publishing.

Mitra, D. L. (2008, November). Amplifying student voice: Students have much to tell us about how best to reform our schools. *Educational Leadership*, 20–25.

Mitra, D. L., & Gross, S. J. (2009). Increasing student voice in high school reform: Building partnerships, improving outcomes. *Educational Management Administration and Leadership, 37*(4), 522–543.

Sands, D. I., Guzman, L., Stevens, L., & Boggs, A. (2007). Including student voice in reform Students speak out. *Journal of Latinos in Education, 6*(4), 323–345.

UN Women. (2012). *Safe public spaces for women and girls: What does planning and designing safe public spaces for women and girls mean?* UN Women, The United Nations Entity for Gender Equality and the Empowerment of Women. Additional information available at: http://www.unwomen.org/

Walford, G. (2008). "The nature of educational ethnography." In G. Walford (Ed.), *How to do educational ethnography* (pp. 1–15). London, UK: The Tufnell Press.

Welton, A. (2011). The courage to critique policies and practices from within: Youth participatory action research as critical policy analysis. A response to "Buscando laLibertad: Latino Youths in Search of Freedom in School." *Democracy and Education, 19*(1), Article 11.

Wolcott, H. F. (2008). *Ethnography: A way of seeing, 2nd edition*. NY: Alta Mira Press.

Wolcott, H. F. (1994). *Transforming qualitative data: Description, analysis, and interpretation*. Thousand Oaks, CA: Sage Publications.

CHAPTER 5

BUILDING A YOUTH LEADERSHIP FORTRESS

High School Women of Color as Visible Activists

Anjalé Welton, Brooke Brock, and Mercedes Perry

ABSTRACT

Unfortunately, school reform policies and research typifies Black and Latina/o youth as at-risk, a problem, and an overall burden on the education system (Ginwright & Cammarota, 2007; Irizarry, 2011; Valencia, 2010). Regrettably, there is limited "nuanced understanding of how [Black and Latina/o youth as activists] respond, resist, and work to transform school and community" (Ginwright, 2007, p. 404). Women of color notably construct visible spaces where gendered racism (toward women and men) is contested (Collins, 2000; hooks, 1981; Oesterreich, 2007); and this community building should be legitimized as an educational asset or as critical social capital (Ginwright, 2007; also see Yosso, 2005).

As such, we revisit our prior participation in V.O.I.C.E.S. (Verbally Outspoken Individuals Creating Empowering Sistahs), a leadership and empowerment program for high school women of color. Brooke and Mercedes,

Women Interrupting, Disrupting, and Revolutionizing Educational Policy and Practice, pages 79–98

currently undergraduate students at four-year universities, were, at the time of their involvement with V.O.I.C.E.S., high school students and youth facilitators. Brooke was one of the founders of the program. Anjalé, now a university professor in education, was formerly an adult facilitator for the program, project director for several related youth leadership programs, and a full-time graduate student. To prepare for this chapter as co-authors, we spent a course of three months corresponding via an online discussion board to reflect on how our prior role as visible young women activists in V.O.I.C.E.S. placed us in a formidable position to construct critical spaces for youth leadership in secondary schools (see Weis & Fine, 2001). We analyzed our discussion board text using principles of youth activism (Delagado & Staples, 2008; Noguera & Cammarota, 2006) as well as concepts from Black feminist thought and hip-hop feminism, theories that focus on young women of color (Brown, 2009; Hernández & Rehman, 2002; Oesterrich, 2007; Ward, 2001) in order to convey how, as young women activists, we constructed a "space to survive and thrive in the complexities of institutional inequities" and transformed school policies and practices (Oesterrich, 2007, p. 4).

"YOU NEED CULTURAL SALVATION!" DISPELLING STEREOTYPES/RECLAIMING YOUTH OF COLOR SPACES

That's how I choose to live
No more compromises, I see your disguises
Blindin' through mind control, stealin' my eternal soul
Appealin' through material to keep me as your slave

But I get out
Oh, I get out of all your boxes
I get out
Oh, you can't hold me in these chains

I'll get out
Oh, I want of social bondage
Knowin' my condition
Oh, is the reason I must change

See, what you see is what you get
Oh, and you ain't seen nothin' yet
Oh, I don't care if you're upset
I could care less if you're upset

See, it don't change the truth and your hurt feeling's no excuse
To keep me in this box, psychological locks

—Lauryn Hill, "I Get Out" (2002)

A number of widespread discourses, such as policy debates and media outlets in various formats (print, television, and internet), sensationalize youth of color—especially Black and Latina/o youth—as culturally deprived (see Ginwright, Cammarota, & Noguera, 2005). Although the field of education is based on democratic principles, real opportunities are scant, and educational aspirations for youth of color are frequently shattered. We must honor teachers and administrators who authentically care for students and who do the lions' share of the emotional work and commitment to serve as institutional agents (see Stanton-Salazar, 1997) for youth of color by assisting with maximizing their resources and connecting them to educational and social opportunities. However, teachers often get "caught up" in the politics of education due to reform efforts and accountability pressures. Adhering to time-sensitive deadlines, standards, and performance indicators becomes the priority rather than building quality relationships with students and the community—relationships that could yield improved student achievement.

While there are teachers who do care, youth of color are sometimes sent the message from their schooling experiences that mere survival (i.e., mediocrity) is something to strive for. They witness how their black and brown peers are disparately educated on a daily basis by being placed in lower academic tracks, linguistically minoritized, and subjected to excessive surveillance, especially when their citizenship status is questioned. They are disproportionately punished, expelled, and pushed out of schooling due to multiple inequities (Brown & Rodriguez, 2009). This complex set of circumstances creates a "convenient" reproductive route to prison (i.e., the school-to-prison pipeline) and/or economic deprivation (Kim, Losen, & Dewitt, 2010). Even as we, the authors, take the time in this chapter to critically reflect on our own work as visible female activists, we realize that as Black women we bear the burden of having minority status. We await the conversation we must have with our own children about the possibilities of hope in schooling as well as the reality that as Black youth, the educational system is often set up with the expectation that they will fail before they ever enter the schoolhouse door (see Ward, 2000). Parents of color release their children to school with what they hope are protective cloaks, but also with recognition that youth who bear a complex set of marginalized identities must develop skills of resistance in order to navigate antagonistic schooling circumstances (see Yosso, 2005).

According to Ginwright et al. (2005), education and social science research is a major culprit of regenerating the culturally-deprived-youth-of-color narrative and reduces "people's complex interactions with their environment to simple manifestations of maladaptive behavior" and does not accurately portray how education has shifted from a system with "its primary role of supporting youth to largely facilitating punishment and control of young people" (p. 28). Because youth of color are largely "othered," depicted as "uncultured," "at-risk" or in need of "intervention," they carry the weight and blame for school failure as educational policy and reform are set up in such a way that the school itself is rarely required to critically reflect on how it institutionally and systemically fails rather than creating a "dynamic model" to support youth of color (Ginwright et al., 2005, p. 28).

This cultural deprivation narrative is even more damaging when gendered. The texture of our hair as young Black women, the various shades of blackness and brownness of our skin, the curvature of our bodies, and the often-expressive inflection of our voices ("Those Black girls are too loud!") when we are in joyous community with one another is commonly culturally maligned by dominant aesthetic expectations. According to Ruth Nicole Brown (2009), "We lack a language that accurately describes what it means to work with Black girls in a way that is not about controlling their bodies and/or producing White, middle-class girl subjectivities" (p. 2). For this reason, it is important to establish dialogue and spaces within schools that, as Brown affirms, celebrates Black girlhood. However, Brown warns that these school spaces for Black girlhood should not be about "etiquette training, managing girls' behavior, punishing who they are, telling them who they should be, or keeping them busy (meaning not sexually active)" (2009, p. 2). Unfortunately, the racial, cultural, and gendered identities that we want to readily affirm and celebrate are often silenced by policies, curriculum, and pedagogy that fail to adequately represent us or do not even recognize that we exist. Furthermore, the sheer mechanized and standardized pedagogical nature of schooling gives young women of color few opportunities to affirm and, more importantly, voice their identities.

Young women of color must be provided with the metaphorical as well as physical space in schools to "reclaim both cultural and feminist possibilities" in order to counter the above-presented raced and gendered cultural deprivation discourse (Hurtado, 2000, p. 274). Unfortunately, the many ways in which youth positively resist and defy negative stereotypes and engage in transformative and restorative community organizing and civic engagement within schools and the surrounding and global community are often ignored by the policy and research discourse (Ginwright et al., 2005). Thus, we use this chapter as an opportunity to argue against the negative discourse and declare as young women of color: We do not need cultural saving, as the research would suggest, because we possess a multitude of identity and leadership assets!

"WE ALREADY GOT THIS!" THEORETICAL FOUNDATIONS FOR YOUNG WOMEN OF COLOR

The only storylines from our Black history that we were exposed to in our K–12 schooling were that of enslavement, segregation, and the Civil Rights Movement. Black women, with the exception of Rosa Parks, were portrayed as tertiary and not necessarily instrumental to pivotal moments in our history. Now that we are greater architects of our own knowledge and have found epistemologies that better align with our experiences as young Black women, we have come to realize that activism is very much a part of our history and is an innate component of our moral core. Just the other day, Anjalé had the opportunity to experience a commendable moment in a high school classroom where a teacher engaged the students in a discussion about Black feminism. The students read Sojourner Truth's *Ain't I a Woman*, and the teacher noted that Truth was one of the first publicly visible and acknowledged Black feminist activists. Could it be that the deletion of Black women who were visible activists from of our former school curriculum was an institutionalized tactic to conceal from us that "we already got this"? Because as young Black women, empowerment, community, and activism are like breathing to us.

It is important to honor a number of feminist traditions that focus on women of color. Still, we affirm that we are *young* women who racially and culturally identify as Black or African American. Therefore, we use a hybrid of Black feminist thought and hip hop feminism, theoretical foundations that we feel most represents our racialized and gendered experiences and our activist work in V.O.I.C.E.S.

Black Feminist Thought

Black feminist thought recognizes that African American women in the United States experience the intersecting oppressions of race, class, gender, and sexuality. When Black feminism is put into practice as a form of activism, it serves as a dialectical response to the intersecting oppression that Black women experience. According to Patricia Hill Collins (2000), "Black feminist thought aims to empower African American women within the context of social injustice sustained by intersecting oppressions" (p. 22).

History, in general, as well as traditional feminist theory (which largely depicts the White, middle class, heterosexual experience), fails to acknowledge or adequately depict how activism and community work is an innate part of our "being" as Black women and always has been—and always will be—central to "social justice for the Black freedom struggle" (p. 129). For example, the struggle to end Jim Crow during the 1950s and 1960s can be seen as the *first* women's movement of the Civil Right Era—a Black women's movement (Cleaver, 2003). It was Black women who were the backbone of churches that helped build capacity for the Civil Rights movement, who raised money for various organizations such as the National Association for the Advancement of Colored People (NAACP) and the Southern Christian Leadership Conference (SCLC), who sat at lunch counters, who went on Freedom Rides, who insisted their children be plaintiffs in school desegregation cases, who boycotted, led voters' rights campaigns, went to jail, and were the driving force for community empowerment and involvement in civil rights (Cleaver, 2003). And it was Black women's radical activist approaches toward civil rights that provided an example for and "transformed White women's understanding of what women could do" (Cleaver, 2003, p. 49).

Black feminist thought does not only address gender oppression, but is a standpoint from which Black women and any other historically oppressed groups can actively "find ways to escape from, survive in, and/or oppose" any "prevailing social and economic injustice" (Collins, 2000, p. 9). Ultimately, Black feminist thought allows us in our analysis of V.O.I.C.E.S. to reclaim the activists within us, as well as identify why V.O.I.C.E.S was a vehicle for countering the intersecting oppressions we face as young Black women.

Hip Hop Feminism

We use Black feminist thought to explore how V.O.I.C.E.S. was a unique opportunity to be empowered and engage in activism in order to push back against the multiple forms of oppression we experienced in school and our communities. However, hip-hop feminism more adequately represents the "in the moment" sociopolitical, raced, and gendered context and is also a viable theory for understanding the context of young Black women in leadership roles. Like any music genre that responds to an era, socially conscious hip-hop music is the soundtrack of our generation and issues we face as young black women in our respective communities. Accordingly, we identify as part of the hip-hop generation.

For young Black women, hip-hop feminism is a departure from Whiteness and "academically sanitized" feminist theories (Peoples, 2008, p. 26). Hip-hop feminism honors the history that led up to Black feminism, but it also is an evolving theory that aims to remain relevant with our times (Jamila, 2002). According to Pough (2002), hip-hop feminism is a framework "to create spaces—both inside and outside of the classroom—for young women especially to make the kinds of connections to societal issues that they do not make in the clubs on the dance floors" (p. 93). Therefore, we use hip-hop feminism to adapt the essence of the music we find most identifies with our schooling experiences. Finally, hip-hop feminism recognizes the creative expression of activism, "privileges the in-betweenness of a Black girl epistemology or a black feminist standpoint," honors black girls' and women's knowledge, and is "located and interpreted through the community (or communities) in which it is immersed" (Brown & Kwakye, 2012, p. 4). Thus, we assert that as members of V.O.I.C.E.S., for us, hip-hop feminism represents the "real" everyday identity politics that we as young, Black women faced, resisted, and acted upon in high school settings.

V.O.I.C.E.S AND THE (R)EVOLUTION OF VISIBLE ACTIVIST

V.O.I.C.E.S. was part of a larger university/K–12 public school partnership between a research extensive university and several urban school districts in a southwestern state. Initially, the partnership designed a leadership program, called the Community of Brothers in Revolutionary Alliance (C.O.B.R.A.), specifically for young men of color at targeted high school campuses where graduation rates for Black and Latino males were at or below 50%. The program was formatted as a once-a-week class during a school's advisory period where youth, teachers, and community leaders come together to form action-oriented changes in schools. A group of young women began to hear of the program, stumbled into one of the male-only sessions, and asked, "Well, what about us?"

Resistance to Having and Using Our V.O.I.C.E.S.

I am woman, hear me roar
Comin' out fresher and flyer than did before
That's right, I'm well respected
Don't get stupid, I'm well protected
If ya wanna battle I'm well prepared
Me and K-Rock are far from scared, you know what
We're brave, livin' in a cave of gold
Waitin' for the misbehaved to get bold
But as I look around so far so good
MC's behaving just like they should
Hands are folded, no whispering or passing notes
All attention to me ya have to devote
I'm like a teacher's salary I'm makin' a night
On the mic rhymes witty and bright
Maybe that's why they name is Lyte
Yo, bust it, Imma end it right here
DJ K-Rock, you end it over there

—MC Lyte, "I am Woman" (1988)

Lyrically portraying a "braggadocious demeanor," or boasting, is a common artistic license used in hip-hop (Ogbar, 2007, p. 75). Traditionally this braggadocious style in hip-hop is centered in masculinity, as the aim of the lyrical "battle" is to prove one's sexual prowess and domination (Ogbar, 2007). MC Lyte is one of the first few notable female rappers to garner mainstream attention in the 1980s and 1990s. In "I am Woman," MC Lyte attacks the oversexualized boasting of her male predecessors and uses the braggadocious technique to convey her intelligence by stating she is "witty and bright" emphasizing she is not afraid to exercise her voice because she is certainly "prepared to battle." This image of a Black woman as intellectually vocal counters the stereotypical images of Black women in history and in the mainstream media as sexually deviant, loose, vixens, or jezebels (see Collins, 2000).

Sadly, as young Black women, we received very few messages such as MC Lyte's in our schooling that told us we should be boastful of our intelligence. Because Black girls are given few opportunities in school to recognize "their own power and genius," they can be led to disbelieve that they have something important to voice (Brown, 2009, p. 3). As Ruth Nicole Brown found in her work (2009), young Black girls sometimes do not recognize their brilliance. In the same utterance, they can make complex commentary and policy implications about issues that face their communities while, at the same time, believe they are not smart.

Initially, V.O.I.C.E.S. had a shaky start. Not only did we have to prove ourselves to administration that we were "worthy" of having a space to call our own, but we also had to convince the women who signed on to participate that this was indeed a space for them and that in that space their voices mattered. School administrators, unfortunately, envisioned Black and Latino males as the source of high school maladies and, at the onset, did not recognize the need for a program specific to young women. In response, Brooke and some of her peers tapped into their innate leadership skills and "went rogue" by meeting independently to name and craft principles for V.O.I.C.E.S. Initially, the young women organically established a group for themselves and met without formal permission from school administration.

Brooke

This idea [V.O.I.C.E.S.] started with three students. Over time, my leadership responsibilities decreased to primarily planning and leading the meetings. It was a lot of work, but I was dedicated to it. It was extremely difficult, and, sometimes frustrating, getting the other young women interested and involved in V.O.I.C.E.S. and encouraging them to see my vision and understand the importance of the group, especially since I had so much going on in my personal life with my mother being in rehabilitation. The vision took a while to convey to other young women, mainly because this was something new and unlike any other organization/group in the school systems in the surrounding area. Because there was no group like it, there was conflict between some of the young women in the group; some grudges among women remained even when the reasons for the grudges had been forgotten. We also struggled with attracting the right target audience, young women of color, and even young White women who we felt could also benefit from the group.

We realized that in order to create a space to express our voices, we would need some structure. We began setting requirements for participation and taking attendance. I, along with the adult facilitators, felt that it was important to address this issue, so to help ease some of the tension, we came up with ideas for activities for the young women to work together and try to get to know each other better. We also felt it was imperative for the young women to feel important and be active in the process of setting the foundation of the group, so we discussed what we wanted our mission to look like and what we officially wanted our name to stand for.

Of course, we needed "adult supervision" to make everything safe, so the school brought graduate students from the university to "facilitate" the group. They made the young ladies a little hesitant to speak up at first, but they acted as unbiased mediators and eventually created a safe space. What I loved most is that the facilitators respected that we wanted the program to be: student based and student led, and they let that happen and encouraged it along the way. This is what set us apart from C.O.B.R.A., the program for young men of color, and many other youth programs in the area.

Mercedes

I believe the most challenging obstacle faced was the lack of participation and organization. Brooke and I are not very different in nature. We are both naturally inclined to lead and share our opinions. Many times, I found myself to be the only person talking and/or making final decisions, especially once Brooke graduated and I was left as the most senior member and leader of the program. I stayed passionate about V.O.I.C.E.S. in order to motivate and uplift the other young women. It was frustrating at times and I typically found myself taking on many duties—often too many—to keep the momentum of the program going and to encourage participants to keep returning to the sessions.

The students were in control from the beginning. It was students' ideas that were used to implement the program, and students who facilitated the weekly meetings. The basis for every goal V.O.I.C.E.S. set and accomplished was determined by students. The adult facilitators were resource providers and supportive of students working constructively, critically thinking, exploring individual identities, and discovering our true history and cultures.

Anjalé

I recall there were many sessions that seemed disorganized, and there were times when attendance waned. I can admit that, as an adult facilitator, I was a bit unsure of how to support a student-led group that was still not "official" in the eyes of the school administration. It was made obvious by the number of times we were moved to different rooms by administration for our meetings, or were frequently "watched" by school security and administration to see if we were "under control" and "productive" (they never went to "check in" on the kids in yearbook club, so why did they monitor us?) that school personnel in general still perceived V.O.I.C.E.S.

as a bit "rebellious" or not something that would be "necessary" for young women of color.

In the early stages of V.O.I.C.E.S., it was challenging to understand what the program was about for a number of reasons. It was difficult to try to get the "right" kind of participation and commitment from the participants. We experienced resistance early on from women who only wanted to passively, not actively, participate. Not all of the women who participated had an authentic reason for attending. Some enrolled in the class because they did not want to enroll in a more "serious" advisory class such as academic tutoring or study hour. Yet, whatever their reason for attending, at least we got them there.

Initially, it was difficult to plan and decide what the focus would be for each class session. Also, there were several sessions in the beginning where women just sat there in silence. The reluctance early on to speak up could be attributed to the fact that schools, as institutions, rarely place women of color in positions where they can have a voice, decide what the topics of discussion will be, and essentially lead themselves. So when one has not been taught how or ever been given the opportunity to be a leader and have a VOICE, resistance is inevitable. It was evident that most of the young women in V.O.I.C.E.S. had never had the chance to freely speak and have control over the topic of discussion in their academic classes. And this lack of experience with critical dialogue caused trepidation among the young women when it came time to speak up on issues. Simply encouraging the participants to talk was quite a struggle. But that is what happens when there are few moments where youth can speak up and speak out in school. It soon gets to the point that we silence ourselves because we do not know the potential of our own voices.

Rare Moments and Cherished Spaces That Are For Us and By Us

[Monie Love]
Believe me when I say being a woman is great, you see
I know all the fellas out there will agree with me
Not for being one but for being with one
Because when it's time for loving it's the woman that gets some
Strong, stepping, strutting, moving on
Rhyming, cutting, and not forgetting
We are the ones that give birth
To the new generation of prophets because it's ladies first

[Queen Latifah]
I break into a lyrical freestyle
Grab the mic, look into the crowd and see smiles
Cause they see a woman standing up on her own two
Sloppy slouching is something I won't do

Some think that we can't flow (can't flow)
Stereotypes, they got to go (got to go)
I'm a mess around and flip the scene into reverse
(With what?) with a little touch of ladies first

Who said the ladies couldn't make it, you must be blind
If you don't believe, well here, listen to this rhyme
Ladies first, there's no time to rehearse
I'm divine and my mind expands throughout the universe
A female rapper with the message to send the
Queen Latifah is a perfect specimen

—Queen Latifah and Monie Love, "Ladies First" (1989)

Even in the midst of the monitoring eye of the state and its performance mandates, teachers, administrators, and school resource officers (a covert name for police surveillance in schools), V.O.I.C.E.S. was a rare space in a public, comprehensive high school where "ladies" were "first." Previous literature suggests that Black girl voice and "loudness" are forms of resistance to school-sponsored oppression. This is unfortunately correlated to our higher incidence of dropping out or being pushed out of school (Fine, 1991; Fine & Zane, 1991). However, the work of O'Connor, Lewis, and Mueller (2005) suggests that young Black women use their voices as power to foil any practices that disparage their schooling experiences, achievement, and outcomes. The Black women in their research drew upon "Black feminine agency" to create their own spaces as a way to resist inequitable treatment in school (p. 177). We agree in the case of V.O.I.C.E.S., where we created a space that was "for us and by us," that the "loud" and "forceful" way in which we stepped onto the scene and decided to build the program on our own from the ground up despite school administrations' trepidations actually worked in our favor and supported our academic success. We were able to create a protective space where we looked out for our fellow Black and Brown "sistahs" by providing the academic support and monitoring of each other that we did not always receive from the teachers and counselors.

The name V.O.I.C.E.S. was carefully crafted by the program founders as a textual representation of the activist space we were trying to create for high school women of color. So, even before we had a physical space within the high school to call our own, creating a bold, dynamic name gave us a "presence" and proclaimed to our peers, teachers, and administrators that "we have arrived," so "stay tuned" to witness our evolution. The founders passed around several iterations of the program name and finally approved Verbally Outspoken Individuals Creating Empowering Sistahs, and even the spelling of "Sistahs" went through a series of spellings to ensure it adequately represented the message we were trying to convey. Eventually, the program founders presented a program proposal to the high school administrators and university representatives. Once we gained approval to be a "legitimized" program, we crafted our own curriculum for the program based on pillars that we called *beams*. As women, our hips are the center of our bodies. We envisioned our hips as "beams" that are a strong foundation for our stature. The curriculum and discussions in our weekly class sessions were based on the following *beams*: (a) academic leadership, (b) peers supporting peers, (c) intercultural communication, (d) critical consciousness, (e) self-definition, and (f) conflict resolution.

Brooke

I do agree that the opportunity and environment of V.O.I.C.E.S. is unique because there are not many programs like it, especially those that are student based and student led. Rarely do groups of minorities get to meet to openly and honestly discuss matters that pertain to struggles and issues concerning those particular groups. As I have learned in college, the only place where this seems to be the norm is at a historically Black college or university. I did not fully understand the power of groups of young people coming together for discussion until college. I somewhat realized the importance in high school, but did not fully understand V.O.I.C.E.S. and its power and potential until college. If I had known what I understand now, V.O.I.C.E.S. could have been so much more powerful.

Why are women resistant to becoming leaders? Because we do not see very many women in leadership positions that look like us, that come from where we have come from, doing what we want to do . . . or better yet what we believe we want to do. People are afraid of what they do not know, and most of us did not know how to lead or understand the power behind leading.

Mercedes

I was not present for the actual beginning of V.O.I.C.E.S. I did not attend a single session until the last few weeks of the first installment of the program. However, I was very interested and outspoken. I understood the importance of it as soon as I saw that girls who had "issues" or conflicts with each other all year round were able to be in the same space, work together, and voice their opinions. So the program lightened the hostility that we young women of color were struggling with among ourselves. I think I realized how much we had in common in that space, even if it was for just a short amount of time.

Anjalé

I remember one of the school administrators, an administrator of color who was a strong advocate for V.O.I.C.E.S., admitted to me that "some of the teachers here don't really care about the Black kids." This administrator noticed that while there were some students of color who dynamically stood out as leaders, most were ignored by teachers and administrators as these relationships were quite strained. Yes, the program aimed to restore positive student of color–teacher relationships, but, in the meantime, it was peer-to-peer/"sistah-to-sistah" relationships—one of the program's *beams*—that helped the women receive social and academic supports that that they did not always formally receive in school. Thus, this was *our* space where for at least the first five minutes of every class we had a rant session where we *listened* and were *attentive* to whatever was on our minds that we wanted to share.

Sistahs Supportin' the Brothas

A lover and a fighter and he'll knock another out
Don't take him for a sucka 'cuz it's not what he's about
Everytime I need him, he always got my back
Never disrespectful for 'cuz his momma taught him that
Whatta man, whatta man, whatta man, whatta mighty good man

—Salt 'n' Pepa, "Whatta Man" (1993)

Though the program was centered on empowering young women of color, the founders were deeply troubled by the level of surveillance Black and Latino young men encountered in their schools on a daily basis. Therefore, the young women also initiated opportunities to partner with C.O.B.R.A., the young men's program, in an effort to rebuild trusting relationships between school adults and Black and Latino students specifically. Collins (2000) unpacked the nature of relationships between Black women and men, which she coined as the "love and trouble tradition" where Black women are caught in a bind of being overpowered by and living for the love of a Black man (p. 152). Even though throughout history it was necessary for Black men to dutifully protect Black women from economic and sexual exploitation under the guise of slavery and Jim Crow, Collins (2000) asserted there is a fine line between *protecting* Black women and *controlling* them. However, the complex way in which Black women experience race, class, and gender oppression means that we have to acquire a since of self-reliance, independence, and empowerment to survive and thrive. This is when we get caught in the quandary of "love and trouble" as our empowerment challenges Black manhood as they wonder whether we still need *protecting* (Collins, 2000). Furthermore, the sexual politics between Black men and women is largely situated under the guise of Whiteness that places heterosexist and Eurocentric standards of how gender should be performed, especially when it comes to what constitutes a traditional family structure and ideology (Collins, 2000).

For V.O.I.C.E.S., it was important that C.O.B.R.A., the young men's group "always had their backs." Audre Lorde (1984) declared that Black women can be further empowered as individuals when:

> Black women and Black men who recognize that the development of their particular strengths and interests does not diminish the other do not need to diffuse their energies fighting for control over each other. We can focus our attentions against the real economic, political, and social forces at the heart of this society which are ripping us and our children and our worlds apart. (p. 46)

V.O.I.C.E.S. and C.O.B.R.A. aimed to turn this "love and trouble tradition" on its head as both groups realized that in order to establish a positive representation within the high school for youth of color at large, the two groups must join forces and build greater strength in numbers to challenge the racial politics in the school.

Brooke

There is no doubt that C.O.B.R.A. is the reason V.O.I.C.E.S. exists. It was our example that a unique group could be created that focused on bringing students together to teach them the power of unity. I think V.O.I.C.E.S. helped C.O.B.R.A. gain a different perspective when we marched into one of their meetings demanding to start a young women's group! I think some may have thought we were a joke, but they soon learned we were serious and we would make it happen. We had unwavering support from C.O.B.R.A. when getting started. They may have not known how we would operate, but they trusted us to make it happen. The difference between V.O.I.C.E.S. and C.O.B.R.A. was that V.O.I.C.E.S. was mainly student based and student led, whereas C.O.B.R.A. was student based, staff led. But I think the young men saw the young women stand up and take charge of the meetings, and it made them want to do the same. We modeled for the young men how to lead the meetings.

V.O.I.C.E.S. also thought it would be beneficial if we had a meeting with C.O.B.R.A. once a month to get the male perspective on many issues and topics of discussion. Our meetings allowed us to have insight and get questions answered. We also met together once a year with student groups from the other nine campuses for various workshops, discussions, and awards. It was great seeing all of everyone together. I believe the other programs for young women and men of color at all campuses had a shared responsibility to continue to be examples of leaders in our communities. All of us getting together showed that we thought we were more than just a number or statistic. We had voices! We wanted more.

Our Struggle Is Our Source for Activism

I'm from a place in Harlem
Where the streets they look like Africa
And the trees are in better condition that the homes so abandoned
P.S. 197

Where I study my academic stare run
And the books so worn and torn I can't think
How they tried to cripple me
Understood the lost side of me
Thank god I had a good teacher on the side of me
Showed me the right thangs to do
Overcame the obstacles
Haters stand up for the things that we've been through ooh

Blays Road Stand up! (uh)
Pre K Stand Up! (uh)
East Coast Stand Up! (uh)
Come around my way

Here we got these buildings called projects but they ain't three stories
They fill about ten on the block April flow go up by twenty
Stories I tell be true story kids cut school and watch Maury
Like if they ain't intellect in what's affecting my life I can't respect them
People who come from where I'm from get it
But we still gotta make a difference
Stand up tall so the world can get it

Teach kids pride instead of "Outside"
Show another side an' they show gon' rise
Stop letting responsibility fall
I can tell you ain't been around my way at all

Why don't you come around (way)
So you can see what my (way)
Eyes been seeing why (way)
Where we need directions (way)
Respect in every lesson (way)
Way, why don't you come around

—Lil Mama, "Stand Up" (2008)

Finally, though we might not have readily identified as feminists or have been aware that our leadership in V.O.I.C.E.S. could be categorized as feminist activism, our personal struggles did serve as the impetus for our call to lead. Pough (2002) described how hip-hop helped her make sense of her personal struggles and embodied the promise of the hip-hop generation:

Black women all my life. My mother was a single parent and she worked hard to make sure that my sisters and I had the things we needed. She did not call herself a feminist. But she left an abusive husband and told any other Black man who could not act right where the door could hit him. Having female presence in my own home notwithstanding, there was something particularly inspiring about that presence personified in my own generation. Hip-hop gave me that. (p. 89)

Brooke

I do not know what made me take that position of leadership to start V.O.I.C.E.S. I can only say that I thought the idea was great and that I was passionate about what it could do and become (of course what I had in mind and how it is being conducted now is a little different). I was dedicated to making it happen. I guess I did not have that fear of the unknown. My entire childhood was filled with uncertainty. I never knew when our lights or electricity or water would be cut off when I got home from school. I never knew when my brother and I would have to move and leave our friends behind or when my mother would go to jail again. I never knew when we would eat some days. I did not know when our house would be randomly broken into and I/we would be held at gunpoint. I did not know when I would find my mother's crack pipe. I did not know I would not have much of a childhood because I had to raise my younger brother because of my mother's addiction. All I knew was that I had overcome all of those situations. I knew that I would not be where I was at the time without my faith in God and all the wonderful people He placed in my life to help me along the way. I knew that because I was determined to make a better life for myself and my family, and people knew my story, that people believed in me and were willing to help me achieve my goals and dreams. I did not take this for granted because these great people that I speak of are the ones that made V.O.I.C.E.S. possible.

My life's experiences helped me build leadership skills. Having to overcome all of the uncertainty, but always keeping a positive outlook on life and believing that I am not a product of my environment, shaped me to lead. I give all the credit to God for blessing me with that mindset. Because of my belief in God and being grateful for blessings, I want to use my life's experiences to encourage the next person, to encourage those that look like me, those that come from where I come from, those that want to do the things I want to do. That is why I chose the word *voices*, because voices are powerful. Voices can make someone smile or ruin someone's day. Voices can move a crowd of people to change the world for good, or for bad. I understood the positive power of the voice in high school and followed my heart to speak out and share my story. I dare not remain silent if I know that my story could encourage another person to break stereotypes, shatter statistics, and change the world.

Mercedes

My parents and family in general have struggled most of their lives. Around the time that V.O.I.C.E.S. was first conceived as a program, my father was diagnosed with cancer. This was a hard time for me, but God kept peace over my heart through V.O.I.C.E.S. I never believed that sacrifices were meant to go to waste. There was no way that I was going to allow my situation to hold me down. This was the mentality that V.O.I.C.E.S. helped me quickly adopt, especially because of the success that I was able to witness

Brooke experience. While I was a member, this was the mentality that I encouraged others to have as well. I had a voice and I needed to be heard.

I had a challenging childhood. Even though it was rough, there were always people in my life who loved me, supported me, and consistently motivated me in everything I aspired to do. I believe that these things made a huge difference and are the reasons why I believe in myself. I was never very impressionable or susceptible to peer pressure. There are some women who are too prideful to allow themselves to be taught because they are more concerned with the image they hold in the eyes of their peers than their own success. This pride in personal image was evident in the petty disagreements and grudges that some women of color held against each other. I blame this on the media because it is constantly bombarding young women with idealistic views of body image and stereotypes instead of focusing on women who are leaders in the world and portraying them as the role models that young women should follow.

Anjalé

Watching the women struggle to find a space for activism reminded me of what I felt as a young Black female, raised by a single mother, who tried to make sense of my identity, especially considering that in my entire K–12 schooling, I was *always* the only brown face in my advanced courses. Being the "only one" made me even more eager to prove people wrong about me by becoming class president, honor society president, and reaching the top ten percent of my graduating class. I was honored when Mercedes once told me that I was her role model and an example of what a capable, accomplished Black woman looks like, and I wondered if she realized that she was the same for me—a reflection. I was in awe of the innate leadership skills the women possessed. I remember at our annual Youth Summit, Brooke was disappointed in how loud and unresponsive the youth in the crowd were when she introduced a guest speaker. Brooke paused, commanded her peers' attention and then gave them all a mini-lecture on respecting a guest. I was astounded by how her peers responded to her, immediately became silent, and then gave the guest speaker the attention and respect that Brooke requested.

I started working with V.O.I.C.E.S. at the end of my 2nd year of my doctoral program, and what a disenchanted year that was. It was then I began to lose sight of why I pursued the doctorate in the first place and felt that the academy, the ivory tower, might have positioned me further and further away from the population I was so passionate about—young people of color. Working with V.O.I.C.E.S. reminded me why I got into the academic game in the first place, and I was reinvigorated by the youth's persistence and leadership. To be quite honest, if I had never been presented with the chance to work with V.O.I.C.E.S. and the community-engaged work that I accomplished with the youth in general, I do not think I would have remained in my doctoral program.

GENDERING YOUTH VOICE: THE ULTIMATE LEADERSHIP FORTRESS, THE ULTIMATE PRAXIS

As visible activists in V.O.I.C.E.S., while we did have the support of adults, we were the primary agents of praxis. Giroux (1997) laments we need more "radical educators" who work alongside youth to promote the "production of struggle" for youth voice (p. 141). In most instances, schools still struggle with the politics of authentically fostering the space for youth from historically marginalized groups in order to individually and collectively assert their voices to address issues and policies that impact their schooling experiences (Giroux, 1997, p. 141). Therefore, our experience as visible activists in V.O.I.C.E.S. can serve as an example of how we as young adults have leadership assets that older adults can learn from. It was the young women in V.O.I.C.E.S. who initiated the bridges and restored relationships with teachers and administrators. Though, at the time, we did not know that our work could be labeled as such, during our tenure in V.O.I.C.E.S. we engaged in praxis rooted in the Black feminist tradition. We were essentially cultural workers (see Collins, 2006) with a political agenda to transform the school by first creating improved schooling conditions for young women of color, developing young women leaders, and challenging school adults' stereotypical perceptions and interactions with all students of color.

According to Black feminist thought, Black women are natural cultural workers and community activists, as activism can take shape in any space or organization (Collins, 2000). So it is no surprise that the founders of V.O.I.C.E.S had a spontaneous reflex to make an activist space for themselves. V.O.I.C.E.S introduced activities such as district-wide youth summits held at the partnering university to expand the visible impact of the program. The young women extended invitations to school administrators and district leaders to witness their youth-led sessions where a number of topics emerged such as leadership, middle to high school transitions, sexism, and school-sponsored racism. The leadership program "created a space for [youth of color] to be recast and heard...as political actors" (Ginwright, 2007, p. 411). In order for the program to gain any credibility, the students challenged school adults' beliefs about how young women of color should be engaged in school. V.O.I.C.E.S., a program created by young women and for young women, was initially met with pushback from school administrators, but with a subsequent 94% college attendance rate, the school district soon recognized the potential of the program, and that when given the opportunity, the leadership of high school women of color can transform campus culture.

Due to the program's success in contributing to the increased academic achievement of youth of color as well as convincing school administrators to "reconsider" the leadership potential of youth of color, the school district expanded the program to one additional high school and five middle schools, and the university decided to expand by placing V.O.I.C.E.S. in additional school districts. The founders of V.O.I.C.E.S. never imagined that their courage to be visible activists in their own school would one day have such a far-reaching impact. Consequently, as visible activists, the young women "reconstituted images" of both women and men of color from "civic problems to civic problem solvers" (Ginwright, 2007, p. 41).

REFERENCES

Brown, R. N. (2009). *Black girlhood celebration: A hip-hop feminist pedagogy*. New York, NY: Peter Lang.

Brown, R. N., & Kwakye, C. J. (2012). Wish to live: the hip-hop feminism pedagogy reader. New York, NY: Peter Lang

Brown, T. M., & Rodriguez, L. F. (2009). School and the co-construction of dropout. *International journal of qualitative studies in education, 22*(2), 221–242.

Cleaver, K.N. (2003). Racism, civil rights, and feminism. In A. K. Wing (Ed.), *Critical race feminism: A Reader* (pp. 48–56). New York, NY: New York University Press.

Collins, P. H. (2000). *Black feminist thought: Knowledge, consciousness, and the politics of empowerment*. New York, NY: Routledge Press.

Collins, P. H. (2006). *From black power to hip-hop: Racism, nationalism, and feminism*. Philadelphia, PA: Temple University Press.

Delagado, M., & Staples, L. (2008). *Youth-led community organizing, theory, action*. New York, NY: Oxford University Press.

Fine, M., & Zane, N. (1991). Bein' wrapped too tight: When low-income women drop out of school. *Women's Studies Quarterly, 29*, 77–99.

Ginwright, S. A. (2007). Black youth activism and the role of critical social capitalism in Black community organization. *American Behavioral Scientist, 51*(3), 403–418.

Ginwright, S., & Cammarota, J. (2007). Youth activism in the urban community: Learning critical civic praxis within community organizations. *International Journal of Qualitative Studies in Education, 20*(6), 693–710.

Ginwright, S., Cammarota, J., & Noguera, P. (2005). Youth, social justice, and communities: Towards a theory of urban youth policy. *Social Justice, 32*(3), 24–40.

Giroux, H. A. (1997). *Pedagogy and the politics of hope. Theory, culture, and schooling*. Boulder, CO: Westview Press.

Hernández, D., & Rehman, B. (2002). *Colonize this! Young women of color on today's feminism*. New York, NY: Seal Press.

Hill, L. (2002). I get out. On *MTV Unplugged 2.0*. New York, New York: Columbia. (July 21, 2001).

hooks, b. (1981). *Ain't I a woman*. Cambridge, MA: Sound End Press.

Hurtado, A. (2000). *Construction sites: Excavating race, class, and gender among urban youth*. New York, NY: Teachers College Press.

Irizarry, J. G. (2011). *The Latinization of U.S. schools: Successful teaching & learning in shifting cultural contexts*. Boulder, CO: Paradigm Publishing.

Jamila, S. (2002). Can I get a witness? Testimony from a hip hop feminist. In D. Hernandez & B. Rehman (Eds.), *Colonize this! Young women of color on today's feminism* (pp. 382–394). New York, NY: Seal Press.

Kim, C. Y., Losen, D. J., & Dewitt, D. T. (2010). *The school-to-prison pipeline: Structuring legal reform.* New York, NY: New York University Press.

Lil Mama (2008). Stand up. On *Voice of the young people.* New York, NY: Zomba/Jive.

Lorde, A. (1984). *Sister outsider: Essays and speeches by Audre Lorde.* New York, NY: Crossing Press.

MC Lyte. (1988). I am woman. On *Lyte as a rock.* New York, NY: First Priority Music/Atlantic Records.

Noguera, P., & Cammarota, J. (2006). *Beyond resistance! Youth activism and community change: New democratic possibilities for practice and policy for America's youth.* New York, NY: Routledge.

Oesterreich, H. A. (2007). From "crisis" to "activist': the everyday freedom legacy of Black feminisms. *Race, ethnicity, and education, 10*(1), 1–20.

Ogbar, J. O. G. (2007). *Hip-hop revolution: the culture and politics of rap.* Lawrence, KS: University Press of Kansas.

Peoples, W. A. (2008). "Under construction": Identifying foundations of hip-hop feminism and exploring bridges between Black second-wave and hip-hop feminisms. *Meridians:Feminism, Race, Transnationalism, 8*(1), 19–52.

Pough, G. D. (2002). Love feminism, but where's my hip-hop: shaping a Black feminist identity. In D. Hernandez & B. Rehman (Eds.), *Colonize this! Young women of color on today's feminism* (pp. 382–394). New York, NY: Seal Press.

Queen Latifah and MC Lyte. (1989). Ladies first. On *All hail the queen.* New York, NY: Tommy Boy Records.

Salt N' Pepa. (1993). Whatta man. On *Very necessary.* USA: Next Plateau/London Records.

Stanton-Salazar, R. D. (1997). A social capital framework for understanding the socialization of racial minority children and youths. *Harvard Educational Review, 67*(1), 1–40.

Valencia, R. R. (2010). *Dismantling contemporary deficit thinking: Educational thought and practice.* New York, NY: Taylor and Francis.

Ward, J. V. (2000). Raising resisters: The role of truth telling in the psychological development of African American girls. In L. Weis & M. Fine (Eds.), *Construction sites: Excavating race, class, and gender among urban youth* (pp. 50–64). New York, NY: Teachers College Press.

Ward, J. V. (2001). Raising resisters: The role of truth telling in the psychological development of African American girls. In L. Weis & M. Fine (Eds.), *Construction sites: Excavating race, class, and gender among urban youth.* New York, NY: Teachers College Press.

Weis, L., & Fine, M. (2001). *Construction sites: Excavating race, class, and gender among urban youth.* New York, NY: Teachers College Press.

Yosso, T. J. (2005). Whose culture has capital? A critical race theory discussion of community cultural wealth. *Race, Ethnicity and Education, 8*(1), 69–91.

CHAPTER 6

AFRICAN AMERICAN FEMALE STUDENTS AT HISTORICALLY BLACK COLLEGES AND UNIVERSITIES

Historical and Contemporary Considerations

Marybeth Gasman

ABSTRACT

This chapter examines the historical and contemporary experiences of Black female students at HBCUs using a gender lens. Beginning with the pejorative treatment of Black female college students by White missionaries in the 19th century, moving to the often invisible role of Black female students in the 1960s campus and civil rights protests (invisible due to the male domination of most civil rights activities), and concluding with an exploration of the lives and aspirations of Black female students in the current day, I will illuminate Black female student experiences through historical inquiry.

Women Interrupting, Disrupting, and Revolutionizing Educational Policy and Practice, pages 99–108
Copyright © 2014 by Information Age Publishing
99

Issues of racial equality have long received special attention at historically Black colleges and universities (HBCUs). One consequence of this focus, however, is that issues of gender equality are sometimes swept under the rug—rarely discussed, except among a small group of feminists (Cole & Guy-Sheftal, 2003). In the words of Black feminist scholar Patricia Hill Collins (1999), many Black college women have found themselves in the position of "outsider-within"—meaning that their gender puts them in a disadvantaged position within the racialized Black college community.

This chapter examines the historical and contemporary experiences of Black female students at HBCUs through a gender lens (Ferree, Lorber, & Hess, 1998). I will illuminate Black female student experiences through historical inquiry, beginning with the pejorative treatment of Black female college students by White missionaries in the 19th century, moving to the often invisible role of Black female students in the 1960s campus upheaval/protests, civil rights protests (invisible due to the male domination of most civil rights activities), and concluding with an exploration of the lives and aspirations of Black female students in the current day.

THE BEGINNINGS OF BLACK COLLEGES

Most Black colleges were founded in the aftermath of the Civil War, with the exception of three in the north: Lincoln and Cheney Universities in Pennsylvania and Wilberforce in Ohio (Anderson, 1988). With the end of the Civil War, the daunting task of providing education to over four million formerly enslaved Blacks was shouldered by both the federal government, through the Freedman's Bureau, and many northern church missionaries (Anderson, 1988). As early as 1865, the Freedmen's Bureau began establishing Black colleges, resulting in staff and teachers with primarily military backgrounds. During this period, most Black colleges were colleges in name only; like many White colleges in their infancy, these institutions generally provided primary and secondary education. From their beginnings, most Black colleges, unlike their historically White counterparts, provided coeducational training. Black women, like Black men, were seen by the White missionaries and Whites in general as potential workers in need of training (Cross Brazzell, 1992; Watson & Gregory, 2005).

The benevolence of the White missionaries was tinged with self-interest and, sometimes, racism (Anderson, 1988; Cross Brazzell, 1992). The missionaries' goal in establishing these colleges was to Christianize the freedmen (i.e., convert formerly enslaved people to *their* brand of Christianity). And while some scholars see the missionaries' actions as largely well meaning (Jencks & Riesman, 1968), many others do not (Anderson, 1988; Watkins, 2001). According to a more radical group of scholars, the idea of a

Black menace was at the forefront of the minds of these missionaries, who believed that education would curb the "savage" tendencies of the former slaves but should not lead to full-blown social equality (Anderson, 1988; Watkins, 2001). The education provided to Black college students was a mixture of liberal arts and industrial training: classical texts were taught side by side with manual labor skills for men and household duties for women, both for their own homes as well as for those White homes in which they might work. Unlike many White women, Black women did not have the option of whether to work outside the home. Many Black colleges also provided teacher training for both men and women (Anderson, 1988).

With the passage of the second Morrill Act in 1890, the federal government again took an interest in Black education, establishing public land-grant Black colleges and universities. This act stipulated that those states practicing segregation in their public colleges and universities would forfeit federal funding unless they established agricultural and mechanical institutions for the Black population. Despite the wording of the Morrill Act, which called for the equitable division of federal funds, these newly founded institutions received fewer monies than their White counterparts and thus had inferior facilities (Gasman, 2007). Just as before the Act, women who attended these schools learned household duties, such as how to cook, clean, make brooms, and sew (Spivey, 2006). On the other hand, men were trained in brick making and laying, farming, blacksmithing, and other forms of manual labor (Spivey, 2006). This kind of industrial curriculum was the norm for women and men at many private Black colleges as well, causing Black intellectuals, such as W.E.B. Du Bois and Mary Church Terrell, to call for more classically focused curricula at these institutions. Black Feminists today have argued that an industrial curriculum for women, including classes in millinery, sewing, cooking, and household management was central to White control of Black women. This curriculum, according to some Black scholars, perpetuated the Black mammy image that Whites found comforting. The Black woman (the Black college student) was, in the eyes of many Whites, "a harmless, ignorant woman whose main pleasure was to take care of them" (Collins, 2001, p. 33).

It was not until the turn of the 20th century, however, that most Black colleges seriously began to provide a college-level, liberal arts education (Anderson, 1988). Institutions such as Fisk in Tennessee, Dillard in Louisiana, and Howard in Washington, DC exemplified this approach, schooling their male and female students in the classics. For the most part, these colleges prepared women for teaching positions in schools and colleges and for public service. Moreover, it is important to note that, much like their White counterparts, these women were expected to enroll in home economics courses to complement their academic skills.

During the early years of Black colleges, female students were sheltered by the mostly White female administration; their lives were shaped by institutional policies designed to control their behavior (Perkins, 1996; Watson & Gregory, 2005). In the eyes of the White missionaries, Black women had been stripped of their feminine virtue by the experiences of slavery and, as such, had to be purified before they could assume the responsibilities of the home (Cross Brazzell, 1992; Gray White, 1999). Typically, during the late 1880s, female Black college students were not allowed to leave the campus without a member of the administration escorting them. By contrast, Black men were free to come and go as they pleased. At most institutions, the dean of women lived on campus in order to watch over the fragile and impressionable young college girls (Bell Scott, 1997; Perkins, 1996). The dean of men, on the other hand, lived off campus as did the other upper level administrators (Bell Scott, 1997; Perkins, 1996). During the mid 1920s, many female students at Black colleges and universities urged campus administrators to grant them greater autonomy, noting that it would help them learn self-reliance—a skill that they saw as essential to assuming leadership roles (Perkins, 1996). These same women fought vehemently against the repressive religious customs used to rear their race and gender (Watson & Gregory, 2005). These practices were generally imposed by White and Black male administrators, many of whom were also ordained Baptist ministers. In particular, the administrators often used the philosophies of the apostle Paul as an excuse to relegate women to second-class status. Women were told that, according to the Bible, patient waiting was to be held above the development of one's talents (Watson & Gregory, 2005). For example, at Howard University, during the 1920s and 1930s, President Mordecai Johnson fought vehemently with Lucy Diggs Slowe, the dean of women, over issues of women's equality. Slowe demanded of Johnson that the female students at Howard have equal living conditions—to no avail. Interestingly, Johnson was an ordained Baptist minister. Moreover, in one instance, Slowe acted as a representative of several female students who had been sexually harassed by a Black male professor. As a result, she received a letter attacking her credibility and that of the students. Under Johnson's presidency, despite his amazing skill at institution building, this type of interaction was a common occurrence (Bell Scott, 1997; Eisenmann, 2001; Gasman, 2006; Nidiffer, 1999).

In spite of the heavy hand of religion and the resulting sexism, Black colleges during the late 1800s and early 1900s offered a surprising number of opportunities for Black female students to participate in traditionally male activities. For example, at Talladega College, women were able to join the rifle club (Anderson, 1988; Thelin, 2004). On the other hand, women participated in social service sororities such as Alpha Kappa Alpha and Delta

Sigma Theta (Giddings, 1988; Parker, 1978). While sometimes focused on the superficial aspects of appearance and socialization, these organizations were also active in suffrage and civil rights activities as well as other national causes (Gasman, 2005, 2008).

During the 1950s and early 1960s, Black women on Black college and university campuses were instrumental in the Civil Rights movement. Women at both Bennett and Spelman Colleges participated in sit-ins and lunch counter demonstrations (Brown, 1998; Lefever, 2005). The administrators of these women's colleges, now Black rather than White, were, by and large, supportive of the student actions. However, this was not the case at all Black colleges and universities. At some public Black institutions, which were under the close supervision of state government authorities, administrators declined to help both male and female student protesters who had landed in jail (Williamson, 2004).

Many of these young HBCU women were fearless, working diligently to make change within their communities and within the country as a whole (Cole & Guy-Sheftal, 2003). For example, Barbara Harris and Diane Nash, both Fisk University students, were jailed along with 63 other male and female students who protested Nashville's segregated lunch counters. Although they were offered an opportunity to make bond ($100), they chose to go to jail because, in their minds, paying the bond would be a capitulation to the South's Jim Crow government (Ashley & Williams, 2004; Cole & Guy-Sheftal, 2003; Gasman, 2007). Ironically, as these female students were fighting on behalf of civil rights, they were still being treated as fragile accessories to men by their college administrations. For example, at the same time that students at Bennett College were marching in the streets and attempting to desegregate lunch counters, they were required to take a course called the "The Art of Living," which focused on becoming a successful homemaker (Bell Scott, 1979, 1997).

In the early 1970s, Patricia Gurin and Edgar Epps (1975) completed a research study that sought to understand the advantages and disadvantages gained by Black male and female students at HBCUs. Surveying 5,000 African American students, this study was comprehensive and its results compelling. The researchers found that undergraduate women at HBCUs were considerably disadvantaged. In particular, the educational and career goals of female students were significantly lower than those of their male peers. Not only were these Black women less likely to aspire to the PhD, but they were more likely to opt for low-prestige careers in the female sector of the nation's job market (e.g., teaching and the health professions). This seminal research also showed that the patriarchal environments at many HBCUs compounded the problem (Gurin & Epps, 1975; Harper, Carini, Bridges, & Hayek, 2004). Other researchers have found that social passivity and disengagement on the part of Black women, most likely caused by institutional environments, helped explain why these individuals did not have higher career aspirations (Bell Scott, 1979; Hine, 2005; Hine & Thompson, 1999; Thompson, 1973; Washington & Newman, 1991).

Scholars in the mid 1980s found that although women were actively engaged in the classroom and in extracurricular activities, they spent less time interacting with individual faculty members (Bonner, 2001). This practice could result in fewer discussions about graduate school and less support for non-female career fields. Moreover, Fleming (1984) found that men at Black colleges were dominant in both the classroom and social settings and that women were less competitive. In Fleming's own words, "the big issue for women on black campuses is their fear of using assertive skills" (p. 145). More recently, researchers have shown more equal gains for men and women from the HBCU experience (Bonner, 2001; Harper et al., 2004). It appears that women have overcome some of the barriers placed before them, breaking away from passivity. However, at many campuses, an atmosphere persists that encourages women to cede to male counterparts in class discussions and in student leadership positions (Bonner, 2001; Guy Sheftal, 1982; Harper et al, 2004).

Studies have also shown that African American female students at HBCUs feel a higher level of anxiety than their male counterparts (Bonner, 2001; Fleming, 1984). In addition, when surveyed, they felt less competent than males. Sadly, other studies have revealed that female students were more willing to take on positions and roles that made them seem less competent in order to avoid threatening their male peers (Washington & Newman, 1991). According to Fleming (1984), at Black colleges,

> women who become a little more assertive in college, but not as much as men, suffer from feelings of unhappiness... [and] women who give little thought to suppressing assertiveness find that they are less popular by the senior year. It looks, then, as if women invest in not asserting themselves so that they can maintain the approval of men. Perhaps this is our root of female competence anxiety. (p. 145)

Despite these feelings of insecurity, women's academic performance at HBCUs outpaces that of Black males. A recent study showed that at most HBCUs, the percentage of Black women on the honor roll was larger than the percentage of women enrolled at the institutions. For example, at Clark Atlanta University in 2005, women accounted for 69% of the student body but made up 84% of the dean's list. Likewise, at Howard University, women made up 60% of the student body but accounted for 70% of the honor roll. On average, the percentage of women on dean's lists at HBCUs exceeded their enrollment by 10% ("Women dominate," 1995).

LOOKING FORWARD

Currently, the nation's HBCUs enroll approximately 250,000 African American students, with a large proportion attending private, four-year institutions. Black women make up the majority of the student population at most Black colleges. For example, at Dillard University, women account for almost three quarters of the student body. Moreover, at Fisk and Hampton Universities, women make up 70% of all students enrolled. According to the *Journal of Blacks in Higher Education* ("Women dominate," 1995), even at Tuskegee University, "which is known for its strong programs in the agricultural sciences (a discipline not considered to be a favorite course of study among women), women are now a majority of the student body" (p. 46). When looked at as a whole, HBCUs grant roughly 28% of bachelor's degrees, 15% of master's degrees, 9% of doctoral degrees, and 15% of professional degrees awarded to African Americans. Black women outpace Black men at all educational levels. Despite generally favorable statistics for degree attainment for women, the majority of these degrees are in traditionally female-dominated programs. Over 70% of Black women's degrees earned at HBCUs are in the health professions or education (Hayes & Boone, 2001). Black women, like White women, hold positions in service areas and are less likely to hold jobs in the sciences. Here certain Black colleges are trying to make gains. For example, of the Black women who enter graduate programs in the sciences, 50% are from Spelman and Bennett Colleges—schools that have special programs preparing their students for scientific fields (www.uncf.org). Moreover, HBCUs represent the top 20 institutions overall in the placement of Black women in graduate programs in the sciences at all U.S. institutions of higher education. Xavier University in New Orleans, in particular, sends more Black women into U.S. medical schools than any other institution in the country (www.uncf.org).

Some recent research has shown that Black college and university women are now selecting majors that were once exclusively male—including science, technology, engineering, and math (STEM). And Black colleges are having tremendous success in their efforts to graduate Black women. For example, according to 2003 data from the Department of Education's IPEDS survey, of all African American female bachelor's degrees conferred, Black colleges produce 38% in the biological sciences, 41% in chemistry, 40% in computer science, 40% in math, and 40% in physics (Gasman, Perna, Yoon, Drezner, Lundy-Wagner, & Gary, 2007). Given their lack of financial resources, it is downright astonishing that Black colleges have such great success in educating African American women (Kim & Conrad, 2006). Sadly, there is little empirical research that captures the success rates of Black colleges in STEM or other disciplines.

In moving forward with research on African American women enrolled at Black colleges, we need to ask more theoretical questions. What existing gender theories can be applied to the lives of women at Black colleges? Why were certain kinds of education and particular roles deemed appropriate for Black college women? How does the treatment of Black women at Black colleges reflect a difference in how Black and White women were (and are) seen in society? How have gender disparities played out at Black colleges? A number of talented female scholars have explored issues pertaining to African American women in higher education. In order to respect and appreciate the role that Black female students at Black colleges have played, it is imperative that we have richer research in this area—research that contextualizes these women within the larger Black college context, and smaller, individual investigations that delve deeply into these women's actions.

REFERENCES

Anderson, J. (1988). *The education of Blacks in the south, 1860–1935.* Chapel Hill, NC: University of North Carolina Press.

Ashley, D., & Williams, J. (2004). *I'll find a way or make one. A tribute to historically Black colleges and universities.* New York, NY: Amistad Publishing.

Bell-Scott, P. (1979). Schoolin' 'respectable' ladies of color: Issues in the history of Black women's higher education. *Journal of National Association or Women's Deans and Advisors of Colored Schools,* 22–28.

Bell Scott, P. (1997). To keep my self-respect: Dean Lucy Diggs Slowe's 1927 memorandum on sexual harassment of Black women. *National Women's Studies Association Journal,* 9.

Bonner, F. (2001). Addressing gender issues in the historically Black college and university community: A challenge and call to action. *The Journal of Negro Education, 70*(3), 176–191.

Brown, L. B. (1998). *The long walk: The story of presidency of Willa B. Player at Bennett College.* Danville, VA: Bennett College Women's Leadership Institute.

Cole, J. B., & Guy-Sheftal, B. (2003). *Gender talk: The struggle for women's equality in African American communities.* New York, NY: Random House.

Collins, A. C. (2001). Black women in the academy: An historical overview. In R. O. Mabokela & A. L. Green (Eds.), *Sisters of the academy: Emergent Black women scholars in higher education* (pp. 27–43). Sterling, VA: Stylus Press.

Collins, P. H. (1999). *Black Feminist thought: Knowledge, consciousness, and the politics of empowerment.* New York, NY: Taylor & Francis.

Cross Brazzell, J. (1992). Brick without straw: Missionary-sponsored Black higher education in the post-emancipation era. *Journal of Higher Education, 63*(1), 26–49.

Eisenmann, L. (2001). Creating a framework for interpreting U.S. women's educational history: Lessons from historical lexicography. *History of Education, 30*(5), 453–470.

Fleming, J. (1984). *Blacks in college.* San Francisco, CA: Jossey-Bass.

Gasman, M. (2005). Sisters in service: African American sororities and the philan-thropic support of education. In A. Walton (Ed.), *Women, philanthropy, and education* (pp. 194–214). Bloomington, IN: Indiana University Press.

Gasman, M. (2007). *Envisioning Black colleges: A history of the United Negro College Fund.* Baltimore, MD: Johns Hopkins University Press.

Gasman, M. (2008). Eyes firmly fixed on the prize: African American fraternities and sororities and their role in the Civil Rights Movement. In M. W. Hughley & G. S. Parks (Eds.), *Empirical studies of Black Greek letter organizations.* Louis-ville, KY: University of Kentucky.

Giddings, P. (1988). *In search of sisterhood: Delta Sigma Theta and the challenge of the Black sorority movement.* New York, NY: William Morrow, 1988.

Gray White, D. (1999). *Too heavy a load: Black women in defense of themselves, 1894–1994.* New York, NY: W.W. Norton.

Gurin, P., & Epps, E. (1975). *Black consciousness: Identity and achievement.* New York, NY: John Wiley & Sons.

Guy-Sheftal, B. (1982). Black women and higher education: Spelman and Bennett colleges revisited. *The Journal of Negro Education, 51*(3), 278–287.

Harper, S., Carini, R., Bridges, B., & Hayek, J. (2004). Gender differences in student engagement among African American undergraduates at historically Black colleges and universities. *Journal of College Student Development, 45*(3), 271–284.

Hayes, B., & Boone, L. R. (2001). Women's health research at historically black colleges and universities. *American Journal of Health Studies, 17*(2), 59–65.

Ferree, M., Lorber, J., & Hess, B. (Eds.). (1998). *Revisioning gender.* Lanham, MD: AltaMira Press.

Hine D. C. (2005). *Black women in America.* New York: Oxford University Press.

Hine, D. & Thompson, K. (1999). *A shining thread of hope. A history of Black women in America.* New York, NY: Broadway Books.

Jencks, C., & Riesman, D. (1968). The academic revolution. New York, NY: Double-day Books.

Kim, M., & Conrad, C. F. (2006, June). The impact of historically Black colleges and universities on the academic success of African American students. *Research in Higher Education, 47,* 399–427.

Lefever, H. G. (2005). *Undaunted by the fight: Spelman College and the Civil Rights Move-ment.* Macon, GA: Mercer University Press.

Nidiffer, J. (1999). *Pioneering deans: More than wise and pious matrons.* New York, NY: Teachers College Press.

Parker, M. (1978). Alpha Kappa Alpha: In the eye of the beholder. Washington, DC: Alpha Kappa Alpha Sorority.

Perkins, L. (1996). Lucy Diggs Slowe: Champion of the self-determination of Af-rican American women in higher education. *The Journal of Negro History, 81*(1/4), 89–104.

Spivey, D. (2006). *Schooling for the new slavery: Black industrial education, 1868–1915.* New York, NY: New World Press.

Thelin, J. (2004). *A history of American higher education.* Baltimore, MD: Johns Hop-kins University Press.

Thompson, D. (1973). *Private Black colleges at the crossroads.* Westport, CT: Green-wood Press.

Washington, V., & Newman, J. (1991). Setting our own agenda: Exploring the meaning of gender disparities among Blacks in higher education. *The Journal of Negro Education, 60*(1), 19–35.

Watkins, W. (2001). *The White architects of Black education: Ideology and power in America, 1865–1954.* New York, NY: Teachers College Press.

Watson, Y., & Gregory, S. T. (2005). *Daring to educate: The legacy of early Spelman college presidents.* Sterling, VA: Stylus Publishers.

Williamson, J. (2004). 'This has been quite a year for heads a falling': Institutional autonomy in the civil rights era. *History of Education Quarterly, 44*(4), 489–511.

Women dominate the honor rolls at Black colleges. (1995). *Journal of Blacks in Higher Education, 6,* 46–47.

CHAPTER 7

REFORMING SCHOOL REFORM

The Need for Addressing Gender and Sexuality Issues in Teacher Preparation Programs

Cathy A. R. Brant

ABSTRACT

When one considers that over three-fourths of teachers in the U.S. are female (and mostly straight), coupled with the rash of reports detailing the demise of LGBTQ students, it becomes clear that addressing gender and sexual identity in teacher preparation programs is critical to creating a "safe space" for all students. This chapter argues that simply taking a gender-neutral or sexuality-blind stance not only perpetuates the status quo, but also weakens education reform efforts that claim to strengthen student outcomes.

In a book about women interrupting, disrupting, and revolutionizing policy and practice, it is important to include the voice of the teacher and the emerging understanding that addressing "diversity" also includes gender and sexual identity issues. At first glance, teacher preparation programs

Women Interrupting, Disrupting, and Revolutionizing Educational Policy and Practice, pages 109–124
Copyright © 2014 by Information Age Publishing
109

may not seem to be "gendered" or "sexualized" places where expanding our purview of diversity to include gender and sexual identity issues is essential. However, when one considers that over three-fourths of teachers in the U.S. are female (IES, n.d.), coupled with the rash of reports of bullying and harassment of, often leading to dire consequences for, LGBTQ students (Dotinga, 2013), it becomes clear that addressing gender and sexuality issues in teacher preparation programs is critical to creating a "safe space" for all students, ultimately undergirding the purposes of schooling while also accomplishing social justice. Thus, not only are university teacher preparation programs gendered and sexualized spaces, so too, are public school classrooms. Simply ignoring this vulnerable population, or taking a gender-neutral or sexuality-blind stance, is unacceptable because it not only perpetuates the status quo, but also weakens education reform efforts that claim to strengthen student outcomes. School reform efforts must be reformed further to include more holistic diversity training for educators. I argue the need for issues of gender and sexuality to be addressed in teacher education programs, in the ways that race, class, and disability are, as well as suggest solutions for addressing these issues in teacher education.

BACKGROUND

It is challenging to precisely count those who identify as gay, lesbian, bisexual, transgender or queer (LGBTQ), especially in the case of youth, yet studies measuring same-sex attraction, same-sex behavior or both of American youth produce an estimate of 1–9% and, most likely, 5–6% percent of the total population (Human Rights Watch, 2001). The numbers of youth who identify as transgender or those who have non-normative gender expressions are even more difficult to estimate. Regardless of the exact number of students who identify as lesbian, gay, bisexual, transgender, or queer/questioning (LGBTQ), at some time in their teaching career, every teacher will wind up working with students or students who come from families with LGBTQ members.

With this reality, it is important to consider the experiences of LGBTQ youth in schools. Sixty-one percent (61%) of LGBTQ students surveyed felt unsafe at school because of their sexual orientation, and nearly 40% felt unsafe because of how they expressed their gender. Eighty-five percent (85%) of students were verbally harassed (e.g., called names or threatened) at school because of their sexual orientation and 64% were verbally harassed because of their gender expression. Forty percent (40%) of the students surveyed were physically harassed (e.g., pushed or shoved) at school in the past year because of their sexual orientation and 27% were because of their gender expression. Nineteen percent (19%) of students reporting being physically assaulted (e.g., punched, kicked, injured with a weapon) because of their sexual orientation, and 14% were physically assaulted because of their gender expression (Kosciw, Greytak, Diaz, Bartkiewicz, 2010).

A similar study was also conducted in regards to the climate for LGBTQ youth in elementary schools (GLSEN and Harris Interactive, 2012). In this study, 1,065 elementary school students in 3rd to 6th grade and 1,099 elementary school teachers of Kindergarten to 6th grade in schools across the country participated in an online survey. Forty-five percent (45%) of the students reported that they hear comments like "that's so gay" or "you're so gay" from other kids at school sometimes, often, or all of the time. Nearly half of teachers (49%) said that they heard students in their school use the word "gay" in a negative way sometimes, often, or very often. More than a quarter of the students (26%) and teachers (26%) reported hearing other students make comments like "fag" or "lesbo" at least sometimes. Almost one in ten of elementary school students (8%) report that they do not conform to traditional gender norms—that is, boys who are perceived to think, act, or look like girls, or girls who are perceived to think, act, or look like boys. Students who do not conform to traditional gender norms are less likely than other students to feel very safe at school (42% vs. 61%) and are more likely than others to agree that they sometimes do not want to go to school because they feel unsafe or afraid there (35% vs. 15%).

These statistics make it clear that this is a population that teachers need to be prepared to work with. Although most teacher education programs attempt to prepare future teachers to work with students from other marginalized groups (African American, the poor or working class, etc.), they are not being adequately prepared to recognize or address gender or sexual identity issues in their classrooms.

THE SCHOOL EXPERIENCES OF LGBTQ STUDENTS

The literature suggests that many students who "come out" and reveal their gender identification or sexual orientation to friends, family, or peers, during their middle or high school years experience moderate to severe levels of bullying, harassment, and hostility from their peers (GLSEN and Harris Interactive, 2012; Holmes & Cahill, 2004; Kosciw et al., 2010; Vaccaro, 2009). The impact of bullying and harassment due to LGBTQ students' gender and/or sexual identities can produce a number of negative effects including isolation from friends and family, depression, drug and/or alcohol use and addition, low self-esteem, lack of engagement in schools, academic failure, and fighting (Beam, 2007; Holmes & Cahill, 2004; Kosciw et al., 2010; Meyer, 2010; Wilkinson & Pearson, 2009).

Homophobia, the fear of and/or discrimination based on sexual orientation, and transphobia, the fear and/or discrimination of those who express their gender(s) in non-normative ways, is not always overt as in the verbal and physical harassment of LGBTQ students; it is often much more subtle and embedded in the day-to-day practices of schools. Sexuality is not a topic that is covered explicitly in most American schools, but when it is covered it is done so in a way that the only sexuality that is addressed is heterosexuality (Epstein, O'Flynn & Telford, 2000; Friend, 1993). The presence of gay and lesbians in history and literature are ignored. Additionally, an even more subtle homophobia exists within the institution. This subtle homophobia takes the form such as a lack of sensitivity to alternative family structures or rigid assumptions about the role of gender in students' lives (Blackburn, 2003; Cosier, 2009; Epstein et al., 2000; Maney & Cain, 1997; Quinlivan & Town, 1999).

As a result, students use a variety of strategies to help them cope with the institution that does not accept their non-normative gender and sexual identities. Friend (1993) identified five main strategies, including passing for straight, accommodation, heterosexual overcompensation, overachievement, and confronting the oppression to build self-empowerment. Passing involves "acting" straight in homophobic contexts, especially school, but also possibly at home. A similar idea to passing is that of covering, or "ton[ing] down a disfavored identity to fit into the mainstream" (Yoshino, 2007, p. ix). The strategy of accommodation (Blackburn, 2003; Friend, 1993) is one where closeted lesbian, gay, bisexual, transgender, or queer/questioning kids contribute to the homophobia of the school by making gay jokes or harass other queer students who are out in an attempt to maintain their own cover or passing. The idea behind this strategy is that no one will identify the person as gay or lesbian if they appear to have a dislike for homosexuality or those who express the gender in ways different from the norm.

A third strategy LGBTQ students use is heterosexual overcompensation (Friend, 1993). Often students using this strategy will live two separate lives, a public heterosexual life and a private homosexual life. When not in school, they may get involved with queer online forums or other places they feel safer in expressing their true identities (Driver, 2007, 2008). When in school, though, they do everything possible to continue to cover and pass. Some may even take heterosexual partners and engage in heterosexual activity so that there can be "no doubt" of their gender or sexual identities by their peers. Friend (1993) also discusses the strategy of overachievement. When using this strategy, LGBTQ youth take one of two approaches: proving themselves to be exceptional in academics, art, music, and so on, or "rather than trying to be exceptional, others may try to be the exception" (p. 229) in which they try to become the token gay, lesbian, or trans who is not like them.

The final strategy discussed by Friend (1993) is confronting oppression to build self-empowerment. Students who employ this strategy actively resist homophobia, transphobia, and heterosexism in their schools (Blackburn, 2007; Friend, 1993; Vaccaro, 2009). They may do this by starting a chapter or a Gay-Straight Alliance (GSA) in their school or by bringing their same-sex or gender nonconforming partner to a school dance. Students may confront oppression through more negative routes. They may actively choose to drop out of schools, under the argument that the schools do not meet their needs. Sometimes, in especially large cities, there are alternative schools that cater to LGBTQ students (Beam, 2007; Friend, 1993), but unfortunately these types of schooling environments are the exception, not the rule.

Sixty-two percent (62%) of students who were harassed or assaulted in schools did not report the incident to school staff, believing little to no action would be taken or that the situation would become worse. Thirty-four percent (34%) of the students who did report an incident said that school staff did nothing in response. Even more startling is that students reported experiencing homophobia and transphobia from their teachers, who are overwhelmingly straight females with little to no training in gender or sexuality issues. Sixty percent (60%) of students reported ever hearing homophobic remarks from their teachers or other school staff. Over half (59%) of students heard teachers or other staff make negative comments about a student's gender expression at school (Kosciw et al., 2010). Schools are a place where students are supposed to feel safe. These statistics reveal that LGBTQ students, in fact, do not. They do not feel that going to authorities in the school will do anything to stop the harassment and bullying.

REFORMING SCHOOL CULTURES

Cosier (2009) argues that school experiences do not need to be negative for queer youth when teachers and administrators are committed to equity and social justice in their buildings. There are things educators can do at both on a classroom level and on a school level. The most basic is making your classroom a "safe space" (Cosier, 2009). Students of all gender identities and sexual orientations benefit from knowing that they have an ally in their teachers. This can be communicated by acts including displaying queer-friendly symbols in classroom, not tolerating any homophobic or heterosexist peer-to-peer harassment, and letting students know that any bullying and harassment will not be tolerated and will be met with consequences. The safe space concept, although ideal, is still flawed. Teachers cannot be aware of everything that goes on within the classroom at all times. Students are also aware that although a given classroom may be safe, they still leave

that classroom during the day and are still susceptible to bullying and harassment. When claiming that their classrooms as safe spaces, teachers need
to be aware of the realities students may live outside of those four walls.

There is substantial literature about ways that teachers create a curriculum that is LGBTQ inclusive across the subject areas and grade levels.
In the early years, students can investigate gender roles and stereotypes
(Meyer, 2010). Teachers can engage in critical conversations with young
students about what happens when individuals cross gender boundaries,
for example, when boys play with "girl toys." Other discussions can revolve
around what jobs men and women can or not cannot do. Another way to
begin to address gender and sexuality issues is through literature (Rowell,
2007). There are a number of picture books that present nontraditional
family structures including those with two moms or two dads. As Rowell
points out, in many of these books, homosexuality is not the main theme
to the book, but instead, there are characters in the book that are gay and
lesbian. There are other books that specifically talk and address stereotypes
around gays and lesbians. There is an increasingly growing body of queer-
themed young adult literature (Blackburn & Buckley, 2005; Clark, 2010a,
2010b; Martino, 2009; North, 2010).

Martino (2009) argues that merely including texts with queer themes or
queer characters is not enough. Instead, he asserts that what is needed is a
curriculum in which teachers teach students to see heteronormativity and
critique it. In confronting issues of oppression of marginalized populations,
one response is the use of critical literacy, which involves "reading, writing,
questioning, and revising the word as well as the ideologically constructed
world" (Young, 2009, p. 109). Blackburn and Buckley (2005) take this even
further in specifically addressing LGBTQ oppression: a queer-inclusive
curriculum.

> A queer-inclusive curriculum is one that offers students a variety of experi-
> ences and varying characters and narrators who define themselves as lesbian,
> gay, bisexual or queer (who suspend sexual and gender identities), or those
> who implicitly claim a normal identity. Our guiding pedagogical concern is
> how best to have students comprehend and critique the social binaries that
> have cultural currency in their own lives; for example young/old, logical/
> emotional, gay/straight. (p. 210)

Critical, queer-inclusive literacy gives teachers and students to explore
the existence and effects of heteronormativity and heterosexual privilege
in their own lives (Gonzales, 2010; Kumashiro, 2001, 2002; Meyer, 2010;
Quinlivan & Town, 1999; Smith, 2009; Young, 2009). Lastly, it gives queer
students the opportunity to see themselves represented in the curriculum.
This may allow them to realize that they are not alone in their experiences.

Gay, lesbian, bisexual, transgender, and queer/questioning (LGBTQ) curriculum can be brought into other content areas in addition to literacy. In fact, scholars (Crocco, 2008; Jennings, 2006; Kumashiro, 2002; Meyer, 2010; Thornton, 2010) have pointed out the lack of and the need for LGBT issues to be addressed as a part of the social studies curriculum. For example, Jennings emphasizes the importance of acknowledging the LGBT identity of historical figures that are traditionally included in textbooks, such as Alexander the Great, Susan B. Anthony, Langston Hughes, and J. Edgar Hoover. Additionally, Thornton argues that oftentimes LGBT individuals, such as social activist Jane Addams, are completely omitted from the curriculum. These authors also argue that while various social movements are included in history lessons (e.g., women's suffrage, the 1964 Civil Rights Act, Chicano labor movement), social studies teachers need to make connections between these movements and gay and lesbian civil rights issues.

Students can be given the opportunity to discuss current events relevant to gay, lesbian and transgendered/transsexual people including same-sex marriage, gay and lesbian adoption and local Gay Pride events (Meyer, 2010). Additionally, Meyer suggests when the topics of healthy relationships and sexual activities are discussed in health classes, that same-sex relationships are included. When discussions of HIV and AIDS arise, teachers can correct misconceptions explaining to students that these diseases impact all people, not just gay men. Finally, Meyer calls for awareness to the language being used throughout the curriculum. Just as there has been a trend to include more diverse-sounding first and last names in examples and problems, Meyer argues that LGBTQ relationships can be included in problems and examples.

As discussed throughout Blackburn, Clark, Kenney, and Smith's (2010) book, teacher activism to fight homophobia and heteronormativity in schools is critical. Regardless of their own sexuality, teachers can establish Gay and Straight Alliances (GSAs) (Cosier, 2009; Gonzales, 2010; Meyer, 2010; Schey & Upstrom, 2010). GSAs are spaces in which students, regardless of gender and sexual identities (those who identify as straight, gay, lesbian, LGBTQ allies, or those who choose not to identify) unite. GSAs can have a number of functions. They can be places where LGBTQ students and allies can come together to find ways to learn more about each other. They can also be places where these students work together to create and implement programs in order to educate other students in the school. Kumashiro (2002) encourages all schools to provide places for oppressed students to go for support. Similarly, Meyer recommends encouraging the administration to permit school-wide initiatives, such as "National Day of Silence" and "Wear Pink Day." Finally, it is important that policy changes (Cosier, 2009) are put into place. One of the most critical policy changes involves schools' discrimination policies. In order to better protect queer students, these policies should have clear and specific language involving sexual and gender diversity (Kumashiro, 2008; Meyer, 2010; Schey & Upstrom, 2010). In other words, rather than policies stating that discrimination or bullying will not be tolerated in the school environment, they should include statements that the discriminations or bullying based on race, class, gender, sexual orientation, and so on will not tolerated in the school. This type of inclusive language sends a much clearer message as to the school administration's position on bullying. It also allows teachers to be more assertive when addressing issues of bullying in the classroom based on gender or sexual orientation because of the explicit language in school policy.

CHALLENGES TO REFORMING SCHOOL CULTURES

The research on teachers' attitudes about gays and lesbians and about addressing gay, lesbian, and gender issues has shown that teachers are hesitant to address these issues in schools. Some believe that talking about sex and sexuality are jobs best left for parents (Clark, 2010a; Kumashiro, 2004; Meyer, 2010; Robinson & Ferfolja, 2001). Teachers are concerned that addressing these issues in the current political climate can put their jobs in jeopardy (Clark, 2010a; Kumashiro, 2004; Robinson & Ferfolja, 2001; Rowell, 2007). Teachers also believe that they should not impose their values on their students and that it is up to the parents to address moral and value issues at home (Bower & Klecka, 2009; Clark, 2010a; Kumashiro, 2004; Robinson & Ferfolja, 2001). Finally, although some teachers would be willing to address sexuality, homophobia, and transphobia in schools, they feel that their teacher education programs have not adequately prepared them to do so (Clark, 2010a; Kumashiro, 2004).

Several studies have investigated preservice teachers' attitudes about LGBTQ people, including both parents and students. Maney and Cain (1997) reported that nearly one half of the 200 preservice teachers surveyed in their study agreed that male homosexuality is a lifestyle that should be condemned. Additionally, another study yielded that preservice teachers had greater negative attitudes toward gay males than toward lesbians (Wyatt, Oswalt, White, & Peterson, 2008). When broken down into subgroups, Mudrey and Medina-Adams (2006) also found that female preservice teachers have more negative attitudes about homosexuality than male preservice teachers. Second, they found that part-time students had a more negative attitude than their full-time counterparts. Finally, Mudrey and Medina-Adams found that students who self-identified as having a minority racial or ethnic background had more negative attitudes than nonminority preservice teachers.

Bower and Klecka (2009) also examined the attitudes and perceptions of practicing teachers about the lesbian mothers of their students. They found that the ten practicing teachers they worked with held some assumptions and norms about both lesbian mothers and practicing teachers. The teachers felt that the lesbian mothers were more concerned with their own needs than the needs of their children. The teachers expressed the opinion that the lesbian mothers should not be making any types of decisions about their personal or social lives that would have a negative impact on their children. For example, the teachers did not connect antibullying, antibias curricula with teaching about diversity and respect. They did not realize the impact that good diversity pedagogy can have on both the LGBT and heterosexual students in the classroom. The participants also felt that addressing LGBT issues in the curriculum could offend some parents and that teachers should not go against the moral lessons that are being taught at home (Bower & Klecka, 2009). The attitudes, assumptions, biases, and beliefs held by teachers can impact both curriculum and pedagogy, but also the way in which the teachers interact with all parents and students of various identity compositions.

In my own study of preservice teachers' sense of self-efficacy in working with and working for LGBTQ students and their families (Brant, 2014), I found that 83% of the 69 preservice teachers surveyed responded that they believe that *they could* work with LGBTQ students and parents reasonably well, if they had time to prepare, while others responded that they were quite confident that this would be easy for them to do. The preservice teachers were also asked about their self-efficacy in regards to their ability to plan instructional activities that reduce prejudice and dispel myths about LGBTQ people. Several respondents indicated a conflict between their desire to include this type of material in the curriculum and actually to be able to do. A few responses are shared below:

"I foresee difficulty in parent perceptions and viewpoints for doing this, but I could do it."

"I can only provide students with lessons that the school will let me. I see some schools having no tolerance for lessons about race, gender, religion, or sexual orientation."

"Even though I do feel strongly about this issue, I don't know that I would risk a job over [not being able to teach about these issues there] . . . I think that I would be looking for other jobs."

These responses reflect a societal view that schools are not the place to address issues of sexuality and gender, especially gender nonconformity. It is clear that elements of the teacher education process need to be reformed to help lay the groundwork for the self-efficacy preservice teachers need for teaching about and teaching for LGBTQ students and their families in a way that is affirming and empowering.

INCLUDING GENDER AND SEXUALITY ISSUES IN THE TEACHER EDUCATION PROGRAM

Just as teacher education is responsible for teaching preservice teachers about instructional methods, content, and classroom management, it is also responsible for teaching these teachers to address issues of diversity and social justice in the classroom. While most teacher education programs in the country cover some sort of diversity issues in their program, sexual orientation is one of the least explicitly covered diversity topics. Additionally, the topic of sexual orientation was predominantly covered in a foundations type class and not carried across the teacher education program as other diversity issues, such as social class, race, and special needs (Sherwin & Jennings, 2006). Kumashiro (2004) raises the point that there is no perfect format for teaching about LGBTQ issues in teacher education, but carefully planned and implemented educational interventions can have a positive effect on preservice teachers' knowledge and attitudes regarding gays and lesbians (Butler, 1999).

Similarly, Wolfe (2006) raises a few major points with the preservice teachers she works with. First, children are exposed to issues of gayness and gay oppression from a young age in out-of-school contexts, being presented with images of nonheterosexual relationships on televisions and movies, as well as other forms of media, and that many elementary-aged students think that the term gay is a negative one. Second, the goal of acknowledging LGBTQ families and issues in the classroom is a way to make the school more inclusive to all. It is up to teachers to create classrooms in which students and their families feel comfortable. Third, dealing with sexuality issues in class has nothing to do with talking about sex, in most cases, and is, instead, about relationships, families, and love. Finally, regardless of whether or not a teacher feels that homosexuality is "right" or "wrong," they must not articulate those feelings to their students.

Just as teacher educators want the preservice teachers they work with to make safe spaces in the classrooms in which they will teach, they must also do so in their own classrooms, especially when addressing diversity issues.

When the teacher education classroom serves as a safe space for students to express their contradictions, doubt and questions as well as their resistance and connection to issues of race, culture *and* gender, we create opportunities for queering the gaze of future teachers. (Asher, 2007, p. 71, emphasis added)

According to Copenhaver-Johnson (2010), we must attempt to "challenge, rather than alienate students as we engage in critical discussions about systems that enable race, ability, gender, linguistic, class, and heterosexual privilege" (p. 17). The goal is to have teacher education students use the materials presented in teacher education programs to examine their own sexuality and gender as well as preconceptions about students and families vis-à-vis gender and sexual identities. Then it is important to understand and flesh out the connections between those conceptions and homophobia and gender oppression and to think critically about how they enact change in their classrooms (Swartz, 2003).

One pedagogical strategy being used to address queer issues in the teacher education classroom involves using specific assigned readings, both personal narratives and academic journal articles (Clark, 2010a; Copenhaver-Johnson, 2010; Vavrus, 2009; Wolfe, 2006) followed with critical discussion. By engaging teachers in critical dialogue, they can begin to interrogate their own thinking in relationship to the readings. As an offshoot of the critical discussions in classrooms, teachers should be encouraged to engage in critical reflection (Robinson & Ferfolja, 2001), which is often best accomplished through written assignments (Clark, 2010a; Copenhaver-Johnson, 2010; Vavrus, 2009). These assignments allow the students to help tell their own stories about their experiences with LGBTQ people and issues or their experiences with heterosexism, homophobia, and transphobia.

An additional pedagogical strategy is the use of guest speakers, which can include gay and lesbian students or parents or teachers who are currently doing ally work in their own classrooms (Evans & Broido, 2005; Wolfe, 2006). There are also a number of films that address LGBTQ issues in education (Clark, 2010b; Copenhaver-Johnson, 2010; Mulhern & Martinez, 1999; Wolfe, 2006). Some of these films show how queer issues are being addressed in classrooms at all grade levels, while other films look deeply into the lived experiences of LGBTQ people, especially their experiences in schools. These films can help teachers understand the way that their responsiveness (or lack of responsiveness) to the topic can either significantly help (or hurt) gay, lesbian, transgender, and ally students.

Finally, just as the use of children's and young adult literature can be used in PreK–12 classrooms, it can also be used in teacher education classrooms (Clarke, 2010a, 2010b; North, 2010; Wolfe, 2006) to help teachers ease into these issues, as well as give them resources to use in their own classrooms. There are a growing number of picture books, short stories, and young adult novels that address sexuality issues, heterosexism, and homophobia.

CONCLUSIONS AND RECOMMENDATIONS

There are several difficulties when addressing gender and sexuality issues in any classroom. The first hurdle for some is to understand that teacher education programs and K–12 institutions are gendered and sexualized places where gendered and sexualized educators teach students with what Norton (2004) calls "a constellation of identities" (p. 47). The "politics of gender" make many uneasy (Lugg, 2003; Marshall, 1992), while "the introduction of sexual orientation—immediately laden with morality, religious intolerance, ignorance and lack of experience—creates unexpected challenges" (Mulhern & Martinez, 1999, p. 247). Some teacher educators argue that length of time in any course is not adequate enough to address such heavy topics as gender and sexual identity issues (Robinson & Ferfolja, 2001; Vavrus, 2009).

Additionally, teacher educators are often limited in their amount of time to address these issues as only a part of a "multicultural" or "diversity" unit or education course. Preservice teachers may also be resistant to the addition of LGBTQ to the "diversity" content in teacher preparation programs. *Recall that prior research indicated that female preservice teachers, in comparison with their male counterparts, expressed more negative attitudes toward gender and sexual nonconformity. Since an overwhelming majority of the education profession is female, this has enormous implications for disrupting the status quo and reforming school cultures.* Resistance to including gender and sexuality in diversity issues can take a number of forms, including vocal opposition to learning about these topics, silence during class discussions, and refusal to complete required classroom assignments. As Copenhaver-Johnson (2010) notes, "the 'problem' of the resistant student does not always reside with the student. It is important to reflect on the ways in which we instructors inadvertently create environments that reinforce resistance" (p. 33). Copenhaver-Johnson raises an important point in that it is easy for teacher educators to blame the teacher education student for his or her resistance. Instead, teacher educators need to look closely at their own teaching practices and reflect upon strengths, weaknesses, and areas in need of improvement (Clark, 2010a; 2010b; Copenhaver-Johnson, 2010; Kumashiro, 2004).

It is important for teacher educators to remember that covering issues of diversity in any classroom can be challenging, especially when one is not a member of the group being discussed. It is difficult to speak for the needs of any group, let alone a group with which they do not affiliate. Teacher educators run the risk of unintentionally perpetuating stereotypes, heteronormativity, and homophobia (Robinson & Ferfolja, 2001) through the materials used in class as well as the way in which the teacher presents material to the class. It is critical that teacher educators reach out to LGBTQ sources and experts to make sure that what they are presenting to their students is accurate and as bias free as possible. Even the most well-intentioned, social justice-oriented teacher educator may inadvertently perpetuate his or her own homophobia or the homophobia of his or her students (Copenhaver-Johnson, 2010; Mulhern & Martinez, 1999). A final element to consider relates to the fluidity and contextual nature of identities discussed earlier in this chapter. There is no one uniform student experience, and LGBTQ students are especially vulnerable. Teacher educators need to understand this and communicate it to their teacher education students.

In order for schools to be safe for LGBTQ students, there needs to be action on many levels. First, school districts need to ensure antibias language in their policies that explicitly covers discrimination based on sexuality and gender expression. Second, teachers must create safe spaces in and out of their classrooms. They must not tolerate any type of bullying and harassment, and let students know that they have a place, if need be, for them to come to report such incidences. Teachers also need to talk about gender and sexuality issues and include the contributions of LGBTQ people in their curriculum. Finally, teacher educators need to give the preservice and inservice teachers they work with the tools to effectively implement new strategies in their own classrooms. If issues of gender expression and sexual orientation are addressed at each of these junctures in teacher education and P–12 educational institutions, the greater the potential for educators (mostly women) to interrupt how gender and sexual identity issues are perceived, disrupt how LGBTQ students are received and revolutionize school environments as safe havens for all students.

REFERENCES

Asher, N. (2007). Made in the (multicultural) U.S.A.: Unpacking tensions of race, culture, gender, and sexuality in education. *Educational Researcher, 36*(2), 65–73.

Brant, C. A. R. (2014). *Pre-service teachers' perspectives on methods, pedagogy and self-efficacy related to gender and sexuality as a part of their multicultural teacher education.* (Doctoral Dissertation, The Ohio State University).

Beam, C. (2007). *Transparent: Love, family, and living the T with transgender teenagers.* Orlando, FL: Harcourt Books.

Blackburn, M. V. (2003). Losing, finding, and making space for activism through literacy performances and identity work. *Penn GSE Perspectives on Urban Education, 1, 2*(1), 1–23.

Blackburn, M. V. (2007). The experiencing, negotiation, breaking and remaking of gender rules and regulations by queer youth. *Journal of Gay & Lesbian Issues in Education, 4*(2), 33–54.

Blackburn, M. V. & Buckley, J. F. (2005). Teaching queer-inclusive English language arts. *International Reading Association, 49*(3), 202–212.

Blackburn, M. V., Clark, C. T., Kenney, L. M. & Smith, J. M. (Eds.). (2010). *Acting out: Combating homophobia through teaching and activism.* New York, NY: Teachers College Press.

Bower, L., & Klecka, C. (2009). (Re) considering normal: Queering social norms for parents and teachers. *Teaching Education, 20*(4), 357–373.

Butler, K. L. (1999). Preservice teachers' knowledge and attitudes regarding gay men and lesbians: The impact of a cognitive educational intervention. *Journal of Health Education, 30*(2), 125.

Clark, C. T. (2010a). Inquiring into ally work in teacher education: The possibilities and limitations of textual practice. In M. V. Blackburn, C. T. Clark, L. M. Kenney, & J. M. Smith (Eds.), *Acting out! Combating homophobia through teacher activism* (pp. 37–54). New York, NY: Teachers College Press.

Clark, C. T. (2010b). Preparing LGBTQ-allies and combating homophobia in a U.S. teacher education program. *Teaching and Teacher Education, 26,* 704–713.

Copenhaver-Johnson, J. F. (2010). Learning about heterosexism as a teacher educator: The resistant student as a catalyst for change. In M. V. Blackburn, C. T. Clark, L. M. Kenney, & J. M. Smith (Eds.), *Acting out! Combating homophobia through teacher activism* (pp. 17–36). New York, NY: Teachers College Press.

Cosier, K. (2009). Creating safe schools for queer youth. In W. Ayers, T. Quinn, & D. Stovall (Eds.) *Handbook of social justice in education* (pp. 285–304). New York, NY: Routledge

Crocco, M. S. (2008). Gender and sexuality in the social studies. In L. S. Levstik & C. A. Tyson (Eds.), *Handbook of research in Social Studies Education* (pp. 172–196). New York, NY: Routledge.

Dotinga, R. (2013, May 16). Anti-gay bullying tied to teen depression, suicide: Suicide thoughts more likely for kids victimized over sexual orientation, research finds. *US News and World Report.* Retrieved from http://health.usnews.com/health-news/news/articles/2013/05/16/anti-gay-bullying-tied-to-teen-depression-suicide

Driver, S. (2007). *Queer girls and popular culture: Reading, resisting and creating media.* New York, NY: Peter Lang.

Driver, S. (2008). Introducing queer youth cultures. In S. Driver (Ed.), *Queer youth cultures* (1–18). Albany, NY: State University of New York Press.

Epstein, D., O'Flynn, S., & Telford, D. (2000). "Othering" education: Sexualities, silences, and schooling. *Review of Research in Education, 25,* 127–179.

Evans, N. J., & Broido, E. M. (2005). Encouraging the development of social justice attitudes and actions in heterosexual student. *New Directions for Student Services, 110,* 43–54.

Friend, R. A. (1993). Choices, not closets: Heterosexism and homophobia in schools. In L. Weiss & M. Fine (Eds.), *Beyond silenced voices: Class, race and gender in United States Schools* (pp. 209–235). Albany, NY: State University of New York Press.

GLSEN and Harris Interactive. (2012). *Playgrounds and prejudice: Elementary school climate in the United States, a survey of students and teachers.* New York, NY: Author.

Gonzales, J. (2010). Risk and threat in critical inquiry: Vacancies, violations and vacuums. In M. V. Blackburn, C. T. Clark, L. M. Kenney, & J. M. Smith (Eds.),

Acting out! Combating homophobia through teacher activism (pp. 74–87). New York, NY: Teachers College Press.

Holmes, S. E., & Cahill, S. (2004). School experiences of gay, lesbian, bisexual and transgender youth. *Journal of Gay & Lesbian Issues in Education, 1*(3), 53–66.

Human Rights Watch. (2001). *Hatred in the hallways: Violence and discrimination against lesbian, gay, bisexual, and transgender students in U.S. schools.* New York, NY: Author.

IES. (n.d.). *Fast facts.* Produced by the Institute of Education Sciences. Retrieved from http://nces.ed.gov/fastfacts/display.asp?id=28

Jennings, K. (2006). "Out" in the classroom: Addressing lesbian, gay, bisexual and transgender (LGBT) issues in social studies curriculum. In E. W. Ross (Ed.), *The social studies curriculum* (3rd ed., pp. 255–264). Albany, NY: State University of New York Press.

Kosciw, J. G., Greytak, E. A., Diaz, E. M., & Bartkiewicz, M. J. (2010). *The 2009 National School Climate Survey: The experiences of lesbian, gay, bisexual and transgender youth in our nation's schools.* New York, NY: GLSEN.

Kumashiro, K. K. (2001). "Posts" perspectives on anti-oppressive education in social studies, English, mathematics, and science classrooms. *Educational Researcher, 30*(3), 3–12.

Kumashiro, K. (2002). *Troubling education: Queer activism and anti-oppressive pedagogy* (1st Ed.). New York, NY: RoutledgeFalmer.

Kumashiro, K. (2004). Uncertain beginnings: Learning to teach paradoxically. *Theory Into Practice, 43*(2), 111–115.

Kumashiro, K. (2008). *The seduction of common sense: How the right has framed the debate on America's schools.* New York, NY: Teachers College Press.

Lugg, C. (2003). Sissies, faggots, lezzies, and dykes: Gender, sexual orientation, and a new politics of education? *Educational Administration Quarterly, 39*(1), 95–134.

Maney, D. W., & Cain, R. E. (1997). Preservice elementary teachers' attitudes toward gay and lesbian parenting. *Journal of School Health, 67*(6), 236.

Marshall, C. (1992). *The new politics of race and gender.* New York, NY: Routledge.

Martino, W. (2009). Literacy issues and GLBTQ youth: Queer interventions in English Education. In L. Christenbury, R. Bomer, & P. Smagorinsky (Eds.), *Handbook of adolescent literacy research* (pp. 386–399). New York, NY: Guilford Press.

Meyer, E. J. (2010). *Gender and sexual diversity in schools.* New York, NY: Springer.

Mudrey, R., & Medina-Adams, A. (2006). Attitudes, perceptions, and knowledge of pre-service teachers regarding the educational isolation of sexual minority youth. *Journal of Homosexuality, 51*(4), 63–90.

Mulhern, M., & Martinez, G. (1999). Confronting homophobia in a multicultural education course. In W. J. Letts & J. T. Sears (Eds.), *Queering elementary education: Advancing the dialogue about sexualities and schooling.* Lanham, MD: Rowman & Littlefield.

North, C. (2010). Threading stitches to approach gender identity, sexual identity, and difference. *Equity and Excellence inEeducation, 43*(3), 375–387.

Norton, A. (2004). *95 Theses on politics, culture, and method.* New Haven, CT: Yale University Press.

Quinlivan, K., & Town, S. (1999). Queer pedagogy, educational practice and lesbian and gay youth. *Qualitative Studies in Education, 12*(5), 509–524.

Robinson, K. H., & Ferfolja, T. (2001). "What are we doing this for?" Dealing with lesbian and gay issues in teacher education. *British Journal of Sociology of Education, 22*(1), 121–133.

Rowell, E. H. (2007). Missing!: Picture books reflecting gay and lesbian families. *Young Children, 62*(3), 24-30.

Schey, R., & Upstrom, A. (2010). Activist work as entry-year teachers: What we've learned. In M. V. Blackburn, C. T. Clark, L. M. Kenney, & J. M. Smith (Eds.), *Acting out! Combating homophobia through teacher activism* (pp. 88–102). New York, NY: Teachers College Press.

Sherwin, G., & Jennings, T. (2006). Feared, forgotten, or forbidden: Sexual orientation topics in secondary teacher preparation programs in the U.S.A. *Teaching Education, 17*(3), 207–223.

Smith, J. M. (2009). Montana 1948: Crossing boundaries with queer theory. In A. O Soter, M. Faust, & T. Rogers (Eds.), *Interpretive play: Using critical perspectives to teach young adult literature* (pp. 161–174). Norwood, MA: Christopher-Gordon.

Smolkin, L. B., & Suina, J. H. (1999). Cross-cultural partnerships: Acknowledging the "equal other" in The Rural/Urban American Indian Teach Education Program. *Teaching and teacher education, 15*, 571–590.

Swartz, P. (2003). Bridging multicultural education: Bringing sexual orientation into the children's and young adult literature classrooms. *Radical Teacher, 66*, 11–16.

Thornton, S. J. (2010). Silence on gays and lesbians in social studies curriculum. In W. C. Parker (Ed.), *Social studies today* (pp. 87–94). New York, NY: Routledge.

Vaccaro, A. (2009). Intergenerational perceptions, similarities and differences: A comparative analysis of lesbian, gay, and bisexual Millennial Youth with Generation X and Baby Boomers. *Journal of LGBT Youth, 6*, 113–134.

Vavrus, M. (2009). Sexuality, schooling, and teacher identity formation: A critical pedagogy for teacher education. *Teaching & Teacher Education, 25*(3), 383–390.

Wilkinson, L., & Pearson, J. (2009). School culture and the well-being of same-sex-attracted youth. *Gender & Society, 23*(4), 542–568.

Wolfe, R. B. (2006). Choosing to include gay issues in early childhood teacher preparation coursework: One professor's journey. *Journal of Early Childhood Teacher Education, 27*(2), 195–204.

Wyatt, T., Oswalt, S., White, C., & Peterson, F. (2008). Are tomorrow's teachers ready to deal with diverse students? Teacher candidates' attitudes toward gay men and lesbians. *Teacher Education Quarterly, 35*(2), 171–185.

Yoshino, K. (2007). *Covering: The hidden assault on our civil rights.* New York, NY: Random House.

Young, S. L. (2009). Breaking the silence: Critical literacy and social action. *English Journal, 98*(4), 109–115.

PART III

UNDERSTANDING AND STRENGTHENING
LEADERS' LIVED EXPERIENCES

CHAPTER 8

"I'M EITHER NICE OR I'M A BITCH"

Gender Entrapment and Black Female Principals

Noelle Witherspoon Arnold

ABSTRACT

This chapter conceptually explores the actions that one Black female principal employs to achieve socially just outcomes for students, and the subsequent
labels placed upon this principal. According to her practice, this principal
discusses being measured against the labels of "nice" or "bitch" when she
does not conform to the "nice" image. This chapter identifies the ways in
which this principal problematizes the gender and raced constructions of
"nice" and "bitch." Forced into supporting district leadership or policy, this
principal manifests a form of "gender entrapment" (Richie, 1996) articulated
through labels constructed for her. By examining and analyzing interviews
with this principal, this chapter also explores how she continues to reconstruct these labels in the interpretation of policy to interrogate marginality,
promote social justice, and initiate social activism in her school.

Women Interrupting, Disrupting, and Revolutionizing Educational Policy and Practice, pages 127–144
Copyright © 2014 by Information Age Publishing
127

Women have multiple labels—"some self-applied, others culturally imposed. . . .
Each of us speaks from a place that has been turned upside down
and inside out by inequities in a social system that is anything but just"

—Cannon, Johnson, & Sims (2005, p. 139)

There is a "gender order" (Gramsci, 1971) inherent in schools and bureaucracies that work against women. According to foundational works by women in educational leadership, "embedded in organizations are subtle innuendos, images, and language that exclude many women such as dominant masculine images of leaders and administration" (Blackmore, 1993, p. 29). Traditional models of educational leadership have long upheld a male model of leadership as the norm and measured the leadership and effectiveness of women accordingly (Shakeshaft, 1979). These leadership theories have often affirmed the primacy of bureaucracy and masculinity (Skrla & Benestante, 1998) and situated themselves as grand narratives in the field. In addition, aspiring leaders and principals are socialized to give primacy to certain behaviors considered as authentic or real leadership, and atypical behaviors are dismissed as deviant or deficient (Marshall, 1996). Current administrative licensure agencies have reduced school administration and leadership to a set of value-free knowledge, dispositions, and performances that mirror current masculine leadership practice and technocratic skills (Witherspoon & Taylor, 2010). For the purpose of this chapter, rather than focusing exclusively upon the masculine and technocratic terrain of leadership, the central questions were, What results when one contests traditional leadership terrains? and How are women labeled as result? When women principals challenge traditional masculinist (Blackmore, 1999) endeavors of the principalship, ensuing labeling and resistance can occur.

Many researchers have posited that to be accepted in educational leadership, women must exhibit a male-modeled leadership frame (Witherspoon, 2010). However, due to the path of many female principals, notions of good leadership are still grounded in feminization of teaching (Grumet, 1981; Blackmore, 1999). Because of this, even feminine discourses of educational leadership can be essentialized into merely abstract notions of what it means to be a female in educational leadership (Blackmore, 1999). Women can be accepted if they conform to a "feminized" version of leadership. This chapter highlights the idea that female educational leaders often exhibit traditional male tendencies for legitimization in leadership, which often result in the "bitch" label. This chapter also highlights a "new" *required* model of leadership that encompasses traditional female labels such as "nice." This type of leadership and what are often considered women's ways of leading entrap women in feminized notions of leadership and position them as self-sacrificing, altruistic, and nice—and further entrap "tougher" women leaders as pathological, deviant, and disruptive (Witherspoon, 2008).

Traditional knowledge and practice domains of educational leadership are being interpreted and challenged by the "marginal" hermeneutics such as those of gender, race, and class (Witherspoon, 2009). Educational leadership has been slow to embrace the standpoint of women and even slower in valuing the intersection of gender with race. There are few studies that identify the collective position of Black women principals (Witherspoon, 2009); those that do tend to exoticize and eroticize urban school realities and issues of student achievement. "By producing counter-hegemonic Black feminist discourses ... [we may] unmask and scrutinize the power of racist and sexist practices operating in school systems" (Bloom & Erlandson, 2003, p. 352) and contest even those in which women are complicit. Womanist theory (Walker, 1983) offers an alternative lens to recast leadership in ways that trouble traditional notions of leadership and notions of women in leadership.

In this chapter, I examine the professional life of one Black female principal. I draw upon a reanalysis of a larger life narrative study conceptualized as spiritual narrative research concerning the import of the spirituality of principals and how that spirituality influences the principal practice. This paper considers the work of Philomena Essed (1991), who coined the term "everyday racisms" to describe the intersecting oppressions that Black women face in society. These intersections can traverse race, gender, class, religion, and sexual orientation, among other things. What is absent in the original analysis is an unpacking of the consequences associated with the work of justice-making in schools and complex realities of gender and professional norms of educational leadership.

Using the lens of gender entrapment (Richie, 1996), this chapter highlights the ways in which gender entrapment was articulated as labels in the lives and work of the participants. Furthermore, this lens illuminated the ways in which these labels were subsequently used as a means to interrogate marginality, promote social justice, and initiate social activism in schools. The findings of the larger study illustrated how principals engaged in everyday acts of justice and reconstruct labels set for them. What emerged from this particular reanalysis was a complex mixture of self-labeling and years of identity construction and a re-presentation and reappropriation of negative labels into actual principal practice. What is absent in the original analysis is an unpacking of the consequences associated with the work of justice-making in schools and complex realities of gender and professional norms of educational leadership.

GENDER ENTRAPMENT

Certain languages, norms, metaphors, and gender scripts underlie the assumptions, expectations, and images of educational leadership (Blackmore,

2002; Hirsch, 2009). Blackmore (2002) states that "women are often expected to show strength in the face of adversity, discrimination, and resistance, all while retaining niceness throughout" (p. 57). Using this concept of nice as a hermeneutic, this chapter offers alternative standpoints counter to traditional notions of women and educational leadership work. The "masculine enterprise of leadership" (Blackmore, 1993) has often embodied women, in prescribed roles, labels, and typecasts of femininity, leadership, and professionalism. One could argue that this is particularly true for Black women. This chapter argues that when a woman veers from certain "entrapments," she is often located as deviant.

Beth Richie's (1996) model of gender entrapment appropriated the meaning from the legal term of meaning to "lure an individual into a compromising act" (Richie, 1996, p. 14). Richie's original work specifically applied to incarcerated women who commit crimes. Richie found that the majority of these women often experienced prior social victimization contributing to their subsequent criminal behavior. Richie's theoretical formulation of gender entrapment "was used to describe what occurs to women who are marginalized in the public or professional sphere because of their race, ethnicity, gender, and class" (Lempert, 1997, p. 369).

In Richie's model of gender entrapment, four elements were salient: (a) feminist theories of identity development; (b) culturally specific ideas of leadership development and socialization; (c) the multiplicity, everydayness, and intersection of variables contributing to entrapment; and (d) social constructions of gendered and raced arrangements concerning women and their work. Her model helped to highlight how some women are "forced or coerced into crime by their culturally expected gender roles, the violence in their relationships and their social position in the broader society" (1996, p. 133). In this same vein, this chapter explores a type of violence that occurs to women professionally who are simultaneously marginalized in the public sphere when they contest these expected gender roles in leading schools. This chapter also highlights the collision that occurs among in certain social controls and justice-making process when "one seeks to create transformations in the conditions under which women make decisions" (Lempert, 1997, p. 369).

As true to the four elements of gender entrapment, one can see how womanist theory and intersectionality (Crenshaw, 1991) provide a framework with which to explore the ways in which the life and experiences of one principal illuminate and problematize the gendered and raced social constructions of "nice" and "bitch." These frames offer a unique standpoint and analysis of both of these constructions. Forced into supporting district administrators, policy, or notions of leadership, this principal's story thematically highlights gender entrapment as articulated labels constructed for her. By reexamining and reanalyzing interviews with this principal, this chapter also explores how she reconstructs and reappropriates these labels in the interpretation of policy to interrogate marginality, promote social justice, and initiate social activism in schools.

Because of the intersection of contexts, identities, and the master narratives of society upon the individual, it is important for the focus of this research to explore the intersection of these sociocultural narratives and multilayered meaning systems (gender, race, educational leadership, social justice, and schooling) in gender entrapment.

METHODS

I began with a reanalysis of an original study of Black female principals. These principals lived and worked in various regions of a southern state in the United States, were at different career stages, led schools at the elementary and secondary organizational levels, and held either bachelor's, master's, or doctoral degrees in education. The participant discussed in this chapter was most willing to discuss the marginalizing experiences she had encountered in her principalship. She was also willing to discuss alternate ways of interpreting and implementing policy in her schools, whether or not their interpretation and/or implementation were consistent with district intentions. At the time of the initial study, Bobbie was in her 32nd year in education. Her career in school administration was unique in that she worked as an assistant principal for three years, a principal for two, and returned to an assistant principalship later in her career. She served as a teacher at the elementary level, during which time she was a school and district Teacher of the Year. She also served for three years at a university as a Teacher in Residence in which capacity she taught undergraduate methods courses in science and classroom management.

At the time of the initial discussions, Bobbie had just completed her doctorate in educational administration and was the principal at an all-Black middle school. This middle school was in another year of successive identification by the state department of education as "low-performing." This school is located in an area of town characterized by low human and fiscal capital, few capital improvements, and a majority of students who qualify for free and reduced lunch.

Subsequent interviews and conversations were held during a period of intense unrest in the schools over what Bobbie described as discriminatory practices by the local school district administration and the school board against the schools located in her particular cluster school zone and against Black principals in the district. Bobbie was initially hired for this school and then terminated after one year. Bobbie filed a lawsuit and won, and was returned to her school for one year. Citing the need for "an experienced administrator," district administrators, in Bobbie's words, "demoted" her to her current position as an assistant principal. Bobbie frequently spoke of her actions to achieve what she considers "right" outcomes for her students and her community and that this is what "got her in trouble."

For this chapter, a new phase of analysis focused on this participant's professional story to answer the research questions:

1. What are descriptions of gendered and raced role articulations?
2. What tensions occur when enacting alternative forms of leadership counter to the traditional schooling norms?

"Life history and narrative approaches have emerged as important research over the last decade . . . and offer exciting alternatives for connecting the lives and stories of individuals to the understanding of larger human social phenomena" (Hatch & Wisniewski, 1995, p. 113). Most researchers agree that the basic premise of narrative inquiry lies in examining "how individuals talk about and story their experiences and perceptions of the social contexts they inhabit" (Goodson & Sikes, 2001, p. 1). In this case, a narrative approach served to allow individuals to rename their racialized, gendered, and professional roles and identities beyond the static boundaries and practices that I am describe as gender entrapment. For this chapter, one participant's narrative was reanalyzed through the frames of gender entrapment.

Positioning Analysis

Just as it is not always clear what counts as narrative, it is sometimes just as difficult to explicate how one does narrative analysis (Dauite & Lightfoot, 2004). According to Mischler (1995), there are three types of narrative analysis. Narrative analysis can be done by examining reference, function, or structure. Reference describes the analysis of the relations between events and their presentation and representation. In particular, reference examines the relationship "between what was told and the interpretations and actual texts that they mean to interpret" (Chandler, Lalonde, & Teucher, 2004, p. 253). Function describes the reasons for which a story is told, what it is meant to do, and why it is told at a particular time (Coffey & Atkinson, 1996; Hendry, 2007). Structure concerns itself with formal, structural properties of a story involving matters such as sociolinguistics, story organization, and literary elements (Labov, 1982; Riesmann, 1993).

This manuscript represents another wave of analysis that highlights positioning analysis and stories of identity (Baumberg, 2003; Labov, 1972). Positioning analysis focuses on the identities people construct for themselves as they engage in narratives. That is, in storytelling, individuals often high-light ways in which they behave that are counter to pre-established selves or behaviors. In this reanalysis, I isolated large narrative units in the tran-scripts to identify themes that emphasize ways in which the participants constructed themselves. A new phase of analysis for this chapter included coding categories of narratives for Richie's (1996) model of gender entrap-ment: (a) feminist theories of identity development; (b) culturally specific ideas of leadership development and socialization; (c) the multiplicity, ev-erydayness, and intersection of variables contributing to entrapment; and (d) social constructions of gendered and raced arrangements concerning women and their work. It is important to note that my method for explor-ing narratives involved the totality of the story being told and not torn apart in analysis (Mitchell & Lewter, 1986, p. 8). The analysis that follows pays particular attention to the formation of a sense of self in the face of differ-ent discursive pulls. What emerged from this analysis was a complex mix-ture of self-labeling, labeling, and an intricacy of identity construction. This identity construction yielded intersections between spirituality, the body, and leadership socialization. What also emerged was the re-presentation and re-appropriation of negative labels and other constructions. This high-lights the issue of how much the construction of a sense of self in this seg-ment is due to "acts of identity" that can be traced back to the individual's and others' discourses that seemingly impose themselves onto participant structures and individual sense-making strategies.

Stories of Identity

Narrative analysis takes as its object of investigation the story itself. I limit discussion here to first-person accounts in interviews of the participant's experience. In putting aside other kinds of narratives (e.g., about the self of the investigator, what happened in the field, media descriptions of events, or the "master narratives" of theory), my research focused on life events in which the participant was disruptive. This accounts for experiences that contest against the backdrop of expected biographies. Personal narratives serve many purposes—to remember, argue, convince, engage, or entertain their audience (Bamberg & McCabe, 1998). Consequently, investigators have many points of entry: Personal narratives can be analyzed textually (Gee 1986; Labov, 1982), conversationally (Polanyi 1985), culturally (Mat-tingly & Garro, 2000; Rosaldo 1989), politically/historically (Mumby 1993; White 1987), and performatively (Langellier, 1989). When we tell stories about our lives, we perform our (preferred) identities (Langellier, 2001). As Goffman (1969, 1981) suggested with his repeated use of the dramaturgical metaphor, social actors stage performances of a desirable self to preserve "face" in situations of difficulty, thus managing potentially "spoiled" identities. Similarly, gender identity is performed or imposed by audiences in social situations. In this participant's case, identity is a "performative struggle over the meanings of self" (Langellier, 2001, p. 3)

FINDINGS

It's not about being nice, or being a lady or not upsetting people. It about representing a full-bodied view of womanhood encompassing outrageous, audacious, courageous, and inquisitive behavior. . . . It's about being capable and competent. It's about being a force to be reckoned with.

—Audrey Thompson

Because Bobbie's narrative highlighted "nice" and "bitch," it is important to explore these "hermeneutics of suspicion" (Floyd-Thomas, 2006b, p. 208). These terms highlight a "nitty-gritty hermeneutic" (Harris, 2006, p. 212) and interpret Black women's stories and everyday experiences without "sugarcoating" oppressive realities. However, Bobbie's narrative emphasizes women's capacity to "outwit, outmaneuver, and outscheme" (Copeland, 2006, p. 228) systems and structures of subjectivity and involves "debunking, unmasking, and disentangling" (Cannon, 1995, p. 138) dominant ideologies surrounding gendered and raced notions of work, justice-making, and leadership. Using "nice" and "bitch" as hermeneutical tools, this chapter highlights what happens when a woman falls outside of the traditional patriarchal roles. Consider the pervasive images of former British Prime Minister Margret Thatcher labeled as the "Iron Maiden" or current United States Secretary of State Hillary Clinton. Regardless of party affiliation, the image of women in power positions is often seen as "acting out of place." However, the depiction of first ladies like Laura Bush, a former librarian, or Michelle Obama, as dutiful mother to young children, ties into the narrative of "nice" that patriarchy imposes.

Defining Nice

Bobby helps define how she interprets what people mean by referring to her as "nice" several times during our conversations:

So much of who I am and what I have experienced professionally happened to me way before I even became a principal. Ever since I was little, I knew what was expected of me as a female, as a Black person, and as the daughter of my Christian parents. "Looking nice and being nice was very important in my family. It feels the same way with some folks in my district too. You gotta look a certain way. On the one hand they want you to dress certain ways, but then you gotta stay pretty too."

For some people, *nice* means one thing and *bitch* means one thing. They think if you are nice you can be stepped on and will take anything. On the other hand, sometimes when you are trying to do the right thing, you get called a bitch. I don't care what they think. For me, I don't want to be called nice. I don't know, somehow it says to me that I am not doing my job. It's when they call me bitch is when I know I am doing my job. So I'll be the bitch any day.

This stuff does not happen to me until I step through the door of the school. The central office is worse. How is it that in others areas of my life these things do not happen, but professionally... (Participant trails off)

I mean to right the wrongs that I see in my school—whether those wrongs have to do with me or not. Whatever that costs me, whatever I have to do, that's what I will do.

Being nice is a ubiquitous adjective for White middle-class females in this culture and is a contradictory position in which to be situated for some. The continuing presence of nice as discourse, tells us that "nice" as a gendered marker, a mental habit, remains secure. Nice works as a site where "power...is remade at various junctures within everyday life (constituting) our tenuous sense of common sense" (Butler, Laclau, & Zizek, 2000, p. 14 as found in McRobbie, 2009, p. 12). "Nice is common sense in women's lives, whether they embrace, reject, and/or worry over its presence" (Bettis & Adams, 2010, p. 1).

Defining Bitch

Long held as a derogatory word, and reserved for women, "bitch" was often applied when a woman was deemed as "unpleasant, fretful, or querulous." However, second-wave feminism brought about a recoup of the word "bitch" to identify strong women. No longer is the word associated simply with the relationship of women, men, and sexuality.

Early and current usage of "bitch" still implies subservience toward the user. When viewing this from a feminist or womanist standpoint, this largely applies to the users as men (Wurtzel, 1999). However, new appropriations of "bitch" by women are about self-naming, empowerment, and emancipation (Williams, 1993). From this standpoint, it would be appropriate for Black women to "take back" and contest any label rooted in the intersecting of oppressions (Collins, 2000). While Bobbie did not pronounce herself as a feminist or womanist (in fact, she often reaffirmed many traditional notions of being female), she wanted to be seen as "not nice." Bobbie associated being "not nice" or a "bitch" as a useful *technical professional* skill.

Embracing the bitch label, in the manner she appropriated it, gave a Bobbie a professional identity to justice work in her school and community:

> Any time a Black woman challenges the status quo, you are always gonna be seen as angry or bitchy. However, then folks know not to mess with you! I was considered a troublemaker, so they expected it. They knew I would speak up, they knew I would fight for resources for my school and community. Rather than deal with me, they gave me what my kids needed.

SOCIALIZATION AND SCRIPTING

"Whether socialization is taking place within or outside the family unit, it is based on organizing principals (beliefs, ideology, values)" (Curry, 2000, p. 59). Exploring what (and whose) beliefs, ideology, and values shape the identity of the school leader becomes particularly important. In the gender entrapment model, theoretical, and social variables grant examination of a multiplicity of factors. In applying these ideas to Bobbie, analyzing gender entrapment origins became particularly salient. While Bobbie discussed much of her personal and professional experience in interviews, she clearly has different ideas concerning the meanings and construction of "nice" in these different contexts. This chapter focuses on instances of early gender scripts as they relate to her personal life; however, these personal experiences shed light on the tensions between professional leadership and social justice that shaped her leadership.

Social role theory and its relation to the socialization of gender expectations clarifies certain gender differences. According to Rose and Frieze (1993) gender roles are acquired during early childhood and adolescence. At a very early age, Bobbie was socialized into a conception of what it meant to be "nice," one clearly rooted in the body and early leadership behaviors. Bobbie frequently referred to her parents and other adults and what they taught her about relations with others.

The Nice Body: Dress and the Beauty Myth

"Central to the act of performing leadership is the body" (Blackmore, 1999, p. 170). Bobbie made frequent references to being highly conscious of her bodily appearance and of being different as she talked about her childhood and her experiences as an educational leader. Even when not asked, Bobbie commented on her appearance and personal dress both personally and professionally. What was also interesting was that these comments frequently came up in conversations about her father. From an early age, a feminine idea of beauty and appearance was important to Bobbie.

He often bragged that I was the prettiest woman in the world. I was his pride and joy. I could do no wrong.

Other male mentors, teachers and colleagues reinforced these same ideas.

Kids made fun of me because I had sandy blondish red hair with green eyes. I also had pink lips. Most black kids did not look like me. I thought I was the ugliest girl in the world. I used to pray to God every night to make me pretty. I could not stand being different. Ironically, people are now paying hundreds of dollars today to have eyes like mine! I played dress-up in my mother's hats, shoes, gloves, dresses. Wearing lipstick was my favorite thing. I had lipstick all over the place. And in my free time, I made clothes for my Skipper doll. She had an outfit for every occasion. I gave Skipper to a little girl when I turned twelve. I felt I no longer needed her.

"For the minority of women...female sexuality requires more overt control through codes of dress, language and manner" (Marshall, 1996, p. 6). What was interesting to me was that Bobbie sought not to "minimize her female presence" (Marshall, 1996, p. 6), but to play it up and exaggerate it. Suits and minimal makeup were not fixed elements of her wardrobe and "getting ready" practices. In fact, Bobbie mentioned that she rarely wore suits and pants (or what is traditionally considered professional) for those in leadership roles. Men often alluded to her appearance when describing her professionally and personally.

My male colleagues would say I'm nice, I will tell you what I think, I'm a very professional, attractive, and smart female. Females generally do not like me at first. Many feel after looking at me that I'm stuck up, that I think I'm all that and a bag of chips. Other professional women are intimidated by my appearance. A nice man I knew always gave me tips on how to dress and keep myself looking gorgeous. He thought all women should look beautiful at all times. My friend gave me some advice after I completed my doctorate degree. He said, "You will have a hard time getting a job because you are a beautiful, smart, attractive Black woman. This will count against you. Women will be jealous of you and hinder your progress. I know that my appearance has helped me.

This "gaze on the female body is a subtle form of control both within and outside organizations" (Blackmore, 1999, p. 172). Bobbie exhibited some compliance with accommodating the male desire; but for Bobbie, she attempted to assert control over male feminine notions and reappropriate them to her advantage.

Bucking Nice: "Bitch"

"For the most part little girls are still raised to be followers" (Curry, 2000, p. 3). This notion certainly affected Bobbie in her personal life, but her personal life was always a place in which these notions could be contested and were not static accounts of nice. For instance, although Bobbie was raised to "be a lady and be nice," her family contested traditional notions of "nice." Bobbie had an early association with women and leadership that as she stated "had an impact on her future goals":

> My mother was the boss and the strength of the family. My mother taught me about life, business, and people. I was ready for the world when I left home. My mother warned me about all types of situations and life experiences. She would always say, "Trust no one. Treat everyone with respect...and keep a smile on your face...[but] do not be a door mat for anyone." My mother made me the strong woman I am today.

Bobbie's relationship to her parents and other adults put an early face on her leadership personality and style. A misreading or silencing of the cultural and historical influences of her leadership personality and style encouraged and perpetuated a deviant notion of leadership.

> If you are a young or middle-age Black woman who is ambitious, intelligent, well-groomed, confident, and not afraid to stand up for your beliefs, you will have a hard time. If you do not sell yourself out and others who look like you, you won't make it. Kiss much butt and you might have a chance.

Women's success in jobs traditionally considered masculine, especially those involving leadership, was largely based on their adoption of traditional masculine traits, such as being aggressive, outspoken, unemotional, and competitive (Cikara & Fiske, 2009). Any exhibition of directness or agency by females has caused these women to be labeled as overbearing or "bitch."

Second- and third-wave feminism brought about a co-opting and reappropriation of the word "bitch" to identify it with the idea of being a strong, capable woman. Early and current usage of "bitch" still implies subservience toward the one who labels. However, Bobbie's narrative makes "bitch" less about the one who labels, and more about self-naming, empowerment, and emancipation (Williams, 1993). So, from this standpoint she "takes back" and contests any label rooted in oppressions (Collins, 2000). Bobbie associated being *not-*"nice" or "bitch" as technical skills she wanted to possess. At one point, Bobbie replied:

> I don't care what people call me. If I am a bitch so be it. I am fighting for my kids. And if that is what that means, then I will take it. In the workplace, nice is a sign of weakness. At work, when I am in charge, I don't care whether people like me or not.

By shunning and reappropriating this assigned identity, Bobbie clearly rejected often reifying notions of what it meant to be a female principal.

Women in educational leadership demonstrate "contradictory experiences of achievement and discrimination" (Chase, 1995, p. 31) and exhibit these experiences culturally and contextually (Blackmore, 1999). Bobbie saw herself as receiving more support from the men in her profession than women and, particularly, other Black women. When the discussions turned professional, Bobbie displayed a gender-neutral position in discussing herself as a school leader. She placed great emphasis upon traditional leadership traits and practices: "I am ambitious, professional, a workaholic with high work ethics. Often I am too ambitious for my own good."

It is interesting that use of the word "bitch" had mainly been issued in the professional rather than a personal setting. In fact, Bobbie mentioned that negative labels were applied mostly by other females (other leaders and teachers alike) in an educational setting; thus highlighting a sometimes "female complicity in hegemonic masculinities" (Blackmore, 1999, p. 188). These women in education are sufferers of gender entrapment and socialization as well in which it is jarring to the system when other women eschew traditional notions of leadership. At Bobbie's low-performing school, there had been only male principals prior to her. According to Bobbie, and other district personnel, males had been positioned specifically as if they were the only ones to offer a "firm hand" and "control the school and teachers" for restructuring. This district, like much of the field of educational leadership, continues to privilege a hard management discourse (Blackmore, 1999). Denigrating words and images are often applied to individuals when they refuse to accept limiting notions in society (Collins, 1991).

A NEW NARRATIVE OF LEADERSHIP

Dantley (2003) argued that educational leadership "accepts labels seen as administrative or management as descriptors of educational leadership practice" (p. 182). Dantley wrote:

> The field is being challenged to consider a cacophony of voices that dispute the normative discourse of hierarchical and bureaucratic syntax, empirical and positivist idioms, and expressions of efficiency and productivity that have been borrowed from the classic business discourse. These new voices are communicating and language or spirituality, libratory praxis, and democratic dialogue.... Essentially, educational leadership is being challenged to engage in a broader conceptualization of its purpose. (p. 182)

Prescriptive ideas of leadership have implications for women and principals of color and their acceptance, socialization, and effectiveness in the principalship (Enomoto, Gardiner, & Grogan, 2000; Shakeshaft, 1999; Tillman, 2003). Current educational leadership research still reveals a tendency to identify "leadership" or "administration" as male in spite of studies that show that women use different leadership styles than men (Witherspoon, 2008). New paradigmatic research must be undertaken that challenge descriptive criteria, conceptual categories and taxonomies that define leaders to account for counter-narrative (i.e., gendered, contextual, political, social, etc.) influences upon leadership.

> When the annals of Eurocentric history generally define leaders as male and of non-African descent, and when the annals of...history focus mostly on white women leaders, what of the (in)adequacy of scholarship, research, and instruction devoted to Black women leaders...in society? And what are the methodological implications for...traditional categories of constructed leadership behaviors to be assessed in light of complex nature of Black women's lives and history? (Martin, 1998, p. 56)

Over the past 70 years, educational leadership concepts have been drawn from patriarchal management ideology, and this model of leadership seems to have failed (Murphy, 2002). How effective is an institutional structure that continues to marginalize or pigeonhole individuals based upon individuals' gender, race, and class?

It has been said that "the practice of educational leadership has very little to do with either education or leadership" (Murphy, 2002, p. 181). Asking women to remain "in their places" and to "be nice" and often conform to essentializing notions of a woman's way of leading is to invite derogatory brands and images of women when she eschews these notions. Educational leadership is in a unique position to explore the deep meanings and practices of women administrators so that women have a voice in their own profession, and can make themselves known and heard. These practices also have an ability to invite emancipation, reflexivity and praxis.

Greer Litton Fox (1977) argued that "normative restriction embodied in such value constructs as 'good girl,' 'lady,' or 'nice girl' acted as powerful regulatory mechanism that shaped all girls and women's behaviors, no matter their race, social class standing or whether they were in the company of men or women" (p. 805). The work of women in educational leadership highlight *nice* and *bitch* and the complicated and incongruous ways in which these social constructions influence the way in which women mediate patriarchy and gender structures in educational leadership.

This chapter does not propose a framework for what we "ought" to do in leadership. Rather, the importance of this chapter lies in underscoring and "busting" the discourse of how niceness constrains, shapes, and coerces professional identities of women educational leaders. It also is meant to give women leaders encouragement to use the hermeneutic of *nice* and *bitch* to interrogate the status quo in schools. Bobbie's narrative reveals there is a time and a place for niceness and there is a time and a place to forgo niceness. Bobbie's story foregoes niceness as a form of protest and mandates she be reckoned with.

"Being nice in the workplace is not a benign quality; whether women identify with being too nice or not nice enough, whether they resist being nice altogether, or whether they appropriate it and use it to their advantage, the tyranny of niceness is always operating" (Bettis & Adams, 2010, p. 3), and this continues to entrap women in pre-articulated roles of leadership. Disrupting gender entrapment debunks taken-for-granted notions of sexes. *Nice* or *bitch* is not, however, an acceptable elaboration or shorthand for female leadership while essentialists treat gender inherent as biological deficits rather than social constructions.

Doing research on women's personal and professional histories and experiences may add to the understanding of social justice and contribute to a more full-bodied view and to enlarge the scope of social justice in schools. In fact, Rizvi (1998) has written, "Social justice is embedded within discourses that are historically constituted and that are sites of conflicting and divergent political endeavors. Thus, social justice does not refer to a single set of primary goods, conceivable across all moral and material domains" (p. 47).

While there is no one way to enact or define social justice, grappling with gender entrapments in educational leadership allows us to inspect the multiple ways justice is lived in the ordinary lives of women. When this inspection is brought to the forefront, oppression as impetus in social justice in schools provides us with unique ways to approach and "right wrongs" (Baumberg, 2003; Labov, 1972).

REFERENCES

Bamberg, M. G. W. & McCabe, A. (1998). Editorial. *Narrative Inquiry 8*(1):iii–v.

Baumberg, M. (2003). Positioning with Davie Hogan—Stories, tellings, and identities. In C. Daiute & C. Lightfoot (Eds.), *Narrative analysis: Studying the development of individuals in society.* London, UK: Sage.

Bettis, P., & Adams, N. (2010). *Nice at work in the academy.* Unpublished paper.

Blackmore, J. (1993). "In the shadow of men": The historical construction of administration as a masculinist enterprise. In J. Blackmore & J. Kenway (Eds.), *Gender matters in educational administration and policy* (pp. 27–48). London, UK: Falmer Press.

Blackmore, J. (1999). *Troubling women: Feminism, leadership, change.* Philadelphia, PA: Open University Press.

Blackmore, J. (2002). Troubling women: The upsides and downsides of leadership and the new managerialsm. In C. Reynolds (Ed.), *Women and school leadership: International perspectives* (pp. 49–69). Albany, NY: SUNY Press.

Bloom, C. M., & Erlandson, D. A. (2003). African American women principals in urban schools: realities, (re)constructions, and resolutions. *Educational Administration Quarterly, 39*(3), 339–369.

Butler, J., Laclau, E., & Zizek, S. (Eds). (2000). *Contingency, hegemony, and universality.* London: Verso.

Cannon, K. G. (1995). *Katie's canon: Womanism and the soul of the Black community.* New York: Continuum Press.

Cannon, K. G., Johnson, A. P. G., Sims, A. D. (2005). Womanist works in word. *Journal of Feminist Studies in Religion, 21*(2), 135–146.

Chandler, M. J., Lalonde, C. E., & Teucher, U. (2004). Culture, continuity, and the limits of narrativity: A comparison of the self-narratives of native and non-native youth. In C. Dauite & C. Lightfoot, *Narrative analysis: Studying the development of individuals in society* (pp. 245–266). Thousand Oaks, CA: Sage Publications.

Chase, S. (1995). *Ambiguous empowerment: The work narratives of women superintendents.* Amherst, MA: Massachusetts University Press.

Cikara, M., & Fiske, S. (2009). Warmth, competence, and ambivalent sexism: Vertical assault and collateral damage. In M. Barretto, M. K. Ryan, & M. T. Schmitt (Eds.), *The glass ceiling in the 21st century* (pp. 49–71). Washington, DC: American Psychological Association.

Coffey, A., & Atkinson, P. (1996). *Making sense of qualitative data: Complimentary research strategies.* Thousand Oaks, CA: Sage.

Collins, P. H. (2000). *Black feminist thought: Knowledge, consciousness, and the politics of empowerment* (2nd ed.). New York, NY: Routledge.

Copeland, M. S. (2006). A thinking margin: The womanist movement as critical cognitive praxis. In S. M. Floyd-Thomas (Ed.), *Deeper shades of purple: Womanism in religion and society* (pp. 226–235). New York, NY: New York University Press.

Curry, B. K. (2000). *Women in power.* New York, NY: Teachers College Press.

Daiute, C., & Lightfoot, C. (Eds.). (2004). *Narrative analysis. Studying the development of individuals in society.* Thousand Oaks, Sage Publications.

Essed, P. (1991). *Understanding everyday racism: An interdisciplinary theory.* Newbury Park, CA: Sage Publications.

Floyd-Thomas, S. M. (Ed.). (2006b). *Deeper shades of purple: Womanism in religion and society.* New York: New York University Press.

Fox, G. L. (1977). "Nice girl": Social control of women through a value construct. *Signs: Journal of Women in Culture and Society 2,* 805–817.

Gee, J.P. 1991. A linguistic approach to narrative. *Journal of Narrative and Life History, 1,* 15–39.

Goffman, E. (1969). *The presentation of self in everyday life.* NY: Penguin.

Goffman, E. (1981). *Forms of talk.* Oxford: Blackwell.

Gramsci, A. (1971). *Selections from the prison notebooks of Antonio Gramsci* (Q. Hoare & G. N. Smith, Trans.). New York City, NY: International Publishers.

Grumet, M. (1981). Pedagogy for patriarchy: the feminization of teaching. *Interchange, 12*(2/3), 165–183.

Harris, M. L. (2006). Womanist humanism. In S. M. Floyd-Thomas (Ed.), *Deeper shades of purple: womanism in religion and society* (pp. 54–76). New York: New York University Press.

Hendry, P. H. (2007). The future of narrative. *Qualitative Inquiry, 12*(4), 487–499.

Hirsch, M. (2009) *Women in educational leadership: Agency and Communion.* Saarbruck-en, Deutschland: VDM Verlag.

Labov, W. (1972). *Language in the inner city: Studies in the Black English vernacular.* Philadelphia, PA: University of Pennsylvania Press.

Labov, W. (1982). *The social stratification of English in New York City.* Washington, DC: Center for Applied Linguistics

Langellier, K. (1989). Personal narratives: Perspectives on theory and research. *Text and Performance Quarterly 9*(4), 243–276.

Langellier, K. (2001). You're marked: Breast cancer, tattoo, and the narrative per-formance of identity." In J. Brockmeier & D. Carbaugh (Eds.), *Narrative and identity: Studies in autobiography, self, and culture.* Amsterdam and Philadelphia: John Benjamins.

Lempert, L. B. (1997). The other side of help: Negative effects in the help-seeking processes of abused women. *Qualitative Sociology, 20*(2), 289–309.

Marshall, J. (1996). *Women managers moving on: Exploring career and life choices.* Lon-don, UK: Routledge.

Mattingly, C. & Garro, L. C., (Eds.). (2000). *Narrative and cultural construction of ill-ness and healing.* Berkeley: Univ. of California Press.

McRobbie, A. (2009). *The aftermath of feminism: Gender, culture and social change.* Thousand Oaks, CA: Sage Publications.

Mischler, E. G. (1995). Models of narrative analysis. *Journal of Narrative and Life His-tory, 5,* 87–123.

Mitchell, H. H., & Lewter, N. C. (1986). *Soul theology: The heart of American black cul-ture.* San Francisco, CA: Harper and Row.

Mumby, D. K. (1993). *Narrative and social control: Critical perspectives.* Newbury Park: Sage.

Murphy, J. (2002). Reculturing the profession of educational leadership: New blue-prints. *Educational Administration Quarterly, 38*(2), 176–191.

Polanyi, L. (1985). "Conversational Storytelling." In T. A. Van Dijk (Ed.)., *Handbook of discourse analysis.* London: Academic Press.

Richie, B. E. (1996). *Compelled to crime.* New York, NY: Routledge.

Riessman, C. K. (1993). *Narrative analysis.* Newbury Park, CA: Sage.

Rizvi, F. (1998). Some thoughts on contemporary theories of social justice. In B. Atwel, S. Kemmis, & P. Weeks (Eds.), *Partnerships for social justice in education* (pp. 47–56). New York, NY: Routledge.

Rosaldo, R. (1989). *Culture and truth: The remaking of social analysis.* Boston: Beacon Press.

Rose, S., & Frieze, I. H. (1993). Young singles' contemporary dating scripts. *Sex Roles, 28,* 499–509.

Shakeshaft, C. (1979). *Dissertation research on women in educational administration: An analysis of findings and paradigm for future research.* Unpublished doctoral dis-sertation, Texas A&M University, College Station.

Skrla, L., & Benestante, J. J. (1998). On being terminally female: Denial of sex-ism in educational administration is no protection of its effects. In C. Funk, A. Pankake, & M. Reese (Eds.), *Women as school executives: realizing the vision* (pp. 57–61). Commerce, TX: Texas A&M University Press.

Thompson, A. (1998). Not the color purple: Black feminist lessons for educational caring. *Harvard Educational Review, 66,* 522–554.

Walker, A. (1983). *In search of our mothers' gardens.* San Diego, CA: Harcourt Brace Jovanovich.

Williams, D. S. (1993). *Sisters in the wilderness: The challenge of womanist God-talk.* Marynoll, NY: Orbis Books.

Witherspoon, N., & Taylor, D. (2010). Spiritual W.E.A.P.O.N.S: Black female principals and religio-spirituality. *Journal of Educational Administration and History, 42*(2), 133–158.

Wurtzel, E. (1999). *Bitch: In praise of difficult women.* New York, NY: First Anchor Books.

CHAPTER 9

AFRICAN AMERICAN WOMEN EDUCATIONAL LEADERS IN TURNAROUND SCHOOLS

Narratives on Transforming Urban School Communities

Cosette M. Grant

ABSTRACT

There is little knowledge on how best to prepare African American women urban school principals to succeed in turnaround schools. Furthermore, scant literature exists that has identified ways in which African American women principals are mentored toward the attainment of their leadership positions. Concurrently, African American female principals in urban turnaround schools receive limited support or resources, which hinders their leadership success in urban schools (Bloom & Erlandson, 2003). Therefore, this chapter illuminates shared common lived experiences of African American women leaders of urban turnaround schools and helps us understand how they make sense of their leadership roles in marginalized settings. This qualitative research utilizes narratives to assess effective strategies for African American women principals

Women Interrupting, Disrupting, and Revolutionizing Educational Policy and Practice, pages 145–173
Copyright © 2014 by Information Age Publishing

transforming turnaround schools. Findings have implications for leadership preparation and practice and provide additional justification for diverse leadership to enhance student achievement.

According to President Barack Obama, America can no longer afford to support the status quo of our current education system, and to be a successful country, we must embrace innovative reform efforts for turning around America's lowest-performing schools (U.S. Department of Education, 2010a). Additionally, the Obama administration has focused national attention on improving the academic achievement of all students. In response to this federal discourse, educators, policymakers, and others have sought remedies to turn around chronically low-performing schools. As a consequence, school districts, especially in urban areas, are challenged to meet the increasing requirements of ensuring learner proficiency and create high-performing schools. School districts acknowledge the need to recruit, hire, train, and sustain high-performing school leaders (Hall, 2008).

Accordingly, Arne Duncan, the U.S. Secretary of Education, describes creating flexible funding mechanisms to foster innovation, including awarding districts with School Turnaround Grants, which use a portion of these grants to fund partnerships of failing districts with educational nonprofit organizations that will assist in turnaround model implementation (USDOE, 2010a). Additionally, the U.S. Department of Education has implemented the Race to the Top (RTTT) program (USDOE, 2011b), which funds economic-stimulus grants. Specifically, RTTT targets states that, in exchange for receiving large federal grants, commit to improving education standards that prepare students for college, implement comprehensive data systems to track student growth and instructional accountability, attract high-quality educators for all schools, and target the turnaround of the nation's lowest performing schools (U.S. DOE, 2010b).

Concurrently, principals, especially African American women in urban schools, maintain that very little support exists as they embark on the challenges of being a principal post-NCLB, not to mention the difficulties and challenges that new principals face. In this regard, Murtadha and Larson (1999) contend that "principals of color, especially African-American women, typically emerge as the leaders of urban schools that are undersupported and economically depleted" (p. 6). They also assert, "They [women of color] are expected to establish and carry out educational agendas that clash with what they and the community see as vital to the education of African-American children" (p. 6). As urban communities across the United States experience changing racial and ethnic demographics, school leaders are confronted with the needs, perspectives, and "funds of knowledge" that students from diverse backgrounds and their families bring to the school (Johnson, 2007). Yet, the myth remains that the ideal leader for most schools conforms to a White, masculine stereotype, particularly at the secondary level (Brunner & Peyton-Caire, 2000; Murtadha & Larson, 1999; Shakeshaft, 1989). For example, in 2003–2004, ethnic minorities, both men and women, represented only 24% of principals in the United States (Strizek, Pittsonberger, Riordan, Lyter, & Orlofsky, 2006). The numbers are more dismal for African American women leaders when categories are disaggregated by gender and race as well. Furthermore, African American women leaders are disproportionately found in urban school environments that have been exhausted of resources and lack support (Bloom & Erlandson, 2003).

While the importance of effective school leadership is undisputed, few studies have been conducted that document the experiences of African American school principals in urban school contexts (Tillman, 2007). One of the only things researchers know with any certainty is that the number of African American women in leadership positions in U.S. public schools is slim (Allen, Jacobson, & Lomotey, 1995). Moreover, educational literature offers limited knowledge construction regarding African American women principals (Alston, 2000; Collins & Lightsey, 2001; Henry, 2001; Lomotey, 1989). Because African American women in leadership positions are rare, their voices are seldom heard (Alston, 1999, 2000; Jackson, 1999). And because they have been so few in number, there is little research about African American women in educational leadership, their professional aspirations, the obstacles they face as they pursue their goals, and the roles of mentors and sponsors in advancing their careers (Allen, Jacobsen, & Lomotey, 1995). Further, deficit theories and misogynistic notions constrain the advancement of African American women into leadership positions (Bloom & Erlandson, 2003). These limitations include difficulty in usurping the male dominance position, stereotyping, self-imposed barriers, circuitous pathways with lack of mentors, and inadequate training or coaching in managing issues of power and control (Blakemore, 1999; Collins, 1991; Grogan, 1999; Hill & Ragland, 1995; Shakeshaft, 1989).

In response to mounting pressure stemming from the federal No Child Left Behind Act (NCLB), school districts across the United States have been confronted with the challenge of developing effective training programs in urban schools. Moreover, districts face additional obstacles in regard to providing assistance and accommodation for educational leaders (many of whom are African American women) who face exceptional resource deficits. To support these efforts, school districts strive to find effective models to build the leadership capacity of school leaders to turn around low-performing schools (Petzko, 2008). As such, mentoring has emerged as a professional development tool for building effective educational leaders. An important avenue to prepare new and qualified principals is through mentorship programs, as the mentoring relationship is seen as a way to improve how school leaders are prepared to carry out their craft in the "real world" (Daresh, 1995, p. 7).

Historically, mentoring has played some part in the training and development of novice principals (Crow & Matthews, 1998; Daresh, 1986; Hobson, 2003; Weingartner, 2009). Mentoring has been a known strategy for building leadership capacity as part of professional development and training (Bloom, Castagna, Moir, & Warren, 2005; Browne-Ferrigno & Muth, 2004; Daresh & Playko, 1990), yet we know little about successful mentoring models effective in developing African American female principals. There is little empirical evidence that identifies how such a knowledge base is enacted. Further, it is unclear what strategies, techniques, training, and other inherent qualities make for a successful African American female principal with regard to turning around low-performing schools.

Therefore, this study attempts to fill the void in the literature on African American women educational leaders' lived experiences in urban school settings, by featuring narrative findings of two African American female principals that participated in a formal mentoring initiative for principals who have effectively led turnaround schools in an urban school district. The needs and challenges commonly identified by these women are addressed; these include issues of race, gender, and class. Individual profiles, through narrative storytelling, were used to display their leadership behaviors within this urban school context. Each woman recounted the realities (successes and limitations) of her actual work, the reconstructions of deeply held leadership belief systems, and the personal resolutions evolving from her leadership experiences within schools.

Finally, this study draws on unique data, combining interviews, observations, and self-reflection of the two study participants (Principal Thelma and Principal Louise—pseudonyms) as most salient for developing them as urban school leaders. In order to better understand ways in which they were able to make use of mentoring pathways and opportunities that led to their success, the following two research questions guided this study: (a) What specific mentoring strategies (if any) were useful to your transition as a principal in a turnaround school?; and (b) What specific mentoring activities (if any) were effective in turning around your school? This chapter concludes with a discussion of the findings and offers implications that subsequently emerged.

LITERATURE REVIEW

Schools across the nation are expected to focus on delivering a high quality educational product as evidenced by No Child Left Behind (NCLB, 2001). Still plagued by the ever-widening achievement gap, lack of student retention, and the lack of equity amongst schools, our nation continues to seek innovative solutions that will provide a turnaround of our current educational crisis. Competent principals are major contributors in the success of a school (Marzano, Waters, & McNulty, 2005). Since principals can have an impact on student learning outcomes, their professional development and competence has become an important focus in the mission to improve U.S. schools.

Challenges to Turnaround Leadership

School principals play an integral role in increasing academic achievement. In fact, research reveals that effective school leaders can raise a low-performing school's overall student achievement by as much as 10 points out of 100 when other factors are equal (Waters, Marzano, & McNulty, 2005). Turnaround leadership concerns the kind of leadership needed for turning around a persistently low-performing school to one that is performing acceptably as measured by student achievement (Fullan, 2005). "Assessing the roles of strong interventions for failing schools is quite complicated," even in the narrow sense, because the combination of intended and unintended consequences is difficult to sort out (Fullan, 2005, p. 174).

With the knowledge that principals play an important role in school turnaround (Carter, 2000), school districts are faced with the challenge of finding ways to build the skills, knowledge, and abilities of its school leaders. Moreover, as newly minted principals enter the ranks of this multifaceted position from preparation programs, most have emerged with beginners' skill sets, and they are left to figure out how to effectively meet the wide range of complex challenges faced by school leaders, especially in urban schools (Farkas, Johnson, Duffett, & Foleno, 2001; Perez, Uline, Johnson, James-Ward, & Basom, 2011; Sanders & Kearney, 2008; Searby, 2010). They enter the position prepared to be competent; however, the position of principal requires that they take on much more that what was originally expected or taught during their preparation programs. In reality, many novice principals enter the position feeling unsupported and without the guidance and coaching necessary to effectively lead a school (Grissom & Harrington, 2010; Searby, 2010).

In the case of new principals, administrators are being asked to do something that they are not necessarily prepared to do (Elmore, 2005). In fact, school administrators feel enormous pressure to keep up with NCLB requirements despite the fact that many urban schools across the country have multiple factors thwarting principals' good intentions. For example, urban schools have social, economic, and cultural conditions that perpetuate their unsuccessful gains.

The changing role of a principal has brought new challenges that deal with influencing the social, economic, and political context of a school. Goodwin, Cunningham, and Eagle (2005) suggested that the role of a school administrator has been transformed from that of a building manager to that of the leader of a community organization. Goodwin et al. (2005) indicated that new principals are not fully prepared to take on the responsibilities of their jobs. Principals are spending more time on the job and have increased responsibilities, while also being held responsible for meeting or exceeding goals established by NCLB (2002). Goodwin et al. (2005) suggested that the quality of prospective principals should improve by having better preparation, recruitment, and professional development. Accordingly, the key lies within preparation before and after someone decides to take on the role of principal (Goodwin et al., 2005). However, it is unclear from the literature what strategies, techniques, training, and other inherent qualities make for a successful principal, particularly in a turnaround setting.

Increasingly complex and demanding, the urban school principalship continues to evolve around a leader not only in an educational institution context, but as a social agent as well. Over the years, educational researchers have tried to explain why patterns of social chaos and inequity tend to surface in poor, minority schools (Anyon, 1997; Kozol, 1991; Noguera, 1996). Agreement exists about the key role of the principal in urban schools, although conditions of professional practice often tend to be characterized by "situational and contextual variables that determine the appropriate application of professional skills" (Cistone & Stevenson, 2000, p. 435). Similarly, African American principals perceive responsibilities toward African American children emanating from their own experiences relating to race and class (Pollard, 1997).

Moreover, urban school leadership requires the principal to understand the long-range effects of poverty, the disparities widespread in local school funding procedures, the impact of neighborhood unemployment on crime within the school, the necessity of interagency collaborations, and causal factors for low parental involvement (Bloom & Erlandson, 2003). To add, Portin (2000) has conducted studies on the urban school principalship and lists three challenges to leadership in the urban principalship:

> The urban principalship may be more challenging along characteristics of entrepreneurial requirements, managing social complexity, and political skill... [relying] more on political leadership skill... to make a case for the interests of their schools in a system of competing needs for limited resources.... Urban principals will need to develop expertise in communicating the unique characteristics of their school that suffer when schools are ranked and

compared against criteria that fail to account for the unique challenges of their community. (p. 503)

Additionally, Murtadha and Larson (1999) contend that despite their credentials and abilities, African American women principals or urban schools in particular, lack support and are economically deprived. Moreover, they (women of color) are expected to establish and carry out educational agendas despite these overwhelming challenges within the schools and community. Yeakey, Johnston, and Adkison (1986) (cited in Hill & Ragland, 1995, p. 20) refer to those souls who accept such challenges as taking on the role of a "messiah" or eventually becoming a "scapegoat" (p. 21). Often, this is the only opportunity African American women will have to become a leader of a school.

Dillard (1995) posited that when caring for students, African American women principals who serve marginalized urban communities do not engage in traditional leadership activities "as they have been traditionally conceptualized" (p. 542). Instead, they consider culture and community context and focus beyond the school. Furthermore, some African American women principals lead differently than their White colleagues, in part because they have been excluded from established power structures. Restricted access to resources and frustration with exclusionary bureaucracies prompted creativity and risk-taking in their leadership roles. Yet African American women principals have become skilled at uniting and engaging stakeholders in marginalized school settings into action (Brooks, 2009; Johnson, 2007).

Developing Turnaround Leaders

Few research-based sources exist regarding the application of turnaround efforts in schools (Boyne, 2006; Leithwood & Strauss, 2008; Murphy & Meyers, 2008). However, the research on successful turnaround initiatives in schools affirms the critical importance of leadership (Public Impact, 2008). The complexity of school turnaround precludes a simple approach. Effective turnaround requires competent leaders skilled at solving problems and influencing others to support and participate in the change initiative. Cincinnati Public Schools (CPS), for example, opted to replace two principals and sought high-potential leaders to fill the vacancies in underperforming schools.

However, successful student achievement attributable to effective leadership in urban schools is difficult to measure because of the limited research in this area. The irony is that from these dismal portraits of abandonment and neglect emerge African American women principals, who tackle these critically ill schools and over time create schools that become "beacons of light within the darkness of their communities" (Bloom & Erlandson, 2003, p. 347). Telling their stories can inform and enlighten our current theoretical formulations about what it feels like to be an invisible change agent who works "on the inside," yet with only illusionary career opportunities in the future (p. 347).

As the faces of urban public school students in America become more diverse, the faces of leadership in America's urban schools should also reflect similar demographic changes. Shakeshaft (1999) dispelled the myth that the number of aspiring principals of color remains relatively low. In fact, "women and minority candidates are certified in much larger numbers than they are chosen for administrative positions" (p. 100). There are detractors; however, few women, and even fewer African American women, receive the necessary mentoring and/or encouragement to pursue educational leadership roles (Grogan & Brunner, 2005). With very few districts headed by women (Brunner, Grogan & Prince, 2003), this means few role models for women considering or assuming leadership roles. To address this, educational systems must deliberately mentor more women and especially more African American women. Although mentoring is referenced in the context of women superintendents, the same recommendations are applicable to African American women principals in urban districts.

The Importance of Mentoring

Leithwood and Steinback (1995) consider mentor relationships as one effective strategy for addressing the theory-to-practice disconnect characterized by administrator preparation programs. Studies show that by integrating professional knowledge and practical experience through mentoring, protégé learning can be enhanced and transferred to new job settings (Björk & Rinehart, 2005; Villani, 2005). Others report that mentoring provides adults with assistance at various career and life stages and should be considered a vital part of the career development process for leaders (Daresh & Playko, 1990).

Supported by social learning theory, mentoring provides direct and observational learning to help novices acquire work patterns and skills and build personal efficacy for successful leadership (Bandura, 1977; Kram, 1985). Crow and Matthews (1998) use the metaphor of a journey to explain mentoring benefits, saying, "Principals are both following others' maps and actively generating their own maps. Mentoring, if successful, provides a map and the support for the administrative journey" (p. 17). Aiken (2002) reported that mentoring helps protégés develop social maps that assist them in their understanding of school culture, their roles as leaders, and their fit with peers and supervisors.

Related to mentoring outcomes, Fagenson (1989) found that workers who are mentored report higher levels of job satisfaction, career advancement, recognition, and security than nonmentored peers. Levinson, Darrow, Klein, Levinson, and McKee (1978) reported that mentoring provides both professional and personal development for protégés, with mentors serving varied roles as advisors, sponsors, and teachers. Further, classical mentoring provides an intense developmental relationship that extends over time and provides protégés with a wide range of both career and social assistance (Whitely, Dougherty, & Dreher, 1991). Aiken (2002) identified five mentoring outcomes that include helping protégés (a) find their voice and vision, (b) form alliances and networks, (c) develop their leadership persona, (d) clarify their balance between custodianship and innovation, and (e) make connections with the larger community.

Moreover, mentoring can be either formal or informal, with a majority of mentoring relationships beginning informally as result of interest and willingness on the part of the mentor and protégé (Phillips-Jones, 1983). Basic to maintaining effective mentoring relationships that promote protégé learning is the need for pairs to develop trust, share common beliefs, determine roles, create opportunities for a nurturing relationship, and monitor progress on job performance and role adjustment (Milstein, Bobroff, & Restine, 1990). Success factors vital for effective formal mentoring experiences include (a) program definition, planning, and structure; (b) selection and training of mentors and protégés; (c) resource allocation for mentoring; and (d) evaluation of mentoring experiences (Wunsch, 1994). Programs that do not include vital components likely result in weaker mentoring relationships and outcomes (Hamilton & Hamilton, 1992).

With the emergence of more formalized mentoring programs for school leaders, this study attempts to fill a need by analyzing mentoring relationships beyond the informal mentoring processes. Additional empirical research is needed to identify determinants of mentoring relationship success. Only a few studies have examined protégé–mentor relationships in school settings and even fewer for African American women leaders in urban schools. Ensher and Murphy (1997) measured similarities of protégés–mentors participating in a short-term, youth work development program, finding that protégés who identified similarly with mentors reported higher levels of satisfaction with the experience. Noe (1988) studied protégé-mentor similarities for participants in a short-term aspiring principal program, finding that protégés in heterogeneous gender mentor pairing used mentors more effectively than those in homogeneous mentor pairing.

Race studies show that protégés mentored by someone of like race spent more time in mentoring activities and reported a greater mentor liking (Ensher & Murphy, 1997). Thomas (1990) reported that like-race mentoring relationships provided a higher level of psychosocial support than those provided in unlike-race relationships.

Few studies explore mentoring relationships between protégés and mentors in formal mentoring programs for school administrators—despite the growing number of mentoring programs being implemented. However, for the purposes of this study, a *mentor* is a person who initiates assistance, helps, provides supports, or teaches skills necessary to successfully perform in a job (Mendez-Morse, 2004). Sheehy (1976) described a mentor as "one who takes an active interest in the career development of another person—a nonparental career role model who actively provides guidance, support, and opportunities for the protégé" (p. 36). Also in this study, *mentoring* refers to the relationship in which a more experienced person takes under their tutelage a less experienced person in order to provide career and psychosocial development is referred to as mentoring. Mentoring is further defined as "the establishment of a personal relationship for the purpose of professional instruction and guidance" (Ashburn, Mann, & Purdue, 1987).

Mentoring Principals

With regard to principals, Daresh and Playko (1990) contend that "mentoring to assist present and future leaders is a powerful tool that may be used to bring about more effective school practice" (p. 44). The use of mentoring, especially in urban schools, has potential value in creating highly effective principals as these first-time leaders engage in learning innumerable school tasks, procedures, policies, and practices that are designed to produce positive student achievement results (Daresh & Playko, 1990; McCreary-King, 1992; McGough, 2003; Mendez-Morse, 2004).

University programs alone will never be enough to prepare principals for the day-to-day challenges of the job (Yirci & Kocabas, 2010). As Yirci and Kocabas (2010) implied, there are some insufficient points in the traditional methods used to train school principals. Pre-service and in-service education activities which school principal candidates have to take are generally full of theoretical knowledge, and they hardly ever contain a connection to practice (Yirci, 2010). Through the process of mentoring, new school principals receive support from an effective and experienced principal in the most troubled period of their professional life (Boris-Schacter & Vonasek, 2009; Daresh, 2004; Grissom & Harrington, 2010; Hall, 2008; Hansford & Erlich, 2006; Hobson & Phenis-Bourke, 2005; Peters, 2010; Rayner, 2009; Yirci & Kocabas, 2010). This assistance comes in the form of peer support and real-world applicability. It takes place in a real school environment. With this practice, the most problematic period of time in the profession is easily overcome and provides each candidate with actual administrative behaviors, which cannot be learned through preservice and inservice training

(Boris-Schacter, 2009; Daresh, 2004; Grissom & Harrington, 2010; Hall, 2008; Hansford, 2006; Hobson, 2005; Peters, 2010; Rayner, 2009; Smith, 2007; Yirci & Kocabas, 2010).

Mentoring of principals in turnaround schools. Many urban school districts across the United States are currently following the reform movement of turnaround schools. These turnaround programs are a result of the No Child Left Behind mandate that requires a school that has continuously been in academic emergency for five years even after interventions have be set in place will be restructured by the state or district (NCLB, 2002). There are many options of how to enact this process, and one is the turnaround program where the school is restaffed and a new leader is appointed or hired to come in and "fix" the problem. Herin lies the problem: that there are a large number of low-achieving schools and a smaller number of effective principals in low-income districts (Darden, 2011). However, there is literature that supports low-income districts going through reforms and becoming successful with time (Scribner, Crow, Lopez, Murtadha, 2011). Moreover, the federal government and states are looking for effective models that will help their districts flourish. Hence, the University of Virginia Darden School funded by the U.S. Department of Education has been working with Cincinnati Public Schools (CPS) on such turnaround issues (Darden, 2011) and trying to determine what is making the program work.

Mentoring support of African-American principals in turnarounds. In addressing equity and diversity in mentoring, mentors need a focus on both the needs of the students, particularly those currently underserved in schools, and the needs of diverse new teachers and principals. Such work means focusing on the specific needs of new principals, including addressing their cultural and linguistic identifications and how those may impact their leadership in schools of underserved communities (Achinstein, 2010). Achinstein and Ogawa's (2011a) study focused on new principals of color as a potentially promising population in terms of diversifying the leadership in urban schools and in impacting urban high-need schools where students of color are schooled.

METHODS

This investigation of principals' perceptions of the effects of mentoring in a turnaround school uses Erlandson, Harris, Skipper, and Allen's (1993) naturalistic inquiry methodology as a means for increasing knowledge for practice using narrative storytelling to design explanatory and exploratory questions about the subjects' social setting (Erlandson et al., 1993). Naturalistic inquiry, conducted to understand human experience and to interpret the perceived realities of the research participants, allows the participants to construct reality within their social settings. Harrison (1995) uses this methodology to reduce the invisibility and silences of women of color in the world by concluding, "In the process of redefining educational administration's critical project[s] and of reconstituting education authority, we must offset the persistent pattern of relegating the work of women—and that of women of color in particular—to the discipline's periphery" (p. 242). The use of the naturalistic inquiry design sought "a deep understanding and explication of social phenomena as they are observed in their own contexts" (Erlandson et al., 1993, p. 16). Bounded by these positions, the research questions emerged to investigate the realities about the role of race and gender in leadership, thoughts about the urban turnaround school, and training and mentoring options for the participants.

In particular, this study examined the principals' perceptions of their mentoring experience with regard to developing and supporting practices or behaviors they believed beneficial in creating effective schools and positive student achievement outcomes. Further, it explored their perceptions of changes that could be made within mentoring in order to best support future participants in their professional growth and development. A qualitative methodology utilizing individual interviews and content analysis of documents was selected for this study. This qualitative approach was selected based on the guidelines suggested by Bogdan and Biklen (1998), Hakim (2000), Marshall and Rossman (1999), Miles and Huberman (1994), and Shavelson and Towne (2002).

Further, this research approach seeks understanding of "how people interpret their experiences, construct their worlds, and what meaning they attribute to their experiences" (Merriam, 2009, p. 5). Creswell (2009) explained that a qualitative study is a strategy of inquiry where the researcher explores in depth a program, an event, an activity, a process, or individuals.

Theoretical Framework

As the suppression of the ideas of African American women in research and epistemological knowledge construction remains a force that undermines the economic, political, and social revitalization within the African American woman's world, black feminist thought (BFT) is a theory that centralizes and validates the intersecting dimensions of race and gender uniquely experienced in the lives of African American women. As an emerging number of African American women are assuming leadership positions in challenging school settings, it is helpful to deconstruct their daily lives as leaders to provide direction for future leaders who may find themselves in similar circumstances.

To this end, one framework that is useful for understanding the experiences of African American women principals in turnaround schools is standpoint theory. Standpoint theory provides legitimacy and rationale to how African American women principals lead their schools, especially schools with low-performing circumstances. In this regard, some African American women principals lead differently than their White colleagues, in part because they have been excluded from established power structures. Restricted access to resources commonplace in schools where African American women principals lead compounded with frustration from exclusionary bureaucracies in many cases prompts creativity and risk-taking in their leadership roles. Standpoint theory uses language and stories to produce alternative realities. Yonezawa (2000) explained that "standpoint theory proposes that people gain knowledge through their positions or social locations. They use the term *positionality* to capture how people's positions in the larger social structure (e.g., race, class, gender, and sexuality) influence what they are aware of and their interpretations of events" (p. 111).

Therefore, African American women would view the world from discrete perspectives based on their social positions, or positionality, within the confines of the larger social structures of race and gender (Collins, 1991; Guy-Sheftall, 1995; Scott, 1982). However, in this study, looking at how African American women principals view themselves and their work helps one to understand more comprehensively why principals "behave, respond, and act the way they do in specific situations in essence creates new knowledge and understanding that clarify an African-American woman's standpoint for African-American women" (Collins 2002, p. 469). Furthermore, what is important to note with regard to standpoint theory is to recognize that African American women leaders demonstrate difference in regard to class, sexuality, background, experience, and school environment, but they hold similarities as a "category."

Participants

The participants were identified and selected using purposeful sampling based on established criteria (Patton, 2002). The participants were two female principals in an urban turnaround school who self-identified as African American, were within three years of a new principal position in a turnaround school, participated in the turnaround initiative, and stated that they were mentored in their current position. The participants' ages ranged from 45 to 60 years old. Richness of professional background and willingness to participate in a series of personal in-depth interviews were the primary considerations in identifying participants for the study.

Interviews

The interviews focused on three areas: participants' backgrounds in education, with emphasis on their experiences being mentored in the mentoring program; their personal reflections on the constructed meaning of leadership as principal in an urban turnaround school setting; and their perceptions of success in a turnaround school setting. Each interview was approximately one hour. The interview questions encouraged participants to tell their stories about specific mentoring experiences during their early stages as principal in an urban turnaround school. The interviews were audiotaped. Interview questions focused on concern with the lack of mentoring of African American female principals as a mechanism for diversifying leadership in urban school districts and as a catalyst for improving pedagogy and culture in urban school settings.

Analysis

With social constructivism as the applied worldview, the analysis of principal interviews, field observations, and documents from the program provided data to inform meaning, find emerging patterns and themes, and support a theory about the use of coaching and mentoring as a strategy to build principal capacity and impact student achievement (Creswell, 2009; Glaser & Strauss, 1967). This qualitative study relied upon an analysis of the participants' perceptions of mentoring in order to gain knowledge of what they deemed as supportive in creating the leadership practices associated with effective turnaround schools as well as diversifying leadership in urban school districts.

Using Erlandson et al.'s (1993) interactive process of data analysis, themes emerged from the transcriptions of the interviews. The data analysis followed Lincoln and Guba's (1985) techniques of unitizing data, creating and deleting categories as the researcher reads and rereads each unit, developing descriptive sentences that distinguish each category from the others, and starting over with each unit to refocus and refine category placement (cited in Erlandson et al., 1993).

Limitations

Study delimitations include the following: (a) the research site is located in a specific geographical region and district, (b) research subjects are African

American women principals who have led the same school site for the past three years, and (c) principals have participated in the professional development program during the past three years of their professional careers.

The findings presented in this study are not monolithic; therefore, they are not the view of all African American women principals or women in general. The findings are representative of the two women studied and interviewed. The cross-cultural themes revealed here are not intended to suggest that only African American women principals know how to effectively lead urban turnaround schools.

FINDINGS: NARRATIVES

This section delineates how the two women principals operated in the world of work, constrained by race, gender, and class. This exploration depends on the words and verbal recitations of both participants to fully dislodge the perspectives that created their personal philosophies regarding self, schools, and community. By presenting counterhegemonic African American feminist discourses such as these, the findings of this study accommodate the activist aim—to unmask and scrutinize the power of racist and sexist practices operating within public school systems. Listening to the underrepresented, yet significant, voices of African American women principals, leaders in turnaround schools may begin to change minds and social constructs about the "others" in America's urban school districts.

The findings were organized in individual narratives addressing both research questions while informing the conceptual framework. Each narrative was unique; however, there were common themes across the two study participants. Their stories did not follow the predicted path of survival to comfort in their roles as principal. They alluded to their preparation as a key factor in their success as new principals. This confirms the importance of mentoring while transitioning into the role of a new principal in a challenging school environment.

Findings also confirm the literature on African American women principal placements in challenging urban schools. Theses principals addressed student performance challenges as a competing priority to leadership training and development. This order of action is also present in the literature on successful urban principals in challenging schools. Findings confirm the effectiveness of mentoring. Time, fit between mentoring and the principalship, constant engagement, and feedback from mentors were important factors for successful school turnarounds as principal.

Finally, the narratives highlight the similarities between the two principals' experiences as it pertains to the two research questions. To this end, there are four common themes specific to mentoring experiences and activities for the study participants that were claimed to be effective in turning around their schools: supporting new principals in urban turnaround schools, mentoring leaders to lead in a dynamic educational environment, mentoring activities focused on student achievement in low-performing schools, and mentoring African American women principals as a catalyst for diversifying school leadership.

Theme 1—Supporting New Principals in Urban Turnaround Schools

Both principals attended an orientation program that trained them in leadership. Both principals commented that new principal orientation was a valuable support provider to the new principals. Both principals indicated that they had an informal mentor or buddy system in place for new principals, where the novice principals could work with and be guided by a more experienced administrator/principal. Accordingly, Browne-Ferrigno and Muth (2004) contend that principals' training, in order to be most effective, should now consist of collegial-peer relationships that are left upon "conditions of trust, openness, risk taking, problem identification, problem solving, and goal setting" (p. 490). Based upon this idea, it was the goal of this research to determine the principals' perception of their participation in the CPS mentoring training program initiative and how the program supported changes that helped them develop effective school leadership behaviors. The research examined data to determine what principals felt worked or did not work in this professional development model and their suggestions for future leadership training models.

In terms of encouraging and supporting additional professional development, Principal Thelma and Principal Louise both indicated the value of mentoring their first year. Not surprisingly, they were placed in two of the lowest performing schools in the district. There was leadership transition, moving from a history of experiencing an authoritarian leadership style to two that were more participatory. The needs assessment process was, as Principal Thelma noted, "an evolving piece," because professional development (PD) planning had previously been a more top-down process. Both principals indicated that they had relied more on administrators/mentors to identify and develop training activities, specific to improving instruction. For the purpose of this study, both Principal Louise and Principal Thelma noted that their knowledge of curriculum and assessment was central to their turnaround work, "because a solid curriculum and aligned assessments are the backbone in making meaningful changes and improvements to instruction."

Theme 2—Mentoring Leaders for Dynamic Educational Environments

As leaders in turnaround schools in the same school district, possessing a strong self-image and cultural understanding of their own personal histories allowed the study participants to recognize that the origin of problems in urban schools were not solely caused by the students' and parents' lack of resources or unwillingness to participate. Rather, low academic achievement must be viewed within the larger structural context of public education's bureaucratic and exclusionary practices. Both women reflected on their upbringings under segregationist laws and practices. It was apparent to the two study participants that a collective consciousness of identity supplied the Civil Rights movement the energy necessary to produce a deeply subversive movement of mass resistance and social transformation. Building on this collective consciousness, they used their awareness of the bureaucratic culture and the political processes present in schools to market a vision for their schools. Despite their differences, these two principals share certain traits and beliefs. Most notably, they were both strong principals who hold their students and their teachers to the highest standards. Both believe that children of all races and income levels can meet high academic standards (Carter, 2000).

A U.S. Department of Education report on nine urban success stories, including schools in Milwaukee, Detroit, Chicago, and East St. Louis, cited school leadership and accountability as key ingredients (Dana Center, 1999). The report indicated that school leaders created a collective sense of responsibility for school improvement. Accordingly, in terms of accountability, Principal Thelma asserted,

> "The way I originally saw things is that we are in these difficult schools, the kids are poor, the parents are not committed." However, mentoring on specific accountability has shifted this notion: "We are all accountable for student achievement and so we need to work through these factors instead of using them as excuses."

Furthermore, she stated:

> One of the first things I said when I came here as Principal is that these children can learn—they will learn. You've got to give it to them. That's my continuing message, although it's not always highly accepted, but it's getting better.

In her new role as principal, Principal Louise spent time planning staff development activities to raise the consciousness level of the teachers about racist teaching practices. According to Principal Louise, "Many teachers refused to openly participate, but that did not stop my mission....However,

I was clear about how we needed to change the rate of achievement for my students—African American students."

In this regard, research suggests that one area of misunderstanding stems from the way in which African Americans and Caucasians experience themselves within the American culture researcher (Scheurich, 1993). Further, racist institutional policies, legal statutes, and oppressive social structures have defined people of color as a group. White skin color relegates Americans into a privileged class; Black skin color determines African Americans' outsider status. Whites, covered by their Whiteness, move fluidly within society and, unaffected by racist policies and laws, possess an individualistic orientation, whereas Blacks are grossly affected by such policies.

Many theoretical formulations of successful leadership nourish the development of an individualistic style. In schools, the competitive American culture promotes and cherishes the individualistic style for academic success. This notion of individuality clashes with the African American cultural group dynamic of racial uplift and equal opportunity and access in education. Being and becoming number one pales in comparison and importance when juxtaposed against other issues within the African American community. It is within this dichotomous environment that African American women must carve out their place. Principal Louise's story supports this claim. In her case, she shared how the preceding principal tried to maintain the status quo, which made things worse. She further indicated how she almost made that mistake. Consequently, Principal Louise was placed in her school as part of her district's plan to provide competent leaders in low-performing schools while diversifying the leadership in response to the rapidly transforming demographics in the school system.

After being named principal of a large, inner-city school in 2009, Principal Louise was astonished about the opportunity to improve a school in her community. Entering with a vision for improvement, Principal Louise described why she accepted the position of principal at a high school with a history of student failure and district neglect. One of her ardent philosophical beliefs is that "I will always work in a community where I live." Working hard, she tried to turn around the tide of indifference and despair. She shared:

> The school was looking for a leader. There was a feeling of hopelessness and helplessness at that school. There was a high turnover of principals for some time. The school was one of the lowest performing schools in the district and the challenge was to turn it around. The entire school was considered at risk and it was located in a high poverty area. The building was in poor condition. When I started, there were eight teaching vacancies to fill before school began. It was a challenge. But I knew I could turn things around. I knew that one component of my leadership was change for the sake of school improvement.

In this regard, Principal Thelma shared that she was also located in one of the lowest-performing schools in the districts. She indicated that when she was asked to take on this new role, she shared with central administration, "I don't mind being asked to do things if I am being supported." Accordingly, she said:

> For consequent years, Principal Thelma did her best to use her clout, charisma, servant leadership style, and community connections to restructure the school instructionally, organizationally, and fiscally.

Working long hours and building new programs within the schools, while trying to maintain a stable staff in the school, seemed like an overwhelming task. Nevertheless, these two women expected that they could do the job. This case in point speaks to what is referred to as the "messiah status"—the ability to make change despite the odds (Hill & Ragland, 1995). In recalling her fierce determination to overhaul the failing school, Principal Thelma's voice reflected the unmistakable sound of defeat.

Theme 3—Specifically Focusing on Strategies to Raise Student Achievement

Turnarounds are one of the only proven strategies for quickly achieving success in low-performing schools (Duke, 2009). Regarding goals focused on student learning, both principals received follow-up and support on mentoring activities from their individual mentors. More evidence for adequate time for learning, integration, and reflection was found at both schools. Each Thursday, students were released early from school so that new principals could engage in professional development and dialogue activities, according to Principal Thelma and Principal Louise. These sessions were structured and organized by central administration. Further, to support the effective implementation of school improvement and provide school leaders with leadership and instructional expertise, and better capacity, Principal Thelma and Principal Louise were provided with bi-weekly structured activities around capacity building. Principal Louise exclaimed: "I don't mind being required to do more if I am being supported."

Both principals maintained a different level of investment in their schools and themselves as African American women principals. Principal Louise further described the difference relative to prior reform efforts in the following manner:

"I feel more supported now than ever. In my first year, I felt more out there on my own, left to my own devices, even though I had a support team. I thought I was grasping at straws and trying to figure it all out. I feel 110% more supported now."

Referred to as "getting the big yes" in the turnaround literature (Hassel & Hassel, 2009, p. 22), providing support to principals and altering policies that may impede school turnaround efforts are critical to effective turnaround initiative. One African American female principal in that study indicated:

As it relates to this particular urban district, the sentiments regarding district investment and support reflect a paradigm shift for the central office. Rather than functioning as a bureaucratic organization charged with procedures and compliance as was the case previously, there is seemingly a concerted effort in working to create the right conditions for all principals in turnaround schools to succeed.

That said, many factors contribute to poor performance. However, the key means of improving performance is professional development and the commitment by central administration of principals in turnaround initiatives, ensuring that students are consistently provided high-quality instruction. Principal Thelma noted, "Since then I have learned to focus on instruction and getting into classrooms....I have reflected on the prioritization of student learning for the purpose of achievement." On this same point, both principals maintain that there has been a culture shift in the district as a result of enhanced mentoring support—"namely, teacher behavior used to be more teacher centered, making sure they [the teachers] were happy versus what is best for the students."

Theme 4—Mentoring African American Women Principals to Diversify School Leadership

Indeed, 50 years after *Brown*, Orfield and Lee (2004) reported that K–12 schooling in the United States has experienced a "substantial slippage toward segregation in most of the states that were highly desegregated in 1991" (p. 2). Orfield and Lee also noted that

the vast majority of intensely segregated minority schools face conditions of concentrated poverty, which are powerfully related to unequal educational opportunity. Students in segregated minority schools face conditions that students in segregated white schools seldom experience." (p. 2)

Therefore, African Americans must establish the agenda for the education of their children. This agenda must include increasing the number of African American teachers, principals, and Superintendents who interact with, nurture, guide, and protect African American children (Tillman, 2007). In this regard, Principal Thelma shared in her experience that she modeled this notion in as a holistic approach to encouraging her environment:

> I demanded much from my teachers, and I demanded much from myself. That is the only way you can get people to follow you. They have to know that you are working just as hard as they are.... It's all about the care and development of our children, our future.

The African American woman principal in Dillard's (1995) study viewed caring for children as "a lifelong responsibility" (p. 552) and, thus, behaved (like Principal Thelma) based on the belief that she needed to change the system to work on behalf of the students.

To add, Mills (1998) acknowledged the dual positions that African American women confront because of the "devastating interaction of the double hegemony" (p. 16). African American women deal with sexist and racist norms that value women for their bodies and their beauty and seldom for their minds or thoughts. Mills further added that "African-American women feel the tugs of both sisterhood and African-Americanness, and...adjudicating between them in times of conflict can be a difficult task indeed" (p. 17). Although Principal Thelma and Principal Louise understood how racist practices functioned to constrain and maintain their career advancement, they did not discuss in the interviews the sexist discriminatory practices operating in their workplace.

DISCUSSION AND CONCLUSION

The purpose of this study was to illuminate commonalities of African American principals as leaders of urban school environments and to understand how they make sense of their leadership roles. The narratives that emerged during the interviews provided perspective and a voice that is absent in the education literature, that which pertains to the dual role of African American women as leaders and social agents answering the call to action to improve, and thus transform, urban schools and communities therein. The findings summarize the similarities in the lived experiences of the two African American women principals with regard to the overarching research inquiry specific to mentoring activities that were acclaimed as most salient to their leadership success and school turnaround.

As the narratives unfolded, I found myself, as an African American woman and as a researcher on issues by and about African American women educational leaders, inclined to identify with "truth" in each shared experience. What was found was that there were multiple truths from both women. Some of their experiences overlapped in theme and delineation, and similar to Dillard's (1995) findings, the women participants certainly incorporated culture and community contexts into their leadership priorities and strategies. However, I did not get a sense from the participants of how the community was embracing (or not) the turnaround initiative. Further study is warranted to learn of instances of responsiveness from the communities of African American women leaders of urban schools transforming schools thus communities.

Accordingly, African American women principals in urban schools develop strength, identity, and a sense of community consciousness that drives them to work in low-performing schools (Bloom & Erlandson, 2003). The participants of this study had developed similar identities as leaders and social agents who operated from their own experiences, past and present, of forces of marginalization in schools and communities that led them to serve urban school communities. Coincidentally, that force of marginalization in a culture that expects centeredness and assimilation produced women who have followed their dreams and lived up to visions of excellence for them. These women were not deterred by the political exigencies of the dominant culture. Both principals indicated that culture and experiences, with emphasis on mentoring, positively influenced their leadership styles.

As noted in previous research on African American female principals in turnaround schools, there remains a paucity of research. This article focused on African-American female principals' persistence in their positions in relation to the concepts of leadership in turnaround schools. This analysis of the role mentoring of aspiring principals contributes to the scant literature and lack of social justice embedded practices in turnaround school literature that has clouded the importance of the lived experience to our understanding of the imperative to provide technical support, through mentor and coaching measures for more African American principals, especially women who find themselves most often in low-performing schools. This could serve as a model for diversifying leadership and policy in schools.

Given this, the findings of this study have potential implications for leadership preparation and practice for African American women. First, if African American women leading urban schools are experiencing success with nontraditional notions of leadership, how can we explore alternate ways of theorizing and understanding Black feminist thought to construct new interpretations of realities for African American women in education? The framework can be an important lens through which to examine the formation and structure of lived realities for any group of color. More research using standpoint theory to create knowledge construction that is emancipatory, antioppressive, and politically active can add power and dimension to those working within racialized environments. Researching within one's own community may add value to the current scholarship on African American women and other women of color.

Finally, given the powerful influence that self-identity and cultural consciousness (Collins, 1991) are believed to have on the lives of African-Americans as whole, and as demonstrated by the two women principals, researchers should explore methodologies that will permit increasingly sophisticated studies of the meanings and interpretive effects of racism, sexism, and classism in the identity and cultural development of African American women. If the task of politically active scholarship is to counter the European-derived cultural and social perspectives and versions of history associated with White dominance, then using any and all alternative means of deconstruction of this privileged epistemology is required for future scholarship development of researchers.

REFERENCES

Achinstein, P. (2010). *Evidence, explanation, and realism: Essays in philosophy of science.* Oxford University Press.

Achinstein, B., & Ogawa, R. T. (2011a). *Change(d) agents: New teachers of color in urban schools.* New York: Teachers College Press.

Aiken, J. A. (2002). The socialization of new principals: Another perspective on principal retention. *Education Leadership Review, 3*(1), 32–40.

Allen, K., Jacobson, S., & Lomotey, K. (1995). African American women in educational administration: The importance of mentors and sponsors. *Journal of Negro Education,* 409–422.

Alston, J. A. (1999). Climbing hills and mountains: Black females making it to the superintendency. In C. C. Brunner (Ed.), *Sacred dreams: Women and the superintendency* (pp. 79–90). Albany, NY: SUNY Press.

Alston, J. (2000). Missing in action: Where are the African-American female school superintendents? *Urban Education, 35*(5), 525–531.

Anyon, J. (1997). *Ghetto schooling: A political economy of urban educational reform.* Teachers College Press.

Bandura, A. (1977). Self-efficacy: Toward a unifying theory of behavioral change. *Psychological review, 84*(2), 191.

Björk, R. L., & Rinehart, J. (2005). Improving educational leadership: Alternative and conventional approaches. *AERA Division A Newsletter: School Leadership News, 11*(1), 3–5.

Blakemore, J. (1999). *Troubling women: Feminism, leadership, and educational change.* Buckingham, UK: Open University Press.

Bloom, G., Castagna, C., Moir, E., & Warren, B. (2005). *Blended coaching: Skills and strategies to support principal development.* Thousand Oaks, CA: Corwin.

Bloom, C. M., & Erlandson, D. A. (2003). African American women principals in urban schools: Realities, (re)constructions, and resolutions. *Educational Administration Quarterly, 39*(3), 339–369.

Bogdan, R. C., & Biklen, S. K. (1998). Foundations of qualitative research in education. *Qualitative Research in Education: An Introduction to Theory and Methods,* 1–48.

Boris-Schacter, S., & Vonasek, G. (2009). Dear Gayle, Dear Sheryl using e-mail for a principal mentorship. *Phi Delta Kappa, 90*(7), 490–494.

Boyne, G. A. (Ed.). (2006). *Public service performance: Perspectives on measurement and management.* Cambridge University Press.

Brooks, S. M. (2009). A case study of school-community alliances that rebuilt a community. *School Community Journal, 19*(2), 59.

Browne-Ferrigno T., & Muth, R. (2004). Leadership mentoring in clinical practice: Role socialization, professional development and capacity building. *Educational Administration Quarterly, 40*(4), 468–494.

Brunner, C., Grogan, M., & Prince, C. (2003). *The American Association of School Administrators' national study of women superintendents and central office administrators: Early findings.* In American Association of School Administrator's Women's Conference, Washington, DC.

Brunner, C. C., & Peyton-Caire, L. (2000). Seeking representation: Supporting African American female graduate students who aspire to the superintendency. *Urban Education, 31*(5), 532–548.

Carter, S. (2000). *No excuses: Lessons from 21 high-performing, high-poverty schools.* Washington, DC: Heritage Foundation.

Cistone, P. J., & Stevenson, J. M. (2000, August). Perspectives on the urban school principalship. *Education and Urban Society, 32*(4), 435–442.

Collins, P. H. (1991). *African-American feminist thought: Knowledge, consciousness, and the politics of empowerment.* New York, NY: Routledge.

Collins, P. H. (2002). Learning from the outsider within: The sociological significance of African-American feminist thought. In C. S. Turner, A. L. Antonio, M. Garcia, B. V. Laden, A. Nora, & C. Presley (Eds.), *Racial and ethnic diversity in higher education* (pp. 103–126). Boston, MA: Pearson Custom.

Collins, K. W., & Lightsey, O. R., Jr. (2001, August). Racial identity, generalized self-efficacy, and self-esteem: A pilot study of a mediation model for African-American women. *Journal of African-American Psychology, 27*(3), 272–287.

Creswell, J. W. (2009). *Research design: Qualitative, quantitative, and mixed methods.* Thousand Oaks, CA: Sage.

Crow, G. M., & Mathews, L. J. (1998). *Finding one's way: How mentoring can lead to dynamic leadership.* Thousand Oaks, CA: Corwin Press.

Dana Center. (1999). *Hope for urban education: A study of nine high-performing, high-poverty, urban elementary schools.* Austin, TX: University of Texas at Austin, Charles A. Dana Center. Retrieved from http://www.ed.gov/pub/ urbanhope/

Darden. (2011). http://www.darden.edu/uploadedFiles/Centers_of_Excellence/PLE/KeysToSuccess.pdf http://www.darden.virginia.edu/web/Darden-Curry-PLE/UVA-School Turnaround/Components/

Duke, D. L. (Ed.). (2009). *Differentiating school leadership: Facing the challenges of practice.* CA: Sage.

Daresh, J. C. (1986). Support for beginning principals: First handles are highest. *Theory Into Practice, 25,* 168–173.

Daresh, J. C. (1995) Research base on mentoring for educational leaders: what do we know? *Journal of Educational Administration, 33*(5), 7–16.

Daresh, J. C. (2004). *Helping leaders: A practical guide to administrative mentoring* (2nd ed.). Thousand Oaks, CA: Corwin Press.

Daresh, J. C. (2006). *Beginning the principalship: A practical guide for new school leaders.* Thousand Oaks, CA: Corwin Press.

Daresh, J. C., & Playko, M. A. (1990). Mentoring for effective school administration. *Urban Education, 25*(1), 43–53.

Daresh, J. C., & Playko, M. A. (1994). Aspiring and practicing principals' perceptions of critical skills for beginning leaders. *Journal of Educational Administration, 32*(3), 35–45.

Dillard, C. (1995). Leading with her life: An African-American feminist (re)interpretation of leadership for an urban high school principal. *Educational Administration Quarterly, 31*(4), 539–563.

Duke, D. L. (Ed.). (2009). *Differentiating school leadership: Facing the challenges of practice.* CA: Sage.

Elmore, R. F. (2005, June). Accountable leadership. *Educational Forum, (69)*2, 134–142). Taylor & Francis Group.

Ensher, E. A., & Murphy, S. E. (1997). Effects of race, gender, perceived similarity, and contact on mentor relationships. *Journal of Vocational Behavior, 50*(3), 460–481.

Erlandson, D., Harris, E., Skipper, B., & Allen, S. (1993). *Doing naturalistic inquiry: A guide to methods.* Newbury Park, CA: Sage.

Fagenson, E. A. (1989). The mentor advantage: Perceived career/job experiences of protégés versus non-protégés. *Journal of Organizational Behavior, 10*(4), 309–320.

Farkas, S., Johnson, J., Duffett, A., & Foleno, T. (2001). *Trying to stay ahead of the game: Superintendents and principals talk about school leadership.* New York, NY: Public Agenda. Retrieved from http://www.publicagenda.org/files/pdf/ahead_of_the_game.pdf

Fullan, M. (2005). *Leadership and sustainability: System thinkers in action.* Thousand Oaks, CA: Corwin Press.

Glaser, B., Strauss, A., 1967. *The discovery of grounded theory.* Aldine Publishing Company, Hawthorne, NY.

Goodwin, R. H., Cunningham, M. L., & Eagle, T. (2005). The changing role of the secondary principal in the United States: An historical perspective. *Journal of Educational Administration and History, 37*(1), 1–17.

Grissom, J. A., & Harrington, J. R. (2010). Investing in administrator efficacy: An examination of professional development as a tool for enhancing principal effectiveness. *American Journal of Education, 116*(4), 583–612.

Grogan, M. (1999). Equity/equality issues of gender, race and class. *Education Administration Quarterly, 35*(4), 518–536.

Grogan, M., & Brunner, C. C. (2005). Women leading systems: What the latest facts and figures say about women in the superintendency today. *School Administrator, 62*(2), 46.

Guy-Sheftall, B. (Ed.). (1995). *Words of fire: An anthology of African-American feminist thought*. New York: The New Press.

Hakim, C. (2000). *Work-lifestyle choices in the 21st century: Preference theory: Preference theory*. Oxford University Press.

Hall, P. (2008). Building bridges: Strengthening the principal induction process through intentional mentoring. *Phi Delta Kappan*, 449–452.

Hamilton, S. F., & Hamilton, M. A. (1992). Mentoring programs: Promise and paradox. *Phi Delta Kappan, 6*, 546–550.

Hansford, B., & Erlich, L.(2006). The principalship: How significant is mentoring? *Journal of Educational Administration*, 36–52.

Harrison, F. (1995). Writing against the grain: Cultural politics of difference in the work of Alice Walker. In R. Behar & D. Gordon (Eds.), *Women writing culture* (pp. 233–245). Berkeley: University of California Press.

Hassel, E. A., & Hassel, B. C. (2009). The big u-turn: How to bring schools from the brink of failure to stellar success. *Education Next, 9*(1), 21–27. Retrieved from http://educationnext.org/the-big-uturn/

Henry, A. (2001). Looking two ways: Identity, research, and praxis in the Caribbean community. In B. M. Merchant & A. I. Willis (Eds.), *Multiple and intersecting identities in qualitative research* (pp. 61–68). Mahwah, NJ: Lawrence Erlbaum.

Hill, M. S., & Ragland, J. C. (1995). *Women as educational leaders: Opening windows, pushing ceilings*. Thousand Oaks, CA: Corwin Press.

Hobson, A. J. (2003). Student teachers' conceptions and evaluations of 'theory' in initial teacher training (ITT). *Mentoring & Tutoring, 11*(3), 245–261.

Hobson, A., & Phenis-Bourke, N. (2005). Head to head: A systematic review of the research evidence on mentoring new head teachers. *School Leadership and Management*, 25–42.

Jackson, B. L. (1999). Getting inside history—against all odds: African-American women school superintendents. In C. C. Brunner (Ed.), *Sacred dreams: Women and the superintendency*. Albany, NY: State University of New York Press.

Johnson, L. (2007). Rethinking successful school leadership in challenging U.S. schools: Culturally responsive practices in school-community relationships. *International Studies in Educational Administration (Commonwealth Council for Educational Administration & Management (CCEAM)), 35*(3), 49–57. Retrieved from http://search.ebscohost.com/login.aspx?direct=true&AuthType=ip,url,cookie,uid&db=a9h&AN=32512777&site=ehost-live&scope=site

Kozol, J.(1991). *Savage inequalities: Children in America's schools*. Crown Publishers, New York.

Kram, K. E. (1985). *Mentoring at Work: Developmental relationships in organizational life*. Glenview, IL: Scott Foresman.

Leithwood, K., & Steinbach, R. (1995). *Expert problem solving: Evidence from school and district leaders*. SUNY Press.

Levinson, D. J., Darrow, C. N., Klein, E. B., Levinson, M. H. & McKee, B. (1978). *The seasons of a man's life*. New York: Knopf.

Lincoln, Y. S., & Guba, E. G. (1985). *Naturalistic inquiry*. Beverly Hills, CA: Sage.

Lomotey, K. (1989). *African-American principals: School leadership and success: Contributions in Afro-American and African studies* (No. 124). New York, NY: Greenwood.

Marshall, C., & Rossman, G. B. (1999). *Designing qualitative research* (3rd ed.). Thousand Oaks, CA: Sage.

Marzano, R., Waters, T., & McNulty, B. (2005). *School leadership that works: From research to results.* Alexandria, VA: McREL.

McCreary-King, K. (1992). Mentoring principals: Who does it and when? *National Association of Secondary School Principals, 76,* 116–120

McGough, D. (2003). Leaders as learners: An inquiry into the formation and transformation of principals' professional perspectives. *Educational Evaluation and Policy Analysis, 25*(4), 449–471.

Mendez-Morse, S. (2004). Constructing mentors: Latina educational leaders' role models and mentors. *Educational Administration Quarterly, 40*(4), 561–590.

Merriam, S. (2009). *Qualitative research: A guide to design and implementation.* San Francisco, CA: Jossey-Bass.

Miles, M. B., & Huberman, A. M. (1994). *Qualitative data analysis.* Thousand Oaks, CA: Sage.

Mills, C. W. (1998). *Blackness visible: Essays on philosophy and race.* Cornell University Press.

Milstein, M., Bobroff, B. M., & Restine, L. N. (1990). Rethinking the clinical aspects in administrative preparation: From theory to practice. *Educational leadership in an age of reform.* New York: Longman.

Murphy, J., & Meyers, C. V. (2008). *Turning around failing schools: Leadership lessons from the organizational sciences.* Thousand Oaks, CA: Corwin Press.

Murtadha, K., & Larson, C. (1999, April). *Toward a socially critical, womanist, theory of leadership in urban schools.* Paper presented at the annual meeting of the American Educational research Association, Montreal, Canada.

No Child Left Behind Act of 2001. (2001, December 13). *Title I: Improving the academic achievement of the disadvantaged* [107th Congress, 1st Session]. Washington, DC: George Washington University, National Clearinghouse for Bilingual Education.

No Child Left Behind Act, 20 U.S.C. Sections 6301 et seq. U.S.C. (2002).

Noe, R. A. (1988). An investigation of determinants of successful assigned mentoring relationships. *Personnel Psychology, 41,* 457–479.

Noguera, P. (1996). Confronting the Urban in Urban School Reform. *Urban Review, 28*(1), 1–27.

Orfield, G. & Lee, C. (2004). *Brown at 50: King's dream or Plessy's nightmare?* The Civil Rights Project, Harvard University. Retrieved from www.civilrightsproject.harvard.edu

Patton, M. Q. (2002). *Qualitative research and evaluation methods.* Thousand Oaks, CA: Sage.

Perez, L., Uline, C., Johnson, J., James-Ward, C., & Basom, M. (2011). Foregrounding fieldwork in leadership preparation: The transformative capacity of authentic inquiry. *Educational Administration Quarterly, 47*(1), 217–257.

Peters, A. (2010). Elements of successful mentoring of a female school leader. *Leadership and Policy in Schools,* 108–129.

Petzko, V. (2008). The perceptions of new principals regarding the knowledge and skills important to their success. *NASSP Bulletin, 92*(3), 224–250.

Phillips-Jones, L. (1983). Establishing a formalized mentoring program. *Training and Development Journal, 2,* 38–42.

Pollard, D. S. (1997). Race, gender, and educational leadership: Perspectives from African American principals. *Educational Policy, 11*(3), 353–374.

Portin, B. S. (2000). The changing urban principalship. *Education and urban society, 32*(4), 492–505.

Public Impact. (2008). *School turnarounds: Actions and results.* Lincoln, IL: Center on Innovation and Improvement. Retrieved from http://www.centerii.org/survey/downloads/Turnaround%20Actions%20and%20Results%203%2024%2008%20with%20covers.pdf.

Rayner, S. (2009). Educational diversity and learning leadership: S proposition, some. *Educational Review,* 433–447.

Sanders, N. M., & Kearney, K. M. (2008). *Performance expectations and indicators for education leaders.* Council of Chief School Officers.

Scheurich, J. J. (1993). Toward a White discourse on White racism author(s). *Educational Researcher, 22*(8), 5–10.

Scott, P. B. (1982). Debunking Sapphire: Toward a nonracist, nonsexist social science. In G. T. Hull, P. B. Scott, & B. Smith (Eds.), *But some of us are brave: African-American women's studies* (pp. 85–92). Old Westbury, NY: Feminist Press.

Scribner, S. M., Crow, G. M., Lopez, G. R., & Murtadha, K. (2011). "Successful" principals: A contested notion for superintendents and principals. *Journal of School Leadership, 21,* p. 390–421.

Searby, L. J. (2010). Preparing future principals: Facilitating the development of a mentoring mindset through graduate coursework. *Mentoring & Tutoring: Partnership in Learning, 18*(1), 5–22.

Shakeshaft, C. (1989). *Women in Educational Administration* (Rev. ed.). Newbury Park, California: Sage Publications.

Shakeshaft, C. (1999). The struggle to create a more gender-inclusive profession. *Handbook of research on educational administration, 2,* 99–118.

Shavelson, R. J., & Towne, L. (Eds.). (2002). *Scientific research in education.* National Academies Press.

Sheehy, G. (1976, April 5). The mentor connection: The secret link in the successful woman's life. *New York Magazine,* 33–39.

Strizek, G. A., Pittsonberger, J. L., Riordan, K. E., Lyter, D. M., & Orlofsky, G. F. (2006). *Characteristics of schools, districts, teachers, principals, and school libraries in the United States: 2003–2004 schools and staffing survey.* Washington, DC: National Center for Education Statistics.

Thomas, D. A. (1990). The impact of race on managers' experiences of developmental relationship: An intra-organizational study. *Journal of Organizational Behavior, 11,* 479–492.

Tillman, L. C. (2007). Halls of anger: The (mis)representation of African-American principals in film. In D. Carlson & C. P. Gause (Eds.), *Keeping the promise: Essays in leadership, democracy and education* (vol. 305, pp. 357). New York, NY: Lang Publishing.

U.S. Department of Education (USDOE). (2010a). *A blueprint for reform: The reauthorization of the Elementary and Secondary Education Act.* Washington, DC: Author.

Weingartner, C. J. (2009). *Mentoring for Principals: A Safe, Supportive and Simple Approach.*

Whitley, W., Dougherty, T. W., & Dreher, G. F. (1991). Relationship of career mentoring and socioeconomic origin to managers' and professionals' early career success. *Academy of Management Journal, 34,* 331–351.

Wunsch, M. A. (1994). *Mentoring revisited: Making an impact on individuals and institutions.* San Francisco: Jossey-Bass.

Yirci, R., & Kocabas, I. (2010). The importance of mentoring for school principals. *The Connexions Project,* 1–7.

CHAPTER 10

INTERRUPTING NO MORE

Why Women Leave the Position
of Superintendent

Kerry K. Robinson

ABSTRACT

The life of a female superintendent is a complex one. When sharing stories of their lives, women often emphasize the difficulty of juggling many things at once, including home and family. According to many of these women, they ultimately left the superintendency to regain their lives. Getting back their home lives, their families, and the care of selves that they had neglected during their tenure in the position was the primary reason for exiting the position. Only through sharing their experiences did they begin to realize whether or not they had successfully multitasked as well as they thought they had. The appearance of having things under control despite the struggle of multiple responsibilities was important. Using the stories of women who held the position and left, this chapter explores why women felt the need to exit the superintendency in order to reclaim balance in their lives.

I have always been fascinated by the position of superintendent. When I was a little girl, I remember wondering what it took to be in charge of not

Women Interrupting, Disrupting, and Revolutionizing Educational Policy and Practice, pages 175–191
Copyright © 2014 by Information Age Publishing
All rights of reproduction in any form reserved.

only a school, but also an entire school system. What did that mean? Did the superintendent make every decision that occurred in the district? Did the superintendent get to that position because he (at that time I had only seen male superintendents) had expertise in all of the positions within the system? If there was ever a lack of substitutes, did the superintendent fill in? I knew the superintendent decided when to call a snow day, but did the superintendent ever drive the school bus?

As I grew older and entered the field of education and worked my way from teacher to school-level administrator and then to district-level administrator, I still kept my eye on the superintendency. I came to realize that the idea of a do-it-all superintendent that I held in my youth was quite exaggerated in most cases. In some situations, however, there were superintendents who did seem to be doing more than the average person could handle. In most cases, those superintendents were women. Those women were the superintendents I wanted to learn more about. Those are the women whose stories I wanted to hear. I wanted to know how they were able to "do it all."

When listening to the stories of those women superintendents, they always emphasized the fact that they had tried to juggle a million things at once, including home and family. In fact, when the women left the superintendency, they indicated it was to regain their lives. Getting back their homes, their families, and the care of selves that they had neglected during their tenure in the position was the primary reason for exiting the position. When sharing their experiences, they verbalized whether or not they had actually multitasked as well as they thought they had. Many explained that while the idea of keeping up the appearance of having it all under control was one of their main objectives, they knew that there were aspects of their lives that were unsuccessful. They believed that the only way to bring balance back to those neglected areas was to leave the superintendency. Using the stories of women who held the position and left, this chapter explores why women felt the need to exit in order to reclaim their lives.[1]

CHALLENGES FOR WOMEN IN POSITIONS OF POWER

Women in positions of power often feel the need to prove themselves beyond what is typically expected of their male counterparts. They feel the need to do more and work harder to battle naysayers and to demonstrate they can be successful in their positions (despite being women), especially those positions that are typically held by men (Grogan & Brunner, 2005; Ottino, 2009; Skrla, 2000). Additionally, there is an unnatural expectation for women of being able to keep all parts of their life balanced. According to Hewlett (2002), however, it is impossible for women to "have it all."

Part of the stress that women in district leadership positions face is due to their personal belief systems. For many women educational leaders, not only is there the anxiety associated with the burdens of the challenging and visible position of superintendent, but there is also the pressure of the demands of being a wife and mother and the desire to spend quality time with their children (Smith, 1993). Regardless of marriage and family status, Deem and Ozga (1997) found that women often feel they must portray perfection as well as "all the characteristics of masculine, rational management in order to counteract inappropriate or hostile assumptions about women managers" (p. 35). As one study participant explained:

> People always have their eyes on the superintendent. In my case they were on me even more since I am a woman superintendent. I needed to look like I was cool, calm, and confident in every situation. I couldn't let people know what I was feeling inside because I knew that people were counting on me and looking to be as an example. I didn't want anyone to claim that this proves a woman can't do it if I say I'm stressed out. But I will tell you, I was stressed out!

At some point, according to the women participants, living the adage of "never letting them see you sweat" catches up with them.

WOMEN NAVIGATING THE SUPERINTENDENCY

> A lot of times people forget that superintendents have lives outside of the district. For example, I have very elderly parents that live next door to me. Well, every morning I go over and make sure that they have everything they need for the day before I leave. I give my mother her shot. I put my dad's compression socks on. These things all occur before 7 a.m.... You know, we're people, too, and your staff and the community need to see that human side of you. People need to know that you're a wife, and you're a mom, and a daughter, and a superintendent. You run everything. At the end of my day, I go home and do laundry and I cook. I do all those things. I go to the grocery store and I babysit grandkids. I do all those things. Believe it or not, I'm not just the superintendent.

While a number of the participants admitted they "reluctantly" or "accidentally" went into administration, they chose to continue the trip up the leadership ladder because they believed they could make a difference for students. This passion for children was the driving force behind these women continuing their careers in administration. The women also pointed out that making a difference for students was their primary reason for pursuing an advanced degree. However, no matter their focus at the time (degree, job search, success in a position), these women noted their commitment to put 100% of their effort into what they were doing to achieve better results for students.

When asked to describe themselves, the women used terms like "type A," "workaholic," "driven," "overachiever," and "superwoman." In fact, when I asked these women to go into greater detail about their perceived drive, they provided me with example after example of how high achieving this collective group was. Some of the highlights include facts such as:

- One participant has six degrees
- One participant has two doctorates
- One woman has eight endorsements on her teaching license
- Two of the women completed their doctorates in three years while working full-time

Living this superwoman-like existence was extraordinarily challenging. Some of the women felt that having a perfect family was a part of the super-woman persona. They emphasized that they managed to work, spend quality time with their spouses, and interact with children (or grandchildren) all in the span of a typical day, as it was all part of what was expected of them as women. Other women explained that they needed to reorganize the importance of certain activities (as one participant verbalized):

> This is the way I am. I don't know how to "turn it down a notch." I put all my effort into whatever I'm working on. I know people always talk about how great women are at multitasking, but in my case, I really put my primary focus on my career. I knew I had these other things to do (having a husband, taking care of my kids), but those took more of a backseat to my career. I put all my focus back on them once I left the position.

WHAT THE WOMEN SUPERINTENDENTS LEFT BEHIND

The women in the study explained that family often played a large role in their decisions not only to accept positions, but to leave them as well. Numerous studies on women in administrative positions emphasize the necessity of having to juggle multiple roles in order to perceive success in the position (Brunner & Grogan, 2007; Dana & Bourisaw, 2006; Funk, 2004; Grogan & Brunner, 2005; Lane-Washington & Wilson-Jones, 2010). Loder (2005) found that a great deal of women's stress comes from the struggle of having to be an instructional leader, wife, mother, caretaker, and more.

For the women in my study, ascension to the superintendency caused a forced isolation from some or all aspects of family life. These women shared that decisions of all types were deliberated over within the family. Unfortunately, these decisions often meant having to "give up" aspects of family in order to gain and succeed in the position. This might mean missing family dinners, bedtimes, Saturday soccer games, date nights with spouses, and Sunday church services. Furthermore, it often meant having to live separately from their partners and families for extended periods of time.

For the women in this study, their ages also often played a large part in their decisions to leave the superintendency. A number of the older women in the study had much more "traditional" views of a woman's role in life. They believed that there was the expectation for them to be wives, mothers, and homemakers, and their careers often conflicted with those role expectations. They expressed that they were leaving the superintendency in order to reclaim that "other" part of their lives.

Relationships With Spouses

It is no surprise that the position of superintendent is extraordinarily demanding. Often, this requires the commitment of leaving home early each morning and not returning until late in the evening. Most of these women's spouses understood that this type of schedule came along with the territory of their wives in roles as superintendents. As one woman explained of the demands of the position:

> I was out probably three nights a week. We had a lot of things that were going on there [in the district]. I had a lot of night meetings; I had a lot of committees, a lot of community committees, and review committees, and all this kind of stuff. I was out probably three times a week, sometimes four times a week. My husband used to say to me in the morning, "I'll see you when I see you."

Their schedules became more exaggerated the higher up the administrative ladder they climbed.

Long days were the norm for these women, not the exception. A number of participants spoke of weathering fifteen- or sixteen-hour days for seven days a week while they served as superintendents:

> I left at 6:00 in the morning and I got home at midnight, 1:00 o'clock, 2:00 o'clock. Sometimes the school board meeting would go till 2:00. . . . I remember one night I got home from work and I hadn't eaten, so I got a bagel and I sat down in bed with the bagel and it was 10:00 o'clock and I said, "Oh god this is so great, it's an early night." He said, "Alice, you are sick, 10:00 o'clock at night is not an early night." But for me it was.

However, long days away and seven-day work weeks still proved better than the alternative that many women faced: Living in separate residences from their husbands while serving in the superintendency. Multiple women in the study lived apart from their husbands and families while they were in the position of superintendent. Two of these women lived apart for more than one superintendency. They believed this was the price they had to pay in order to get the position. As one woman explained: "At one time I was a finalist for four different superintendencies in three different states. I told my husband, I don't know where I'll be living, but it won't be here with you. That's the only thing for sure I know right now."

When one of the women attained a superintendency, her husband would often not have the opportunity to move because of his own job constraints. Having multiple households was something that came to be expected with gaining the position for women. This meant that most of their time with their husbands was spent apart:

> By the second year, I had a house in Linville, a house in Plainfield, and we had a beach home. It was like, "Where am I going to be? Who's on first?" It was a crazy deal. It became tougher on the home front, because of our separation. For the eight years I was superintendent, we were separated at least four of them in fact, probably closer to five. I didn't want to be by myself any more.

All of the women used the same phrase when they were discussing the time that they lived apart from their husbands: *commuter marriage*. Not only did they want to talk about their own experiences with commuter marriages, they were quick to bring up the names and situations of other women superintendents who had also experienced commuter marriages. Collectively, this group agreed that this commuter marriage phenomenon had a great effect on the length of tenure for the superintendent.

When spouses lived apart so that they could each have a career, the time the couple was able to spend together revolved around the school division's schedule. These women spent months (and in some cases years) living separate lives from their husbands and described their relationships as "weekend/holiday marriages." Quite a few other women explained that their weekly "dates" with their spouses involved attending high school sporting events.

> We did Friday night football. That was our Friday night date. In Mountainside our schools played one another a lot so I could almost hit all high schools on Friday night because they'd be playing each other so I'd go one quarter, one quarter, one quarter, and one quarter. So I saw everybody in the community in one night.... That was just part of becoming part of the community, and when you're a superintendent you do that.

These weekend "dates" were referenced by quite a few of the women as one way that they were able to make their relationships work. Having these dates out in public, however, meant that it was just another instance where the superintendent was "on" at all times.

While a number of women lived within the constraints of commuter marriages, there were some who were quick to point out that this arrangement was not ideal, especially for young couples:

> Now, that's not the way you can live as a young family and so I'm fully aware that the model I am talking about is not a model that can be copied by younger women. It is simply not. But, the women who came before me in the superintendency, either they had no children, or their children were grown and their husbands were able to follow them to their superintendency, or they were divorced. . . . I can tell you it's a different sort of life.

Young or old, living apart from families and spouses took a toll on women superintendents. Living in a community alone only seemed to increase the "workaholic" nature of the women in this study. These women felt if there was no one to go home to, there was no rush to get home for the night. As one woman shared:

> I spent way more time at the office and I think part of the draw of hiring a person like me even as superintendent is that I didn't have a family to go home to. So I could stay until 8:00, 9:00 at night or 10:00. I didn't have a problem with meetings at night, I was 24/7. So you know, "silly me."

Raising Children (or Not)

The topic of children often came up with the majority of participants in this study. Some of the women explained that they made the choice to not have children because of their career paths. They understood that there would be a conflict between raising children and continuing to climb the administrative ladder to the superintendency. These women explained they needed to address/explain their choice to not have children, as if it was unnatural for a married woman to be childless. One woman shared the story of her initial interview in a community where the subject of children was inquired about early on in the process. She said, "When I walked into that room, they asked me very tough questions, many that were totally inappropriate. 'Why don't you have children?' I was asked that question more than once." Many times, however, childless women were viewed as ideal superintendents by school boards:

> Board members never hesitated in offering, "Oh, she doesn't have children. Of course she can work until three in the morning, because I'm sure her husband can cook something in the microwave himself." It was almost like I was being penalized, because I didn't have to pick someone up at day care,

or I didn't have a child who had strep throat. I felt that there was just a very uneven expectation that people held me to.

The Superintendent and Her Health

While all of the women talked about the positives aspects related to the position of superintendent, they also provided plenty of examples of how stressful the position of superintendent could be. Because of this constant stress, many of these women believed the position had detrimental effects on their health:

> I really would say that I didn't take the time to take care of myself and it took a toll on me. I didn't want to take the time out because I wanted to get done what I needed to get done. When you finally look up from your desk or your computer it is 8 o'clock at night and you say, "Well I'll do that tomorrow," but the same thing happens over and over. The superintendency I have a feeling a lot of people don't really realize the pressure or the full extent of the job that is involved. It's a stressful job and it's a time consuming job.

The long days/nights and the seven-day workweek expectation that they put upon themselves also proved to be too great. One woman explained, "I worked 14 hour days for those years including weekends, and the stress on me was just too much." There were no down times on the job and, because of that, the women believed the only way to stop the speeding roller coaster was to walk away:

> The job sucks too much energy out of you. People suck energy out of you all the time. So, it doesn't mean you become impersonal, it means that you find your own way to keep your energy level up. Yeah, I definitely had the energy sucked out of me. I lost my health, I lost my innovation. I didn't lose my passion, but it wasn't fun anymore. And, I always told myself that if it wasn't fun anymore, I needed to be doing something else or leave.

The Ballooning (or Shrinking) Superintendent

As the women explained, the position of superintendent required long hours behind their desks or behind the wheel of a county-issued automobile. This didn't leave much time in their days for exercise. One woman explained that she, unfortunately, let her main stress reliever (exercise) go while she served in the position. "I didn't exercise as much as I should have. I used to walk before I was in the superintendency, but that had to go by the wayside."

The challenge of healthy eating was also something that was shared in a number of the women's stories. Most of the time, fast and convenient won out over healthy eating options:

I gained a lot of weight that was probably the biggest thing that happened to me. Because I often didn't get dinner and I would get to the McDonald's on the highway between Frazier County and Rural Creek. I'd go through the drive-thru and it would be 9:30 or 10 o'clock at night. I'm getting the Big Mac and the fries. The people at the drive-thru knew me. Many times that would be the only thing I'd really eaten all day and I was eating on the way home. I know it was terrible for me, but it was because of my lifestyle. I gained a lot of weight.

Another superintendent said she spent a lot of time thinking about what had caused her weight problem while she was in the position. She realized that food was her way to deal with what was going on around her.

I had struggled with a bit of a weight problem when I was in the superintendency. You know it's interesting they say people acclimate to the community and the people around you in what they eat and how they act and how they behave, and I fell right into that and I gained about 50 pounds. The way I dealt with things was you know maybe I will make cookies, maybe I will make a cake, maybe I will eat this pie, whatever. When I left the superintendency I think I had realized I am truly an emotional eater, too, because I had kind of eaten my way through the stress of whatever. You realize then, at post-superintendency, that you are just stuffing down all the other stuff. For me it was just a manifestation of what I was trying to deal with, but really didn't know if I could deal with it publically because I had to be the one person that was cool and confident and approachable.

Chronic Health and the Superintendency

Some of the women found that not taking care of themselves over long periods of time manifested in serious health conditions. For some, this became a primary consideration in whether they would be able to continue as superintendents:

My blood pressure would spike when there would be a crisis, but then it would go back down. The doctor was confused and I was confused because most of the time it was quite low but if anything happened it would go so high, it was off the wall. After that happening a few times, he finally put me on two different types of medication to help it. There were other issues as well. I had stomach issues, ulcers. I had flare-ups of so many different things. It takes a toll. I needed to spend time taking care of myself because I certainly wasn't doing a good job of it while I was superintendent.

Poor health proved to not only play into when a woman decided to leave; it often also determined whether or not she would work again:

Well, the position definitely impacts your health. I firmly believe that, and [it was] another reason why I decided that when I retire, I'm finished. I'm not going to continue to put myself through more stress. Part of it was my body and what I felt had been done to my body, the abuse basically.

Many of these women realized that mental and physical hardships were tangible reasons to put the job behind them and try to recapture the lives they had prior to the superintendency.

Lingering Health Issues Post-Superintendency

Even after leaving the position, a few of the participants shared that they were still suffering long-term effects that the job had on their physical bodies. For example, some women continued to take medication years after they left the position. Eileen described the long-term effects of stress in this way:

I was tired of it. I was sick. My body had gone into total, I don't know what. The stress had taken its toll on me, I guess would be the best way to put it. And some of that has still carried over if they say that stress is part of it. I had something called polymyalgia rheumatica, which is... they don't know what causes it, but it's stress, and it's part of the exoskeleton, and it's extremely painful and I went on Prednisone. I didn't come off Prednisone until last year. So, that was four years of taking Prednisone. When I came off Prednisone, I found that my whole body had fibromyalgia. But, the Prednisone has just covered taking care of one. So, the stress had just totally deteriorated my body, my health, and everything else.

In addition to chronic conditions, a few of the women also shared they worked with therapists after leaving the superintendency to help "get over" the position. One woman explained:

I had to go into therapy because I couldn't sleep and I was diagnosed with post-traumatic stress disorder, actually, because I never knew when the attacks were coming. My therapist explained that it was all related to my tenure in the superintendency. I'm glad I left when I did so I can hopefully reverse these effects.

WHAT THE WOMEN RECLAIMED POST-SUPERINTENDENCY

After deciding that they did not want the superintendency to interrupt and disrupt their lives any longer, these women purposefully made a point to get back to doing the things they felt they were not able to do while they were in the position. This meant leaving a large part of their work identities behind and pursuing things they perceived they had failed to do for many years. As one participant shared:

I told my colleagues when I am gone, I am gone.... I think many people have a hard time giving up the identity of the superintendent. You have to get to know yourself again because you are certainly more than your job. Now, I am guilty just like many of the others of putting my whole self into my career for many, many years. I worked nights and days and weekends always. But there is more to you than just your job. You have to see what else is out there. I was in this nonstop pace a long time. But it was time for me to leave and start living a full life again.

Rekindling Family Relationships

One thing that women were interested in doing was reestablishing a stronger connection to family members. While serving in the position, women experienced loneliness and they had the tendency to keep things bottled up inside since there was no one to share with who would understand what they were experiencing:

I never told my kids what went on and I think one of the hardest things is my husband wasn't there to let me vent since we were living apart and that became very difficult. . . . This made me really lonely. I was lonely to begin with, because I was in a place where I didn't have any friends. I only had working colleagues and associations. But then I didn't have anyone to share my day with. The more I was longing for simple daily conversations with my family I knew it was time to go.

Spending more time with their spouses also proved to be a strong desire for leaving the position. As one woman explained:

Most male superintendents have wives that stay home. They don't have careers. I think there is something to be said for that. I know when I was superintendent there were many times I wished I had a stay-at-home wife. Now some females do have a spouse that is retired and he can help keep the home fires because as a superintendent you don't have time to focus on the home fires. Once I retired, I was able to devote the time to being an equal partner in our marriage. Before then, I know my husband needed to accept the fact that I couldn't devote 100 percent of myself to us.

Paying Back My Husband

While a number of women shared how they were looking forward to spending time with their spouses, these stories often closely resembled guilt-ridden narratives of regret. For women who retired from the position, they explained it was often to "pay him back" (their husbands) for all of the sacrifices they made during their superintendencies. As Gwen explained her retirement life:

I am enjoying my retirement. It's very happy. When we talk about what we're going to be doing, well I don't take lightly the fact that he gave up a lot. He did not pursue a lot of his interests because of my career. So now it's sort of, "What you want to do? I'm ready to go, whatever." I always want to check with him first because I know I'm like 30 years in debt.

It appeared that the idea of retirement was thought about much more often when a woman's spouse had already retired. There was a pressure to retire so that the couple could start a new chapter in their lives and begin doing more things together:

So, I'd been thinking about retiring. I would say in the last couple of years I was noticing that I wasn't quite as ready to jump up and run anywhere like I previously had been doing. Also, my husband was retired and he kept saying that he wanted to travel more. I was interested in traveling as well, but I was also intrigued about having time to just not be doing anything, or just new things.

Retiring to spend time together was sometimes the ultimate race against the clock for these women. Olivia explained that her husband was the sole reason for her retirement and departure from the superintendency:

When I retired I was 61 not quite 62—so see I could have worked till I was 65 easily, my health was good [and] I could have worked. I still had the support from my board. . . . My husband was a fair number of years older than I and I really wanted us to have a period in our lives, another chapter in our life that I was—I think was perceptive enough that that chapter wasn't going to be but "so long." And he was not—he wasn't really ill, but he had some things wrong with him and I just had a feeling. . . .

But I always knew that my family was my top responsibility and I wanted to spend some time with my husband because when I was superintendent I slept at home and that was about it. I didn't know how to do the superintendency any other way. I didn't spend very much time at home. I was rarely ever at home. . . . So I did want that time with my husband . . . and so we spent, before he died we had almost eight years, which I value and treasure. So that's why I left. I didn't leave because I didn't like it anymore. I didn't leave because I was tired of the politics of it all. I didn't leave because I didn't want to work so hard. My overriding reason for leaving was that I just felt that if I were going to have some times together and good memories that I needed to separate from that.

Grandchildren

For many of the women who felt they missed out on opportunities with their children, they were determined not to make the same mistakes with their grandchildren. The arrival of grandchildren provided the opportunity to be more involved with their families. One woman shared the differences her grandchildren will experience:

I have two sons and the older son just had a baby. While I was superintendent, with my schedule I was lucky if I got to see him [my grandson] every 2 or 3 weeks because remember, it's not only the time you put in at the office, but from the time you get home and grab a bite to eat then you're back at it again until 12 or one clock in the morning and then you try to sleep and it's still on your mind. It's so, so much going on and so many decisions to make. One day my son said, "Mom, you know Craig (Craig is my grandson) he's going to be grown up before you know it" and then he indicated to me that he resented, well not resented really, but he would have liked for me to have spent more time with him too as he was growing up. This had a profound effect on my decision to leave. I realized I didn't want to miss what was going on with my grandson and while I couldn't get back those past years with my son, I was going to be involved with him and his family now.

These women felt compelled to reestablish this part of their lives. Family took on a more central role than it had while they were in the position of superintendent. The women took the opportunity of having grandchildren to try and make up for time lost with their own children.

"Having a Life"

All of the time focused on the position of superintendent made for extremely long days, weeks, and months over a period of years. This particular schedule of always "being the superintendent" was mentioned as a major consideration in leaving. The women longed for days where they could get back to a sense of normalcy:

I think when I left the superintendency, my husband and I saw six movies in the theater in a month. I don't think I saw six movies during the entire tenure of my superintendency, and that includes watching them at home on cable. It was nice that my husband and I would have the chance to just do things together when we wanted.

One of the areas that often emerged when talking about "having a life" was having the time to travel. While the women all had vacation time while they were in their positions, there was never an opportunity to really leave the position behind when they went away. With the prevalence of cell phones and laptops, a superintendent was always easily within reach. This was one of the first adjustments they made after leaving their positions: realizing their time was once again their own:

Immediately after I retired we went to Florida for two months. If we had not done that, I would probably still be working right now because it took me a long time to relax. I sat there thinking, I need to be on the phone, I need to be in a meeting, I need to be on my computer, I was edgy. Then I realized that I really didn't HAVE to be doing any of those things anymore. I could sleep late! I could do whatever I wanted, WHENEVER I wanted!

The adjustment of having time to do "whatever" was another conversation that occurred many times throughout the women's stories. The challenge was to recapture all of the opportunities that had been missed while they were superintendents. In a number of cases, this meant having the chance to read for pleasure again. As one woman commented:

So now that I'm retired, I do a lot of things that I never had time to do. One thing is reading. I love reading books but I was always so driven to stay current. I was reading any research I could get my hands on to make sure we were always at the forefront. I didn't have time to read the bestsellers, unless they were related to work, the leadership books; I read the leadership bestsellers. And now I can read for pleasure. I don't have to worry about "proper books." In fact, I can go to a movie or go to a museum when I want. I can finally do all the things that I didn't have time to do when I was in that position. It might not seem like much, but it is really a big deal.

In most cases when describing their new lives, the women overemphasized just how different it is now that they are no longer following the breakneck schedule of the superintendency:

I wanted to have time to play tennis and visit with friends. Let me clarify, when I said not do anything, I meant work. I knew I would fill my days with other activities, but they would not be work. I would be doing things that I wanted to do but never had time to do while I was working. I mean there are so many cultural events that go on in the middle of the week that I could never go to because I had a meeting or an event at a school or a major report due.

Reestablishing Health

In the words of one of the participants,

Well, the position definitely impacts your health. I firmly believe that, and another reason why I decided that when I retire, I'm finished. I'm not going to continue to put myself through more stress. Part of it was my body and what I felt had been done to my body, the abuse basically. I have to say that health really did contribute to my decision to not only retire, but to not work again after I had retired. I needed to try and repair myself. I needed to spend time taking care of myself because I certainly wasn't doing a good job of it while I was superintendent.

When speaking of their overall well-being, a number of the women approached their health as trying to reverse the damage they had done while they were in the position. It was finally the time to focus on their selves and make good health a priority. As one woman explained:

> It wasn't till after I left that I took the time to let that telephone cord that I had become completely unwind and just get better. That's when I decided I would reclaim my health. By taking the time and focusing on myself and not on the 4,000 students and 510 employees that I spent so much time focused on previously, I lost 80 pounds and finally went back to being me again.

DO WOMEN REALLY HAVE TO LEAVE?

There has been a great deal written on the topic of women administrators and work–life balance (Byington, 2010; Chávez, 2012; Loder, 2005; Olesnie-wicz, 2012). Often, these studies attempt to identify societal constraints and to address gender stereotypes while identifying and providing strategies for success and support systems for women. While some research finds that societal pressures compel women to make choices to fill more domestic roles (Gordon & Galloway, 2008; Vasquez-Guignard, 2010), often, it is the expectations that a woman puts on herself that cause the greatest challenge. In fact, many women do not feel capable of truly balancing home and work, and ultimately decide to choose one or the other to be successful. The women in this study voiced the challenge of trying to be successful superintendents at the same time they enjoyed the other aspects of their lives. Consequently, a number of these superintendents felt they had to interrupt their personal lives in order to enact the position in the way they felt was needed. One way to address the unequal balance is to reconceptualize the position of superintendent. This means the position must not be conceptualized around male norms. It is imperative that the experiences, successes, and challenges of both men and women in the superintendency are included in the literature so that reconceptualization can occur.

> Currently the superintendent is mostly described as a CEO, a business metaphor that doesn't necessarily evoke images of social change. Team leader, movement leader, pastor, mother, and human rights advocate are all descriptions that ring of change, much more so than does CEO. Translating the work of leadership and administration into the work of change is likely to appeal to women. This is where meaning-making is most likely to occur. (Grogan & Shakeshaft, 2011, p. 91)

While visions of the position of superintendent undergo transformation, so must the expectation of what occurs outside of the position. A new model for work–life balance in leadership is called for, particularly for the health of women. Instead of the "double whammy of impossible expectations" (Spar, 2012, p. 38), women need to have access to support systems and a sense of collaboration and shared responsibilities in both home and work environments.

NOTE

1. The findings in this chapter are part of a large study on women who left the position of superintendent (see Robinson, 2013). This interview study included twenty women who departed the position of superintendent in a southern state. In some cases, the women went on to other superintendencies. However, in most cases, the women in this study left the position altogether.

REFERENCES

Brunner, C. C., & Grogan, M. (2007). *Women leading school systems: Uncommon roads to fulfillment.* Lanham, MD: Rowman & Littlefield.

Byington, M. K. (2010). *Principal balance: Life role balance among women in secondary school administration.* Unpublished doctoral dissertation, University of Nebraska, Lincoln. Retrieved from http://digitalcommons.unl.edu/dissertations/AAI3428254

Chávez, V. (2012). *!Si se puede! How Latina principals successfully balance work and family life.* Unpublished doctoral dissertation, University of Southern California, Los Angeles. Retrieved from http://digitallibrary.usc.edu/cdm/ref/collection/p15799coll3/id/15765

Dana, J. A., & Bourisaw, D. M. (2006). *Women in the superintendency: Discarded leadership.* Lanham, MD: Rowman & Littlefield Education.

Deem, R., & Ozga, J. (1997) Women managing for diversity in a post modern world. In C. Marshall (Ed.), *Feminist Critical Policy Analysis: A perspective from post secondary education* (pp. 25–40). New York, NY: Falmer.

Funk, C. (2004). Outstanding female superintendents: Profiles in leadership. *Advancing Women in Leadership Journal, 16.* Retrieved from http://www.advancingwomen.com/awl/spring2004/FUNK.html

Gordon, S. P., & Galloway, H. (2008, October). *Barriers faced by women: A study of female superintendents.* Paper presented at the Annual Meeting of the University Council for Educational Administration, Orlando, FL.

Grogan, M., & Brunner, C. C. (2005). Women superintendents and role conception: (Un)Troubling the norms. In L. Björk & T. J. Kowalski (Eds.), *The contemporary superintendent: Preparation, practice, and development.* Thousand Oaks, CA: Corwin Press.

Grogan, M., & Shakeshaft, C. (2011). *Women and educational leadership.* San Francisco, CA: Jossey-Bass.

Hewlett, S. A. (2002). Executive women and the myth of having it all. *Harvard Business Review, 80*(4), 66–73.

Lane-Washington, L., & Wilson-Jones, L. (2010). Women superintendents: Challenges, barriers and experiences as senior level leaders. *National Forum of Educational Administration and Supervision Journal, 27*(4), 1–6.

Loder, T. L. (2005). Women administrators negotiate work–family conflicts in changing times: An intergenerational perspective. *Educational Administration Quarterly, 41*(5), 741–776.

Olesniewicz, J. (2012). *Balancing work and family: How female superintendents succeed at work and home.* Unpublished doctoral dissertation, University of Southern California, Los Angeles. Retrieved from http://digitallibrary.usc.edu/cdm/ref/collection/p15799coll3/id/16039

Ottino, K. L. (2009). Diminished aspiration: Women central office administrators and the superintendency. Unpublished doctoral dissertation, University of Minnesota, United States – Minnesota. Retrieved from http://conservancy.umn.edu/bitstream/50960/1/Ottino_umn_0130E_10281.pdf

Robinson, K. (2013). *The career path of the female superintendent: Why she leaves.* (PhD Dissertation, Virginia Commonwealth University—Virginia). Retrieved from https://digarchive.library.vcu.edu/handle/10156/4138

Skrla, L. (2000). The social constructional of gender in the superintendency. *Journal of Education Policy, 15,* 293–316.

Smith, V. (1993). Flexibility in work and employment: The impact on women. *Research in the Sociology of Organizations, 11,* 195–216.

Spar, D. (2012, October 1). American women have it wrong. *Newsweek, 160*(14–15), 38–48.

Vasquez-Guignard, S. J. (2010). *Latina university professors: Insights into the journeys of those who strive to leadership within academia.* Doctoral dissertation. Retrieved from ProQuest Digital Dissertations. (UMI 3432923)

CHAPTER 11

COLLABORATIVE FEMINISM AT WORK

Networking for Success

Whitney Sherman Newcomb

ABSTRACT

Developing successful careers in universities for women often means negotiating conflicts that arise due to women's minority status. The relationships that women faculty form with other women in the academy may be of particular importance to identity construction, developing a research agenda and effective research strategies, and overcoming feelings of isolation. The purpose of this project was to identify narratives of women who have experienced success in the academy in departments of educational leadership through collaborative relationships with other women faculty. Individual standpoints were collected of the lived experiences of these women. Themes were developed during data analysis unique to this particular group of women and included the following: double jeopardy—being a woman and identifying as a feminist; empowerment through knowledge; social webbing; drawbacks; and paying it forward through activism.

Women Interrupting, Disrupting, and Revolutionizing Educational Policy and Practice, pages 193–211

Though research supports the notion that leadership based on women's ways of knowing can facilitate more inclusive schooling environments (Irby & Brown, 2002), faculty preparing leaders for the K–12 setting are predominantly male. In 2003–2004, although women received 47% of PhDs, they accounted for only 35% of tenured or tenure-track faculty nationwide (NCES, 2005) and were most well-represented at community colleges and disproportionately represented at lower ranks. While full-time non-tenure-track positions are being filled in disproportionate numbers by women (Harper, Baldwin, Gansneder, & Chronister, 2001), only 26% of full professors are women (AAUP, 2001). Women are 58 percent of instructors, 54 percent of lecturers, and hold 51 percent of unranked positions. The percentage of women with tenure fell from 1998 to 2007 (Marcus, 2007). Furthermore, pay equity remains an unresolved concern in academe (Curtis, 2004; Porter, Toutkoushian, & Moore, 2008). U.S. national reports of average faculty salaries indicate that the gender pay gap persists across all ranks (AAUW, 2007). While women have made advances, literature indicates that much work is left to be done toward the realization of gender equity in university settings.

THE WORK ENVIRONMENT FOR WOMEN FACULTY

According to Dickens and Sagaria (1997), developing thriving careers in universities for women often means negotiating conflicts that arise due to women's minority status. Universities have little understanding of the challenges that women face (Ward & Wolf-Wendel, 2004). Riger, Stokes, Raja, and Sullivan (1997) reported that departments with fewer women are seen as more hostile and chilly environments. Their work was based on interviews with 20 women faculty about informal socializing, mentoring, sexist attitudes and comments, professional isolation, remediation policies and practices, and physical safety to assess the perception of climate for female faculty. Data from the interviews with women were used to develop a survey instrument that measured a larger number of both male and female faculty perceptions. Women perceived their work environments as "chillier" than men and scored significantly lower than men on the subscales developed from the interviews categories described above. Similarly, Acker and Feuerverger (1996) interviewed women faculty members of education and found that they reported working excessively hard in comparison to their male colleagues, taking responsibility for supporting both colleagues and students, being "good department citizens," and taking greater responsibility for the nurturing and housekeeping side of academic life.

Stokes, Riger, and Sullivan (1995) identified such barriers to women in the work setting as dual standards and opportunities, discriminatory attitudes and behaviors, and the struggle of balancing work and personal responsibilities.

In regard to dual standards and opportunities, they found that though functionally irrelevant, gender often produces differences in opportunities for mentoring and rewards between male and female faculty. Junior women have difficulty finding mentors because senior men find them riskier than junior males or are uncomfortable mentoring women. In regard to discrimination, the extent of sexist attitudes and comments ranged from subtle to blatant, sometimes resulting in the greater report of women being harassed than men (typically by someone holding a higher academic rank). Furthermore, in regard to work–life balance, although many universities have adopted family-friendly policies (i.e., parental leave, stopping of the tenure clock for new parents), the ease with which women are able to take advantage of these policies depends on one's department head and colleagues, who are sometimes unsupportive when home conflicts with professional demands. It is women who report the work–life balance as a struggle because they still retain the status of primary caregivers for childrearing. Central to Stokes et al.'s (1995) study, and seminal to the development of the one reported here, was their identification of the lack of informal socializing/networks for women that denies and cuts them off from resources and information vital for promotion (see also Sherman, 2005). Because of this, little scholarship exists on how women mobilize themselves and one another and whether or not they network to combat sexist practices (Hart, 2008).

The relationships that women faculty form with other women in the academy may be of particular importance to identity construction, developing a research agenda and effective research strategies, and overcoming feelings of isolation. Though evidence exists that formal networks for women have been powerful in the past, they are currently in decline due to lack of support from both university and local school contexts (Coleman, 2010). Studies of collaborations between women at research institutions who share a gender consciousness and similar research interests are limited but have the potential for highlighting women's ways of combating their exclusion from traditional mentoring and networking. The purpose of this project was to identify narratives of women who have experienced or are experiencing success in the academy in departments of educational leadership through collaborative relationships with other women faculty. It seems only logical to believe that increasing the number of successful women in university departments of educational leadership through collaborative mentoring and networking might lead to an increased number of women graduate students and leaders in K–12 education in the United States and worldwide. Mentorship provides women graduate students additional capital for success (Mansfield, Welton, Lee, & Young, 2010) and has proven successful for the attainment of leadership positions as well (Sherman, 2005; Sherman, Beaty, Crum, & Peters, 2010; Sherman, Munoz, & Pankake, 2008; Sherman & Wrushen, 2009).

MENTORING, COLLABORATION, AND NETWORKING

While Moore and Sagaria (1991) provided insights into women's isolation from male networks and positions of power, others have demonstrated women's success through caring and collaborative networking with one another (Belenky, Clinchy, Goldberger, & Tarule, 1986; Coleman & Rippin, 2000; McNae, 2010; Noddings, 1986; Tannen, 2001). This is largely due to women's gender socialization being focused on building and maintaining relationships (Gilligan, 1982). According to Dickens and Sagaria (1997), "The values and relationships that have long been associated with women in Western culture—nurturance, reciprocity, intimacy, mutuality, and care and concern for others—appear repeatedly both implicitly and explicitly in the literature on collaboration" (p. 82).

McNae (2010) demonstrated that girls and young women benefit from co-construction and shared leadership activities while developing their sense of self. Additionally, Shapira, Ara, and Asaiza (2010) found that women principals of Arab schools in Israel were successful in a culture where women leaders are not the norm, due to their reliance on networking between themselves and with their surrounding school communities. According to Gilligan, traditional gender socialization encourages women to seek out horizontal connections rather than vertical connections with others. This has been problematic for women in the work setting because while women are more comfortable with and seek out relational connections, hierarchical structures are the norm (Tannen, 2001).

Mentoring as a practice has traditionally been enacted as unidirectional and hierarchical (Tannen, 2001) as it has involved giving (imparting knowledge to a neophyte) rather than receiving and modeling best practice. In traditional didactic mentoring relationships, an organizational hierarchy exists that scaffolds men's gender-role socialization (Tannen, 2001). However, women are often not successful with this model of mentoring because what comes more naturally to them is akin to a webbing model where more than one individual is networked relationally (Tannen, 2001). At the very least, women are not successful with the didactic model because they are not often "tapped" to be mentored (Sherman, 2005).

Limbert (1995) studied two models of mentoring between women faculty members: mentoring between a veteran and junior faculty member and a peer mentoring model between women in the university setting. Limitations to the first model—too few veteran women to serve as mentors and veteran women who have not been allowed into male networks and thus have limited power—make the second more appealing and natural to women due to gender socialization. Limitations to the first model also occur in K–12 schooling in the United States (Sherman, 2005; Sherman et al., 2008; Sherman, & Wrushen, 2009). Advantages to the second model include opportunities to merge and exchange multiple networks between members to build upon the original network and less of a tendency to become overly dependent on a single person.

Appley and Winder (1977) identified a theory of collaboration that runs counter to traditional narratives of competition based on three characteristics: Individuals in groups share mutual aspirations and common conceptual frameworks; interactions between individuals are characterized by concepts of fairness; and common conceptualizations lead to individual's consciousness of motives and caring toward others and a commitment to work with others as a matter of choice. It is upon the above premise of collaboration that the current study was founded.

METHODOLOGY

I developed a qualitative study based upon a purposeful sample of tenure-track/tenured women faculty in departments of educational leadership in the United States. This report focuses on one group of women from this sample in particular. This group of women consisted of veteran tenured faculty, tenure-track faculty who were several years into their positions, tenure-track faculty new to their positions, and a doctoral student. Ages ranged from 30 to 70 years of age and ethnicities were either White or Hispanic. Participants represented four institutions of higher education across two states.

These women met to collaborate on writing and research on a regular basis for approximately two years. The group was initiated by a mentor and mentee who had made contacts with several other women with similar research interests at annual research conferences. They met together for long weekends at one another's houses, and expenses were shared and split evenly between all members so that no one person had a greater burden in regard to travel or food/accommodation expenses. An agenda was established for each meeting and presentations and publications planned together. Sometimes the group worked together as a whole, and other times, two or three members of the group broke off to work on projects together in smaller groups. The group met approximately five times outside of getting together at annual research conferences over a two-year span. The collaborative is no longer formally active due to the women participants' schedules becoming more complicated, but the women continue to work together outside of the formal collaborative and remain in touch with one another for support.

Individual standpoints were collected of the lived experiences of these women, upon which qualitative inquiry is founded (Denzin & Lincoln, 1994). Research questions included: How do women faculty experience success in the academy? and How and why do women collaborate with other women faculty? For the larger project, I utilized the "snowballing" approach

(McMillan & Schumacher, 2001) to sampling by contacting women faculty known to be engaged in collaborative professional relationships with other women and letting the rest of the sample evolve by having women who were interviewed recommend other women. The group of women for this report was a subset of the larger group of women with whom I formally collaborated for two years (and, thus, my perspective is included as a participant).

Data analysis was conducted throughout data collection. I followed Mc-Cracken's (1988) four-step description of the one long interview beginning with a review of the literature combined with researcher self-examination, followed by consideration of possible interpretive paradigms, followed by the development of a questionnaire, and concluding with interviews conducted simultaneously with data analysis to allow for the emergence of categories and relationships in relation to what the literature says about women leaders.

The five women faculty who were engaged in the two-year long collaborative relationship were interviewed in individual sessions lasting approximately 60–90 minutes in a standardized, open-ended manner to allow for freedom in response (Patton, 1990) and to curb variation (Rossman & Rallis, 1998). I was interviewed by a colleague so that my perspective as an active member of the group could also be included (and I was interviewed first so that other participants' responses would not influence my own since I conducted the rest of the interviews). Interview questions were developed based on Rayle, Bordes, Zapata, Arrendondo, Rutter, and Howard's (2006) interview protocol including open-ended questions in categories such as the culture of the research university, collaboration, networking, and feminism. Findings are not representative of all women. However, information gained is useful to gaining a more complete understanding of women's lived experiences as university faculty through realities that were constructed from their own personal and collective standpoints.

FINDINGS

Paying attention to Rayle et al.'s (2006) thematic categories, themes were developed during data analysis unique to this particular group of women. The following themes are described below: double jeopardy—being a woman and identifying as a feminist; empowerment through knowledge; social webbing; drawbacks; and paying it forward through activism.

Double Jeopardy—Being a Woman and Identifying as a Feminist

Each of the women in this collaborative group described difficulties being accepted as a woman in their departments. Three described instances of not being heard or taken seriously because of stereotypical assumptions about women:

> Being a woman in south [state] has been a real eye opener for me because I've never been a minority and here, I am a minority. So, it's like a double whammy. I have found women are not expected to be bold and intelligent and decision makers and so I'm kind of running up against that. And, my department...the men are very respectful, but it is very obvious to me that my opinion really doesn't count. I know I can give it and everyone will shake their head and say thank you for sharing, but that's about it.

> I have missed opportunities because of assumptions people make about me based on gender. I'm the last person invited to participate on committees, but the first person expected to be at social events.

> When I first became a professor, I spoke out regularly...but got tired of not being heard or, worse, having the man sitting next to me patted on the back for making a suggestion I'd just made five minutes before him. This muted me for a time, but I eventually made my way back. Now, when I make suggestions, people listen, but think I'm too bossy!

For one woman, not being heard made her invisible. For another, invisibility was defined by the "stealing" of her ideas from male faculty after being ignored when she spoke. And, for another, being a woman produced silence and invisibility, literally, as her presence was lacking on committees where vital decisions were made. When asked whether their departments support research on women, responses indicated a lingering refusal to accept feminist research as valuable. One assistant professor said a tenured professor in her department said to her, "Why would students write about women...why are women writing about women? There's no value." Another associate professor mentioned that when she applied for her first university position, she was asked why men weren't included in her dissertation on women's experiences with mentoring as if the title of the dissertation was of no consequence. This same professor mentioned that students were not allowed at her doctoral-granting institution to complete dissertations on women because of one professor's perception that "there were too many studies about women." And yet another associate professor made the comment that:

> There's not a lot of support for gender research at my institution. In fact, it isn't taken seriously. Faculty members joke about it. I developed a course to address social justice issues, including gender, and I was not allowed to call it leadership for social justice because it implied that we would support gays and lesbians...so, apparently my institution not only fails to support women, but gays and lesbians as well.

At this woman's university, the topics of gender and sexuality were completely silenced and not allowed in course content.

Several professors talked about the lack of advice and mentoring opportunities from other women at their institutions. One woman talked about her first position and said,

> I think the first thing you do when you secure a job is to get counsel from those that are tenured. And the majority in my department are male. The only female I could seek advice from was another assistant professor a year ahead of me. You find out after a while that the advice that the males provide you is traditional and won't necessarily work for you, and because I'm in a Hispanic-serving institution and am a Latina myself, it was devastating to find out that no woman of color has ever gotten tenure in the department.... That should speak volumes to you about the gender experience in my department.

This woman not only had a lack of women mentors to choose from, but there was no precedent set for an ethnic minority woman ever having received tenure at her institution.

Another talked about the struggle to hold other professors in her department accountable for sexist behavior and traditions. She put it this way:

> You are the one who speaks out when something is not looked at for women. This position isn't pleasant because you have to talk to a group of male professors who are all tenured (not advisable for an assistant professor), but if you don't do it, who will? I have had to tone talk of feminist research down a little and describe it as more of an awareness process.

For this woman, though frustrated with the lack of discussion on discriminatory behaviors and practices, she tried to work within the system she existed in to "play the game" for tenure, but to push boundaries in small, more subtle ways, when possible. It is clear from the women's responses that there is the need for both support to women faculty and a continued push for research on women and minorities. From stereotypical assumptions to outright refusal to acknowledge feminist research as valuable, the women who came together to collaborate with one another for support justifiably needed one another.

Empowerment Through Knowledge

Information and skill building are valuable tools for success. For the graduate student and the assistant professors new to academia, participating in the collaboration helped them understand and learn about the requirements of the position. One of the women put it this way:

This was my first experience in academia and I knew nothing about writing articles. Had it not been for this group, I wouldn't have been exposed to conferences or even exposed to the feasibility of becoming a professor—that in itself was unimaginable for me until this group came together. And once we came together, we helped one another because we wanted to give one another a hand up as we went through the various stages of our careers together. It gave me all of the information...as much as possible to do what I needed to do in this career.

This woman, though a doctoral student in the last year of her PhD program, had received no mentoring or instruction on the rules of the professorate in regard to expectations for writing, demonstrating the detriment of lack of access to information.

Another talked about her initial impetus for joining the group and lack of access to information about the "rules of the higher education game":

My joining had a twofold purpose. First of all, I knew I needed help with the tenure-track position. I was pretty sure that I could do whatever they told me I had to do, but I wanted to do it with class and do it well and I wanted to represent my department and college well. I knew the group would be a good support for that. Second, I knew nothing about higher education and I knew I would get that information through the group.

Another participant was more task-specific and said, "It was extremely helpful to learn how to put a book together. And it was great to work with a full professor who already had that experience!" The participant who was a graduate student the first year of the collaboration gained a faculty position during the second year and said,

A key selling point was the university wanting me to have a line of inquiry...so showing them that I had publications and was working on new projects (all through my work with the collaborative group) and that I could collaborate with other people, and not only other people but people from other institutions, was a huge selling point.

For the assistant professors who were further in their careers and being reviewed for tenure, the group helped them further establish themselves as capable researchers transitioning from assistants to associates. While the women new to the profession gained help beginning their research agendas, those more veteran gained help by both broadening the scope of their research and increasing quantities of presentations and publications to gain tenure and promotion. One made the point that,

I think it was key that we were all researching women in very stages of education and higher education. That helped because we all had information!

It helped that we brought experiences from different universities because it brought different viewpoints. We shared the rules with one another. And we were all in different stages of our careers. We each had our own individual contacts. So that was beneficial because it was like a domino effect of contacts for networking.

Another more experienced woman in the group also said, "Writing and presenting—that isn't everything. We need to know more and we need to share with those new to the field that there is more."

While the professors new to the profession were aware that they needed help with learning the skills required by university tenure-track positions, those with more experience also knew that success in the position was not only about publishing and presenting, but knowing the rules of the game in regard to networking, dividing time between tasks, and responding to stereotypical assumptions and expectations.

Social Webbing

All of the women in the collaborative group understood the power of networking and the relief that having social support could provide to them. All of the women talked about benefits of the networking relationship to be about both skill building and socializing. The primary purpose for joining the group for one assistant professor was to gain a social network that was otherwise absent for her:

At the beginning it was all about the camaraderie and the support and knowing that when I arrived to a conference, I would know someone. And then, as the group matured, or maybe as I matured, I looked at the group and the leadership and how they could help me make choices about being tenure-track and being a good professor in higher education. . . . By simply talking to one another and sharing, we learned.

This professor's needs followed along the lines of Maslow's hierarchy of needs, as social support was primary and not until that was satisfied could the group evolve into more of an academic support for her.

Two of the more experienced women of the group talked about the group serving as a venue for sharing work and as a way to force the organization of time. One said,

I think it was a good way to work with a group of individuals that had a common interest and research agenda on social justice and a good opportunity to develop a network and at the same time work towards tenure and promotion through joint publications and presentations. It was also a social part to it.

Friendships, but academic support as well. I don't have anyone at my institution who I can share things with or who would value my work.

The other said,

I looked forward to getting together with everybody. I really like doing research, but taking the time, making the time, and setting it aside on your own...you don't do it as well by yourself as you do when you plan it with a group. You all hold each other accountable for making progress.

All of the women indicated utilizing the group for two purposes: to gain a type of social support that facilitated friendships between members, more formal didactic mentorships, which helped them become further networked in the field, and to gain academic skills in publishing and presenting. One of the women in the group new to the field talked about a specific instance of how the group worked not only to network her with the other members, but with those outside of the group as well:

I was also introduced to another woman through my mentor (who was also in the collaborative group) who shared my research interest, and that professor's help was seminal too. She opened her arms and I knew right away that my connection with the first professor had led to a wealth of resources....I have published four journal articles from that relationship alone. Powerful women have really paved the way for me.

Another woman who had more experience in the field spoke of webbing as a strategy she uses to secure her own position in the field as a woman. She put it this way:

I was fortunate enough as a graduate student to have good mentors who paved the way for me and networked me at conferences before I even gained a position. When I ran into other new professors in the field during my first years as a professor, I realized that I was lucky rather than the norm and that my own position could be jeopardized in the field if I didn't actively recruit and support other women. So, for me, one way to do that is through what I call webbing. I have mentors who introduce me to their mentors and social networks and I, in turn, introduce these women to other new women in the field to create a spider web of support readily available.

For at least two of the women who were already well networked into the field, they utilized the collaborative group to create wider circles of support more far-reaching in the field. For these women who had already experienced academic success in their positions and were less needy in regard to publications and presentations, webbing other women into the field was a way of securing their positions in the field in the future.

Drawbacks

While the women spent very little time in discussion about drawbacks from participation in the collaborative group, they were keenly aware of any tensions that had arisen between group members and spoke candidly about what one called "bumps in the road." One woman talked more about disappointment in herself for letting the group down at a time in her life where personal circumstances made it difficult for her to complete a task taken on by the group together:

> There was some negativity due to circumstances in my life at the time.... I allowed myself to get off track for a while there and it in turn affected my level of performance, I guess. I had a lot of issues with the book we were publishing and wasn't getting any support from my institution and it had a huge effect on my relationship with some of the group members for a while. They were disappointed in me, and understandably so . . . there's no ill will, but I do not have the same kind of relationship with some of the members anymore because of that. And I take a lot of responsibility for that. I was going through a hard time, but I should have handled it differently. When you work in a group, you have other people counting on you . . . and that just adds pressure.

Another theme that developed from two of the women was the importance of noting the purpose for the group from the beginning. For instance, both women indicated that while social support was important to them, they entered the group at a time when the need to produce publications and presentations at high volumes was at the forefront of their reasons for joining the group. These women were looking to participate in a collaborative relationship with women on their academic level and who had enough experience in the field to hit the ground running. While they both talked about the importance of bringing in new people to the group, they cautioned that it is best to keep a balance between members who need a lot of support and those who do not. One said,

> Had we had a few women who had a little more experience in the group, perhaps we would have had more opportunities. Some of us were doing a lot more of the giving than the receiving if that makes sense. It isn't that I'm complaining about that, because I do think it is my duty to mentor other women . . . it's just that care should be taken to make sure everyone's needs are being fulfilled.

One final drawback to participating in the group came to light for two of the women new to the field at the time they joined the group. Both women talked about isolating themselves from other groups or networks that may have been available to them due to the fact that they clung so closely to the collaborative relationship studied here. One of the women explained, "I may have isolated myself because I had the group to depend on. I depended on them and didn't go out and search for other collaborations and relationships. So it actually may have been positive and negative for me."

For the women new to the field, they indicated that they were so thankful to be part of a group that they failed to seek out connections other than those that were established through the webbing effect.

Paying It Forward Through Activism

The women were asked to describe their thoughts on being feminist researchers, taking action as feminists, and whether participating in the collaborative group had encouraged them to return the favor and give someone else a hand up. Every single woman in the collaborative is actively mentoring both students and other professors new to the field in formal and informal ways.

They are chairing dissertations: "I'm chairing a dissertation on women, so I know for sure that person is going to make it through. I set the example so that my students know how things can look differently."

They are mentoring women doctoral students: "Certainly the collaborative made me a better mentor for young women in our doctoral program considering higher education."

They are mentoring other faculty members in their departments: "I'm working with a young professor who is an African American male working toward tenure and he's showing isolationism—we're able to share experiences with one another."

Two of the women are frequently seen in tow of new doctoral students at conferences and work with their students on publications and presentations. These same professors have given a hand up to numerous professors new to the field and to graduate students who have now gained academic positions. There seems to be little room for doubt in regard to how powerful these women view the act of networking and no hesitance toward lifting others up. One woman explained the impact the collaborative had on her success as a mentor: "I had a better sense of what was helpful rather than superficial and could meet the needs of some others better after participating in a collaborative relationship myself."

Perhaps due to the women's definitions of feminism came their desire to actively collaborate with and mentor other women in the field. Their words indicated a commitment to care for others through actively sharing knowledge. One woman spoke of feminism as a way to promote a female presence in the workplace:

Feminism to me means that we have to keep a presence in the workplace and be a model of the female leaders. I think we're still trailblazing in certain ways when you look at presidents and provosts still being male for the great majority.

Another spoke of the fact that being in a collaborative group with a specific focus on women's ways of understanding helped her to value herself:

Being a feminist helps me to value myself and to see the importance at looking at things from the female perspective ... it helps me realize there is more than one way to see things. Just because you're surrounded by males in a male world doesn't mean that is the way things should be or that those are the only experiences that exist.

Another explained that feminism, to her, means helping other women up to level the playing field: "I really am strongly in support of feminism and women supporting women and giving one another a step up and seeing another woman not as a person to step on but as a person to pull up along with me." She went on to say, however, that it is also our responsibility to actively shape our roles and stereotypes about women: "Always reminding people that gender issues permeate the workplace and striving to pass knowledge along to others so that they don't replicate what we went through."

DISCUSSION

The findings of this study are in line with research that has demonstrated women's success through collaborative networking (Belenky et al., 1986; Coleman, 2010; McNae, 2010; Noddings, 1986; Tannen, 2001). Since the beginning of the collaborative relationship, one graduate student gained a tenure track position at a university; two assistant professors were awarded tenure and promotion to associate professors; and two assistant professors, during the writing of this manuscript, were getting ready to go up for tenure and expected to have no problems. One monograph was edited and published by the group, and one book was in press by two members of the group. Approximately seven book chapters were published or were in press during the writing of this manuscript. Over fifteen peer-reviewed publications and numerous conference presentations were the result of collaborations that came from within or stemmed from this collaboration, confirming Limbert's (1995) assertion that women tend to merge networks between members to expand opportunities and confirming Tannen's (2001) assertion that a webbing model of mentorship is more natural for women. Furthermore, as women faculty in departments of educational leadership who research women's experiences in K–12 leadership and write from feminist perspectives, this group's impact is far reaching and flows from the academy to the K–12 educational environment.

There were no indications by the women in this collaborative relationship that competition was a driving force behind their network or that competition resulted between the members. Instead, because they shared a desire to conduct feminist research on women leaders, their motives were driven by thoughts of caring for one another and an overall commitment to help one another gain positions, tenure, and promotion and to extend this help to graduate students and aspiring women K–12 leaders. Similar to Appley and Winder's (1977) theory of collaboration, these women spoke of a commitment to work with one another by choice. They made the time to meet with one another at research conferences and outside of research conferences on their own time. And, the major drawback to participating in the collaborative was the pressure of knowing others were relying on you for project completions. Because of their care for and dedication to one another as friends and as colleagues, they worked not only for themselves, but out of feelings of responsibility for the success of others.

The rate at which the women in this collaborative experienced success in such a short period of time indicates that collaborative networks are powerful tools for women faculty and could also possibly serve to benefit women leaders practicing in K–12 education. According to Dickens and Sagaria (1997), developing thriving careers requires the negotiation of conflicts. Riger et al. (1997) identified such conflicts for women as lack of participation in informal socializing, lack of mentoring, sexist attitudes, professional isolation, and gender/family-friendly policies that may not actually be embraced by those in university settings. The collaborative effort described here helped the women participants overcome several of the conflicts noted above. The empowerment they gained through the sharing of both formal and informal knowledge about university "norms" and the negotiation of expectations was crucial to both gaining faculty positions and advancing in them and was effective at combating the lack of informal socializing, the lack of mentoring, and professional isolation. The social webbing that occurred between members of the collaborative and between larger groups of women connected to some of the women in the collaborative was effective at combating the lack of socialization, the lack of mentoring, and professional isolation as well. One of the most vital lessons learned from the collaborative is the power that social webbing and networking hold for creating a cyclical movement toward the constant mentoring of women through paying it forward. This study suggests that women who empower themselves through networking and social webbing are more likely and able to help other women new to the field by mentoring and facilitating social relationships for them. When studying and learning from the themes that emerged from the interviews, it became apparent that while many of the conflicts Riger et al. (1997) highlight were effectively alleviated; responding to sexist attitudes and changing policies and practices were less effectively combated. The women spoke of encountering sexist attitudes and assumptions but did not share strategies they had used to push change. They worked more quietly behind the scenes and tried to find ways to push their agendas and personal careers forward without jeopardizing their opportunities for tenure and promotion.

Looking ahead, further research is needed on how veteran women in the field of educational leadership were able to negotiate stereotypical assumptions and behaviors as well as research on how they have pushed or plan to push policy now that they hold more secure, tenured positions in their departments. New research might also compare women who participate in collaborative networks with women who participate in traditional didactic mentoring relationships or with women who have experienced no mentoring or networking at all—across both university and K–12 environments. Further study on how networks can become the norm rather than the exception for women through formal efforts through professional and academic organizations and through integration into doctoral programs preparing women for academic positions is also warranted. Care should be taken by those seeking to establish collaborative networks to ensure a good balance of participants with varying levels of experience so that the needs of all can be more efficiently met. The women who participated in this collaborative relationship not only ensured their survival and success in academia, but they were actively striving to ensure the survival of other women in both the academy and K–12 settings. And, as indicated by the women's discussion of what it is like to be women professors conducing feminist research, much work is left to be done to change stereotypical perceptions.

APPENDIX A

Interview Guide

What is the culture of the university for women? For you in particular?

What is it like to be a feminist scholar?

What was the purpose of developing the collaborative relationship?

Were other mentoring relationships/networks/networks of power available to you? Or were you isolated from these? How? Can you give an example?

Describe the collaborative relationship in terms of attributes and drawbacks.

What were the effects of the collaborative relationship on your personal well-being (self-esteem, stress, loneliness, power)?

How did the relationship help you evolve as a scholar?

How has the collaborative relationship affected your commitment to mentor and collaborate with others?

What does feminism mean to you? How are you able to enact this? What are actions key actions you take as a feminist?

REFERENCES

AAUP, American Association of University Professors. (2001). *Statement of principles on family responsibilities and academic work.* Retrieved from http://www.aaup.org/AAUP/pubsres/policydocs/contents/workfam-stmt.htm

AAUW, American Association of University Women. (2007). *Behind the pay gap.* Retrieved from http://www.aauw.org/research/upload/behindPayGap.pdf

Acker, S., & Feuerverger, G. (1996). Doing good and feeling bad: The work of women university teachers. *Cambridge Journal of Education, 26*(3), 401–422.

Appley, D. G., & Winder, A. E. (1977). An evolving definition of collaboration and some implication for the world of work. *Journal of Applied Behavioural Science, 13*(3), 279–281.

Belenky, M., Clinchy, B., Goldberger, N., & Tarule, J. (1986). *Women's ways of knowing: The development of self, voice, and mind.* New York, NY: BasicBooks.

Coleman, G., & Rippin, A. (2000). Putting Feminist Theory to Work: Collaboration as a Means Towards Organizational Change. *Organization 7*(4), 573–87.

Curtis, J. W. (2004). Faculty Salary and Faculty Distribution Fact Sheet 2003–04. AAUP Director of Research, for the Committee on Women in the Academic Profession. Retrieved from http://www.aaup.org/AAUP/pubsres/research/2003-04factsheet.htm

Denzin, N., & Lincoln, Y. (1994). *Handbook of qualitative research.* Thousand Oaks, CA: Sage.

Dickens, C. S., & Sagaria, M. D. (1997). Feminists at work: Collaborative relationships among women faculty. *The Review of Higher Education, 21*(1), 79–101.

Gilligan, C. (1982). *In a different voice: Psychological theory and women's development.* Cambridge, MA: Harvard University Press.

Harper, E. P, Baldwin, R. G., Gansneder, B. G., & Chronister, J. L. (2001). Full-time women faculty off the tenure track: Profile and practice. *The Review of Higher Education, 24*(3), 237–257.

Hart, J. (2008). Mobilization among women academics: The interplay between feminism and professionalism. *NWSA Journal, 20*(1), 184–208.

Irby, B. J., & Brown, G. (2002). Women leaders: Creating inclusive school environments. In J. Koch & B. Irby (Eds.), *Defining and redefining gender equity in education* (pp. 43–58). Greenwich, CT: Information Age.

Limbert, C. A. (1995). Chrysalis, a peer mentoring group for faculty and staff women. *NWSA Journal, 7,* 86–99.

Livingston, A., & Wirt, J. (2005). *The condition of education 2005 in brief (NCES 2005-095).* Washington, DC: U.S. Department of Education.

Mansfield, K. C, Welton, A., Lee, P., & Young, M. (2010). The lived experiences of female educational leadership doctoral students. *Journal of Educational Administration, 48*(6), 727–740.

Marcus, J. (2007). Helping academic families have families and tenure too: Universities discover their self-interest. *Changes, 39*(2), 27–32.

McCracken, G. (1988). *The long interview.* Newbury Park, CA: Sage.

McMillan, J. H., & Schumacher, S. (2001). *Research in Education* (5th ed.). New York, NY: Longman.

McNae, R. (2010). Young women and the co-construction of leadership. *Journal of Administration, 48*(6), 677–688.

Moore, K. M., & Sagaria, M. D. (1991). The situation of women in research universities in the United States: Within the inner circles of academic power. In G. Kelly & S. Slaughter (Eds.), *Women's Higher Education in Comparative Perspective* (pp. 185–200). Dordrecht, The Netherlands: Kleiwer Academic Publishers. Reprinted in J. S. Glazer, E. M. Bensimon & B. K. Townsend (Eds.). (1993). *Women in Higher Education: A Feminist Perspective.* Needham Heights, Massachusetts: Ginn Press, Simon & Schuster.

Noddings, N. (1986). *Caring: A feminine approach to ethics and moral education.* Berkley, CA: University of California Press.

Patton, M. Q. (1990). *Qualitative evaluation and research methods* (2nd ed.). Newbury Park, CA: Sage Publications.

Porter, S. R., Toutkoushian, R. K, & Moore, J. V., III. (2008). Pay inequities for recently hired faculty, 1988–2004. *The Review of Higher Education, 31*(4), 465–487.

Rayle A. D., Bordes V., Zapata A., Arrendondo P., Rutter M., & Howard C. (2006). Mentoring experiences of women in graduate education: Factors that matter. *Current Issues in Education, 9*(6). Retrieved from http://cie.asu.edu/volume9/number6/index.html

Riger, S., Stokes, J., Raja, S., & Sullivan, M. (1997). Focus on female faculty: Measuring perceptions of the work environment for female faculty. *The Review of Higher Education, 21,* 63–78.

Rossman, G., & Rallis, S. (1998). *Learning in the field: An introduction to qualitative research.* Thousand Oaks, CA: Sage.

Shapira, T., Ara, K., & Asaiza, F. (2010). Arab women principals' empowerment and leadership in Israel. *Journal of Educational Administration, 48*(6), 704–715.

Sherman, W. H. (2005). Preserving the status quo or renegotiating leadership: Women's experiences with a district-based aspiring leaders program. *Educational Administration Quarterly, 41*(5), 707–740.

Sherman, W. H., Munoz, A., & Pankake, A. (2008). The great divide: Women's experiences with mentoring. *Journal of Women in Educational Leadership, 6*(4), 239–259.

Sherman, W. H., & Wrushen, B. (2009). Intersecting leadership knowledge from the margins: Women secondary principals. *Journal of School Leadership, 19*(2), 171–198.

Sherman, W. H., Beaty, D., Crum, K., & Peters, A. (2010). Unwritten: Young women faculty in educational leadership. *Journal of Educational Administration, 48*(6), 741–754.

Stokes, J., Riger, S., & Sullivan, M. (1995). Measuring perceptions of the work environment for women in corporate settings. *Psychology of Women Quarterly, 19*(4), 533–549.

Tannen, D. (1990). *You just don't understand: Women and men in conversation.* New York, NY: HarperCollins.

Tannen, D. (2001). But what do you mean? Women and men in conversation. In J. M. Henslin, (Ed.), *Down to earth sociology: Introductory readings* (11th ed.) (pp. 168–173). New York: Free Press.

Ward, K., & Wolf-Wendel, L. (2004). Academic motherhood: Managing complex roles in research universities. *The Review of Higher Education, 27*(2), 233–257.

PART IV

PRESSING FORWARD TO CHANGE THE FUTURE

CHAPTER 12

USING THE SENSES IN REFLECTIVE PRACTICE TO PREPARE WOMEN FOR TRANSFORMING THEIR LEARNING SPACES

Christa Boske

ABSTRACT

This chapter seeks to push at current conceptual boundaries within the field of educational leadership in understanding relationships between preparing women candidates to lead for social justice through the senses—ways in which school leaders perceive their lived experiences and relation to others. The author examines how three K–12 female public school leaders came to understand what it meant to lead for social justice through their sense-making by exploring their ways of knowing through artmaking. These spaces afford women opportunities to deepen their ways of knowing and responding to the needs of those they serve, especially for those who live on the margins due to race, class, gender, and other differences from the mainstream. This case study is significant to furthering extant literature because it examines how these women make sense of what it means to lead for social justice through the senses. Specifically, it does so through the use of auditory/video reflec-

Women Interrupting, Disrupting, and Revolutionizing Educational Policy and Practice, pages 215–244
Copyright © 2014 by Information Age Publishing
215

tions and artmaking in an effort to create spaces for school leaders to shift their sense-making from text to audio/visual artmaking—a formal curricular decision grounded in the recognition of rich meanings and imaginative possibilities embedded in nontext-based, sensual understandings. Findings suggest these women brought to their work a more explicitly caring and collaborative ethic to promoting social justice work in schools.

While beliefs, values, and traditions from which we have come are immensely powerful in shaping our ways of knowing and responding to the world, we need to take seriously their impact on our work in schools. Those who prepare educators have a responsibility to consider the implications of contemporary educational issues, including the urgency to speak in our own voices, while clearly relating to established theoretical traditions. William Pinar (1975), a curriculum theorist who emphasizes the method of *currere*—the infinitive form of curriculum emphasizing the significance of experience, contends there is a need to examine interrelationships. This examination is critical to creating comprehensive curriculum, which deepens understanding. Pinar identifies this process as *reconceptualism*, which, in its literal definition, is constant redefinition, but with a theoretical framework; he contends a phenomenon is underway. The purpose of this chapter is to further examine sense-making and artmaking as a possible phenomenon within the field of educational leadership for female school leaders as they *reconceptualize* their ways of knowing and responding to oppressed populations. These transforming learning spaces offer divergent perspectives to educators with embedded possible controversy when contrasted with the rest of the field. Research findings (see Boske, 2009, 2011a, 2011b, 2012a, 2012b, 2012c, 2013; Shapiro, 2006) suggest this *reconceptualization* of school leadership preparation is a fundamental dialectical relation among knowers, knowing, and the known (also see Pinar, 1994). The transformation offers a redefinition of self, constructed through the discourse and scholarship of those who engage in this process.

The task of preparing school leaders is continual, careful, and insistently pressing the limits of what it takes to create critical comprehensive experiences for women. The literature on school administration often ignores women administrators and focuses on their male counterparts (Grogan & Shakeshaft, 2011; Shakeshaft, 1989). Specifically, women's history in school is different than men's. Women often share similar experiences including a commitment to family, raising children, and, of course, growing up female. These experiences shape women's perspectives and ultimately their ways of knowing and responses to the world around them. Therefore, those who prepare school leaders may reconsider what it means to reconceptualize school leadership preparation. They may inquire how women understand what Langer (1953) refers to as *mind of meaning* and *meaning of mind*, which suggests the mind becomes a place in which interpretations are made, and within these interpretations are the creation of symbols, signs, and meanings that encompass a total range of human feeling.

Treating women's experiences as sources of insight and exemplifications of the mind affords those who prepare school leaders with opportunities to engage in the very forms of their own experiencing. In this sense, Pinar's (1975) and Langer's (1953) works encourage us to engage in a similar kind of self-reflection that is meant to make us more familiar with the lived feelings involved in making meaning, symbolic formation, and transformation. These symbolic forms become ways in which we live, lead, and become human. The role of language in informing experiences, the encounter with sense-making, and the process of making meaning through art attempt to help us understand the mind as achievement. The mind affords spaces for higher-order processes of feeling and experience. They become embodied in the symbols that reveal pivotal ways in which school leaders deepen their ways of knowing and feeling. These new ways of being are situated within diverse contexts and, when applied, encourage leaders to be inspired—for imaginative possibilities (Boske, 2009).

The fusion of conceptual-constructive dimensions of Pinar's (1975) and Langer's (1953, 1972) work encourage those who prepare school leaders to reconsider to what extent efforts focus on deepening understanding of what it means to be a woman in educational leadership. Refocusing inquiries encourages us to look within and turn attention away from what exists toward what does not. As new ideas emerge, others fade, and new ones are created. These new learning spaces offer school leaders opportunities to understand how development occurs, collectively, professionally, and personally. Often times, they will encounter opposing values, beliefs, and experiences; however, these experiences create spaces in which ideas or forces meet each other, transform, and hopefully offer more comprehensive ways of knowing for the learner.

Because men and women live through multilayered lived experiences, they are storytelling organisms who, individually and collectively, lead storied lives. Their ways of knowing and responding to the world are essential to understanding the way they think and learn. Women's lives and how they are composed should be of interest to educators, school leaders, and those in higher education settings, because they invite in-depth understanding regarding their lived experiences, which are often ignored in the literature (see Grogan & Shakeshaft, 2011). In order to initiate and maintain an increased intellectual state, inquiry must center on understanding learning and teaching; how it takes place; and undertaking different beliefs, values, and assumptions within diverse contexts. Such efforts have the potential to discover links to learning, teaching, and leading. With this perspective in mind, experience is therefore the starting point. It begins from within—understanding self, people, and their relation of self to others and to their environment (e.g., Dewey, 1934, 1938, 1961).

This chapter seeks to push current conceptual boundaries within the field of educational leadership in understanding relationships between preparing women candidates to lead for social justice through the senses—ways in which school leaders perceive their lived experiences and relation to others. Throughout the chapter, I examine how K–12 female public school leaders and I, as a faculty member, came to understand what it meant to lead for social justice through their sense-making by exploring their ways of knowing through artmaking. I begin with a brief overview of sense-making and artmaking, the significance of preparing school leaders to lead for social justice, and the considerations made to utilize sensual reflective practice as a transformative pedagogy in order to link the senses to social justice work in schools. Next, I present cases of aspiring female school leaders. The chapter concludes with understanding the implications of this reflective practice in preparing women school leaders to address issues of justice in U.S. public schools.

It is important to articulate how I construct differences between sense-making and artmaking for school leaders. Sense-making is the process by which school leaders draw meaning from their lived inquiries while engaging in complex reflective processes. Artmaking and audio/video technology are essential tools used to provide spaces to construct meaning making through the senses. Such spaces afford opportunities to deepen their ways of knowing and responding to the needs of those they serve, especially for those who live on the margins due to race, class, gender, and other differences from the mainstream. Because of inherent challenges in preparing school leaders to take a more critically conscious stance toward deepening their empathic responses toward children and their communities, especially with issues centered on social justice and equity (Lopez, 2003; Marshall & Oliva, 2010; Tooms & Boske, 2010), there is a need to engage school leaders in sense-making, by which they give meaning to experiences (Boske, 2009, 2011a, 2011b, 2012a, 2012b, 2012c, 2013; Brown, 2004, 2006; Shapiro, 2006).

THE NEED

School leaders are often not prepared to engage in transformative curriculum leadership. Instead, women are traditionally prepared to understand their roles as managers of systems rather than deepening their empathic responses and connections with school communities. Those concerned with student learning recognize the need to pay closer attention to the impact of the nation's deepening cultural texture, racial tensions, and increasing percentage of students from historically disenfranchised populations (U.S. Bureau of Census, 2010) and the influence such changes will continue to have on the nation's schools, colleges, and universities (Gay, 2010). Scholars—including Sonia Nieto, Geneva Gay, Jeffrey Brooks, Lisa Delpit, Gerardo Lopez, Patrick Slattery, Michael Dantley, Linda Tillman, and Gloria Ladson-Billings—are concerned about the serious academic achievement problems among children and families who live on the margins. The underachievement of minority children calls for systemic, holistic, authentic, comprehensive, and curriculum transformative interventions in U.S. public schools (e.g., Gay, 2010; Henderson & Gornik, 2007; Sleeter & Grant, 2009). This broad-based and systemic curriculum reform requires deeper and more comprehensive analysis of schools, which needs to be collectively addressed with transformative curriculum leaders who focus on raising consciousness (Burns, 1978; Eisner, 1994; Noddings, 1984).

School leadership programs that emphasize the need for personal transformation require critical thought and reflection with regard to beliefs, lived experiences, and cultural identity. Attempts may include building the capacity and will to transform school leaders to deliver policies and practices that address the lived realities of disenfranchised populations. Sometimes these discussions center on disparities facing children of color (Ladson-Billings, 1994), school policies that fail to serve marginalized populations (Marshall, 1993; Marshall & Gerstyl-Pepin, 2005), or longstanding achievement gaps between mainstream and marginalized children in U.S. public schools (Apple, 1993; Darling-Hammond, 1997; Marshall & Oliva, 2010). School leaders must interrupt practices that perpetuate the belief that some groups of children are intrinsically more able than other groups of children due to class, skin color, language, sexual identity, or gender (Shields, 2003). In light of this, the leader-in-training should be made aware of leadership as a powerful intervening variable in determining whether children from diverse backgrounds are successful (Reyes, Scribner, & Parades-Scribner, 1999; Scheurich & Skrla, 2003). In this way, those who prepare school leaders must reconsider how programmatic decisions that influence curriculum content and pedagogy foster transformational experiences for aspiring school leaders (Boske & Tooms, 2010b). One means of promoting the courage and skill set necessary to sustain social justice and equity work in schools is to provide them with safe spaces to reflect on the impact of sense-making on their school leadership identity.

Although school leaders make meaning from engaging with their environments, those who prepare school leaders tend not to consider to what extent the senses (i.e., sight, smell, sound, taste, and touch) influence how women understand the influence of the senses impacting community norms, attitudes, and values as preferences. The way school leaders make sense of their environments is derived from these senses, which are embedded throughout school practices, curriculum, pedagogy, and policy. Therefore, sense-making can be understood as a political act, engaging women school leaders in assuming that what makes sense to them is but one possible interpretation among a myriad of possibilities.

There is an urgency to deepen understanding regarding how to create spaces in which school leaders promote and address issues of social justice and equity in U.S. public schools. This increased attention is aligned with arts-based principles centered on understanding sensory ways of *knowing*. Artmaking is recognized as an experiential mode of inquiry that reveals insights and ways of understanding that impact our capacities for knowing (e.g., Cahnmann-Taylor & Siegesmund, 2008; Dewey, 1934; Eisner, 2008; Kridel, 2010; Malewski, 2009). Utilizing artmaking for *making sense* of our lived experiences through sensory exploration creates spaces for school leaders to consider their actions and reflect upon their impact (e.g., Ellsworth, 2005; Springgay, 2008). This chapter is significant to furthering extant literature of women school leaders by examining curriculum through the senses. Specifically, it does so through the use of auditory and video reflections in an effort to create spaces for women to shift their sense-making from text to audio/visual artmaking—a formal curricular decision grounded in the recognition of rich meanings and imaginative possibilities embedded in nontext-based, sensual understandings.

LEADING FOR SOCIAL JUSTICE IN U.S. PUBLIC SCHOOLS

Leading for social justice is a highly emotional endeavor requiring courage, integrity, imaginative possibilities, and self-awareness. It is important to acknowledge the ongoing debate and tensions regarding multiple meanings for *social justice*. For the purpose of this chapter, social justice is defined as committing to the moral use of power (Bogotch, 2002), fostering critical inquiry (Brown, 2004, 2006), and promoting social action (Boske, 2012d; Boske & Diem, 2012; Marshall & Oliva, 2010; Tooms & Boske, 2010). As school leaders address issues of marginalization within U.S. public schools, they begin to discover aspects of schooling to which they had previously not attended such as fundamental structural inequities (Darling-Hammond, 2005; Ladson-Billings, 2006), insufficient school funding (Kozol, 1991, 2006) and a lack of highly qualified school personnel within urban and rural communities (Darling-Hammond, 2002, 2005). Within U.S. public schools, children are exposed to the effects of these inequities through the perpetuation of hegemonic school practices, which reproduce and reinforce cultural and educational traditions of White, middle-class, English-speaking, Christian, heterosexual communities (e.g., Gonzalez, Moll, & Amanti, 2005; Marshall & Oliva, 2010; Tooms & Boske, 2010). The impact of social justice and equity issues on the lives of underserved populations is so profound that it has begun to cause those who prepare school leaders to reconsider the academic content and pedagogy of their courses in order to provide spaces for candidates to recognize, analyze, and respond to systemic inequities (e.g., Boske, 2014; Boske & Tooms, 2010; Brown, 2004, 2006; Ladson-Billings, 2006; Marshall & Oliva, 2010).

ARTMAKING AS SENSE-MAKING

In response to concerns raised about the importance of addressing issues of social justice, several scholars contend that artmaking has the potential to deepen empathic responses and increase readiness to interrupt oppressive school practices. Greene (1995), for example, calls for approaches in education that lead to the release of imagination. She connects artmaking to deepening empathy, stressing, "If people cannot imagine a better state of being, they will likely remain stuck or anchored" (p. 52). Eisner (2002) contends artmaking is a vehicle to transform an individual's consciousness, enlarge the imagination, and encourage problem-solving. Artmaking plays a significant role in sense-making, because the act of knowing is interconnected with affect, intuition, and imaginative thinking (Eisner, 2008; Zwicky, 2003). Therefore, artmaking is not about feelings and emotions the artist *has*; it is about which feelings the artist comes to *know* (Langer, 1982). It has been my experience that the inclusion of artmaking offers school leaders opportunities to increase their critical consciousness and examine how identities are constructed, as such scholarship indicates.

One way of understanding processes of artmaking is as a symbolic projection of vital emotional and intellectual tensions between the mind, feeling, and process (Langer, 1972). It is constructed symbolism and presents the artist's "way of feeling" abstractly (Langer, 1953, p. 146). Artmaking produces what Langer calls *presentational* symbols—that is, symbols that give *form to feeling*. Therefore, artmaking reaffirms the significance of lived experiences and personal knowing of what it means to address issues of social justice (e.g., Land & Stovall, 2009)—in this case, in their roles as school leaders.

CONTEXT

In the spring of 2010, a northeastern university revised its educational leadership program. In an effort to promote equity and social justice, they created the Leading for Social Justice course in response to the University Council of Educational Administrators' (UCEA), an international educational school leadership preparation organization, urgent call for preparation programs to promote social justice leaders (e.g., Boske, 2012d; Boske & Diem, 2012; Marshall & Oliva, 2010; Tooms & Boske, 2010a). In order to afford candidates with transformational learning experiences (e.g., Dewey, 1897/2004; Pinar, 1994), programmatic course requirements, curriculum, and pedagogy were revised accordingly. Faculty also engaged in an explicit effort to understand the nuances of educational growth for school leaders, embraced the need for self-understanding, and promoted the significance of visionary work to reframe curriculum conversations and pedagogical practices (e.g., Brown, 2004, 2006; Shields, 2003). And in 2011, faculty created a program mission statement with surrounding school leader representatives and candidates to include the words *social justice* and *equity*.

The Leading for Social Justice course engages students in nontext, sense-making reflective practices, a process including increasing critical consciousness through weekly audio/video reflections (e.g., Boske, 2014; Brown, 2006), experiential service learning (e.g., Bowden, Billig, & Holland, 2008), and artmaking (with guidance from community artist mentors) (Boske, 2009; Shapiro, 2010). For 15 weeks, candidates respond to predetermined questions aligned with Terrell and Lindsey's (2009) cultural proficiency framework via audio and video-recorded reflections, examine lived realities of specific marginalized groups in U.S. schools (e.g., Marshall & Oliva, 2010), conduct equity audits in U.S. schools/colleges (e.g., Kozol, 2006; Skrla, Scheurich, & Bell McKenzie, 2009), and take a critical stance on one social justice issue, translating their often emotional-laden responses into pieces of visual art that, in turn, are exhibited at a university gallery at the end of each semester.

CASES

I inquired how women experience encounters with sense-making in such a way to understand, examine, and make meaning in being in relation with school communities as school leaders. To examine this question, I utilized a case study approach to research, a method that was particularly well-suited to the work because of the ways in which it affords the researcher an opportunity to investigate a contemporary phenomenon within a real-life context across multiple sources of data (Feagin, Orum, & Sjoberg, 1991; Yin, 1994). Data collected for this study consisted primarily of 51 weekly audio/video reflections (three participants and 18 reflections each), field notes, and course assignments (i.e., three equity audits, 33 metaphors, 15 small group reflections, three action research studies, and three artmaking projects).

The remainder of this chapter focuses on these three cases from 2010–2011. Adrianna is a White, married, heterosexual female inner-city teacher in her late twenties. She desires to become an assistant principal within the next five years. Margaret, a White, married with children, heterosexual female works at a suburban middle school. She is in her early thirties and wants to pursue a leadership position within the next few years. Prachi is an Eastern Indian, married, heterosexual woman with children, who works as a teacher in a suburban school. She will pursue a career in educational leadership within the next five years.

Data analysis consisted of examining and categorizing data evidence to address the initial propositions of a study (Yin, 1994). To do this, I utilized a kind of pattern-matching, one of the most desirable strategies for analysis in case studies because of the ways in which this technique compares an empirically based pattern with a predicted one (Trochim, 1989; Yin, 1994). Findings suggest these women brought to their work an explicitly caring and collaborative ethic to promoting social justice work in schools. In addition, they increasingly promoted critical and systemic perspectives to ways of understanding what is necessary to eliminate injustices faced by those they served in schools. Their ways of knowing encourage the need to look within, to interrupt the dominant culture of individualism, and to build bridges between self and community. Analysis yielded the following four emergent themes: (a) Promoting social justice leadership to promote changes for future generations, (b) living personal inquiries through sense-making, (c) a continued sense of development and transformation, and (d) embodied sense-making through artmaking.

PROMOTING SOCIAL JUSTICE LEADERSHIP

These women stressed the shift in their understanding from "school leaders as managers" to addressing issues of social justice and readiness to interrupt oppressive school practices. They emphasized the need to be afforded spaces to critically reflect on issues of social justice through sense-making created spaces to promote imaginative possibilities. For example, Margaret emphasized how the process "allowed her to express things written words alone could not say." Raising their consciousness about the lived realities of children and families from disenfranchised populations played a pivotal role in their sense-making and helped them realize the importance of examining the impact of their ways of knowing in understanding the tensions between their beliefs, responses, and lived experiences.

Throughout this process, they recognized transitioning from written words to audio/video afforded them with an "unfamiliar freedom of responses." They stressed how often they found themselves "enjoying" the reflective spaces in which "they were not interrupted" and "embraced the freedom to express their feelings and thoughts openly." Within these spaces, they deepened their understanding for the need to look within and utilized these self-reflective experiences to "intensely focus" on "what mattered most." They shared moments in which the reflective process offered spaces to "give knowledge," because the process "broadened their scope of knowing." For these women, this space became "sacred." It was within these spaces that new ways of understanding were "rooted in their experiences." As Adrianna noted, "The process of reflecting through video made me acknowledge my tendency to ignore what I was feeling and the need to acknowledge that what I think matters." Within these spaces, the intertwined ways in which they understood themselves as women, partners, colleagues, mothers, and daughters encouraged them to reexamine themselves as school leaders.

As they engaged in the self-reflective process, they began to reconceptualize themselves as leaders of social justice and equity. They came to better understand themselves as leaders for social justice by deepening their critical consciousness. They stressed how moving from traditional text to audio/video deepened their ways of knowing and responding to social justice. For example, Prachi stressed how the reflective process encouraged her to translate her experiences. Metaphors created spaces for personal knowing and reconsidering what it means to respond to the call to lead for social justice and equity issues in schools. This increased awareness and promotion of social justice issues expanded her discourses of schooling and also encouraged Adrianna to begin to identify as a catalyst for making meaningful change in schools. She stressed the urgency to "interrupt the negative conversations in the teachers' lounge when people would put down our kids." Adrianna also emphasized the need to "stand up for the students who were often overlooked." Margaret shared similar insights with her "new found engagement and commitment to social justice by being a bridge for students and families." She contended, "I got it. I'm drinking the Kool-Aid." Prachi concurred and recognized the power from within and the need "to push herself" to lead for meaningful change in schools. For these women, the process of audio/video self-reflection afforded them with spaces to "struggle in the silence" and "look at themselves in new ways." And as Adrianna noted, "I grew in unexpected ways and never realized why I did the things I did, but this process gave me a chance to see the real me. I couldn't hide behind a video. I realize that now, so it gave me a chance to really think about what all of this meant to me a school leader."

IMAGINATIVE POSSIBILITIES THROUGH SENSE-MAKING

Initially, these women described their identities as a combination of positions and tasks associated with their school employment (e.g., disciplinarians, curriculum developers, supervisors). Over time, they began to identify themselves according to their gender, race/ethnicity, sexuality, ability, native language, immigration status, age, class, and religion. Adrianna noted, "I recognized how often I lived what I thought of myself as a woman, but I didn't think about it before. I chose to go into teaching because I wanted to make a difference. I feel the same way in my life outside of work. I have responsibilities to my husband, family, and friends." For these women, they grappled with understanding their learning selves in times of complex meaning making. For example, they initially referred to themselves as "positions at a school." They discovered how often they ignored their lived experiences, voices, and insights. Margaret and Prachi stressed the "need to look within" but recounted how often they were not encouraged to do so in preparation programs, within professional development, and within their community.

As they deepened their new ways of understanding self in relation to self and others, they made connections among their experiences, insights, and feelings. Adrianna compared her "old self" to her "new self" as "saying what other people consider right" to "sharing how she makes sense of the world." Often, these women noted how often they were unaware of their "felt mentality." At times, these concerns centered on peer acceptance, especially for those who were members of the dominant culture. For example, Adrianna revealed her "guardedness" in her role as a school leader when she turned her written replies to weekly reflections into a prewritten script that her boyfriend filmed at her request. In them, she recognized possible consequences of her not being "true to herself." In an effort to come to terms with this tension between "what others want in her" and "what she wants for herself" as a school leader, she decided to "take a risk" and share her ways of knowing by privately filming herself rather than performing for her boyfriend and any other audience, present or implied.

In light of such comments, it is perhaps not surprising their reflections revealed how often they struggled in processes of sense-making that in many ways challenged their traditional approaches to understanding leadership as well as the influence of self as learner. For Adrianna, this process was at times "mentally challenging." These women recognized the need to "choose to serve those who have been forgotten in schools," and as Margaret noted, "to use her voice" and "help people understand what you stand for and why." They internalized a newfound sense of self through this process of sensual meaning making and described how "surprised" they were by their "enthusiasm" and "passion" to promote social justice and equity in schools. As Margaret stressed, "I realize I am ready to fight the fight and want to live what I am learning." Similarly, Adrianna said, "I know it begins with me and I want to work with people at my school to make a difference, especially for the students who don't have a champion."

These women engaged in identity development centering on making connections between lived experiences, assumptions, and responses towards children and families. Through these experiences, they discovered how the process of looking within can create intense emotional experiences. Adrianna, for example, shared how "surprised" she was when she "got emotional" about a documentary, and how her voice "cracked" when she described how the experience influences how she understands what it means to live as a promoter for social justice. As their awareness of self and self-relation to others deepened, so too did their understanding of the role of developing self. They realized their capacity for genuine choice in addressing issues of social justice and equity in schools. For Margaret, this understanding was embedded in the impact of this emotional process in his recognition of the existence of oppression and the role she played as the "bridge" within her school community:

> People are complicated beings whose lives are storied and whose identities are narrtively constructed. My artwork uses faces to represent the leader and student and a connecting rope bridge to symbolize the bridge leader's stewardship and commitment to improving the lives of other. The student's molded face is peeled back to illustrate the complex layers of the human being, the rope bridge adjoins the mouths of these two individuals and focuses attention on the necessity of speaking up to empower disenfranchised students, families, communities, and educational systems.

Adrianna too began to express her new sense of self by positioning herself in spaces in which she could make change within her school community. She initiated dialogue regarding marginalized populations and how to utilize literature to broaden the scope of student understanding. She also initiated the first Gay Straight Alliance within her urban school district to promote safe schools for all students. For these women, their experiences encouraged them to immerse themselves in uncomfortable spaces, to examine the interconnectedness between their ways of knowing, and to respond in culturally responsive ways to those most in need. They realized that "walking the talk" and "living what we believe" were critical to engaging others in their inquiries. These spaces welcomed others into meaningful conversations and often "built bridges" to form alliances with teachers and community members and, ultimately, created forums centered on new discourses.

EMBODIED SENSE-MAKING THROUGH ARTMAKING

These women explicitly noted what they saw as the importance of sense-making through artmaking, a process they felt encouraged them to act on their ways of knowing and the process of arriving at such understandings.

As with the previous sections, Adrianna, Margaret, and Prachi's narratives serve as exemplary lenses that performatively document the kinds of transformations they experienced throughout the reflective process.

Adrianna

Pluralities of people's lived experiences and meaning making are exemplified in Adrianna's artmaking. The multiple images and her personal vision afford viewers with new perspectives of what she sees, feels, and imagines for schools. Adrianna's art translates into content and provides her meaning-making with form. The process affords her a space to deepen her consciousness and refined attunement to engaging authentically and adventurously with a particular consciousness that includes the need for intentional efforts to foster a renewal of self, and self in relation to others.

Adrianna stressed how often she "struggled" with making meaningful change. She often emphasized the need to be "fully present" with "self and self in relation to others." When Adrianna was able to make deliberate efforts to deepen her ways of knowing, she not only engaged in art as maker, but she infused her understanding with the release of her imagination. The process encouraged her to allow her feelings and thoughts to inform and illuminate what needed to be realized. And in this case, Adrianna became engaged to in various modes of seeing and sense-making and grounding these new understandings within her life as an aspiring school leader.

She recognized the reflective nontext based process as necessary to "seeing a whole change…that these little tiny changes being made within a person are worth the growth, and I know they are it's just…you don't always see it right away." Adrianna worked closely with a community artist throughout this process. Her artist mentor lived through Vietnam protests and the Civil Rights movement. Roman and Adrianna often discussed how "unaware" she was regarding significant historical events or people who sacrificed their lives for others' rights (i.e., Ruby Bridges, Emmett Till, Jim Crow, Frederick Douglas, Josiah Henson). As they engaged in meaningful dialogue about the role of race and racism within the foundations of modern culture and policy, Adrianna started to make more concerted efforts to deepen her understanding and implications for leading for social justice in schools through her artmaking (see Figure 12.1). She wanted her artmaking to recognize the need for a new vision as well as realizing the need for educators to attend to their part. She hoped to encourage viewers to "wonder" about the implications of her vision. The process "always held more than what I thought would happen, because it encouraged me to ponder" and "to think about imagining what could be."

Over the course of the semester, Adrianna's responses in her reflective practice documented how artmaking illustrated the deepening understanding and

Figure 12.1 Social justice is like art...if we don't pay attention, it's not there.

empathy in her sense-making—her final art object focused on the need to *look within* in "order to grow as school leaders." For her piece, Adrianna used a clock to represent a "timeline" of events that signified "horrifying beginnings" and "ideal" ends. The ideal depended on the imagination creating openings that were often unexpected; however, they afforded Adrianna opportunities to rethink social justice issues in schools by depending upon her imaginative possibilities.

Adrianna created the clock as a catalyst to provoke meaningful dialogue about the lived experiences of marginalized populations and the role each of us plays to improve the realities of underserved children and their families. Adrianna hoped to engage viewers in an examination of their tendency to perpetuate oppressive practices. Her clock symbolized a vision centered on each of us playing a vital role in leading for social justice from spinning hands, a metaphor for how "those in dominant positions perpetuate the status quo," to artifacts placed at each number on the clock to represent a continuum of change, beginning with slavery and ending at the Human Rights Federation's equal sign. Her use of silver paint symbolized a mirror and the need to look within and acknowledge how each of us perpetuates oppressive practices.

Margaret

An emphasis was placed on social justice work being a highly emotional endeavor. For Margaret, the experience evoked a range of emotions from fear to frustration to shock to anger to enlightenment. She felt frustrated with the system at large because colleagues and school leaders did not seem to "speak the same language" or "find value in what she was learning." We discussed the significance of beginning from within. She recognized the need to become self-aware and to examine the potentially powerful means by which she could help uncover injustices through literature. Throughout this reflective process, she illustrated through her artmaking how she drew the courage, joy, and imagination to address the lack of responsiveness toward issues of social justice. The process engaged her heart, mind, and body in unexpected ways. So much of what needed to be accomplished began with Margaret. She realized that engaging herself through nontext expression, she was able to address repressed thoughts and emotions regarding the service of social justice in schools. Her thoughts centered on "the power of one" and the "need to begin from within." Margaret realized her hard work was essential. She also discovered that by "being the bridge," by internalizing and embodying these new ways of knowing and responding, she could permeate oppressive ideologies and structures within her school. She labored over ways in which to interrupt these practices and concluded that she needed to utilize her position as "teacher" to model what was meant to by "becoming" a social justice leader in schools.

Margaret's social justice stance centered on this statement: School leaders have the moral responsibility to serve, advocate, and bridge the gap for those from disenfranchised populations. Margaret perceived current school leaders as "inadequately prepared with the skills, knowledge, and commitment to interrupt oppressive school practices." She called for candidates in leadership preparation programs to be "astute activists" for underserved populations. Margaret contended that school leaders "needed to be astute activists for underserved populations" and believed "preparation programs should encourage school leaders to be advocates and champions for all children and families." Her position of power as a teacher and graduate student afforded her opportunities to share her new ways of knowing with other school community members. Margaret utilized her audio/video reflections as spaces to look within and process the political implications of her emotions as well as the hierarchical relationship between reason and emotion. She recognized how often issues of social justice were not discussed, because "those" issues are not "in our job description" or are often "ignored." By pushing these concerns aside, school community members were not held accountable to "deal with" or "address" the exclusive nature of school practices/policies in her district.

The restrictive and repressive school practices and policies did not seem to value emotion, critical thought, or intellectual practices. Therefore, she decided to interrupt these distorted school practices by promoting student-centered work, opportunities to empower students, and affording students opportunities to express their authentic selves through artmaking and literature. She utilized literature in her classrooms to foster emotion, engage students in processing what was meant by social justice, and afford them opportunities to have a voice. Margaret believed such efforts have the potential to "reform oppressive practices and promote systemic change." She began by examining herself and proceeded by creating spaces in which students used literature to dialogue about unjust power relations and the need to embody genuine transformation of self by engaging in strong expressions of emotion. She emphasized the need for teachers and school leaders to promote "democratic ideals and values necessary for an equitable and socially just education because they appear more often in rhetoric than in practice."

Margaret utilized the symbol of a bridge, which she embodied within her sense of self and identity as a school leader, to illustrate bridge making as a process (see Figure 12.2). In other words, Margaret embodied a new sense of self and recognized the need *to become* the bridge. Margaret noted how often "bridges symbolize patient stability and an emotional growth or journey." She believed "bridge leaders are culturally proficient individuals who engage in the doing and being of leading for social justice." Therefore, students who are marginalized "need champions willing to bridge the gaps in education." She noted, "My artmaking illustrates the urgency and determination for bridge leaders in education to move us from rhetoric to activism." She continued, "While these bridges are not necessarily physical passageways, they are critical corridors by which disenfranchised people can segue from one place in their lives to another." The making of the

Figure 12.2 Building bridges: Championing for all students.

images offered a way to "break through the boundaries" and "rediscover" herself as an educator and making pathways for something new.

For Margaret, it was imperative that the educational system assist in ridding society of inequities and embedding democratic principles for *all* citizens. She used her "body and soul" in her artmaking and understood this as a metaphor, a tool, for making deeper connections between self and others. The space informed her practice, ways of knowing, and ways of responding. It was "unlike any other experience" because the process afforded "everyone opportunities to gain knowledge about themselves" and "turn these new ways of understanding into wisdom." Margaret emphasized the process does not require "people to be talented or elite artists"; rather, it is a complex process of "making meaning about our role within schools, within our communities, and within society at large." She came to understand that the collective knowing and understanding of self and sharing this experience with her students afforded everyone an opportunity to work as a collective, which made her social justice stance even more significant, because she was *living it.*

Contrary to dominant beliefs, Margaret contended, "In order for educational leaders to bridge gaps in relationships and understanding, it is essential to draw educators and school leaders closer to a realized ideal of education through reformation of their policies and practices." She continues, "Through this work, they will make good on exceeding the unmet, American promise created through marginalization." Her artmaking conveys the urgency for transformative leaders to have the moral courage to critique and rid society of inequities while offering the promise of greater individual achievement. Margaret concluded, "If school leaders enlist the help of others, it becomes easier for them to address and terminate oppression within schools." In other words, they need *to become the bridge*. School leaders who serve with a disposition and epistemological view steeped in democracy are *bridges* that enable purposeful communication and collaboration among all involved and impacted by education in order to overcome oppression in schools. They lead with their "mind, body, and soul."

Prachi

An emphasis was placed on "thinking about what we are doing and why we do what we do, especially for children who live on the margins." Nontexted processes afforded Prachi with spaces to become an active learner, because she was "moved in unexpected ways" and challenged to extend and renew her sense of self. Within that space, Prachi found a "new sense of freedom" and awakened self in search of finding meaning through her life story of self with others. Her artmaking created a space for her to find her voice and to play a participatory role in articulating the needs of her young community. Prachi promotes possibility and hope. Her artmaking urges people to reconsider the extent by which we stop and think about the implications of our practices and responses to children and families in schools. She encourages educators to deepen their awareness and open themselves to become more aware of what is possible.

Prachi's artmaking centers on the need for thoughtfulness, authenticity, and commitment to imaginative possibilities. She emphasizes the need for educators to reflect on their practices. This reflective process includes the need to think critically about young imaginations being freed, to propose new intellectualism, or higher-order thinking, to reconsider authentic responses for meaningful change, and to engage in a renewal of self and others. Her passion centers on serving children identified as English language learners (ELL). She suggests that ELL students "are merely shadows, marginalized, isolated, and often overlooked by the cultural majority, but within them is the power to rise above the waters through support and self-advocacy."

The nontexted-based process afforded her spaces to reconsider how life's events occur within our environment and situate us in specific spaces and periods of time. Reflecting on these encounters through sense-making enabled her to recapture the process of *becoming*, and in this case, of becoming a woman leading for social justice. As a meaning maker, she engaged in understanding her role in constructing and reconstructing realities of those she served—children identified as English language learners. Her artmaking reflects a multitude of perspectives and voices, and she recognized that the construction of this meaning making is never complete. The focus of her work is on a process—deepening of consciousness and the need for action.

Prachi emphasized how often students identified as ELL face challenges associated with linguistic, academic, cultural, and social adjustments in a new cultural and educational environment. Her concerns center on the increasing number of students whose first language is not English and the limited number of teachers who are capable and/or willing to embrace these students in their classrooms. As a result, Prachi noted many ELL students do not receive specialized language services and are often assigned to regular classrooms where they are mainstreamed with English-speaking students, in spite of their limited English language proficiency. She stressed how often "even with multicultural standards and guidelines, preservice teacher education does not adequately prepare teachers to work with linguistically and culturally diverse students."

Prachi stressed how often factors related to the social and cultural background of ELL students may negatively influence their academic performance. She capitalized on her new understanding by translating the tendency for monocultural restoration in schools into artmaking. The children's lived experiences became the focal point of her meaning-making. Prachi noted, "Moreover, for ELL students, the issue is not just about learning English. Rather, it involves critical issues such as their identities in school and their interpersonal relationships with other people. This is why it is very important to introduce their perspective into ESL education discourse in a way that informs both theory and practice." She continues, stating, "Tailoring English as a second language (ESL) teaching to the cultures of the students, that is, incorporating the behavioral and interactional patterns rooted in students' cultures, might be another useful way to help ESL students to achieve and learn to their full potential." Her artmaking illustrates the need for effective culturally responsive school leaders to build inclusive curricula that match the cultural and linguistic backgrounds of the learners and work with their parents to participate more fully in their children's education. Prachi stressed, "The challenge of diversity cannot be denied or overlooked by merely attempting to bridge the achievement gap. We as educators and proponents of social justice need to make a deliberate effort to bridge the growing chasm between language-majority and language-minority students."

The title of Prachi's art is "Hidden Voices" (Figure 12.3). Her artmaking centers on clashing perspectives and contesting voices within public schools and the need to give way for effective dialogue. This dialogue calls for less reactive approaches and the intentional incorporation of holistic school practices that reconsider the significance of voice and story. Prachi emphasized that people who are marginalized often feel discriminated against or shamed because of their identity (i.e., race, ethnicity, class, religion, native language, sexual identity, ability—mental/physical, family structure, gender). For those who are disenfranchised, she contends that discriminatory practices often impact the degree to which they can propose imaginative possibilities, because they tend to be ostracized and silenced by

Isolation   Hope   Self-Advocacy

Figure 12.3   Hidden voices.

those in positions of power. Prachi noted a need for teachers, school leaders, children, and families to be more aware of alternative possibilities they want to pursue, especially if they feel their truths are questioned, ignored, or silenced. The interplay of this complex engagement is represented her artmaking.

Prachi created three coiled pots. The coils are symbolic of the building blocks, which she contends are the foundation of every culture. The earthtone net, to represent "warmth," was made by hand by her community artist mentor, who followed the tradition of net making by Peruvian fishermen using a shuttle. The first pot (on the left) placed on the fisherman's net represents how English Language Learners are trapped in "a web of isolation." Prachi expresses her concern that the "voices of children identified as English language learners are not heard." The second pot (in the middle), is titled "hope." This pot is wrapped in a net and hanging from the ceiling and is symbolic of the support of family, teachers, administrators, and community members who need to provide encouragement and support for children identified as English Language Learners. The last pot (on the far right) is titled "Self-Advocacy." The coiled pot has clay vines and flowers embedded within the piece to represent the "blooming of the child." Because of the support and encouragement received by school community members and family, the child learns to become a self-advocate and feels the freedom to express feelings of pride, accomplishment, and success. Her work urges viewers to reconsider their role in promoting this work and the need to awaken the imagination.

Prachi's awareness of self and self to others through story and understanding left her and others to inquiries in which their perspectives regarding children identified as ELLs were deepened and expanded. These new perspectives engaged her in deepening the consciousness of her colleagues and school leader. The connections made by seeing, hearing, and experiencing enhanced school practices for these children and their families.

DISCUSSION

The implications of these findings suggest that these women promote an evolved vision of leading for social justice through school leadership that extends beyond oneself. They came to understand the immense power of their beliefs, values, and traditions and how these experiences shape their ways of knowing and being. It was through what Pinar (1975) noted as *currere* that the significance of experience of reflective practice and sensemaking encouraged them to speak in their own voices. These voices also emphasized the need to examine interrelationships, especially with those from disenfranchised populations. The reflective nontext-based process reconceptualized their ways of knowing and responding to oppressed populations in schools. The women stressed how these transforming learning spaces offered divergent perspectives that often conflicted with mainstream beliefs and school practices. The reflective process was fundamental to the evolving dialectical relation among the women as knowers, as knowing, and as the known (Pinar, 1994). This transformation afforded Adrianna, Margaret, and Prachi spaces to redefine their sense of self and construct a new self through discourse and scholarship.

The reflective process created critical comprehensive experiences for them. Their histories, experiences, insights, and voices were heard, valued, and celebrated. They shared the need to investigate what it meant to be an educational leader interested in promoting social justice and equity. Their lived experiences were the foundation for their calling. Their lived experiences shaped their perspectives and ultimately their ways of knowing and commitment to serving marginalized populations. They recognized the significance of making meaning, how interpretations are made, and the power of creating symbols, signs, and meanings that encompass a total range of human feeling (Langer, 1953). Their experiences were valued and perceived as sources of insight. Throughout this process, their symbolic forms came to represent the ways in which they were choosing to live and lead. Adrianna, Margaret, and Prachi embodied these symbols that revealed their imaginative possibilities (Boske, 2009).

They came to understand their new ways of knowing and being as imperative to influencing the lives of those they served across schools, within communities, and for future generations. Adrianna, Margaret, and Prachi remind us that *their leadership matters*. They understood reflective sense-making practices as a process through which they recognized themselves as tools of expression. The process was comprised of contiguous interwoven threads that blurred any separation between their artmaking and living their inquiries. Artmaking served as a visual representation that encompassed forms of consciousness and commitment to strive toward expression of self and self to others. Their movements and forms of increased critical consciousness became the access structures to the life of feeling and promotion of social justice work in schools. The process captured the nuances of their personal journeys and echoed their deepest trajectories of thought—what is within must be spoken, and what is spoken must be lived. Their process exemplifies the cognate insight expressed when speaking of significant life experiences. This symbolic transformation occurred because, for each of them, their new sense of self reflected a whole cultural rebirth (Langer, 1953).

Although this work is not necessarily new to extant arts literature regarding classrooms and teaching, there is a dearth of opportunities for future or current school leaders to make sense of their understandings through artmaking. Adrianna, Margaret, and Prachi stressed how often they were not encouraged to share their emotions and remain in control in order to be identified as a professional (see Beatty, 2000). However, after engaging in this process, they realized that controlling emotions often suggest repressing intense emotional responses that may have detrimental effects on their ability and willingness to commit to social justice work (Larson & Ovando, 2001). They also realize the need for intellectual guidance with context specific activities and spaces for reflective narrative practices (e.g., Clandinin, Conelly, & Chan, 2002).

Their insights suggest a framework for understanding the significance of sense-making and the need to promote the visible self for women school leaders (see Figure 12.4). At the outermost layer, these women understood their positions as spaces to make transformational change within larger systems and for future generations. They emphasized the need to engage in this work as antithetical to specific prevailing practices, but also, they recognized the need to aspire to promoting self-work and work with others. It is within this conceptual model (see Figure 12.4) that these women understand the impact of passivity and the need to encourage themselves and others to engage in authentic tensions within social-intellectual relations, and ultimately, to be visible and be heard.

The reflective process invited the cultivation of an internal dialectic. It became a call to examine personal responses to interactions, scholarly readings, colleagues, and the community at large. Their sensibility exhibited their new sense of self as a vital position to understanding and realizing the need to be firm, unyielding, and strong. Through the examination of their histories and origin of life, they formulated new understandings of

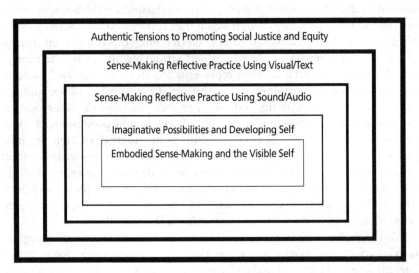

Figure 12.4 Embodied sense-making and the visible self.

self, which led to discovering the nature of intellectual development and the need to actively engage in imaginative possibilities. The reflective process utilized audio/video tools, which encouraged them to venture toward uncharted territory in an effort to better understand the impact of their lived experiences. Adrianna, Margaret, and Prachi stressed that audio/video provided necessary tools to express their experiences, feelings, and insights that "words alone" could not. Their artmaking served as a physical manifestation of their growing understandings about self, self in relation to others, and social justice. The process encouraged them to make dramatic shifts from traditional written prompts, to audio (sound)/video (visual) understandings, to visual metaphors, to new embodied selves, all of which become the impetus of radically understanding oneself in relation to others, especially for those who live on the margins.

Utilizing the senses (sight and sound) encouraged them to give *feeling to form* and *form to feeling* (Langer, 1953). As they moved from text to audio to visual metaphors through artmaking, they *came to know* and *live their inquiries*, which centered on social justice and equity issues facing U.S. public schools. The interconnectedness between the senses afforded them spaces to create multiple meanings centering on an evolving school leadership identity. They made connections between what they saw, heard, felt, and experienced by connecting their emotion-laden experiences through artmaking, directly impacting their ways of *knowing* (Langer, 1982). This sense-making process guided them through a process in which their senses transform their consciousness (Eisner, 2002), deepened their understanding of their beliefs and attitudes towards power (Allen, 1995), and created spaces centered on an ethic of care through imaginative possibilities (Greene, 1995; Noddings, 1984).

Their notion of making sense not only centers on deepening their understanding of sensory exploration, but they engage in actions aligned with revelations from their reflective processes. These new responses encourage understanding the interconnectedness between sense of self, school practices, and impact of responses (Schön, 1983). Understanding the implications of this reflective process range from using text as a way of knowing to understanding the significance of sight and sound to deepening their beliefs as school leaders (Allen, 1995). These spaces serve to uncover the influence of lived experiences as well as marginalized voices through storytelling (Barone, 2002). The process functions as a release, promoting imaginative possibilities centered on understanding their role in interrupting oppressive school practices (see Greene, 1995). They rediscovered their renewed sense of self and renewal. Their new ways of knowing through nontext-based processes created spaces for alternative structures. They challenged the oppressive nature of these structures, critically thought about the implications of those perspectives and practices, and proposed imaginative possibilities through the creation of new experiences. In these ways, sense-making pushed their rigid conceptual boundaries of what it meant to lead as women in schools to understanding how their senses influence their ways of knowing, recognizing structural inequities, and ability to challenge cultural and educational superiority of the dominant culture (i.e., White, middle-class, English speaking, Christian, heterosexual communities) to interrupt oppressive school practices (Gonzalez et al., 2005; Marshall & Oliva, 2010; Tooms & Boske, 2010a). The impact of sense-making transformed their school leadership identities from narrowly defined roles, attitudes, and beliefs about women to new ways of knowing and responding to the world, especially for underserved populations.

IMPLICATIONS

This chapter opens up possibilities to engage women school leaders in authentic ways to deepen their understanding, ways of knowing through sensory experience, and making meaningful systemic change. Experimental exploration and thinking about knowing through sense-making suggests those who prepare school leaders should reconsider how to expand women's ways of knowing about what it means to lead for social justice (e.g., Boske, 2012d; Boske & Tooms, 2010; Theoharis, 2007). The sense-making reflective practice framework affords tremendous possibilities for teaching and learning by placing pedagogy at the center of programmatic practices with knowledge and experience in the making (e.g., Ellsworth, 2005). Sense-making evolves as school leaders engage in a myriad of media that afford them spaces to engage as visual artists. Artmaking creates uncertain spaces to reconceptualize what is meant by leading schools as well as how their identities are viewed within art (e.g., Springgay, 2008). The process is a constant exchange of knowing and not knowing and becoming more comfortable with the intersections of personal and situational experiences. Those who prepare educators may reconsider how they encourage candidates to boldly confront their inquiry and willingness to engage in a process centered on imaginative possibilities. Such examinations encourage educators to continuously reflect on their ways of knowing and implications for marginalized populations, all of which are essential to this *making process.*

Sense-making encourages people to reconsider their ability to engage in new ways of understanding through perception, selection, and responsiveness. The relationship between how they understand themselves as school leaders was reorganized throughout the ongoing dialogue of reflection, metaphor, and artmaking. The experience, therefore, becomes more than finding value in artmaking. It engages candidates with the senses, expanding values of personal knowings, interpretations, and expressions that evolved into a newly constructed school leadership identity. This examination relies heavily on the individual's ability and willingness to engage in meaningful dialogue and active participation in sense-making. These experiences are not only shared with others—they are encouraged to be *felt* and *lived*. As such, these opportunities have the potential to be absorbed by the complexities of relations, support candidates in identifying themselves as a medium or vehicle for learning and change, and utilize pedagogy as a medium for sense-making.

If educational preparation programs promote sense-making reflective practices, sensitivity towards curriculum as medium might deepen understanding through an exchange of self and self, self and other, and self and community. Sense-making through a nontext-based process engages educators in a process of metaphor and play, avoiding rigid boundaries of right versus wrong, and catapults them into imaginative possibilities and renewal of self. The connective process precedes meaningful learning, because it is a transformational medium centering on change of self, and ultimately, change in ways of knowing and responding to the world. The creative process affords a worthwhile direction emphasizing teaching and learning for social justice and equity in schools. The process plays a significant role in educator's expressing the need to have, to desire, and to engage in awareness of self and others. This process, which originates from situated life and considers the plurality of people's lived experiences, is critical to learning how to take a more thoughtful approach to promoting social justice in schools. To think in relation about what we do and why we do what we do affords us spaces to develop a deeper consciousness of ourselves, our struggles, our meaning making, and responding authentically to those we serve. This process engages educators in a specific dialogue—one of hope and renewal.

CONCLUSION

Where there is a prevailing current ethos of radical critical theory and cultural responsiveness in schools, and where the learning process is understood as more than a transmission of knowledge, there is a need to inquire about someone's background, place of origin, expectations, desires, and experience; these ways of knowing are pivotal to the pedagogic process. Challenging repressive notions within leading schools exposes educators to truths, prejudices, and biases that often do not align themselves with the lived experiences of people from disenfranchised populations. And for the purpose of this chapter, they may not align with women's histories. There is a need to interrogate in more detail official educational discourses within universities in an effort to better understand their role in preparing contemporary women school leaders.

Broadly, I am arguing that for women in school leadership to be taken into account, they must first be understood as having been ignored. The pushing away permits those interested in this work to continue to dismantle and navigate the existence of women in leadership and voice needed for its renewal. The emotions and lived experiences of school leaders, especially marginalized populations, are not to be eliminated, ignored, or suppressed. Rather, their emotions are essential to creating socially just practices and policies, because they create new and deeper connections with those served. The challenge is to make multiple voices and visions and to attend to the plurality of consciousness, which has the potential to promote authentic responsiveness, social justice, and equity. It is within these spaces that educators consider contexts such as caring, concern, and integrity. These principles are in response to the call to lead in just ways. Those who prepare educators may need to rethink how their teaching encourages candidates' newly transformed selves to engage in this courageous work. Using their imaginative possibilities is critical to attending to the plurality of consciousness and responsiveness in schools. Therefore, pedagogy and curriculum are vital spaces of encounter, of creating new ways of knowing, and of coming in contact with diverse histories, including gender histories—which, unfortunately, have otherwise been subject to enforced forgetting. But perhaps, because their narratives have been shared in this chapter, opportunities can be imagined, because *now* they have been written.

REFERENCES

Allen, P. B. (1995). *Art is a way of knowing*. Boston, MA: Shambhala Publications.

Apple, M. W. (1993). *Official knowledge: Democratic education in a conservative age*. New York, NY: Routledge.

Barone, T. (2002). From genre blurring to audience blending: Reflections on the field emanating from an ethnodrama. *Anthropology and Education Quarterly, 33*(2), 255–267.

Beatty, B. (2000). The emotions of educational leadership, *International Journal of Leadership in Education, 3*(4), 331–357.

Bogotch, I. (2002). Educational leadership and social justice: Practice into theory. *Journal of School Leadership, 12,* 138–156.

Boske, C. (2009). Imaginative thinking: Addressing social justice issues through MovieMaker. *Multicultural Education and Technology Journal, 3*(3), 213–226.

Boske, C. (2011a). Audio and video reflections to promote social justice. *Multicultural Education & Technology Journal, 5*(1), 70–85.

Boske, C. (2011b). Sense-making reflective practice: Preparing school leaders for nontext-based understandings. *Journal of Curriculum Theorizing, 27*(2), 82–100.

Boske, C. (2012a). Aspiring school leaders addressing social justice through artmaking. *Journal of School Leadership, 22*(1), 116–146.

Boske, C. (2012b). *Educational leadership: Building bridges among ideas, schools and nations.* Charlotte, NC: Information Age Publishing.

Boske, C. (2012c). Sending forth tiny ripples of hope that build the mightiest of currents: Understanding how to prepare school leaders to interrupt oppressive school practices. *Planning and Changing* [Special Issue], *43*(1–2), 183–197.

Boske, C. (2012d). Standing still is no longer an option: Understanding how to prepare school leaders to interrupt oppressive practices. In C. Boske & S. Diem (ed.), *Global Leadership for Social Justice: Taking it from the Field to Practice (Advances in Educational Administration, Volume 14)* (pp. 159–171). Bingley, UK: Emerald Publishing.

Boske, C. (2013). Preparing school leaders for social justice. In I. Bogotch & C. Shields (Eds.), *International Handbook of Social [In]Justice and Educational Leadership.* (289–308). Netherlands: Springer.

Boske, C. (2014). Critical reflective practices: Connecting to social justice. In I. Bogotch & C. Shields (Eds.), I*nternational Handbook of Social [In] Justice and Educational Leadership* (pp. 289–308). Netherlands: Springer.

Boske, C., & Diem, S. (2012). *Global leadership for social justice: Taking it from the field to practice.* Bingley, UK: Emerald Publishing Educational Leadership Book Series.

Boske, C., & Tooms, A. K. (2010a). Clashing epistemologies: Reflections on change, culture and the politics of the professoriate. In G. Jean-Marie & T. Normore (Eds.), *Educational leadership preparation: Innovation and interdisciplinary approaches to the Ed. D. and graduate education* (pp. 33–52). New York, NY: Palgrave MacMillan.

Boske, C., & Tooms, A. K. (2010b). Social justice and doing "being ordinary." In A. K. Tooms & C. Boske (Eds.), *Building bridges: Connecting educational leadership and social justice to improve schools* (pp. xvii–xxviii). Charlotte, NC: Information Age Publishing.

Bowden, M., Billig, S., &, Holland, B.A. (2008). *Scholarship for sustaining service-learning and civic engagement.* Charlotte, NC: Information Age Publishing.

Brown, K. (2004). Leadership for social justice and equity: Weaving a transformative framework and pedagogy. *Educational Administration Quarterly, 40*(1), 79–110.

Brown, K. (2006). Leadership for social justice and equity: Evaluating a transformative framework and andragogy. *Educational Administration Quarterly, 42*(5), 700–745.

Burns, J. M. (1978). *Leadership.* New York, NY: Harper & Row.

Cahnmann-Taylor, M., & Siegesmund, R. (2008). *Arts-based research in education: Foundations for practice.* New York, NY: Routledge.

Clandinin, D. J., Connelly, F. M., & Chan, E. (2002). Three narrative teaching practices—One narrative teaching exercise. In N. Lyons & V. K. LaBoskey (Eds.), *Narrative inquiry in practice: Advancing the knowledge of teaching* (pp. 133–145). New York, NY: Teachers College Press.

Darling-Hammond, L. (1997). *The right to learn: A blueprint for creating schools that work.* San Francisco, CA: Jossey-Bass.

Darling-Hammond, L. (2002). Learning to teach for social justice. In L. Darling-Hammond, J. French, & S. Garcia-Lopez (Eds.), *Learning to teach for social justice* (pp. 1–7). New York, NY: Teachers College Press.

Darling-Hammond, L. (2005). New standards and old inequalities: School reform and the education of African American students. In J. E. King (Ed.), *Black education: A transformative research and action agenda for the new century* (pp.197–224). Mahwahy, NJ: Erlbaum.

Dewey, J. (1934). *Art as experience*. Toms River, NJ: Capricorn Books.

Dewey, J. (1938). *Experience and education*. New York, NY: Collier Books.

Dewey, J. (1961). *Democracy and education*. Old Tappan, NJ: Macmillan.

Dewey, J. (2004). My pedagogic creed. In D. J. Flinders & S. J. Thornton (Eds.), *The curriculum studies reader* (2nd ed., pp. 17–23). New York, NY: Routledge-Falmer: (Original work published 1897).

Eisner, E. W. (1994). *The educational imagination: On the design and evaluation of school programs* (3rd ed.). New York, NY: Macmillan.

Eisner, E. W. (2002). From episteme to phronesis to artistry in the study and improvement of teaching. *Teaching and Teacher Education, 18*(4), 375–385.

Eisner, E. (2008). Art and knowledge. In A. Cole & J. Knowles (Eds.), *Handbook of the arts in qualitative research: Perspectives, methodologies, examples, and issues* (pp. 3–12). London, UK: Sage.

Ellsworth, E. (2005). *Places of learning: Media, architecture, pedagogy*. New York, NY: Routledge.

Feagin, J., Orum, A., & Sjoberg, G. (Eds.). (1991). *A case for case study*. Chapel Hill, NC: University of North Carolina Press.

Gay, G. (2010). *Culturally responsive teaching: Theory, research, and practice* (2nd ed.). New York, NY: Teachers College Press.

Gonzalez, N., Moll, L., & Amanti, C. (Eds.). (2005). *Funds of knowledge: Theorizing practices in households, communities and classrooms*. Mahwah, NJ: Erlbaum.

Greene, M. (1995). *Releasing the imagination: Essays on education, the arts, and social change*. San Francisco, CA: Jossey-Bass.

Grogan, M., & Shakeshaft, C. (2011). *Women and educational leadership*. San Francisco, CA: Jossey-Bass.

Henderson, J. G., & Gornik, R. (2007). *Transformative curriculum leadership* (3rd ed.). Upper Saddle River, NJ: Pearson.

Kozol, J. (1991). *Savage inequalities: Children in America's schools*. New York, NY: Crown.

Kozol, J. (2006). *Shame of the nation: The restoration of apartheid schooling in America*. New York, NY: Crown Publishers.

Kridel, C. (2010). *Encyclopedia of curriculum studies*. Thousand Oaks, CA: Sage.

Ladson-Billings, G. (1994). *The dreamkeepers: Successful teachers of African-American children*. San Francisco, CA: Jossey-Bass.

Ladson-Billings, G. (2006). From the achievement gap to the education debt: Understanding achievement in U.S. schools. *Educational Researcher, 35*(7), 3–12.

Land, R. R., & Stovall, D. O. (Eds.). (2009). Hip hop and social justice. *Equity and Excellence in Education, 42*(1), 433–435.

Langer, S. K. (1953). *Feeling and form: A theory of art*. New York, NY: Scribner.

Langer, S. K. (1972). *Mind: An essay on human feeling* (Vol. 2). Baltimore, MD: John Hopkins University Press.

Langer, S. K. (1982). *Philosophy in a new key: A study in the symbolism of reason, rite, and art* (3rd ed.). Cambridge, MA: Harvard University Press.

Larson, C., & Ovando, C. (2001). *The color of bureaucracy: The politics of equity in multicultural school communities.* New York, NY: Wadsworth.

Lopez, G. R. (2003). The (racially-neutral) politics of education: A critical race theory perspective, *Educational Administration Quarterly, 39*(1), 68–94.

Malewski, E. (2009). *Curriculum studies handbook: The next moment.* New York, NY: Routledge.

Marshall, C. (1993). *The new politics of race and gender.* London, UK: Falmer Press.

Marshall, C., & Gerstyl-Pepin, C. (2005). *Re-framing educational politics for social justice.* Boston, MA: Allyn & Bacon.

Marshall, C., & Oliva, M. (2010). *Leadership for social justice: Making revolutions in education* (2nd ed.). Boston, MA: Allyn & Bacon.

Noddings, N. (1984). *Caring: A feminine approach to ethics and moral education.* Berkeley, CA: University of California Press.

Pinar, W. (1975). *Curriculum theorizing: The reconceptualists.* Richmond, CA: McCutchan Publishers.

Pinar, W. F., (1994). *Autobiography, politics and sexuality: Essays in curriculum theory 1972–1992.* New York, NY: Peter Lang.

Pinar, W. F., Reynolds, W. M., Slatter, P., & Taubman, P. M. (1975). *Understanding curriculum.* New York, NY: Peter Lang.

Reyes, P., Scribner, J., & Parades-Scribner, A. (1999). Delta forces: The changing fabric of American society and education. In J. Murphy & K. S. Louis (Eds.), *Handbook of Research in Educational Administration* (pp. 183–201). San Francisco, CA: Jossey-Bass.

Scheurich, J. J., & Skrla, L. (2003). *Leadership for equity and excellence: Creating high-achievement classrooms, schools, and districts.* Thousand Oaks, CA: Corwin.

Schön, D. (1983) *The reflective practitioner: How professionals think in action.* San Francisco, CA: Basic Books.

Shakeshaft, C. (1989). *Women in educational administration.* Thousand Oaks, CA: Corwin.

Shapiro, L. (2010). Releasing emotion: Artmaking and leadership for social justice. In Marshall, C. & Oliva, M. (Eds.), *Leadership for social justice: Making revolutions in education* (2nd Edition, pp. 242–258). Boston, MA: Pearson.

Shields, C. (2003). *Good intentions are not enough: Transformative leadership for communities of difference.* Lanham, MD: The Scarecrow Press.

Skrla, L., Scheurich, J. J., & Bell McKenzie, K. (2009). *Using equity audits to create equitable and excellent schools.* Thousand Oaks, CA: Corwin Press.

Sleeter, C., & Grant, C. A. (2009). *Making choices for multicultural education: Five approaches to race, class and gender* (6th ed.). Hoboken, NJ: John Wiley & Sons.

Springgay, S. (2008). *Body knowledge and curriculum: Pedagogies of touch in youth and visual culture.* New York, NY: Peter Lang.

Terrell, R. D., & Lindsey, R. B. (2009). *Culturally proficient leadership: The personal journey begins within.* Thousand Oaks, CA: Corwin Press.

Theoharis, G. (2007). Social justice educational leaders and resistance: Toward a theory of social justice leadership. *Educational Administration Quarterly, 43*(2), 221–258.

Tooms, A. K., & Boske, C. (2010). *Building bridges: Connecting educational leadership and social justice to improve schools.* Charlotte, NC: Information Age Publishing.

Trochim, W. (1989). Outcome pattern matching and program theory. *Evaluation and Program Planning, 12*(4), 355.

U.S. Bureau of Census. (2010). 2010 Census data. Retrieved from http://2010.census.gov/2010 census/data/

Yin, R. (1994). *Case study research: Design and methods* (2nd ed.). Thousand Oaks, CA: Sage.

Zwicky, J. (2003). *Wisdom and metaphor*. Kentville, Nova Scotia: Gaspereau Press.

CHAPTER 13

USING FEMINIST PERSPECTIVES TO INTERRUPT AND DISRUPT "GENDER NEUTRALITY" AND REVOLUTIONIZE ORGANIZATIONAL AND POLICY STUDIES

Katherine Cumings Mansfield, Anjalé D. Welton, and Margaret Grogan

ABSTRACT

Revolutionizing the fields of educational policy and organizational studies requires taking a revolutionary approach to policy and organizational research. This chapter aims to show the utility in using feminist perspectives to interrupt and disrupt the long-established practice of utilizing so-called "neutral" frameworks and data-collection tools in educational research endeavors. By taking a historical approach to understanding how we have studied policy and practice in educational leadership in the distant and not-so-distant past, we

Women Interrupting, Disrupting, and Revolutionizing Educational Policy and Practice, pages 245–265
Copyright © 2014 by Information Age Publishing
245

show how the gendering of policy and organizational studies holds promise to push the field forward in new and important ways. We also argue that the current trend of returning to "scientific" educational research is a type of backlash against feminist scholars that must be resisted to ensure a holistic appraisal of policy and organizational studies.

Revolutionizing the fields of educational policy and organizational studies requires taking a revolutionary approach to policy and organizational research. This chapter aims to show the utility in using feminist perspectives to interrupt and disrupt the long-established practice of utilizing so-called "neutral" frameworks and data-collection tools in educational research endeavors. By taking a historical approach to understanding how we have studied policy and practice in educational leadership in the distant and not-so-distant past, we show how the *gendering* of policy and organizational studies holds promise to push the field forward in new and important ways. We also argue that the current trend of returning to "scientific" educational research is a type of backlash against feminist scholars that must be resisted to ensure a holistic appraisal of policy and organizational studies.

HISTORICAL OVERVIEW

The study of educational leadership, similar to other organizational studies, can trace its roots to the initiation of scientific management in the 1890s (Mills & Tancred, 1992; Scott & Davis, 2007; Shafritz, Ott, & Jang, 2005). Adam Smith is credited with having introduced the concept of the division of labor to the Western lexicon in the 1700s, while Max Weber wrote about charismatic leadership in his work on rational organizations in the 1800s. In the 1890s, Frederick Winslow Taylor sought to improve industrial efficiency by pioneering the concepts of scientific management. Then, in the 1920s, Elton Mayo and his colleagues conducted productivity studies at Western Electric's Hawthorne plant in the United States, resulting in a shift from proving the efficacy of Taylorism to analyzing the effects of human psychology on productivity. This trend led to what is referred to as the Human Relations Movement that focused on humanizing the workplace and human motivation in the actualization of individual and organizational goals (Bolman & Deal, 2003; Follett, 1926/2005; Maslow, 1943/2005; Mills & Tancred, 1992; Scott & Davis, 2007; Shafritz et al., 2005).

After WWII, a rationalist perspective was again accentuated—albeit, sometimes critically—during which there was a push in the social sciences to utilize the theories and methods from the hard sciences such as systems theory (Katz & Kahn, 1966; Scott & Davis, 2007; Senge, 1990; Shafritz et al.,

2005). While the field was profoundly influenced by social psychology, academia continued to emphasize quantitative approaches to research (Bolman & Deal, 2003; Scott & Davis, 2007; Shafritz et al., 2005).

The field of policy studies, while embedded in the much older discipline of political science, is relatively new, especially when compared to the field of organizational studies. According to Engelbert (1977), the field of policy studies in university settings can be traced to the 1930s, when it was coupled with an overarching interest in the New Deal politics of the day. While the field is still relatively young, the decade between the late 1960s and 1970s saw exponential growth in attention given to studying policy as an academic field (Engelbert, 1977). According to Engelbert, "no other subject matter in the social sciences has had a comparable flowering or impact within the university setting" (1977, p. 228).

The literature distinguishes between traditional forms of policy analysis that emphasize empirical methods and critical approaches. The founder of the field, Harold Lasswell, envisioned policy analysis as a means to "create an applied social science that would act as a mediator between academics, government decision makers, and ordinary citizens, by providing objective solutions to problems that would narrow or minimize, if not eliminate, the need for unproductive political debate" (Fischer, 2003, p. 3).

According to Fischer (2003), Lasswell's vision also included taking a multidisciplinary approach to constructing policy analysis with an explicitly normative orientation. Moreover, policy analysis was to have a problem-oriented focus that was contextual in nature. Unfortunately, the policy field did not grasp Lasswell's daring vision, but instead "emerged more along technocratic rather than democratic lines" shaped by a limited methodological framework of "neopositivist/empiricist methods" that disregarded a multidisciplinary approach (Fischer, 2003, p. 4).

Similar to prior organizational studies, the traditional approach to policy studies is described by some as a linear process devoid of value judgments that focuses on measureable facts—free of power struggles—that is supported by scientific application of management skills and program design and implementation (Birkland, 2005; Blackmore, 1995; Fischer, 2003; Marshall, 1999; Rochefort & Cobb, 1994).

While organizational studies and educational policy are two distinct fields, they both have similar roots and continue to be closely or loosely connected, depending on the subject under investigation. Historically, educational policy and practice—and how we study the issues bound up in them—have been interconnected and interdisciplinary. This has created a dialectic, which poses questions and suggests answers about what is important and how those issues deemed important should be studied.

Expansion and Modification of Foci

A major shift in the education research field occurred in the 1980s: Academia no longer viewed quantitative, positivist approaches to research as solely legitimate. Qualitative research methods—borrowed from anthropology—were now acknowledged as valid approaches as well. This coincided with the trend of increased interest in cultural explanations of leadership behavior and organizational change as well as the inclination to view organizations as open systems that interact with cultural context (Bolman & Deal, 2003; Cohen, March, & Olsen, 1972; Cook & Yanow, 2005; Kingdon, 2003; Mills & Tancred, 1992; Schein, 1993, 2004; Scott & Davis, 2007; Shafritz et al., 2005; Trice & Beyer, 1993). Business firms, schools, and other groups have gradually become viewed as communities that develop a unique culture characterized by idiosyncratic rituals and symbols, giving each business firm, school, or group its distinctive identity.

The increasing globalization of the economy has made understanding organizational behavior extremely important in the business world as people with diverse backgrounds and cultural values are required to work together effectively and efficiently (Bolman & Deal, 2003; Cox, 2005; Mills & Tancred, 1992; Scott & Davis, 2007; Shafritz et al., 2005). Along with a general swell in critical scholarship across disciplines in academe, the organizational studies field also faced growing criticism for what has been perceived by some as its ethnocentric and procapitalist biases (Acker, 1992; Alvesson & Billing, 1997; Cox, 2005; Gherardi, 1995; Mills & Tancred, 1992; Schein, 2004; Scott & Davis, 2007; Shafritz et al., 2005).

A Critical Nod

Following the critical turn in organizational studies, academics in a variety of fields turned their attention to power in the workplace generally and the role gender plays in organizations specifically. Some researchers catalogued the inordinate number of men in leadership positions, compared to women—especially in female-saturated careers such as education, nursing, and other service professions (Blount, 1998; Brunner & Grogan, 2007; Grogan, 1996; Marshall, 2003; Shakeshaft, 1989; Skrla, 2003a, 2003b; Young, 2003, 2005). Others studied the ways culture socializes men and women to perform in specific ways to fit in organizations (Acker, 1992; Ackerman, 2008; Alvesson & Billing, 1997; Blount, 1998; Christman & McClellan, 2007; Ferguson, 1985; Gherardi, 1995; Hearn & Parkin, 1992; Hochschild, 1983/2003; Kanter, 2005; Ruddick, 1989; Scott & Davis, 2007; Sheppard, 1992; Skrla, 2000; Tooms, Lugg, & Bogotch, 2010). Additional scholars focused on analyzing policy through a critical feminist lens to illustrate ways organizational procedures and practices affect women differently than men (Acker, 1992; Alvesson & Billing, 1997; Ferguson, 1985; Gherardi, 1995; Hearn & Parkin, 1992; Kanter, 1977, 1979/2005; Marshall, 1999; Pillow, 2003; Scott & Davis, 2007; Sheppard, 1992). We now discuss the gendering of organizational and policy studies in greater detail below.

THE GENDERING OF ORGANIZATIONAL AND POLICY STUDIES

It is important to point out that as early as the 1920s, female scholar Mary Parker Follett (1926/2005) criticized most aspects of scientific management and coined the terms "power with" rather than "power over" to differentiate shared decision-making from coercion. Follett did acknowledge a positive contribution of Taylorism: that is, his notion of depersonalizing orders. For Taylor (1916/2005), it was not a matter of just the managers giving orders to the workers. Rather, the situation dictated the "orders" for *all* individuals, whether overseer or overseen. Each person did what was needed to facilitate the success of the organization on a case-by-case basis. Follett (1926/2005) took this idea and modified it to include her preponderance for building relationships. She argued, "An order should seek to unite, to integrate, dissociated paths." She critiqued the practice of many "bosses" whose behavior was "harassing," "tyrannical," and who exhibited "overbearing conduct" (p. 153), which led to resentment. Not only did the company fail to benefit for time wasted on avoidable conflict, but the worker lost one of the few things she/he truly possessed: her/his self-respect—and the universal human right to be treated respectfully.

Rather than approach management from the "depersonalized" frame of scientific management or the customary, hyperpersonal response as illustrated above, Follett (1926/2005) advocated approaching management in a way she described as *repersonalizing* (p. 155). That is, our personal relationships with people, regardless of their position in the organization, should be first and foremost in our minds and in our habits as we interact. As such, we should not "divorce" people from their personal and professional situations. Moreover, we should ensure that our communications are done as a "face-to-face suggestion" rather than a "long-distance order" (p. 155). Furthermore, Follett wrote, "we need a new word" for orders because the desire to "govern one's own life is, of course, one of the most fundamental feelings in every human being" (p. 155). Follett's (1926/2005) suggestions were a far cry from Weber's (1922) call for a strict segregation between public and private lives via organizational policy. Follett's (1926/2005) work also argued against Taylor's (1916/2005) supposition that workers were inept and overseers were necessary to enforce the adoption and implementation of the scientifically discovered "one best way."

Gender Role Expectations and Fitting In

In 1983, Arlie Hochschild published the influential book, *The Managed Heart: Commercialization of Human Feeling*. Hochschild began with the thesis that human emotion and feeling was, in large part, social. Culture guided the act of recognizing a feeling by proposing what's possible for us to feel. Hochschild (1983/2003) used the example of the Czech word, *litost,* which refers to an indescribable yearning, mixed with regret and sorrow—an anthology of feelings with no counterpart in another language. It is not that a non-Czech person is incapable of feeling *litost.* Rather, a person who is not Czech has not been *socialized* to recognize this constellation of feelings and name it *litost*. In addition to recognition and naming, Hochschild (1983) reported that people are taught "feeling rules." In other words, we learn to manage our feelings in predictable and acceptable ways: for example, to be happy at a wedding, sad at a funeral, and deferential to a superior at work.

Hochschild took the ideas involved with the socialization of emotional feeling and performing and applied it to organizational behavior and work environments: Human beings perform "emotional labor." That is, workers labor to act in a certain way that matches their job role and others' expectations. Likewise, they labor to induce an anticipated emotion or attitude in customers and/or their superiors while on the job (Hochschild, 1983/2003). Hochschild's work is important because she showed that as a job becomes more heavily service-oriented, the more it becomes labor-intensive emotionally. Moreover, the more a person was expected to perform emotional labor on the job, the more likely that job was designated for a female worker. Accordingly, Hochschild (1983/2003) found that there was a division of labor between males and females: Females were expected to be people-pleasers (e.g., airline stewardesses) and males were expected to be in charge (e.g., airline pilots).

Sarah Ruddick (1989) continued Hochschild's ideas in her theory of "maternal work." According to Ruddick, maternal thinking and maternal work entailed the nurturance and training of children (and women) that resulted in a woman's growth, preservation, and social acceptability. Although she acknowledged that both men and women can do maternal work, women in the home or in so-called gendered professions more often did it. She added that since objectivity, self-control, and detachment were necessary to be taken seriously, win recognition, and make gains in male-dominated professions, women's traditional association with maternal work thwarted their attempts to expand to other professions.

When exploring gender expectations on the job, Ferguson (1985) argued that the practice of expecting women to change to succeed in business was inappropriate and unjust. She criticized the proliferation of the self-help book genre that purported to help women succeed in business by taking on more masculine qualities. Ferguson argued that rather than urging women to amend themselves to fit into organizations imprinted with historical patriarchy, organizations need to be revamped to include the voices of women in policy and practice. In addition to pervading personal and work lives, Ferguson (1985) outlined how the traditional patterns of male-female dominance-subordination even penetrated the language of policy and practice in organizations.

Later, in the late 1990s to early 2000s, Sarah J. Tracy studied emotional labor in service organizations by conducting ethnographies of correctional officers and cruise ship employees, confirming many components of Hochschild's, Ruddick's, and Ferguson's theories (see Tracy, 2000, for an example). Then, Debra J. Ackerman's (2006) study of childcare teachers magnified the various ways women's work was still devalued in our present economy. "Caring work," or any occupation heavy in personal contact and concern about individuals' welfare, was perceived by most as a woman's job. Additionally, she found that caring work has continued to be devalued in our society, resulting in less honor, power, and money. Furthermore, related gender wage differences have acted to reinforce social constructions about appropriate and desirable male and female roles (Ackerman, 2006).

Educational Policy and Practice

Feminist scholars in educational administration have piggybacked on Ferguson's work by developing ways to analyze policy language as well as document the various ways female educational administrators worked to fit into a historically male field. For example, Christman and McClellan (2008) followed what they called "resilient women administrators" to determine characteristics that enabled them to persist despite what they dubbed "living on barbed wire" (p. 3). They found that successful female administrators endured adversity by their ability to move fluidly between markers construed as being masculine and components aligned with femininity. The women they studied identified with masculine terms such as *authoritative, decisive, assertive, rational, competent,* and *competitive.* In addition, they also categorized themselves as *caring, nurturing,* and *collaborative,* which are suggestive of feminine qualities. The women they studied were able to fit in with the organization and maintain resiliency by negotiating "what the literature describes as an interplay of both [feminine and masculine qualities]" (Christman & McClellan, 2008, p. 15).

Other women educational leadership scholars have pushed to develop more "assertive methodologies" that enabled analysts to "reveal the societal contributions to gendered hierarchies and power dynamics in employment, families, religions, schools, businesses, and politics" (Marshall & Young, 2006, pp. 63–64). Shaw (2004) referred to critical feminist policy analysis as a "partial corrective" to traditional forms that ignore women's issues (p. 57). Marshall (1999) concurred and added that other methods are insufficient to ask "gender questions as well as recognizes the power and language dynamics as activists challenge hegemonic policy arenas" (p. 128). Shaw (2004) agreed, stating, "Policy analysis is never value-neutral. However, it is often silent on the issue of gender" (p. 56). Following in the footsteps of Ferguson (1985), more current critical feminist scholars have interrogated how gender, race, and class shape the entire policy process and have specifically asked how women are "represented, reproduced, regulated and restrained" in policy discourse and consequent practice (Pillow, 2003, p. 151).

THE PRESENT PUSH FOR "SCIENTIFICALLY BASED RESEARCH"

Unfortunately, and in spite of the progress made toward more holistic approaches to organizational and policy studies, the past decade has found us circling back to rationality. It is perceived in the popular discourse that we as Americans have lost our way in terms of educating our citizens and have reached an educational crisis rooted in weak university-based education programs and ill-prepared teachers. Schools of education are believed to hold their faculty to much lower research standards than other disciplines, and the U.S. educational system is considered to be generally in decline and losing its foothold on a global scale (Tobin, 2007). Thus, it has become commonplace for educational research to be maligned in the American policy arena—by both Democrats and Republicans—for its perceived low level of rigor and empiricism (Tobin, 2007). To supposedly rectify matters, advocates argue for the application of "scientifically based research" to educational research and practice using the same experimental and quasi-experimental standards as the natural and medical sciences (Shaker & Ruitenberg, 2007). Furthermore, from feminist and other critical perspectives, this return to rationality uses principles meant for highly controlled laboratory settings to make sense of education, which is an inappropriate approach in light of the complex variables and contextual and structural circumstances of education, pertaining to gender, race, class, sexuality, and so on that cannot be narrowly tested (see Erickson & Guiterrez, 2002; Tobin, 2007).

The No Child Left Behind Act of 2001 (NCLB), which reauthorized the Elementary and Secondary Education Act, calls for the use of "scientifically based research" as the foundation for many education programs and for classroom instruction, and since the onset of NCLB, the federal government, think tanks, and corporate entities that produce advocacy research continue to have a growing impact on what apparently constitutes sound educational research and practice (Shaker & Ruitenberg, 2007). While the call for "scientifically based" educational research appeared in the discourse earlier, the advent of NCLB institutionalized the approach by mandating it and tying educational funding to its preponderance. Early on, the policy discourse embraced definitions of scientifically based research that gave qualitative and quantitative research methods equal importance, but by the time NCLB was signed in 2001, the definition of scientifically based research leaned heavily towards quantitative approaches (Eisenhart & Towne, 2003).

In 2000, Representative Castle (R-DE) introduced H.R. 4875 (i.e., the "original Castle Bill"), which outlined a protocol for what counts as scientifically valid research that qualifies for federal research dollars, and this protocol included both "scientifically based quantitative" and "scientifically based qualitative" research standards (Eisenhart & Towne, 2003). The Reading Excellence Act of 1999 (REA), which articulated scientifically based research standards for reading, heavily influenced the language of the proposed H.R. 4875 bill. The REA of 1999 and the original Castle Bill made it clear to educational researchers that the emerging definitions of scientifically based research at the federal level would have a growing impact on their work. Therefore, in fall 2000, the National Research Council (NRC) convened a committee of educational researchers to assert its voice on what should be considered scientifically based research in education (Eisenhart & Towne, 2003). In 2001, this committee released the report Scientific Research in Education (SRE), which proposed that scientifically based research be defined by six guiding principles that are the same regardless of the type of research method (quantitative or qualitative) utilized (Eisenhart & Towne, 2003).

Subsequently, the NRC was called to testify on findings from the SRE before the subcommittee on Education Reform of the U.S. House Education and Workforce Committee. In its testimony, the NRC recommended the development of a federal education research agency (now called the Institute of Education Sciences or IES) and argued that the six principles outlined in the SRE offer a general approach to scientifically based research that gives researchers the flexibility to select methods (not preferring qualitative over quantitative or vice versa) based on their research questions (Eisenhart & Towne, 2003). Shortly after the SRE report was released, NCLB was passed by Congress and signed by President George W. Bush. The SRE report and the original Castle Bill considered qualitative methodologies, but unfortunately NCLB only considers quantitative research, especially randomized trials, as rigorous scientifically based research (Shaker & Ruitenberg, 2007).

After NCLB was signed into law, the federal government continued to reinforce its definition of what constitutes scientifically based research. On February 6, 2002, Assistant Secretary for Elementary and Secondary Education Susan Neuman hosted a seminar where leading experts in the fields of education and science discussed the meaning of scientifically based research and its status across various disciplines, and henceforth according to the U.S. Department of Education's Strategic Plan 2002–2007 the federal government's goal was to transform the field of education into an evidence-based field (Shaker & Ruitenberg, 2007). That same year the original Castle Bill (H.R. 4875) was passed in its final version as the Education Sciences Reform Act (ESRA). According to Eisenhart and Towne (2003), the ESRA "definitions are more inclusive of various research designs and more sensitive to the realities of research in practice than those in the original Castel Bill" and suggest that the NRC's congressional testimony on findings from the SRE report had some impact on the crafting of the ESRA (p. 35). As such, Eisenhart and Towne (2003) would argue that the definition for scientifically based research in education will continue to be contested by policymakers, service providers, and educational researchers.

Vindicating the "Evidence" for Feminist Approaches to Research

Milner (2007) cautions that "in the process of conducting research, dangers can emerge when and if researchers do not engage in processes that can circumvent misinterpretations, misinformation, and misrepresentations of individuals, communities institutions, and systems" (p. 388). Thus, it is important for researchers to be reflexive regarding their positionality when conducting research (Milner, 2007). Scholars who examine the identity politics involved when conducting educational research acknowledge the utility of quantitative research methods but question whether the national push for scientifically or evidence-based research in school reform can fully signify the nuances of identity at multiple levels (individual, group, organizational), especially identities that historically have been and continue to be placed at the margins (Milner, 2007; Tillman, 2009).

The question of what counts as evidence still remains at the crux of the scientifically based research debate. The expansion of standardization and narrow, formulaic measures for evaluating principal and teacher effectiveness and student performance and the growing efforts of private/corporate entities to fund school reform initiatives, are telling and suggest that the ongoing debate on the quality of educational research still leans towards positivist approaches. As popular support for positivist approaches to measure educational progress grows, the key policy problem the U.S. educational reform agenda aims to solve in the first place—the achievement gap—further widens. The exacerbating educational inequities are cause for concern as our nation's classrooms become increasingly diverse and suggest that maybe the regarded positivist-generated "evidence" in the scientifically based research debate might not be the "right" kind of "evidence" to meet the needs of the changing faces of U.S. classrooms. Tillman (2009) calls for a broader paradigmatic approach that fits the "realities of the political, economic, social, and educational landscape of the United States" as our "changing society and particularly the changing contexts of education bring new and often complex challenges" (p. 458). Thus, research methods outside of positivist traditions must also be considered.

In order to counter the over-promotion of positivist approaches to scientifically-based research, several scholarly frameworks have emerged that urge educational researchers consider their own "racialized and cultural positionality in conducting research" (Milner, 2007, p. 397) and design research that is culturally responsive by giving context to participants' racialized and cultural experiences (Tillman, 2009). Quantitative approaches such a quasi-experimental design and randomized trials do not capture the lived experiences and co-constructed narratives that qualitative research is able to render (Tillman, 2009), and therefore greater emphasis and consideration should be given to research approaches that give voice to those who have been silenced, misinterpreted, and misrepresented (Milner, 2007).

The federal government's continuous efforts to emphasize scientifically based research serve as a counterattack against not only the aforementioned cultural responsive and race-conscious frameworks but also feminist methodologies (Lather, 2004). Unfortunately, "evidence" generated from feminist methodologies is commonly delimited as an "embarrassing emotion fest of women's work which can only be interpreted as excess, wild or crazy, bizarre, remote, or meaningless to the task of social policy" (Lather, 2004, p. 766). Moreover, "masculinized language" and "regimes of power" have become so commonsensical that we are oblivious to the hegemony and domination involved in the pursuit of "standards of truth" of scientifically based "evidence" (Lather, 2004, p. 266). As such, feminist methodologies can provide the "evidence" necessary to be all-encompassing of various intersecting identities (gender as well as race, class, sexuality, ability geography), complex policy problems, and the "multiplicity of the social world" (Lather, 2004, p. 768).

RECLAIMING OUR HISTORICAL TRAJECTORY: A CALL FOR FUTURE DIRECTIONS

In an effort to "get back on track," we have outlined a plan for resistance against the present trend to ignore women's issues and feminist perspectives in research generally and organizational and policy studies in educational leadership in particular. We argue that the present trend toward more scientific approaches, as described above, is meant to disrupt the not-so-current past push toward "gendering" organizational and policy studies in education. However, rather than go back to just paying attention to gender, or using gender as a unit of analysis, we argue that the field of educational leadership should be pushed further to critically examining policy and practice via feminist analytical frameworks.

Distinguishing Between Feminisms

Feminist analysis is complicated by the complexity of categories such as gender and race. This is exemplified by the following quotes: "While struggling to 'write against the grain,' feminist analysts also have to address assertions that their work has race, class, and heterosexual biases" (Marshall, 1999, pp. 69–70). "Feminists love to hate essentialism, to track it down in its various places, to identify its disguised reproductions, to ferret it out in fellow feminists, and to assure ourselves that we are not committing its sins" (Ferguson, 1993, p. 81). As Blackmore (1997) explains, "there are instances when we need to universalize the experience of women across culture, race, class and time; and other instances when we need to emphasize specificity and difference amongst women in different contexts" (pp. 441–442). Rather than lament this as a negative manifestation of division among women, Blackmore (1997) advises us to consider it a process of articulating "between the macro and the micro: the particular and the universal" (p. 442) that is expected while conducting research depending on the situation.

Divisions and debates exist within the women's movement, which undermine the strength and acceptance of feminist research, adding fuel to the dominant discourse that proclaims the decline in feminist thinking (Eyre, 2000; Marshall, 1999). It is beyond the scope of this current chapter to tackle these disagreements. The bottom line for this chapter is to acknowledge the difficulties and press for research designs that center on arenas of power and dominance such as school boards and legislative bodies along with policy artifacts such as curriculum guides (Marshall, 1999). Meanwhile, one must be sensitive to Olesen's (2005) observations that the "failure to attend closely to how race, class, and gender are relationally constructed leaves feminists of color distanced from feminist agendas" (p. 236). Thus, Blackmore's (1997) call to purposely fluctuate between micro and macro emphases as context permits or requires is a challenging yet vital strategy. A final quote by Sarah Ruddick (1989) may be helpful:

> There is no litmus test for identifying a "feminist." Internationally and in the United States, feminism is a multifaceted social movement in the process of change and self-creation. When I speak of feminism I refer, minimally, to a politics that is dedicated to transforming those social and domestic arrangements that deliberately or unwittingly penalize women because of their sex. Second, whatever their other polices and interests, feminists focus seriously on the ways that gender—social construction of masculinity and femininity—organizes political, personal, and intellectual life. The feminist assumption is that gender divisions of work, pleasure, power, and sensibility are socially created, detrimental to women and, to a lesser degree, to men, and therefore can and should be changed. Most important, though perhaps controversially, feminists are partisans of women, fighting on their side, sometimes against, often with, men. As women, or in solidarity with them, feminists struggle against any social, racial, economic, or physical abuse that threatens women's' capacity to work and to love." (pp. 234–235)

Using Feminist Theory to Understand Educational Organizations

Since 1992, Joan Acker has justified the need for gendering organizational theory and outlined essential elements of a framework designed to explore gender in organizations as a variable. We agree with Acker (1992) that the proliferation of studies concerning women and the workplace did a fine job of documenting women's persistent difficulties but did not theorize ample explanations as to why gender inequities continued in organizational life. In her attempts to remedy this gap, Acker (1992) offered a description of basic elements she believed were essential to building a viable theory capable of gendering organizational analysis. These building blocks, which can be utilized by other scholars in various proportions to fit particular research projects, included examining gendered processes, interrogating gender and sexuality as organizational resources, and unearthing the gendered substructure of an organization.

First, Acker (1992) defined gender as socially produced patterns of behavior that differentiated people as either masculine or feminine. In other words, a person might be born with the chromosomes that indicated an individual as male or female, but they were not predetermined to exude either feminine or masculine characteristics based on their chromosomal combination. Rather, people were typically socialized to lean toward one binary or the other. Theorists have encouraged us to consider gender as existing on a continuum: If people are given the freedom to develop their full potential without constraints, they will develop some combination of interests, strengths, weaknesses, and propensities that are idiosyncratic to the individual based on a combination of physiological, psychological, and cultural factors (Acker, 1992; Blount, 2005; Fine, 2010).

The first essential element of a gendered theory for organizations that Acker (1992) put forward was to look for gendered processes that take place in the organization. One example would be the production of gender divisions. In other words, one discovers and describes whether there is an existing gender pattern of jobs, wages, power, and subordination, identifying the ordinary organizational practices that produce/reproduce these patterns (Acker, 1992). Are women and men segregated to avoid the possibility of sexual encounters? What symbols do organizations use to describe and ultimately justify gender patterns if they exist? For example, are top leaders referred to as strong, rational, and forceful? Is the organization described as aggressive and competitive or supportive and caring? How would interactions between individuals be characterized as far as various combinations of male-male/male-female/female-female and dominance-subordination/alliances-exclusions? How is sexuality communicated in overt/covert ways? Finally, Acker (1992) promoted the notion of examining the internal mental work of individuals within the organization as they made sense of their work and their place in the organization. Do women and men express that demands are placed on them as far as gender-appropriate behaviors? If so, what are they and what effect do these demands have, if any?

Examining gender and sexuality as organizational resources is the next essential element advocated by Acker (1992). Human bodies—both male and female—are organizational resources. Acker (1992) believed that their materiality enabled thinking and production on the job. Sangster (2007) also found that work conditions directly influenced, and in some cases literally mutated, the body in terms of health and well-being. Acker (1992) and Sangster (2007) both found that the lower a worker was on the hierarchy, the more tightly controlled the corresponding physical body. Conversely, higher-level employees were rewarded with fewer bodily constraints. For example, store clerks could not empty bowels or bladder as the body dictated—only when the time clock or boss indicated permission. Meanwhile, managers had access to the executive washroom as a matter of privilege. In addition, "women's bodies, sexuality, and procreative abilities are used as grounds for exclusion or objectification [while] men's sexuality dominates most workplaces and reinforces their organizational power" (Acker, 1992, p. 254).

Thirdly, Acker (1992) solicited organizational analysts to discover the gendered substructure of organizations. According to Acker (1992), the more obvious manifestations of gender discrimination in the work place, as sketched above, were made possible by a gendered substructure that acted as a foundation for other activities to occur. The gendered substructure was made up of

> the spatial and temporal arrangements of work, in the rules prescribing workplace behavior, and in the relations linking workplaces to living places. These practices and relations, encoded in arrangements and rules, are supported by assumptions that work is separate from the rest of life and that it has first claim on the worker. (p. 453)

One might ask: What organizational policies seem gender neutral but actually contribute to the problems identified in an organization (e.g., lower wages for women)? How does the organizational mission make assumptions about work–home roles and responsibilities? How is company use of time implicated differently for women and men? How is use of space different for men and women? Who is more visible among workers and why? What are some of the underlying processes that maintain gender divisions and identities? Who are the organizational leaders? How are they recruited and selected? Are they male or female? What kinds of gender attributes do they exude (or are expected to exude)? How do they actively influence the culture of the organization? Acker's (1992) three-pronged approach to gendering organizational analysis might be a helpful tool for researchers to determine the role gender plays in organizational culture in K–12 and higher education settings.

Using Feminist Theory to Understand Educational Policy

Unlike what most consider traditional policy analysis, critical policy analysis comes closer to Lasswell's 50-year-old ideal of doing policy work while acknowledging context and group values (Fischer, 2003). In fact, some purport traditional analysis as lacking the sophistication to attempt analysis that takes into consideration the contestable nature of problem definition, research findings, and explanations and arguments for solutions (Blackmore, 1995; Fischer, 2003; Marshall, 1999; Rochefort & Cobb, 1994). Therefore, other tools are necessary that draw from many disciplines while considering the contributions of critical theory, poststructuralism, social constructionism, postmodernism, and discourse analysis (Fischer, 2003; Marshall, 1999; Rochefort & Cobb, 1994).

How this translates into real life is the tendency of critical policy analysts to be "critical" and "get political" as well as to examine taken-for-granted assumptions about societal and subgroup values (Rochefort & Cobb, 1994). Critical policy analysts emphasize description rather than prescription while stressing the subjective foundations of social reality (Fischer, 2003). More-over, critical policy analysts "must consider whether a policy will empower and democratize, and whether it will dispense goods to the 'have-nots' as much as they consider traditional questions such as whether a policy is ef-ficient" (Marshall, 1999, p. 69).

The critical approach illumines the role of rhetoric in the policymaking process; especially as it relates to authority and moral mandates to justify and promote policy decisions (Rochefort & Cobb, 1994). Critical policy theorists are well aware of the discomfort they cause, but do not apologize for their call for "the use of interpretive methods to probe the presupposi-tions that discursively structure social perceptions, organize 'facticity,' and deem events as normal, expected, and natural" (Fischer, 2003, p. 14).

Critics complain that critical policy analysts fall into the trap of relativ-ism whereas Fischer (2003) argues that the relativism cry is an unfair ac-cusation. He insists that the approach is still skeptical: "But rather than anchoring this skepticism in the search for 'truth,' such analysts start with the recognition that different discourses, definitions, and questions lead to different policy prescriptions" (Fischer, 2003, p. 14). And besides, some stories just happen to be more truthful, persuasive, and humane than oth-ers (Fischer, 2003). Thus, exploring the margins is one way to get at a more truthful report of the policy process (Fischer, 2003; Mansfield, Welton, & Grogan, in press; Marshall, 1999; Rochefort & Cobb, 1994).

Feminist critical policy analysis builds on the philosophical underpin-nings of the critical approach but concurrently narrows and expands its purposes by focusing on the effects of policy on women and insists on "pro-ducing new syntheses that in turn become the grounds for further research, praxis, and policy" (Olesen, 2006, p. 236). Olesen (2006) explains:

> [Q]ualitative feminist research in its many variants...problematizes women's diverse situations as well as the gendered institutions and material and histori-cal structures that frame those. It refers the examination of that problematic to theoretical, policy, or action frameworks to realize social justice for women (and men) in specific contexts.... It generates new ideas to produce knowledges about oppressive situations for women, for action or further research. (p. 236)

The purpose of feminist critical policy analysis is to show how numerous policies appear to be gender-neutral on the surface but, in fact, negatively impact women. "Policy analysis is never value-neutral. However, it is often silent of the issue of gender" (Shaw, 2004, p. 56). The approach gener-ally asks how gender, race, and class shape the entire policy process and specifically asks how women are "represented, reproduced, regulated, and restrained" (Pillow, 2003, p. 151).

The components of feminist critical policy analysis are similar to other critical approaches such as critical race theory. Like other critical

frameworks, the feminist approach does not hide the fact that it is ideo-
logical. However, its central focus is gender rather than, say race or class,
(although race and class are interwoven with female identity and policy
issues.) Another commonality with other critical approaches is its use of discourse analysis to uncover ideologies and assumptions embedded in policy
documents, as well as its goal of identifying formal and informal power, politics, and policies that help or hinder human experience (see Eyre, 2000;
Marshall, 2000; Parsons & Ward, 2001).

There is a weaving of ideas from critical and poststructuralist work that
informs questions, arguments, and proposed methodologies. However, the
infusion of feminist theory sets it apart from other critical approaches. Also
unique to feminist critical policy analysis is its reliance on collecting data on
the "lived experiences of women, as told by the women themselves" (Shaw,
2004) or "grounded in women's experience taking its standpoint from the
'other' side of the gender line" (Parsons & Ward, 2001, p. 49) and its emphasis on action research that is meant to transform institutions and lives.

CONCLUSIONS AND FURTHER CONSIDERATIONS

A critical analysis of all education policy documents (intent) as well as practices (interpretation and implementation) is advocated. One might ask how
using feminist perspectives could shed light on the new approaches to the
reauthorization of the Education Secondary and Elementary Act (ESEA)
that are currently under discussion, for instance. Mansfield et al. (in press)
offer an example of how feminist critical policy analysis (FCPA) reveals er-
roneous assumptions and faulty logic in the current national and state approaches to STEM education and helps to explain why STEM policies have
not yet been successful in meeting their goals. What might we learn about
the new Common Core Standards from FCPA? Or about such state education policies as the recently weakened California Beginning Teacher Support and Assessment Program (BTSA)? Or the latest New York state teacher
evaluation system? What do we need to know about the current national
practice of "academic redshirting" in kindergartens across the country?
How well are the various state policies governing charter schools serving
girls and marginalized others? In addition, FCPA could provide valuable
perspectives on the emergence of new state accountability systems being
created under the recent waiver provisions of NCLB. These are just some of
the enormous range of possibilities offered by policy legislation and implementation practices.

In this chapter, we argue that (re)introducing gender embedded in a critical feminist framework might offer new and valuable perspectives on educational policy and organizational studies in education. Extending research that

has already been done would reinvigorate both academic and popular discussions that have for too long been dominated by rational, positivist and other so-called neutral inquiry approaches. The formulation of research questions and appropriate research methodologies would benefit greatly from a critical framework informed by gender issues and issues of intersectionality. Despite the plethora of studies aimed at bringing social justice to our schools, to date, the power of state and national policy to effect significant, positive change in public education has not been well used. Building on earlier education scholarship that has utilized gender as a unit of analysis, bringing attention to a gendered discourse of educational leadership and gendered school/ district organizations, feminist critical approaches have potential to disrupt the status quo and revolutionize the field.

REFERENCES

Acker, J. (1992). Gendering organizational theory. In A. J. Mills & P. Tancred (Eds.), *Gendering organizational analysis* (pp. 248–260). Newberry Park, CA: Sage.

Ackerman, D. J. (2006). The costs of being a child care teacher: Revisiting the problem of low wages. *Educational Policy, 20*(1), 85–112.

Alvesson, M., & Billing, Y. D. (1997). *Understanding gender and organizations.* London, UK: Sage.

Birkland, T. A. (2005). *An introduction to the policy process: Theories, concepts, and models of public policy making.* Armonk, NY: M. E. Sharpe.

Blackmore, J. (1995). Policy as dialogue: Feminist administrators working for educational change. *Gender & Education, 7*(3), 293–314.

Blackmore, J. (1997). Level playing field? Feminist observations on global/local articulations of the re-gendering and restructuring of educational work. *International Review of Education, 43*(5-6), 439–461.

Blount, J. (1998). *Destined to rule the schools: Women and the superintendency, 1873–1995.* Albany, NY: SUNY Press.

Blount, J. (2005). *Fit to teach: Same-sex desire, gender, and school work in the twentieth century.* Albany, NY: SUNY Press.

Bolman, L. G., & Deal, T. E. (2003). *Reframing organizations: Artistry, choice, and leadership.* San Francisco, CA: Jossey Bass.

Brunner, C. C., & Grogan, M. (2007). *Women leading school systems: Uncommon roads to fulfillment.* Lanham, MD: Rowman & Littlefield Education.

Christman, D., & McClellan, R. (2008). "Living on barbed wire": Resilient women administrators in educational leadership programs. *Educational Administration Quarterly, 44*(1), 3–29.

Cohen, M. D., March, J. G., & Olsen, J. P. (1972). A garbage can model of organizational choice. *Administrative Science Quarterly, 17*(1), 1–25.

Cook, S. D. N., & Yanow, D. (2005). Culture and organizational learning. In J. M. Shafritz, J. S. Ott, & Y. S. Jang (Eds.), *Classics of organizational theory* (6th ed., pp. 368–382). Belmont, CA: Wadsworth.

Cox, T. (2005). Creating the multicultural organization: The challenge of managing diversity. In J. M. Shafritz, J. S. Ott, & Y. S. Jang (Eds.), *Classics of organizational theory* (6th edition, pp. 469–475). Belmont, CA: Wadsworth.

Eisenhart, M., & Towne, L. (2003). Contestation and change in national policy on "scientifically based" education research. *Educational Researcher, 32*(7), 31–38.

Elementary and Secondary Education Act, H. R. 4875 (ESEA).

Engelbert, E. (1977, May/June). University education for public policy analysis. *Public Administration Review,* 228–236.

Erickson, F., & Guiterrez, K. (2002). Culture, rigor, and science in educational research. *Educational Researcher, 31*(8), 21–24.

Eyre, L. (2000). The discursive framing of sexual harassment in a university community. *Gender and Education, 12*(3), 293–307.

Ferguson, K. E. (1985). *The feminist case against bureaucracy.* Philadelphia, PA: Temple University Press.

Ferguson, K. E. (1993). *The man question: Visions of subjectivity in feminist theory.* Berkeley: University of California Press.

Fine, C. (2010). *Delusions of gender: How our minds, society, and neurosexism create difference.* New York, NY: WW Norton.

Fischer, F. (2003). *Reframing public policy: Discursive politics and deliberative practices.* Oxford, UK: Oxford University Press.

Follett, M. P. (2005). The giving of orders. In J. M. Shafritz, J. S. Ott, & Y. S. Jang, (Eds.), *Classics of organizational theory* (6th ed., pp. 152–157). Belmont, CA: Wadsworth. (Original work published 1926)

Gherardi, S. (1995). *Gender, symbolism and organizational cultures.* Thousand Oaks, CA: Sage Publications.

Grogan, M. (1996). *Voices of women aspiring to the superintendency.* Albany NY: SUNY Press.

Hearn, J., & Parkin, W. (1992). Gender and organizations: A selective review and critique of a neglected area. In A. Mills & P. Mills (Eds.), *Gendering organizational analysis* (pp. 148–162). Thousand Oaks, CA: Sage Publications.

Hochschild, A. R. (2003). *The managed heart: Commercialization of human feeling.* Berkeley, CA: University of California Press. (Original work published 1983)

Kanter, R. M. (2005). "Power failure in management circuits." In: J. M. Shafritz, J. S. Ott, & Y. S. Jang (Eds.), *Classics of organizational theory* (6th ed., pp. 342–351). Belmont, CA: Wadsworth. (Original work published 1979)

Katz, D., & Kahn, R. L. (1966). Organizations and the system concept. In J. M. Shafritz, J. S. Ott, & Y. S. Jang (Eds.), *Classics of organizational theory* (6th ed., 2005, pp. 480–490). Belmont, CA: Wadsworth.

Kingdon, J. W. (2003). *Agendas, alternatives, and public policies* (2nd ed.). New York, NY: Longman.

Lather, P. (2004). Scientific research in education: A critical perspective. *British Educational Journal, 30*(6), 759–772.

Mansfield, K. C., Welton, A., & Grogan, M. (in press). Troubling the policy discourse: Gender and the STEM crisis. *International Journal of Qualitative Studies in Education.*

Marshall, C. (1999). Researching the margins: Feminist critical policy analysis. *Educational Policy, 13*(1), 59–76.

Marshall, C. (2000). Policy discourse analysis: Negotiating gender equity. *Journal of Education Policy, 15*(2), 125–156.

Marshall, C. (2003). The emperor and research on women in school leadership: A response to Julie Laible's loving epistemology. In M. D. Young & L. Skrla (Eds.), *Reconsidering feminist research in educational administration* (pp. 211–219). Albany, NY: SUNY Press.

Marshall, C., & Young, M. D. (2006). Gender and methodology. In C. Skelton, B. Francis, & L. Smulyan (Eds.), *The Sage handbook of gender and education* (pp. 63–79. Thousand Oaks, CA: Sage.

Maslow, A. H. (2005). A theory of human motivation. In J. M. Shafritz, J. S. Ott, & Y. S. Jang (Eds.), *Classics of organizational theory* (6th ed., pp. 167–178). Belmont, CA: Wadsworth. (Original work published 1943)

Mills, A. J., & Tancred, P. (1992). *Gendering organizational analysis.* Newbury Park, CA: Sage Publications.

Milner, R. H. (2007). Race, culture, and research positionality: Working through dangers seen, unseen, and unforeseen. *Educational Researcher, 36*(7), 388–400.

No Child Left Behind Act of 2001 (NCLB).

Olesen, V. (2005). Early millennial feminist qualitative research: Challenges and contours. In N. K. Denzin & Y. S. Lincoln (Eds.), *The Sage handbook of qualitative research* (3rd ed., pp. 235–278). Thousand Oaks, CA: Sage.

Parsons, M., & Ward, E. R. (2001). The roaring silence: Feminist revisions in the educational policy literature. *Policy Studies Review, 18*(2), 46–64.

Pillow, W. (2003). 'Bodies are dangerous': Using feminist genealogy as policy studies methodology. *Journal of Education Policy, 18*(2), 145–159.

Reading Excellence Act of 1999 (REA).

Rochefort, D. A., & Cobb, R. W. (Eds.). (1994). *The politics of problem definition: Shaping the policy agenda.* Lawrence, KS: University of Kansas

Ruddick, S. (1989). *Maternal thinking: Toward a politics of peace.* Toronto, Canada: Random House.

Sangster, J. (2007). Making a fur coat: Women, the labouring body, and working-class history. *Internationaal Instituut voor Sociale Geschiedenis: IRSH, 52*, 241–270.

Schein, E. H. (2005). Defining organizational culture. In J. M. Shfritz, J. S. Ott, & Y. S. Jang (Eds.), *Classics of organizational theory, 6th edition* (pp. 360–367). Belmont, CA: Wadsworth.

Schein, E. H. (2004). *Organizational culture and leadership* (3rd ed.). San Francisco, CA: Jossey-Bass.

Scientific Research in Education. (2002). (SRE). *National Academy of Sciences* (R. J. Shavelson & L. Towne, Eds.), Washington, DC: National Academies Press.

Scott, W. R., & Davis, G. F. (2007). *Organizations and organizing: Rational, natural, and open system perspectives.* Upper Saddle River, NJ: Pearson.

Senge, P. M. (1990). *The fifth discipline: The art and practice of the learning organization.* New York, NY: Doubleday Currency.

Shafritz, J. M., Ott, J. S. & Jang, Y. S. (2005). *Classics of organizational theory* (6th ed.). Belmont, CA: Thompson Wadsworth Publishing.

Shaker, P., & Ruitenberg, C. (2007). 'Scientifically-based research': the art of politics and the distortion of science. *International Journal of Research and Method in Education, 30*(2), 207–219.

Shakeshaft, C. (1989). *Women in educational administration.* Newbury Park, CA: Sage.

Shaw, K. M. (2004). Using feminist critical policy analysis in the realm of higher education: The case of welfare reform as gendered educational policy. *The Journal of Higher Education, 75*(1), 56–79.

Sheppard, D. (1992). Women managers' perceptions of gender and organizational life. In A. J. Mills & P. Tancred (Eds.), *Gendering organizational analysis* (pp. 151–166). Newberry Park, CA: Sage.

Skrla, L. (2000). The social construction of gender in the superintendency. *Journal of Education Policy, 15*(3), 293–316.

Skrla, L. (2003a). Mourning silence: Women superintendents (and a researcher) rethink speaking up and speaking out. In M. D. Young & L. Skrla (Eds.), *Reconsidering feminist research in educational administration* (pp. 103–128). Albany, NY: SUNY Press.

Skrla, L. (2003b). Normalized femininity: Reconsidering research on women in the superintendency. In M. D. Young & L. Skrla (Eds.), *Reconsidering feminist research in educational administration* (pp. 247–263). Albany, NY: SUNY Press.

Taylor, F. W. (2005). The principles of scientific management. In J. M. Shafritz, J. S. Ott, & Y. S. Jang (Eds.), *Classics of organizational theory* (6th ed., pp. 61–72). Belmont, CA: Wadsworth. (Original work published 1916)

Tillman, L. C. (2009). The never-ending education science debate: I'm ready to move on. *Educational Researcher, 38*(6), 458–462.

Tobin, J. (2007). An anthropologist's reflections on defining quality in education research. *International Journal of Research and Method in Education, 30*(3), 325–338.

Tooms, A. K., Lugg, C. A., & Bogotch, I. (2010). Rethinking the politics of fit and educational leadership. *Educational Administration Quarterly, 46* (1), 96–131

Tracy, S. J. (2000). Becoming a character for commerce: Emotion labor, self subordination and discursive construction of identity in a total institution. *Management Communication Quarterly, 14*, 90–128.

Trice, H. M., & Beyer, J. M. (1993). *The cultures of work organizations.* Englewood Cliffs, NJ: Prentice-Hall.

Weber, M. (1922). Bureaucracy. In J. M. Shafritz, J. S. Ott, & Y. S. Jang,(Eds.), *Classics of organizational theory* (6th ed., 2005, pp. 73–78). Belmont, CA: Wadsworth.

Young, M. D. (2003). Troubling policy discourse: Gender, constructions, and the leadership crisis. In M. D. Young & L. Skrla (Eds.), *Reconsidering feminist research in educational leadership* (pp. 265–298). Albany, NY: SUNY Press.

Young, M. D. (2005). Shifting away from women's issues in educational leadership in the U.S.: Evidence of a backlash? *International Studies in Educational Administration, 33*(2), 31–42.

CHAPTER 14

ACTIVISM AND COMMUNITY ENGAGEMENT TO PROMOTE GIRLS AND WOMEN

To Have Voice and Choice

Rachel McNae

ABSTRACT

New and ever-evolving ways in which young women access information and then act on this information challenge many traditional notions of being a citizen and participating in a school community. Faced with historical learning approaches and patriarchal leadership structures that may not align with increasingly globalized contexts, the contributions of young women can be stifled and underestimated. Changing times must prompt educators to reexamine what it means to be a citizen and active community member. Within these considerations, attention must be paid to the shifting duality of knowledge and power, as educators and young women alike seek to redefine the relationships between teacher, student, school, and the wider community.

This chapter examines the complex notion of global citizenship and interrogates the concept of "voice," highlighting of the role voice can have in engaging young women as committed global citizens. The use of co-constructive

Women Interrupting, Disrupting, and Revolutionizing Educational Policy and Practice, pages 267–301

pedagogies within learning communities is examined as a vehicle for creating democratic spaces in which young women can share in decision-making processes. Obligations for leaders working alongside young women in both educational and community settings are highlighted, and reflective questions are posed to encourage the engagement of alternative approaches to develop leadership and a sense of agency amongst young women.

To find voice is to find identity, and the possibility of agency in the world.
Voice . . . is the inescapable capability, which young people require
to flourish at the turn of the century.
—Ranson, 2000 (p. 286)

The capability of using voice as a means of contributing to change processes within local and global communities is vastly important for young women. As indicated above by Ranson (2000), the notion of being a global citizen is predicated on the concept of voice, a key element of generating engagement and involvement in decision-making processes. The belief that there is a need for young women to participate in decision-making processes within their schools and communities is not a new concept (Alexander & Farrell, 1975). However, while the importance of young women having a voice within their schools and communities is identified in more recent research (see Archard, 2012; McNae, 2010), few researchers and practitioners have interrogated the vital roles young women may play in generating contexts for this to happen.

A growing body of research evidence identifies the importance of the role that dialogue can have in generating a sense of agency and ownership for young women as decision-makers within their schools and communities. Similarly, research investigating youth consultation in these contexts is rapidly expanding, and many researchers espouse the benefits of involving young people in decision-making processes and curriculum design (Lodge, 2005; MacGregor, 2007; Rudduck & Flutter, 2004; Thomson & Gunter, 2005). These bodies of literature frequently exist within mutually exclusive realms, and an interrogation of this literature may provide insight into how the voices of young women are positioned within these growing number of research publications. The literature canvassing the concept of voice and, more specifically, the voices of young women reveals a wide scope in the ways that voice is interpreted and represented and comes with many caveats. This has resulted in the need for researchers to understand what voice is and how the concept, which is not clear-cut or well defined, may be best utilized to engage young women as active citizens within their schools and communities.

The purpose of this chapter is threefold. First, it examines the complex notion of global citizenship and interrogates the concept of "voice," highlighting the role that voice can have in engaging young women as committed global citizens. The case is made for those working with young women to shift away from voice initiatives and encourage seeking opportunities to develop youth–adult partnerships within which meaningful dialogue can take place.

Second, although Denner, Meyer, and Bean (2005) draw our attention to potential benefits of youth–adult partnerships in female leadership development, research and guidance focusing on how to create authentic partnerships and involve students as active participants in school decision making is sparse (Mitra, 2008). The use of co-constructive pedagogies within learning communities is examined as a vehicle for the formation of democratic spaces in which young women can share in decision-making processes and a practical example of such a partnership in action is illustrated. Important considerations to assist in developing these partnerships are shared and the associated challenges outlined.

Finally, the obligations for those leaders working alongside young women in both educational and community settings will be highlighted. Reflective questions are posed throughout the chapter to encourage the engagement of alternative approaches to develop leadership and a sense of agency among young women and to address the unique challenges they face.

BEYOND THE SCHOOL GATES: THE NOTION OF THE GLOBAL CITIZEN

No one had to tell us where milk came from, or how butter was made. We helped to harvest the wheat, saw it ground into flour in the mill on our own stream; I baked bread for the family at thirteen. There was a paper mill too on our stream; we could learn the secrets of half a dozen other industries merely by walking through the open door of a neighbour's shop. No wonder school was a relatively unimportant place—a place where we learned only about the mechanical tools, the three R's, and a smattering about things far away and long ago. Our really important learning, the learning how to live in the world into which we were born and how to participate in its work, was right at hand, outside the schoolhouse walls. (Pratt, 1948 cited in Rogoff, Bartlett, & Turkanis, 2001, p. 5)

Nearly half a century has passed since Caroline Pratt made the statement above. Stirring romantic notions of youth and adolescence for many adults, we catch ourselves daydreaming wistfully back to times of days gone by, and are promptly brought back to current reality, sighing, *"Things were different when I was your age."* Through the comparison of past experiences with the present, we are blinded by the speed of change around us and come to the realization that young women are growing up at a time of increasing domestic and international globalization (Watkins, 2005). We begin to acknowledge the situations where learning takes place for young women are not simply restricted to the four walls of a classroom as Carlsson-Paige and Lantieri (2005) state:

> We are educating our young people in an extraordinary time in human history as they grow up in an increasingly interdependent world. News from around the world is available in an instant; the Internet and mass communications give young people immediate access to ideas and people from all over the world.... [T]here is an increasing awareness among students that a great many issues... are intertwined and affect them personally. (p. 97)

The new and ever-evolving ways in which young women can access information and then act on this information challenge many traditional notions of being a citizen and participating in a school community with its historical learning and leadership structures. Changing times prompt us to re-examine what it means to be a citizen within an increasingly global context and the shifting duality of knowledge and power seeks to redefine the relationships between teacher, student, school, and the wider community.

ENDURING UNDERSTANDINGS OF GLOBAL CITIZENSHIP

Understandings of what it means to be a citizen in a western developed society are constantly evolving (Osler, 1996), and it is inevitable that different communities will have different views of what constitutes citizenship (Wilkins, 2000). Historically, the notion of citizenship was often constructed in official education documents to serve the dominant social and political discourses of communities at the time (Down, 2004). The notion of citizenship has evolved continually since, and it has gained depth in meaning through the increasing democratic focus of communities and greater breadth as its reach extends beyond patriarchal and class structures.

There are however, common features of citizenship illustrated throughout the literature. Burkimsher (1993) reviewed large amounts of literature in this area and concluded that a sense of belonging, the capacity to gain access, and the ability to participate were prevalent characteristics of citizenship. He states, "that without any one of these there is no citizenship" (p. 7). McMurray and Niens (2012) purport that learning about citizenship encourages young people "to develop the social skills and negotiate shared norms and values, such as cooperation, trust and reciprocity" (p. 218) to function within increasingly diverse societies. Further to this, Williams and Humphrys (2003) emphasize the importance of participation within a community. They compare the historical elements of citizenship, "rights, duties, participation and identity" (p. 4), with more contemporary themes such as globalization and the development of "trans-national and global spaces" (p. 4), encouraging *connections and interaction* between individuals from around the world. They concluded that the traditional notion of citizenship must be challenged, as there is a need to accept these global links and changing environments if we are to ensure that young people are to be active citizens in the future.

Griffith (1998), a key writer in the field of global citizenship, encourages an active and holistic approach to defining the global citizen. Believing that global citizenship is a construct that should now be considered to be most appropriate to the third millennium, he states:

> The global citizen is not merely aware of her rights but able and desirous to act upon them. She is of an autonomous and inquiring critical disposition but her decisions and actions are tempered by an ethical concern for social justice and the dignity of humankind. She is, therefore, able, through life whilst contributing to the commonwealth, the public welfare, with a sense of civic duty to replenish society. (p. 8)

Noddings (2005) recognizes the complexity of creating defining criteria and argues that different perspectives such as economics, sustainability, diversity and peace are all key perspectives which need to be considered when attempting to define what a global citizen is. Challenging the traditional and often used economic perspective that emphasizes that a global citizen is a citizen who can live and work effectively anywhere in the world, she argues that social and economic justice, the protection of the earth, social and cultural diversity, and the *education* of people play key roles in what it truly means to be a global citizen. The question could be asked: What role can schools play in the creation of global citizens?

THE LINK BETWEEN SCHOOLS
AND THE CREATION OF THE GLOBAL CITIZEN

Dewey, perhaps one of the most influential educationalists of the 20th century, was aware that for citizenship education, the teaching approach was just as important as the content. His suggestion was driven by the need to educate the "democratic citizen," arguing that problem solving is the best way of developing a critical outlook that is the key to producing actively engaged citizens (Dewey, 1961). His focus on the relationship between the school and society was emphasized in his article "Moral Principles in Education," where he contests that moral training in schools is meaningless unless it related to the wider life of the community and society. More recently, Stoll (2003) argues, "to succeed in a world characterised by rapid change and increased complexity, it is vital that schools can grow and develop, adapt creatively to change and take charge so that they can create their own preferable future" (p. 131).

Griffith (1998) argues that the pedagogical construct of independent learning plays a key role in transforming the policy of educational citizenship into effective practice. Through this means of education, students are encouraged to make decisions about how they will learn and as they develop the qualities of a global citizen, they will have the opportunity to gain independence in their decision making, both as students as a member of a community. However, in a contrast to this, the notion of dependent learning, which is very prominent in today's historical school structures, encourages young people to depend on others for their learning, often the teacher. Through this learning process, the qualities of global citizenship are suppressed and they "learn to become dependent upon the decisions of others, both as pupils and as citizens" (Griffith, 1998, p. 8). Deborah Meier, a more recent champion of democratic education, believes that "we have lost sight of the traditional skills, aptitudes, and habits needed for a democratic way of life" (2003, p. 15) and encourages schools to re-evaluate their role in preparing young people to participate equally as democratic citizens both within and beyond the school walls. It is statements like these that lead us to question the roles that schools play in the preparation of young women for thriving in the wider world.

Griffith (1998) highlights the useful links between learning, education, and the creation of the global citizen. He makes a case for what he defines as *educational* citizenship and suggests that, in order for schools to play a role in the creation of global citizens, we need to embrace:

> A concept of education based upon the premise that the similarities between the qualities of the educated person and the global citizen indicate a symbiotic relationship between education and global citizenship. From this premise it is argued that pupils of all ages should be accorded citizens' rights throughout their education, both to prepare them for full and active democratic citizenship and to improve the educational provision of their state schooling. (Griffith, 1998, p. 8)

Such a belief proposes there is a need to ensure that the learning within schools remains relevant to the lives of young people both inside and outside of the school. Supporting such a philosophy, Tsolidis (2002) advocates that "as educators we have an obligation to remain relevant and prepare young people for futures which will be lived in an ever-shrinking world and within which people are already living globalized lives" (p. 218). Central to the notion of the "global citizen" is the need to teach for what Tsolidis describes as "cultural fluidity" (p. 218). She believes that we need to "imagine our students in a world we may not understand or have experiences—a globalized world where cultural fluidity is the bread and butter of everyday existence" (p. 218). She has no doubt that students in the schools of today are already more adept than their teachers at "assuming this reality and understanding the need for facility with this reality as requisite for their future success" (p. 218). A decade on, the work of Ungerleider (2012) continues to emphasize the importance of engaging young people in education, which focuses on self-awareness, compassion, diverse perspectives on current issues, and capacities for social action.

Favoring the links between learning to be a global citizen within and beyond the school walls, Burkimsher (1993) proposed that citizenship education must be tied to the nature of the school and must be "developed in active and experiential ways in real contexts" (p. 7). In this way:

> Pupils can acquire and practice life skills and supplement more formal ways of learning. This involves pupils going out into the community and the community coming into the school, a partnership between school and community in which each serves as a resource for the other. (Burkimsher (1993, p. 7)

Access to resources and information within a democratic forum, a sense of belonging to a learning community, participating and having voices heard are key areas that have arisen from the aforementioned literature. They are important aspects for schools to take into account when addressing school planning and processes. Resonating with the views of Dewey (1961) previously mentioned, the lived experience is a valued and necessary part of democratic learning to be an active citizen. There is a need for the encouragement of democratic learning environments as a means for young people to participate within this democratic space—a key aspect of being a global citizen. An essential element underpinning the ability for young women to participate within democratic spaces is the provision of opportunities to share their voices.

Some reflective questions for educational leaders:

- In what ways does your organization assist young women to develop as global citizens?
- How do the leadership structures in your organization contribute to creating democratic spaces which young women are welcomed into as active contributors to change?

ENGAGING AND VALUING THE VOICES OF YOUNG WOMEN: THE CASE FOR DIALOGUE IN CURRICULUM DESIGN

Researchers credit student voice initiatives with reengaging youth with school (Fielding, 2004, MacGregor, 2007), improving curriculum and pedagogy in schools (Rudduck & Flutter, 2000), and enhancing school ethos (Russell & Bryom, 2007). It is therefore no surprise that some researchers in educational fields see this area as an important avenue for exploring perceptions and the voices of young women about their lives and experiences to provide schools with alternative sources of knowledge about this group of students. Examples of young people being involved in the processes of informing school planning and policies are becoming increasingly apparent in the literature surrounding school reform (among many examples, see Fielding, 2001, 2004; Innes, Moss, & Smigiel, 2001; Leitch & Mitchell, 2007; Mitsoni, 2006; Shallcross, Robinson, Pace, & Tamoutseli, 2007). In its present form, activities involving student voice range from small group discussions solving school problems or issues (such as bullying), voicing opinions about school issues, to working in partnership with teachers and school communities to develop and implement school improvement strategies (Mitra, 2004).

Involving young women in decision making about their learning can enhance the learning experience. Specific examples relating to young women (for example, see Archard, 2012; Bond, Belenky, & Weinstock, 2000; Denner et al., 2005; McNae, 2010; Mono & Keenan, 2000; Saunders, 2005) show the benefits and complexities of involving young women in decision-making processes. Research illustrates that providing them with opportunities to suggest content and contexts that are meaningful to them and to recommend learning approaches and program structures that suit their learning styles can generate more relevant and engaging learning environments (Scratchley, 2003; Smith & Taylor, 2000). Fielding (2004) supports such a view and states that if we can provide space for student voice, we can "open up very different sets of possibilities for students, for staff, for the school as a learning community and for the school's capacity to engage with its communities in the process of reciprocal renewal" (p. 202). Similarly, Stoneman (2002) demands that adults create space for the voices of young people so that they can be heard. She believes "we desperately need the energy and intelligence of youth plugged into action that will improve society now" (p. 226).

However, many students believe that schools rarely listen to their views or involve them in important decision-making processes that affect their learning (Noddings, 1992) and that adults make assumptions about what is important for young people to know and do, failing to ask young people what they think (Scratchley, 2003). This can result in the creation of "one-size-fits-all" and "top-down" approaches to learning, which are frequently based on adult's own experiences. Morgan and Streb (2003) propose that when students are involved in programs and ideas in which they do not have voice and ownership, they can actually resent being involved and feel it is a waste of time. Stainton-Rogers, Stainton-Rogers, Vyrost, and Lovas

(2004) urge adults to step away from using their own personal experiences on which to design learning experiences. They state:

> If we [school staff] have a concern for what current life is like for today's generation of young people, or what may help them in their futures, we cannot use our own experiences of being young or the aspirations we then held as much of a guide. If we want to promote the life opportunities of young people, if we want to help them to prepare for their futures and make well-informed choices about them, then we need to find out about this "new world" in which they are growing up. (p. 117)

In the present climate, most student voice initiatives are designed as opportunities for trivial opinion sourcing with a focus on management and performance rather than the social and personal development of the student (Rudduck, 2006). Holdsworth (2004) advocates that student voice must not result in what he calls "trivial exercises in temporary engagement" (p. 7) but should contribute to the why of learning, as well as the how and what. He cites frequent examples of such practice illustrated throughout schools, such as asking students to be involved in creating school cafeteria menus, or consulting students in school decision-making processes, only to ignore their voices and recommendations. Holdsworth (2004) urges researchers and practitioners to avoid dangerous tokenistic practices and be reflective when designing or selecting methods to use in student voice initiatives. The important step of acting on the voices of students becomes vital if educators and policymakers are to move from what Hart (1992), and more recently Bragg and Fielding (2005), describe as tokenistic and decorative approaches to the authentic inclusion of young people's voices and move towards engaging students in meaningful actions involving their learning.

Although an increasing number of educationalists advocate for using student voice in educational settings and as part of school decision-making processes, Lodge (2005) highlights that engaging student voice can also be very complex, prompting a call for a more critically reflective approach to student voice inclusion and educational research in this area. Student voice is neither neutral nor authentic as it is produced within dominant discourses of power and control within educational settings (Thomson & Gunter, 2006), and rather than empowering students in decision-making opportunities that impact on their learning, Cook-Sather (2007) emphasizes that some approaches to student voice work in school can actually reinforce dangerous power dynamics and stereotypes.

There is a danger that the process of consulting students can result in the social stratification of schooling being hidden (Arnot & Reay, 2007), and the totalizing of student experiences assumes a collective experience that reinforces the status quo. The notion of "voice" implies that there is one voice for a group of students. Robinson and Taylor (2007) challenge this as being a monolingual assumption that creates an illusion that one voice would represent the voices of many. It must be recognized, therefore, that there is not one single student voice in total, but a collection of the voices of students. Researchers and educators are warned of the essentialization of students' voices and the assumption that the voices of youth will share truthful and informed knowledge about teaching and learning and school reforms (Thomson & Gunter, 2006). Cook-Sather (2007) cautions that the uncensored acceptance and value placed on student voice can lead to the "romanticizing" of student voice. Arnot and Reay (2007) remind us that the voices of young people are no more or less authentic or important than any other stakeholder in the education community—for example, teachers, parents, trustees, and principals.

Bolstad (2011), Lodge (2005), and Byrom, Thomson, and Gates (2007) suggest the need for *dialogue* rather than *voice*, where students become engaged members of conversation in a climate of trust, and where they can share and act upon new ideas. Dialogue between students and teachers can change the power balance between the teacher and the student and can also reduce the possibility of essentializing student voice. The opportunity for dialogue through meaningful conversations and negotiation may allow stakeholders, on both an individual and group basis, to share ideas, thoughts, and beliefs. People involved in the conversation in turn can clarify what is shared, and ideas can also be further developed and more fully understood. This may result in both teachers and students gaining a more thorough understanding of the perceptions involved in the current situation and minimize inherent contradictions in both adult and student interpretations. Fielding and Bragg (2003) encourage all who work and research in the area of student voice to continually address whose voices are heard, which are easiest to hear, and which are difficult to get. Fielding (2004) goes as far to suggest a set of questions to consider throughout student voice activities. These include who is allowed to speak, who gets heard, who is listening, what skills are needed, how people regard each other, what structures and systems are needed, and where there are spaces for making meaning together.

Some reflective questions for educational leaders:

- What opportunities are there for young women to share their voices?
- How do you teach and encourage young women to share their voices?
- Who listens and who gets heard?
- Which voices are silent, not heard, or ignored?
- What happens when young women say things you do not want to hear?
- What action is created from this dialogue?

DEVELOPING AUTHENTIC LEARNING
PARTNERSHIPS WITH YOUNG WOMEN
USING CO-CONSTRUCTIVE PEDAGOGIES

Youth–adult partnerships can provide a context for dialogue to take place, allowing individuals to articulate their points of view and address issues relevant to them personally—all important facets of global citizenry. Youth–adult partnerships are relationships constructed in ways that encourage youth and adults to work collaboratively in creating programmes and taking action on issues of interest. They are relationships based on mutuality between youth and adults in the teaching and learning arrangement. Within this relationship, each person sees herself as a valuable resource, with each age group offering something unique (Zeldin, Petrokubi, & MacNeil, 2007). Mitra (2008) defines youth–adult partnerships as "relationships in which both youth and adults have the potential to contribute to visioning and decision making processes, to learn from one another, and promote change" (p. 222). Recent literature encourages schools to explore youth–adult partnerships. Zeldin, Larson, Camino, and O'Connor (2005) believe: "The divide between the youth and adult worlds is complex, multi-faceted, and sometimes downright inscrutable for parties on both sides of the divide. Researchers have important roles in creating strong and sustainable relationships across generations" (p. 7).

The literature highlights a number of benefits of utilizing youth–adult partnerships. Partnerships can increase commitment from young people towards their community (Zeldin, 2004). Similarly, Manefield, Collins, Moore, Mahar, and Warne (2007), in their extensive account of the historical and changing perception of youth voice in education, believe that partnerships in education are highly valuable and that "involving students as partners in their education strengthens their self-esteem and respect and provides practical agendas for improvement that have student support" (p. 14). Mitra (2008) also acknowledges many benefits of such arrangements ranging from teachers and students working together to gain an outcome that neither group could have reached alone, to addressing equity issues and injustices.

Examples of successful youth–adult partnerships in education are becoming increasingly prominent in educational change literature. Denner et al. (2005) bring to our attention the potential benefits of youth–adult partnerships in female leadership development as a way of addressing the unique challenges faced by adolescent girls and building upon their individual strengths. Investigating the relationships between 164 girl leaders and five adult women leaders in the Young Women's Leadership Alliance over a duration of three years, they found a number of key practices for generating successful programs with young women. These included firstly "legitimizing a range of leadership styles," secondly, "creating a way for all voices to be heard," and third, "creating a norm of respectful disagreement" (Denner et al., 2005, p. 87). With regard to adult leaders being successful in building relationships with the young women, they identified (a) providing guidance rather than instruction, (b) creating of an environment where girls felt comfortable to speak their minds, and (c) acknowledging the importance of building strong peer relationships amongst group members. Zeldin, Larson, Camino, and O'Connor (2005) warned that "strong relationships do not emerge spontaneously" (p. 5), and in order for these to occur, knowledge about youth adult partnerships and a significant amount of effort and planning are required.

Research that focuses on how to create authentic partnerships and involve students as active participants in school decision making is sparse (Mitra, 2008). Bishop and Glynn (1999) emphasize the importance of changing power relations and creating a learning environment where the learners' sense-making processes are used and developed so they can successfully participate in decision-making processes and constructing knowledge. However, it is these levels of participation that draw interest from researchers as they work to theorize the notion of involving students in decision-making processes.

DEVELOPMENTAL FRAMEWORKS
FOR AGENCY AND PARTICIPATION

Hart's (1992) ladder of participation is a model frequently used by many in the area of youth development and student engagement to illustrate how levels of student engagement and the influence of adults can impact on the learning experience for young people. At the bottom of the ladder he shows a tokenistic approach to involving students in decision making that results in minimal student engagement. As they move up the rungs of the ladder, they pass through increasing levels of engagement. At the top rung students have meaningful and student-driven ownership of learning processes and a high level of engagement. This model illustrates the important aspect of not just listening to the voices of students (which he describes as tokenism, decoration and often manipulation), but also creating action from these, which can result in a high degree of participation (which he describes as child-initiated processes with shared decision-making). Similarly, Fielding (2004) emphasizes key aspects of student engagement, calling for a move from dissemination, through discussion and teacher-led dialogue, to student-led dialogue. Hargreaves (2006) similarly focuses on the aspect of student voice and states "Co-construction focuses heavily on the talk that takes place between teacher and learner—their learning conversations"

(p. 18). Bruner (1996) also believes in the restructuring power relations and states that we need to

> characterize the new ideas as creating communities of learners. Indeed, on the basis of what we have learned in recent years about human learning— that it is best when it is participatory, proactive, communal, collaborative and given over to constructing meanings rather than receiving them. (p. 84)

Harry Shier's (2001) "Pathways to Participation" model is a useful tool for reflecting upon and ascertaining an organization's readiness and commitment to young people's participation in decision making. Based around the three areas of processes related to participation, he identifies *opening*— where there is a certain amount of readiness; *opportunity*—where the needs are met for an organization to operate in practice; and *obligation*—where policies support this expectation of youth involvement in decision making.

Bishop and Glynn (1999) purport that such a process can be created within an organization through providing contexts where learning can take place actively and reflectively. The development of youth–adult partnerships is founded on the principles of democratic education (Apple & Beane, 1995). The principles advocate for learning environments that encourage the open flow of ideas, a concern for the common good, trust in the group's ability, and the active use of critical thinking to evaluate experiences and ideas. A variety of learning styles also need to be included and students within the partnership must be given the power to determine which learning styles they need to use in order to learn best. Denner et al. (2005) support this collaborative approach to learning when working with young women. They believe that settings where young women have the opportunity to work together and practice a range of leadership styles in a supportive environment provides them with a forum where they do not have to choose between maintaining relationships or hiding their opinions (which is often the case in female youth peer groups).

Within the partnership relationship, there are some important aspects to consider. Camino (2005) supports the use of youth–adult partnerships but warns that misguided approaches can leave both parties discontented with outcomes. Examples of these approaches include holding the belief that young people need to do everything of importance, adults need to get out of the way and give up their power, and youth must be the key focus for benefit within the relationship. Such discourses can have a negative effect on the youth–adult partnership and leave young people feeling disillusioned and resentful. Culp and Cox (2002) argue that adult and youth partnerships alone are not enough to effectively develop leadership among youth. They state that adults must consider societal trends to project the future contexts in which youth will demonstrate their leadership. When approached in a strategic and authentic way, youth–adult partnerships can provide many benefits. This research used youth–adult partnerships to co-construct the leadership curriculum with young women. It is therefore timely to introduce an example of this practice in action.

Some reflective questions for educational leaders:

- What examples of partnerships with young women are present in your organization?
- What is the focus of these partnerships?
- What support is given to staff and students to develop their skills and abilities to create these authentic partnerships?
- What deliberate strategies are in place to initiate and conclude these partnerships?

CASE STUDY—REVOLUTION: ENGAGING STUDENT VOICE TO CO-CONSTRUCT A LEADERSHIP PROGRAMME WITH YOUNG WOMEN IN A NEW ZEALAND HIGH SCHOOL

Background to this Research:

Sarah shuffles into the hostel meeting room, her slippers scuffing the already worn carpet as she slowly and deliberately moves across the floor. With a Milo carefully balanced on top of a Cosmo magazine, she looks at me and exhales a sigh of what could only be read as frustration. Placing her mug on the coffee table, she looks over to one of her peers, rolls her eyes, and plunges herself into a space on the awaiting couch. "How long will this take, I've got to study," her eyes piercing mine. "...AND I've got better things to do."

As a teacher of young women in a secondary school, I recall the occasion above, stemming from the recent invitation by a school principal to provide leadership guidance for a group of young women in their final year of schooling. I responded to this request by designing and implementing what I thought to be an effective leadership development program for a group of young women aged 16 to 17 years old. Supported by postgraduate study in the area of leadership, I scoured my lecture notes, theories, and course readings to design a program that focused on defining, explaining, and practicing leadership. The program took place the following term, and upon reflection, I am now not surprised about the not-so-positive response I received from the students. As Sarah illustrated in the example from my research journal, the desire to learn, be involved, and be engaged in what should have been a positive learning experience was nonexistent. Upon consideration, I can now see that the content of the program was far removed from the actual contexts in which the young women exercised their leadership, and the definitions and theory were irrelevant to their day-to-day experiences. I now cringe as I reflect and I feel apologetic, and even embarrassed that I subjected anyone to such a learning (or not) opportunity.

After completing the delivery of this leadership program, I thought to myself that there had to be a better way to teach young women about leadership. I was a feminist who was supported by my core value of social justice. What should have been important were the leadership experiences of the young women, not the theories and definitions of leadership. These experiences and the context in which they exercised their leadership should have been central. I set about redesigning how I might go through this process differently. The underpinning philosophy for the design and implementation of the second leadership program described as a case study in this chapter was that it had to be a collaborative process between the young women and me. Also, it was critical that the program be relevant for this group. An imported leadership program created by adults, for adults, was not likely to meet the needs of the young women in a secondary school.

THE FOCUS OF THE RESEARCH

This qualitative action research study was located in an urban girls' Catholic secondary school and examined the leadership perceptions and experiences of 12 young women. The primary purpose of this research was to develop an alternative model of leadership curriculum development, and the research sought answers to the questions: how effective is the process of co-construction in creating a leadership development program for young women, and how effective would this program be in developing young women's leadership?

This research used a collaborative action research approach to co-construct and evaluate a leadership development curriculum with a group of young women. I believed that by understanding their leadership beliefs and their leadership contexts, learning experiences could be designed to develop their leadership practice in a meaningful and relevant way. From my study of the literature and previous work in this area, I believed that the use of adult–student partnerships (presented in the form of learning communities) and the inclusion of student voice in the negotiation and evaluation of a leadership development curriculum would assist in the creation of a leadership program that met the needs of this particular group of students.

Having the voices of the young women as a central part of this research required detailed planning, using a variety of research methods and ensuring that the methods selected allowed for this to happen in a safe and valid way. Methods that also contributed to the formation of the strong youth–adult partnerships were essential. Semi-structured interviews allowed the young women to individually share their voices. Focus group discussions allowed for engaging and interactive discussions between the young women, and also between the young women and me. Field notes and artifacts of students' work from workshop activities provided further means by which to gather important information and observations throughout the research.

DESCRIPTION OF THE RESEARCH

Over 12 months, there were eight phases located within an action research framework. Phase one of the research involved making initial contact with the school involved, fulfilling school access requirements, and selecting students for the leadership program and associated research. The second phase involved informing parents and students of the research at a school assembly and inviting students to be part of the research and leadership program. Twenty participants for the research were randomly selected from a self-nominated list of 56 pupils. Students were given an information pack with a letter that outlined the timeline, the required commitment, and the goals of the program and letters of permission and consent were taken home by students for themselves and parents to sign.

Phase three involved spending time creating a community of learning so that students got to know each other. Team-building activities and icebreaker games were used as a means for group members to get to know each other. Initial focus group interviews were held to ascertain the young women's views of leadership and their perceptions and beliefs about what it meant to be a leader. Extra time was allocated during this phase due to the diverse nature of the group, and more time was required to build an emotionally safe learning environment through further team-building activities and the creation of a group treaty.

The fourth phase involved developing the content and creating the structure for the leadership program. This was done through a second series of focus groups. During these conversations, students shared what they wanted to learn, how they would like to learn it (different learning strategies, both practical and theoretical), and what order the content should follow. Working together, a framework was negotiated that illustrated what the students felt was important to learn, what order to learn it in, and what activities they would use to allow the learning to happen. I also drew on my leadership knowledge and teaching experience to contribute to this and expand the students' ideas about what leadership could be and also offer a variety of teaching and learning approaches.

Phase five involved facilitating and participating in the leadership program. The group met for up to two hours, every week for eight weeks. Following afternoon tea, objectives for the session were shared and students would participate in the planned leadership session. At the end of the session, students evaluated what worked in the leadership program and what did not and made suggestions for future improvements and changes. The students recorded field notes as the evaluation took place. It was somewhere in between phases five and six that the student named the leadership program REVOLUTION. Each letter in the word *revolution* represented a key characteristic of their leadership beliefs—Respect, Enthusiasm, Vision, Outgoing, Lived (walking the talk), Unique, Transform, Integrity, Open, Never-ending.

In the sixth phase a final evaluation of the content and structure of REVOLUTION was made by the participants and changes to the leadership programme were suggested. Using evaluation field notes from each of the previous leadership sessions, students participated in focus group conversations and evaluated the whole of the program, making suggestions as to what might work better, what might have more impact, or what might have been more relevant. During this phase, the students also made a presentation to the board of trustees outlining what the program looked like, why and how they created it, the benefits and challenges, and the changes and ideas they would incorporate the following year.

Phase seven involved the analysis of the information gathered from interviews, observations, field notes, group work sheets, focus group interviews, and program evaluations. Interview transcripts were completed for the interviews, and these transcripts were shared back with the participants. Individually, participants had the opportunity to view the transcripts, make changes, and add information for clarity. These were then posted back in a freepost envelope. The analysis of the transcripts took place through a thematic approach. Transcripts from the interviews were photocopied, and different emerging themes were color-coded and a code book was created. The transcripts were revisited over many weeks for further analysis as new themes came to hand.

The eighth and final phase was an unplanned aspect of the action research and involved the young women sharing the new and improved leadership program with a new group of students the following year. During 2008, the graduates from the leadership program in 2007 offered to work alongside a new group of year 12 students, taking them through the program. This program ran over eight weeks and involved 16 students.

During this time I was merely an overseer. The REVOLUTION graduates called for volunteers through the school notices. Students collected and completed an application form from the school office, which had been drafted, edited, and finalized by the graduates and supported by the year

12 dean. The graduates met and selected 16 students based on criteria that they had generated. The criteria included people who may have had the potential to give back to the school, showed leadership ability, or were keen to explore and develop their own leadership. They then presented this list to the year 12 dean for approval.

The program was launched the following year for the new cohort of students. Previous graduates worked in pairs to plan and present a session that had been allocated to them. They took ownership of collecting and creating resources for this session. After each session was presented, the original graduates evaluated how it had gone and provided feedback to the presenters. This also allowed the two students who were presenting the following week to plan and build on previous material and allow for flow and progression in the learning pathway. At the conclusion of the 2008 program, two final focus group evaluations took place, one with the 2007 graduates who had taught in the program, and one with the 2008 graduates who had participated in the program. These focus groups were run to evaluate the program and the learning that had happened as a result of being involved. This final round of focus groups allowed further ideas for improvements and structural changes for the future to be shared.

SUMMARY OF THE RESEARCH FINDINGS

The findings demonstrated that the process of co-construction provided a valuable opportunity for me to work with the young women in a youth–adult partnership and create a contextually relevant leadership program. The process, although different from what the young women had experienced before, allowed for the sharing of ideas, while at the same time developing understandings about leadership within this particular school context. A number of key themes arose from the findings, and this chapter focuses on the findings related specifically to the following aspects: youth–adult partnerships, the complex and multifaceted nature of co-construction, the role of co-constructive pedagogies in challenging traditional youth development teaching approaches, student voice as an essential element of youth–adult partnerships, and the challenges associated with planning and future sustainability.

Youth–Adult Partnerships Were Essential for Co-construction

The creation of this partnership with the young women had a significant impact on their involvement with the program. The findings highlighted that the young women found co-construction personally rewarding and a source of enjoyment, with the majority of the reasons for this relating to the youth–adult partnership that was created. It could be suggested from the findings that students appreciated the opportunity to work alongside an adult and that even the process of creating the leadership program had its own rewards. Findings emphasized not only the benefits of youth–adult partnerships within the co-construction process, but also the impact that this can have on the young women's future involvement to make decisions about learning and taking responsibility to design opportunities to make learning happen. These findings support key themes in the literature, such as the work of Meier (1993), who highlighted the need for connection, inclusivity, participation, and collaboration. Furthermore, within the learning community and partnership, a sense of *agency* was required (Watkins, 2005). This meant that by coming together as a collective, there was a belief from all members of the learning community that they can make informed choices and take action. By being a part of the learning community, there was also a sense of *belonging* through membership. Respect, inclusion, acceptance, and support are key ingredients for this to occur (Watkins, 2005). Through developing a sense of belonging, there was a growth of commitment within the community, which can illustrate the *cohesion* between community members. This cohesion can assist in the creation of joint action when required. Lastly, recognizing and embracing the differences of others illustrated that *diversity* was a key facet in the creation of the learning community. This may have assisted in creating an inclusive community of difference as described by Shields and Seltzer (1997) in which culturally diverse viewpoints and practices are accepted and celebrated. I believe that youth–adult partnerships provide for new opportunities in youth development. Working alongside adults, young women have the opportunity to share ideas, develop their viewpoints, and be involved in a productive relationship that aids their learning. The uniqueness they bring to the relationship adds richness, and this diversity allows for greater impetus for future change.

The nature of the youth–adult partnership was highly complex. There were many layers to the relationship and these had to be negotiated with care. Camino (2000) states that youth–adult partnerships are "a multidimensional construct. They contain (a) principles and values, which actors use to orient the relationship and to guide behavior; (b) a set of skills and competencies through which the behaviors are focused; and (c) a method to implement and achieve collective action" (p. 11).

Although I was aware of the challenges involved in creating respectful partnerships with young people, I was not aware of the need to formalize these aspects and make them explicit to the group. An area I found that lacked coverage in the literature was the aspect of motivation within these relationships. Of great surprise to me was the source of motivation for these students. The motivation to be involved in the leadership program extended beyond the opportunities to plan and participate in a planned leadership experience. Evidence of this occurring was in the unexpected outcomes after the leadership program took place. The young women provided a leadership breakfast for students within the school who considered themselves leaders. This was set up as an opportunity for them to meet and talk about leadership with other leaders. Interestingly, in the context of youth–adult partnerships, Mitra (2009) speaks of the work of McLaughlin (1993) and the need for "visible victories" (Mitra, 2009, p. 322), where the legitimacy of the relationship can be seen through the accomplishment of a set outcome. She believes that these victories help to legitimate the process and can help to establish credibility of youth–adult partnerships within the school. Furthermore, I also experienced a significant amount of learning. Within the partnership, I too developed my knowledge and understanding about leadership within a particular context. I also came to know a group of young women on a level that perhaps I might not have as a teacher.

Due to the nature of the learning community, the safe and supportive learning environment and the willingness of all involved to work towards a shared vision, it became clear to me that sometimes the visible victories actually make way for invisible strengthening of relationships. I believe this has significant implications for those working alongside students in partnerships. I have learned that in relationships like this it is important to plan for and celebrate the visible victories but also to acknowledge and understand that the invisible victories are also important in enhancing motivation and increasing the young women's desire to strive for leadership opportunities.

As the young women had been involved in the planning and creation of the leadership program there was an increased sense of ownership. I believe this may have led to a greater motivation to be involved and attend the leadership sessions. This finding supports the work of Wallin (2003), who found in her work when identifying leadership opportunities for senior students within Saskatchewan schools, opportunities to be involved in making decisions about their learning kept the students interested and focused. Similarly, Close and Lechman (1997) acknowledged the benefits of including young people in the planning and implementation of a peer mediation program. Their work highlighted the benefits of including young people in sharing their knowledge of conflict resolution with adults to enhance the adults' understanding about issues that were important to them and the best ways to address them. The secondary school students in the study also indicated that opportunities similar to these encouraged them to take more responsibility for their learning and fostered more positive relationships with their peers. In the case of this research, the findings indicated that the design of the youth–adult partnerships allowed opportunities for peer relationships to strengthen and provided opportunities for students to build new friendships. Such a relationship could also be viewed the other way where it was actually the developing relationships that provided the opportunity for the partnership to occur.

Developing a learning community was central to the ease with which the students shared their voices. It took time for the students to open up and share their views. This may have been due to many reasons—firstly, as I was an outsider, a level of trust needed to be established. Secondly, the group that was brought together for the research was a group of students who did not normally mix together, and therefore, the dynamics of the group needed to be addressed to ensure that people felt comfortable. As the size of the group was small, relationships were established quickly. Mitra (2009) suggests that "a youth–adult partnership can only be as big as it is possible for all group members to be known and to have the ability to actively participant [sic] as valuable members of the collective" (p. 328). Although it is deemed important to seek the voices of young people in regard to developing learning curriculum and approaches, I believe that this process is not unproblematic and can be rather complex and, sometimes, deceptive.

Action research carried out by Sanchez (2009) with three young women highlights the importance of "building relational knowledge" (p. 86). She found that through building trusting relationships she was able to "foster and deepen reflective knowledge" (p. 86), and she spent six months of the three years doing so. Similarly, in this research, although the time investment differed, these strong partnerships were foundational to the co-construction process because the process was heavily reliant on them. I feel it is important to highlight that this period of building relationships was not a finite process but continued beyond the planned "getting to know you" time at the beginning of the research. As relationships changed and altered over time in the research, so did the interactions, and consequently the research process; however, it is these initial stages that are essential. All of these aspects required significant negotiations, planning, flexibility, and organization. It is therefore not surprising that one important area warranting discussion that was an essential part of my learning was the fact that co-construction is extremely complex, and people embarking on co-construction will learn as well as teach.

Co-construction was Complex and Multifaceted

Co-construction, although useful and effective in generating a contextually relevant, needs-based leadership program, was also extremely complex. Co-construction is frequently presented as a tool used to generate new knowledge. In the case of this research, co-construction was a useful and engaging learning process that involved the young women and not only generated a leadership program, but also provided an opportunity for them to learn about leadership. However, in the literature, co-construction is often portrayed as an unproblematic and linear process. Hence, when embarking on this research, it was initially designed in a certain way to take into account this linear process. In reality, I found it to be anything but the unidirectional, mechanical, and rational process commonly referred to in the literature (Datnow, Hubbard, & Mehan, 1998). As the process of co-construction got underway, it became obvious that a linear process was not necessarily representative of true co-construction. I discovered that much of the literature failed to take into account the nature of relationships and the impact of the context on the process of co-construction (with the exception of Bishop & Glynn, 1999). Furthermore, although co-construction was touted as an approach that shared power and provided opportunities for all involved being active creators of curriculum, many of the complexities of relationships and processes are overlooked. From this research it became clear that those embarking on co-construction processes with young women need to be comfortable with chaos and be ready for the unknown.

The learning within the co-construction process was multifarious (Barker, 2008) and required significant planning and flexibility. Throughout the co-construction process, the students often revisited their original knowledge and starting point in order to move forward in their leadership thinking. Moreover, while this process generated new knowledge, it also confirmed the existing leadership knowledge and beliefs held by the young women, thus validating existing leadership practices. For example, one student, Jenny, did not realize that the tutoring that she was already doing was leadership until it was made clear to her in the group discussions around what leadership could be. This finding supports the work of Strachan and Saunders (2007), who, in their work focusing on women's leadership development, found that as the women co-constructed their leadership learning opportunities and developed their leadership understandings, the expanding views of leadership validated existing leadership practices that had previously not been viewed as leadership. What I learned was that as the adult I did not have to be the sole provider of knowledge and answers. I believe this to be a strength of the co-construction process, especially when working with larger groups. Participants were able to draw on multiple sources of information to develop their leadership understandings and validate their existing leadership practices. It was useful because the young women were not solely reliant on the teacher and others who had more contextual knowledge, and consequently they were able to make excellent contributions in this area.

Co-construction Challenged Traditional Youth Development Pedagogy

The findings indicated that the complexity of the co-construction process extended into the pedagogical nature of the teaching and learning approaches. The youth–adult partnerships that were utilized in the co-construction process were different from the traditional ways of teaching and learning that the young women were used to, sometimes contradicting the young women's existing beliefs about teaching and learning. Rodriguez and Brown (2009) acknowledge that collaborative work with young people can be difficult, as many "have never been expected to control the terms of their learning or collaborate with adults" (p. 27), and in the case of this research, the young women were not used to working in partnership with an adult, and even scarcer was the opportunity to be involved in decision making about their learning. As noted by Boomer (1992),

> Traditionally, there has been an "apartness" in classrooms. Teachers teach and children learn. Teachers guide and children are guided. Teachers decide what is to be done and children usually try to comply. Teachers accommodate children and children accommodate teachers, but they have different roles. (p. 32)

The young women commented that adult–student partnerships were not frequently utilized in this secondary school setting; therefore, engaging students in this type of partnership challenged their current views of who held important knowledge and who should make decisions about learning. Mitra (2009) argues that the traditional roles of the teacher and the student in schools can restrict opportunities for youth–adult partnerships. In her work exploring the challenges of creating youth–adult partnerships in school she found that such a process "requires intentional effort to push against the institutional pressures that encourage a reversion back to traditional teacher and student role" (p. 318). I learned that relationships are central to leadership development. I believe providing space and opportunities for the relationships in a learning community to flourish was effective in developing strong partnerships with the young women, and this impacted on their leadership development. However, an essential part of this process was recognizing that the process itself did not necessarily fit into the structured and timetabled approach to this research and required a significant amount of flexibility. It could be timely to note that many adult-generated leadership programs and one-size-fits-all approaches to leadership do not necessarily have the luxury of this time and flexibility. Outside providers are expected to meet delivery targets, and timetables frequently inhibit opportunities for providing space and developing relationships. I believe therefore that an investment in building relationships is required as a firm foundation for leadership development.

On many occasions, co-construction shifted the responsibility for the learning from being solely the responsibility of the adult to being a shared responsibility between the teacher and the students as different people took ownership for different parts throughout the co-construction process. Anderson and Sandmann (2009) believe that the underlying concept supporting the success of youth–adult partnerships is mutuality. Within this mutuality, it is recognized that all individuals involved in the partnership have responsibility for the outcome and, therefore, their voices must be recognized and valued. For the partnership to be successful, "both parties must be considered valuable contributors to the decision-making process" (Anderson & Sandmann, 2009, p. 4). Within the context of New Zealand, the Māori concept of *ako* is used to describe the teaching and learning relationship, where the teacher is also learning from the student. I found the co-construction process to be underpinned by this concept. *Ako* is grounded in the principle of reciprocity and also recognizes that "the learner and whanau cannot be separated" (Ministry of Education, 2008, p. 20). Alton-Lee (2003) defines the concept of *ako* as involving the ability to both to teach and to learn. A key facet of *ako* is to recognize the knowledge that all people in the learning arrangement (in this case, the researcher and the students) bring to any learning interactions. This allows for new knowledge and understandings to be created from shared learning experiences (Alton-Lee, 2003).

Such a belief was integral to the design of the co-construction process. However, the findings indicated it took the young women time to get used to this process. Upon reflection, the fact that I had not initially made the roles within the youth–adult partnership as clear as they needed to be may have had some bearing on this. Larson, Walker, and Pearce (2005) note that in order for youth–adult partnerships to be successful, roles for both the adults and the youth must be justified and made clear to all involved in the relationship. Consequently, one aspect essential to creating a sense of *ako* within this research was the provision for student voice within the co-construction process.

Student Voice Was an Essential but Also Challenging Element of Co-construction

Hanvey (2003) argues that while quantitative data through surveys and questionnaires can be useful to gain a broad spectrum of information and can contribute to our understanding of youth as a developmental concept, individual interviews or focus groups using a qualitative framework and asking young people what they think and what their experiences have been can add more richness and keep the context of young people present. This further enriches our understanding of youth (Hanvey, 2003). Holdsworth (2004) makes it clear that, although a range of language is used to describe the involvement of student voice in decision-making and change processes, some descriptions are more limited than others—for example, consultation and involvement could be seen as less participatory than participation and action. I had originally only planned for the sharing of voice within the co-construction process; however, it also became an important part of the learning processes within the leadership program itself. The findings indicated that such a concept was complex and not only was the sharing of voice important in getting messages across, but the withholding of voice was also an important aspect. Gunter (2001) states, "Voice is problematic as it connects with capability and capacity. Some voices are louder than others" (p. 125). Balancing student voice within the process required a significant amount of attention to ensure that all voices were heard. For example, the findings illustrated that some voices were more frequent or prominent in group discussions. What I learned was that student voice was more powerful than I had initially perceived.

Furthermore, it became apparent that although I had planned for the inclusion of student voice within the research process, it remained situated as just that—within the research. When change was sought in terms of leadership structures and decision making within the school, the voices of the young women alone were not enough to create that change, with the only exception being when they requested money to support the program. It might have been useful to extend the notion of student voice outside of the research focus and focus on furthering the young women's understandings about how they can make their voices matter in future decision making within the school. Rodriguez and Brown (2009) see this process as shifting from simply having a voice to being actual agents of change in areas that matter. In order for this to happen further critical engagement *within* and *of* the school context by the young women would have been necessary. I learned that simply having a voice might not be enough to create change. When those sharing voices are not in position to make decisions, it is difficult for change to happen.

Co-construction Required Planning and Time for Future Sustainability

No teachers were included in this research, so I turned to the literature to explore some of the challenges faced by teachers when attempting to implement co-construction processes within their classrooms. A recent and timely example from the New Zealand context, Mansell (2009) highlighted that many teachers found it difficult to utilize co-construction because of the extra time and energy required to make it an effective and meaningful process. Although there was a small amount of flexibility to do this within the context of this research, within the case of broader education, this may not be the case. Mansell found that the everyday requirements of teaching drew a significant amount of teachers' time, making it difficult for them to commit to investing further time in new ideas about curriculum—for example, co-construction. One aspect of the findings in this research related to the need for adequate time in order for the co-construction process to be adequately planned for and strong partnerships formed within the learning community. Mitra (2009) purports that in order for youth–adult partnerships to be successful, "sufficient time and space for relationships to develop and for activities to be designed and implement" is required (p. 319). However, as this research was bound by a research timeline, there was pressure to meet deadlines. This may have influenced the final outcomes of the co-construction process. I discovered that the research timeline needed to be flexible, as it required adjusting so that more time could be spent creating a safe, supportive, and productive learning community.

The co-construction process was far-reaching. It not only shifted leadership beliefs and understandings, but it also developed a shared sense of pride and belonging. This sense of belonging was so powerful that many students returned to the school the following year (after they had left the school) and ran the program again for another group of students. The program became self-sustaining in some ways through these actions of the students; however, the complexity of co-construction was lost on this group. They believed that taking the program and delivering it to another group of students would have the same impact as they experienced. They did not realize the role that co-construction had played in the development of the leadership curriculum and the development of their leadership understandings.

Throughout and even more so, after the REVOLUTION leadership program, there was a disconnection between the students and the school. Literature addressing learning communities comments on the need to involve the wider school community in the learning community itself (Stoll, 2003). However, there is no set boundary or requirement outlined as to who should belong to the learning community and who should be included in the process of group formation and knowledge creation. Therefore, as an outsider coming into a school, I was the sole adult engaging with this group. This, on one hand, was positive as it created an aspect of mystery and difference, as staff members whom the students knew had not initiated the program. Speck (1999) envisions learning communities involving the whole school and community partners beyond the school gates. She also speaks of a school learning community as a community that values and promotes ongoing collaborative processes and recommends that such environments can result in collaborative action. There is dialogue between all stakeholders—the teachers, students, staff, principal, parents, and the school community. Through the reflexive nature of this research I also came to realize that while I had built these relationships within the partnership, I still felt like what Patricia Hill Collins (1991) describes as "an outsider within" (p. 35). However, I did not come to realize this until the final stages of the research when the young women returned to run the leadership program for a new group of students. I have come to realize that although learning communities can be powerful in creating leadership programs, in order for change to happen at a systemic level, the learning community needs to incorporate not just people who are capable of making decisions, but also people who are in positions of influence and can implement suggested changes.

The original design of the leadership programme was based around two contributing parties—me, as the researcher and facilitator, and the young women. The possibility of involving other adults in this process during those initial stages may have had a detrimental effect on the participants and their abilities to speak freely about their leadership aspirations, beliefs, and the things that influenced these. However, these also provided challenges as the program struggled to gain credibility among the students and staff because it was unknown. Robertson (1991) concluded in her collated report titled "ACCO: Achieving Charter Curriculum Objectives: A Teacher Development Programme Using a School Development Strategy," that involving the wider community was paramount if sustainable change was to occur. She states that "an inclusive approach to curriculum development is required" and will be "more likely to overcome institutional barriers to change and sustain the direction of development" (p. 5). Similarly, Senge (1990) highlights the need to acknowledge the broad context in which experiences sit. His seminal work on systems thinking highlights the need to have a good understanding of the whole context that we work within, and only then can meaningful and appropriate action take place. He speaks of the need to "see" systems and understand the dynamics of how key elements connect (p. 231). For example, in this research, once I had left the school, I removed the essential ingredient of the "adult" element from within the youth–adult partnerships. I consider this aspect was key to making the program successful and motivating the young women to remain involved because the students frequently commented on how they enjoyed the youth–adult partnership relationship.

Although the learning community sustained itself once I had left, I believe it still required the adult–student partnership relationship to make it seem like an attractive proposition for learning. Tillery (2009) highlights the value of adult connections with secondary school students and outlined how these relationships enhanced the sense of belonging with the school community. It may therefore have been useful to involve a school staff member and/or a person in the local community throughout the process in order to mentor them through the process to ensure future involvement from the school and "buy in" from the school. What I learned was that in order for change to occur more broadly, beyond the students themselves and more so in the school context, it would be essential for an insider who is placed in a key decision-making role to be involved. They can assist the students in creating sustainable change within the school based upon the needs of the students.

CONCLUDING THOUGHTS FOR LEADERS

The notion of the global citizen, although not a new term, must shift beyond its clichéd status (Tsolidis, 2002) and remain prevalent in education discussions if schools are to play a role in preparing young women to be active contributors to their communities. As schools are challenged with restrictive timetables and increasing administrative demands, the time available for schools to grapple with preparing young women to be engaged community members may not be seen as a priority. However, research has shown that schools can be key places for young women to learn to be global citizens when they model and reflect the qualities of a democratic learning environment. This environment is founded upon authentic partnerships with adults where young women play a key role in planning and developing learning processes, working collaboratively with others, practicing and modeling skills of agency, and generating a sense of belonging, alongside the ability to accept diversity.

The process of exploring and challenging traditional notions of schooling and leadership becomes central to supporting the development of young women as global citizens. Carlsson-Paige and Lantieri (2005) state:

> We need to insist that schools enable all young people to have their ethical, political, social and emotional selves welcomed; their spirits uplifted; and their capacity for active meaningful learning fully engaged. These exceptional practices need to become the norm. Compassionate, insightful, and committed young people and adults will learn how to tackle the profound political, emotional, social and spiritual issues of our time. Preparing young people to be global citizens is to make sure that no child is left behind and that every aspect of the human being is welcomes into our schools. (p. 102)

Many educators and academics believe that lack of student engagement in societal issues can be addressed through the provision of citizenship education programs. However, with many of these based on traditional notions of citizenship, they are far removed from the globalized lives of young people today. Schools must therefore recognize the need to break down the boundaries between school and community and operate within a democratic collective. It is only when these boundaries between school knowledge and life knowledge are broken down that we will see the emergence of global citizens, prepared and willing to play active roles in the community on both a local, national, and global scale.

Educational leaders have an obligation to investigate how learning communities can be created within classrooms, schools, and the wider community. Traditional structures of schools can be questioned and democratic practices sought within and beyond these structures with the obligation to be inclusive of diversity and to be collaborative, trusting, and encouraging of participation. Not only should these structures be in place, but also young women must remain central to these structures and practices. It is through democratic frameworks and relevant learning experiences that students can further explore the characteristics of global citizenry.

The responsibilities that lie with school leaders, staff, and the young women themselves are immense, and if the notion of global citizenship is to be addressed in schools, there are many challenges faced by educational leaders. Schools, and more specifically, teachers, could be encouraged to enlarge their views about what young women can do in schools and create space for student voice to be incorporated in planning and decision making within the school context. However, as Hart (1992) has highlighted, such actions need to be authentic and illustrate to young people that their ideas and suggestions are taken seriously. This increased understanding is essential to further inform processes that schools use to prepare young women for leadership responsibilities, not only within the school context but beyond the school gates.

Due to the significant influence of context on young women's leadership understandings and practices as educational leaders, there is an obligation for school leaders and students to critique the traditional leadership structures of our schools that we present to students. We should aim to seek to model democratic practices within these structures that allow for young women to have a voice in planning their leadership learning and participation, an aspect not frequently planned for or actioned in many school contexts (Brooker & MacDonald, 1999; Cook-Sather, 2002). It is by ensuring that young women are central to the planning of the leadership development approaches and that their voices are valued and acted upon that leadership learning experiences can be designed in ways that actually means something to them now and in the future. There must be a shift in thought surrounding the leadership of schools, with schools encouraging a distributed form of leadership which supports power sharing (Bishop &

Glynn, 1999) and the creation of dynamic working relationships within the school walls and beyond.

Schools and young women alike must recognize the need to break down the boundaries between traditional school structures and the leadership needs of young women. It is only when these boundaries are broken down that we will see an increase in the participation of young women leading beyond the school gates, prepared and willing to share their voices and play active roles in the community on a local, national, and global scale.

REFERENCES

Alexander, W. E., & Farrell, J. P. (1975). *Student participation in decision-making*. Toronto, Canada: Ontario Institute for Studies in Education.

Alton-Lee, A. (2003). *Quality teaching for diverse students in schooling: Best evidence synthesis*. Wellington, NZ: Ministry of Education. Retrieved from www.educationcounts.govt.nz/publications/series/2515

Anderson, K. S., & Sandmann, L. (2009). Toward a model of empowering practices in youth–adult partnerships. *Journal of Extension, 74*(2), 1–8.

Apple, M. W., & Beane, J. A. (Eds.). (1995). *Democratic schools*. Alexandria, VA: Association for Supervision and Curriculum Development.

Archard, N. (2012). Student leadership development in Australian and New Zealand secondary girls' schools: a staff perspective, *International Journal of Leadership in Education, 15*(1), 23–47.

Arnot, M., & Reay, D. (2007). A sociology of pedagogic voice: Power, inequality and pupil consultation. *Discourse: Studies in the cultural politics of education, 28*(3), 311–325.

Barker, M. (2008). How do people learn? Understanding the learning process. In C. McGee & D. Fraser (Eds.), *The professional practice of teaching* (2nd ed., pp.17–46). South Melbourne, Victoria, Australia: Cengage.

Bishop, R., & Glynn, T. (1999). *Culture counts: Changing power relations in education*. Palmerston North, NZ: Dunmore Press.

Bolstad, R. (2011). *From 'student voice' to 'youth–adult partnerships': Lessons from working with young people as partners for educational change*. Working paper from the Families and Communities Engagement in Education (FACE) project. Wellington, NZ: New Zealand Council for Educational Research. Retrieved from http://www.nzcer.org.nz/default. php?products_id=2761

Bond, L. A., Belenky, M. F., & Weinstock, J. S. (2000). The Listening Partners Program: An initiative toward feminist community psychology in action. *American Journal of Community Psychology, 28*(5), 697–730.

Boomer, G. (1992). Curriculum composing and evaluation: An invitation to action research. In G. Boomer, N. Lester, C. Onore, & J. Cook (Eds.), *Negotiating the curriculum: Educating for the 21st century* (pp. 91–97). London, UK: Falmer Press.

Bragg, S., & Fielding, M. (2005). It's an equal thing... It's about achieving together student voices and the possibility of a radical collegiality. In H. Street & J. Temperley (Eds.), *Improving schools through collaborative enquiry* (pp. 105–134). London, UK: Continuum.

Brooker, R., & MacDonald, D. (1999). Did we hear you? Issues of student voice in curriculum innovation. *Journal of Curriculum Studies, 31*, 83–87.

Bruner, J. (1996). *The culture of education.* Boston, MA: Harvard University Press.

Burkimsher, M. (1993). Creating a climate for citizenship education in schools. In J. Edwards & K. Fogelman (Eds.), *Developing citizenship in the curriculum* (pp. 7–15). London, UK: David Fulton.

Byrom, T., Thomson, P., & Gates, P. (2007). My school has been quite pushy about the Oxbridge thing: Voice and higher education choice. *Improving Schools, 10*(1), 29–40.

Camino, L. (2000). Youth–adult partnerships: Entering new territory in community work and research. *Applied Developmental Science, 1*(4), 11–20.

Camino, L. (2005). Pitfalls and promising practices of adult-youth partnerships: An evaluator's reflections. *Journal of Community Psychology, 33*(1), 75–85.

Carlsson-Paige, N., & Lantieri, L. (2005). A changing vision of education. *Reclaiming Children and Youth, 14*(2), 97–105.

Close, C. L., & Lechman, K. (1997). Fostering youth leadership: Students train students and adults in conflict resolution. *Theory into Practice, 36*(1), 1–7.

Cook-Sather, A. (2002). Authorizing students' perspectives: Toward trust, dialogue and change in education. *Educational Researcher, 31*(4), 3–14.

Cook-Sather, A. (2007). Resisting the impositional potential of student voice work: Lessons for liberatory educational research from poststructuralist feminist critiques of critical pedagogy. *Discourse: Studies in the Cultural Politics of Education, 28*(3), 389–403.

Culp, K., & Cox, K. J. (2002). Developing leadership through adult and adolescent partnerships in the third millennium. *Journal of Leadership Education, 1*(1), 41–57.

Datnow, A., Hubbard, L., & Mehan, H. (1998). *Educational reform implementation: A co-constructed process.* Berkeley, CA: Center for Research on Education, Diversity and Excellence, UC Berkeley. Retrieved from http://escholarship.org/uc/item/1470d2c8

Denner, J., Meyer, B., & Bean, S. (2005). Young women's leadership alliance: Youth–adult partnerships in an all female after-school program. *Journal of Community Psychology, 33*(1), 87–100.

Dewey, J. (1936). *Moral principles in education.* New York: Houghton Mifflin.

Dewey, J. (1961). *Experience and nature.* Lasalle, IL: Open Court.

Down, B. (2004). From patriotism to critical democracy: Shifting discourses of citizenship in social studies. *History of Education Review, 33*(1), pp. 14–27.

Fielding, M. (2001). Beyond the rhetoric of student voice: New departures or new constraints in the transformation of 21st century schooling? *Forum, 43*(2), 100–110.

Fielding, M. (2004). 'New wave' student voice and the renewal of civic society. *London Review of Education, 2*(3), 197–217.

Fielding, M., & Bragg, S. (2003). *Students as researchers: Making a difference.* Cambridge, UK: Pearson.

Griffith, R. (1998). *Educational citizenship and independent learning.* London, UK: Jessica Kingsley.

Gunter, H. (2001). *Leaders and leadership in education.* London, England: Sage.

Hanvey, L. (2003). *Social inclusion research in Canada: Children and youth*. Ottawa, ON: Canadian Council on Social Development.

Hargreaves, D. (2006). *A new shape for schooling*. London, UK: Specialist Schools and Academies Trust. Retrieved from http://curriculumdesign.ssatrust.org.uk

Hart, R. A. (1992). *Children's participation: From tokenism to citizenship. Innocenti Essays No. 4*. Florence, Italy: UNICEF International Child Development Centre.

Hill Collins, P. (1991). Learning from the outsider within: The sociological significance of Black Feminist thought. In M. M. Furnow & J. A. Cook (Eds.), *Beyond methodology: Feminist sociology as lived research* (pp. 35–51). Bloomington, IN: Indiana University Press.

Holdsworth, R. (2004). *Taking young people seriously means giving them serious things to do*. Melbourne, NSW: Youth Research Centre, Faculty of Education, University of Melbourne.

Innes, M., Moss, T., & Smigiel, H. (2001). What do children say? The importance of student voice. *Research in Drama Education, 6*(2), 207–213.

Larson, R., Walker, K., & Pearce, N. (2005). A comparison of youth-driven and adult-driven youth programs: Balancing inputs from youth and adults. *Journal of Community Psychology, 33*(1), 57–74.

Leitch, R., & Mitchell, S. (2007). Caged birds and cloning machines: How student imagery 'speaks' to us about cultures of schooling and student participation. *Improving Schools, 10*(1), 53–71.

Lodge, C. (2005). From hearing voices to engaging in dialogue: Problematizing student participation in school improvement. *Journal of Educational Change, 6*, 125–146.

MacGregor, M. G. (2007). *Building everyday leadership in all teens*. Minneapolis, MN: Free Spirit Publishing.

Manefield J., Collins R., Moore J., Mahar S., & Warne C. (2007). *Student voice: A historical perspective and new directions*. Melbourne, Victoria: Office for Education Policy and Innovation.

Mansell, H. (2009). *Collaborative partnerships: an investigation of co-construction in secondary classrooms*. Unpublished doctoral thesis, University of Waikato, Hamilton, New Zealand.

McLaughlin, M. W. (1993). Embedded identities: Enabling balance in urban contexts. In S. B. Heath & M. W. McLaughlin (Eds.), *Identity and inner-city youth* (pp. 36–68). New York, NY: Teachers College Press.

McMurray, A., & Niens, U. (2012). Building bridging social capital in a divided society: The role of participatory citizenship education. *Education, Citizenship and Social Justice, 7*(2), 207–221.

McNae, R. (2010). Young women and the co-construction of leadership. *Journal of Educational Administration, 48*(6), 677–688.

Meier, D. (1993). Transforming schools into powerful communities. *Teachers College Record, 94*(3), 654–658.

Meier, D. (2003). *In schools we trust: Creating communities of learning in an era of testing and standardization*. Boston, MA: Beacon Press.

Ministry of Education. (2008). *Ka Hikitia— Managing for Success: The Māori Education Strategy 2008–12*. Wellington, NZ: Group Māori, Ministry of Education.

Mitra, D. L. (2004). The significance of students: Can increasing "student voice" in schools lead to gains in youth development? *Teachers College Records, 106*(4), 651–688.

Mitra, D. L. (2008). Balancing power in communities of practice: An examination of increasing student voice through school-based youth–adult partnerships. *Journal of Educational Change, 9*(3), 221–242.

Mitra, D. L. (2009). Strengthening student voice initiatives in high schools: An examination of the supports needed for school-based youth–adult partnerships. *Youth and Society, 40*(3), 311–335.

Mitsoni, F. (2006). "I get bored when we don't have the opportunity to say our opinion": Learning about teaching from students. *Educational Review, 58*(2), 159–170.

Mono, A., & Keenan, L. D. (2000). The after-school girls leadership program: Transforming the school environment for adolescent girls. *Social Work In E d u c a - tion, 22*(2), 116–128.

Morgan, W., & Streb, M. (2003). First do no harm: The importance of student ownership in service-learning. *Metropolitan State Universities, 14*(3), 36–52.

Noddings, N. (2005). *Educating citizens for global awareness.* New York, NY: Teachers College Press.

Noddings, N. (1992). *The challenge to care in schools.* New York, NY: Teachers College Press.

Osler, A. (1996). *Learning to participate.* Birmingham, UK: Development Education Centre.

Pratt, C. (1948). *I learn from Children: An Adventure in Progressive Education.* New York: Simon and Schuster.

Ranson, S. (2000). Recognizing the pedagogy of voice in a learning community. *Educational Management and Administration, 28*(3), 263–279.

Robertson, J. (1991). *ACCO: Achieving charter curriculum objectives: A teacher development programme using a school development strategy.* Hamilton, NZ: University of Waikato, School of Education.

Rogoff, B., Bartlett, L., & Turkanis, C. G. (2001). Lessons about learning as a community. In B. Rogoff, C. G. Turkanis, & L. Bartlett (Eds.), *Learning together: Children and adults in a school community* (pp.3–20). New York: Oxford University Press.

Robinson, C., & Taylor, C. (2007). Theorising student voice: Values and perspectives. *Improving Schools 10*(1), 5–17.

Rodriguez, L. F., & Brown, T. M. (2009). From voice to agency: Guiding principles for participatory action research with youth. *New Directions for Youth Development, 123,* 19–34.

Rudduck, J. (2006). The past, the papers and the project. *Educational Review, 58*(2), 131–143 .

Rudduck, J., & Flutter, J. (2000). Pupil participation and perspective: "Carving a new order of experience." *Cambridge Journal of Education, 30*(1), 75–89.

Rudduck, J., & Flutter, J. (2004). *How to improve your school: Giving pupils a voice.* London, UK: Continuum.

Russell, L., & Byrom, T. (2007). Engaging critically with pupil voice. *Improving Schools, 10*(1), 3–4.

Sanchez, P. (2009). Chicana feminist strategies in a participatory action research project with transnational Latina youth. *New Directions for Youth Development, 123*, 83–97.

Saunders, R. E. (2005). Youth leadership: Creating meaningful leadership programmes for young women through the process of co-construction. *New Zealand Journal of Educational Leadership, 20*(2), 15–30.

Scratchley, M. (2003). *Hearing their voices: The perceptions of children and adults about learning in health education.* Unpublished doctoral thesis, University of Waikato, Hamilton, New Zealand.

Senge, P. M. (1990). *The fifth discipline: The art and practice of the learning organization.* London, UK: Random House.

Shallcross, T., Robinson, J., Pace, P., & Tamoutseli, D. (2007). The role of students' voices and their influence on adults in creating more sustainable environments in three schools. *Improving Schools, 10*(1), 72–85.

Shields, C. M., & Seltzer, P. A. (1997). Complexities and paradoxes of community: Towards a more useful conceptualization of community. *Educational Administration Quarterly, 33*(4), 413–439.

Shier, H. (2001). Pathways to participation: openings, opportunities and obligations. *Children and Society, 15*(2), 107–117.

Smith, A. B., & Taylor, N. J. (2000). A new discourse for child advocacy, children's services and research. In A. B Smith, N. J Taylor, & M. Gollop (Eds.), *Children's voices: Research, policy and practice.* Auckland, NZ: Pearson Education.

Speck, M. (1999). *The principalship: Building a learning community.* Upper Saddle River, NJ: Prentice-Hall.

Stoll, L. (2003). The learning community: learning together and learning from one another. In K. Myers & J. MacBeath (Eds.), *It's about learning (and it's about time): What's in it for schools?* (pp.131–160). London, UK: Routledge Falmer.

Stainton Rogers, W., Stainton Rogers, R., Vyrost, J., & Lovas, L. (2004). Worlds apart: Young people's aspirations in a changing Europe. In J. Roche, S. Tucker, & R. Flynn (Eds), *Youth and society* (pp. 76–90). London, UK: Sage.

Stoneman, D. (2002). The role of youth programming in the development of civic engagement. *Applied Developmental Science, 6*(4), 221–226.

Strachan, J., & Saunders, R. (2007). Ni Vanuatu women and educational leadership development. *New Zealand Journal of Educational Leadership, 22*(2), 37–48.

Thomson, P., & Gunter, H. (2005, April). *Researching students: voices and processes in a school evaluation.* Paper given at the Annual Meeting of the American Educational Research Association, Montreal, Canada.

Thomson, P., & Gunter, H. (2006). From 'consulting pupils' to 'pupils as researchers': A situated case narrative. *British Educational Research Journal, 32*(6), 839–856.

Tillery, A. D. (2009). *The moderating role of adult connections in high schools: Students' sense of school belonging.* PhD thesis, Georgia State University. Retrieved from http://digitalarchives.gsu.edu/alesI_diss/6

Tsolidis, G. (2002). How do we teach and learn in times when the notion of 'global citizenship' sounds like a cliché? *Journal of Research in International Education, 1*, 213–226.

Ungerleider, J. (2012). Structured youth dialogue to empower peacekeeping and leadership. *Conflict Resolution Quarterly, 29*(4), 381–402.

Wallin, D. (2003). Student leadership and democratic schools: A case study. *National Association of Secondary School Principals NASSP Bulletin, 87,* 55–78.

Watkins, C. (2005). Classrooms as learning communities: A review of research. *London Review of Education, 3*(1), 47–64.

Wilkins, C. (2000). Citizenship education. In R. Bailey (Ed.). *Teaching Values and Citizenship Across the Curriculum* (pp. 14–27). London: Kogan Page.

Williams, M., & Humphrys, G. (2003). *Citizenship education and lifelong learning: Power and place.* New York, NY: Nova Science Publishers.

Zeldin, S. (2004). Youth as agents of adult and community development: Mapping the processes and outcomes of youth engaged in organizational governance. *Applied Developmental Science, 8*(2), 75–90.

Zeldin, S., Larson, R., Camino, L., & O'Connor, C. (2005). Intergenerational relationships and partnerships in community programs: Purpose, practice, and directions for research. *Journal of Community Psychology, 33*(1), 1–10.

Zeldin, S., Petrokubi, J., & MacNeil, C. (2007). *Youth–adult partnerships in community decision making: What does it take to engage adults in the practice.* Chevy Chase, MD: National 4H Council. Retrieved from http://www.fourhcouncil.edu/pv_obj_cache/pv_obj_id_7288E7A

CHAPTER 15

THE PENSIVE ATHENA

Lessons on Leadership, Career, and Leveraging Change

Autumn Tooms Cyprès

ABSTRACT

Both practitioners and scholars have considered the pragmatics of how women fit within an educational school community relative to job performance. However, there has been a lack of effort to explore the theoretical and conceptual orientations underlying the message of what it means to fit or not fit as a leader. This chapter seeks to explain how fit emerges out of three critical constructs (i.e., social constructionism, hegemony, and identity theory) working contextually to make up a theoretical framework underlying the political actions and speech referred to as "fit." This chapter uses autoethnography to consider lessons relative to the politics leadership and interruption in juxtaposition with fit. The convergence of hegemony, identity, and social construction is considered along with examples of the author's personal experiences with interrupting power structures and reforming educational systems. Questions for consideration are offered in the framework of a decision tree that facilitates a cost-benefit analysis of interruption efforts in relation to career trajectories in academia.

Women Interrupting, Disrupting, and Revolutionizing Educational Policy and Practice, pages 303–315

303

INTRODUCTION

Like many professors, I begin my mornings early with little rituals intended to jumpstart my brain into the excruciating work of translating ideas and life experiences into manuscripts for editors to eviscerate. A cup of green tea is poured and the cats are fed. Then I sit down to my computer and books that reside near a copy of a marble relief called the Pensive Athena (pictured in Figure 15.1). The original was excavated from the Acropolis in 1888. Athena wears a peplos (the power suit of her time) and the Corinthian helmet of wisdom. Her head is bowed, and she's leaning on a spear pointed down at a rectangular object. Some interpret this as tombstone. Others see the rectangle as a mile marker, thus the longstanding debate as to the message in the image. Is this Athena mourning a colleague lost in battle? Or is she pointing the spear of truth at a milestone in reflection of her journey? Is she grieving, or thinking? I prefer the idea of a leader reflecting on what she has identified as the truth. In either case, I am sure she is also exhausted, as leadership is hard work, even for a goddess.

Figure 15.1 Pensive Athena.

Athena's image is a provocative touchstone of leadership considerations. She was a warrior of intellect, in which strategy and the clever negotiation of identity helped many to change the world for the better. She disguised herself when necessary as a man (in the form of *Mentor,* an advisor to the ruler Telemachus) and contributed an androgynous array of skills to the community she served. Nimble as both nurturer and confrontationist, she would have been a formidable school principal and glorious professor.

And so I begin, as Athena may have, to point the spear of truth at the realities of politics and life experiences in an effort to better understand the less traveled road of leadership, fit, and organizational disruption. This chapter is organized into two parts. Part 1 considers the nexus point of politics and identity called *fit* (Tooms, Lugg, & Bogotch, 2010). Part 2 extends such considerations with three personal *tipping point allegories* related to leadership, career politics, and change. This chapter concludes with explorations of the motifs which harmonize Parts 1 and 2.

PART 1: POLITICS AND FIT

This chapter utilizes a poststructural conceptual framework called *fit* (Tooms et al., 2010) to consider how the convergence of identity (Stryker & Burke, 2000), hegemony (Foucault, 1980), and social constructionism (Gergen, 1999) affects politics in terms of both the organization (i.e., academia and school systems) and individual (i.e., professors and principals) leadership. Poststructural considerations of identity and its relationship to politics are rarely considered in tandem. Poststructuralism as an intellectual movement began in Paris and claims such thinkers as Foucault (1975), Derrida (1982), and Barthes (1968). The prefix "post" refers to the movement's rejection of structuralism, or the idea of an independent and superior signifier that asserts knowledge of absolute reality and truth (Capper, 1999; Cherryholmes, 1988; Foucault, 1983; Scheurich, 1997). One of the aims of poststructuralism is to deconstruct such traditional points of view regarding reality and truth. *In other words, poststructuralism views the realities of underlying structures as culturally conditioned, ongoing interpretations, filled with biases and glaring omissions.* At the heart of poststructuralism is the concern with deconstructing the power relationships embedded in the words, texts, and discourse practices that shape our social relationships and status. In this context, discourse and discursive practices include the different ways in which we integrate language with the communicative tools of nonlanguage such as symbols and nonverbal behavior in an effort to give meaning to the world (Gee, 1996). The three interrelated theories explained below are: social constructionism, identity theory, and hegemony. What follows is an explanation of each.

Social Constructionism

The term *social constructionism* was first coined by sociologists Berger and Luckman in their seminal work *The Social Construction of Reality* (1966). In essence, they posited that reality is co-created by humans. According to Gergen (1999, p. 47) there are four contours that best define social constructionism:

1. The terms by which we understand our world and our self are neither required nor demanded by "what there is."
2. Our modes of description, explanation, and representation are derived from relationships.
3. Describing or otherwise representing reality reflexively fashions our future.
4. Reflection on our forms of understanding is vital to our future well being.

These four tenets demonstrate the immense challenge found in sustaining valued traditions and yet creating new realities. Social constructionism invites us to reconsider the nature of leadership in a way that relentlessly considers the blinding potential of "common sense" knowledge and the mundane routines of school.

Identity Theory

Identity can be used as a reference to parts of a self, which are composed of meanings, attached to the roles people play in society (hooks, 1991; Laing, 1966; Stryker & Burke, 2000). I visualize these frameworks as empty picture frames that we wear around our necks in day-to-day interactions. For example, consider that a Catholic, American, female professor is also a mother, wife, member of the local gym, Democrat, football fan, and volunteer at the local art museum. Her children primarily identify her as "mother" rather than "Democrat" or "professor." Why? Because we generally ignore the other contexts of identity (and corresponding frameworks of identity) that are outside of the ones that include our participation.

In terms of sociolinguistics, researchers note that how we explain, model, and understand who we are differs with unique circumstances (Butler, 1997; Gee, 1996; Goffman, 1967; Jung & Hecht, 2004; Kroeger, 2003; Lakoff, 2004; Lather, 1991; Morkos, 2003; Stryker & Burke, 2000). For example, two women sharing at an early morning workout at the gym might use a different set of words to describe particular frustrations with their jobs than they would in front of their children or their bosses.

Hegemony

Hegemony explains that some groups or individuals maintain dominance over other groups of individuals in society through socially constructed persuasions and coercions (Gramsci, 1971). This dominance is achieved through convincing members of subordinated groups to accept, adopt, and internalize the dominant group's definition of what is *normal* (Kumashiro, 2004). This type of veiled oppression is achieved by using mechanisms such as the mass media and mass schooling, which inculcate and reinforce the viewpoint and power of the dominant class (Apple, 2001; Derrida, 1982; Edelman, 1988; Foucault, 1975).

Those subjugated by hegemony are rarely aware of its presence because the messages of what is normal permeate the everyday consciousness of society. Feminist scholars, including Blackmore and Sachs (2007), have explained that women in positions of school leadership choose to operate at work from one of several gender scripts of leadership. These include a "being strong" script, "superwoman" script, and the "social male" script. Curry (2000) explained that hegemonic structures in the United States mandate that women deal with leadership norms within education by constructing a "leader persona" that requires the compartmentalization of certain features of themselves. The hegemonic compartmentalizations stretch across facets of identity that include gender, ethnicity, religion, and sexuality.

Foucault (1975) extended the concept of hegemony when he coined the phrase *panoptic mechanism*. This is in reference to the panopticon, a kind of prison designed by English philosopher Jeremy Bentham. The panopticon allowed an observer to view all the prisoners without the prisoners being able to know if they were being watched or not. Consequently, the prisoners in a panopticon would learn to monitor their own behavior via punishment from their supervisors.

Here is how the administrative panopticon works: If you are always being watched, but yet you do not know who is watching, you edit your own actions in order to follow the rules of those to whom you report. Because fit is rooted in hegemony, which serves as a catalyst for self-surveillance, fit becomes another example of a panoptic structure that maintains the status quo in our educational systems, policies, and practices. It keeps those in power in and those who challenge power out of public school leadership.

All schools (both public and private) not only inculcate members of society in terms of *how to be*, more importantly, they constrain members of society by teaching and reinforcing *how not to be* (Foucault, 1975). This is accomplished through language games. This is based literally on Austrian philosopher Ludwig Wittgenstein's theory of *language games* (1965, p. 71). He explained reality is formed and reformed through the use of the language games which are a series or cycle of interactions that contain covert and overt rules. People use language games to understand these rules, as well as honor, break, or change them. In school administration, words that play a part in power structures and language games include "professional, collaborative and appropriate."

Hegemony influences who fits and who does not fit because it contours the discussions around what it acceptable and unacceptable behavior in societies, organizations, schools, and even classrooms. It frames and contours the margins of tolerance (Charters, 1953) that society creates within school communities. Hegemony influences who works in schools and the kind of behavior deemed useful in order to gain and maintain the social capital granted in accordance with the socially constructed view of what is professional (Blount, 2005; Fryand & Capper, 2003).

PART 2: THE TIPPING POINT ALLEGORIES

Allegory Number One: "But Jefe,[1] This Is Wrong"

The first conversation I had as a school principal was with the superintendent who hired me. Carol (a pseudonym) outlined the political background of my new K–8 school of 1200 students: "Leighton school has always been this public school district's answer to a private academy. Our parents appreciate the advance courses and opportunities like student learning exchanges to Japan. Your job is to keep them happy and the standards of academic rigor high. If these parents are not happy, they have the power to ask for your removal as principal. This will put me in a rough spot. Remember, my job is to make the school board president happy. Your school is full of politics and I don't want any boats rocked."

I really wanted to support my superintendent. And I wanted very much to fit. So when she suggested I look more professional by changing my naturally curly red hair into a newscaster bob and wearing acrylic fingernails, I eagerly asked for the name of her favorite salon. The president of Leighton's PTA shared with me on my first day at work that her parent group was responsible for getting rid of another administrator in the school district. And during my first year at Leighton, the superintendent decided to assuage parents who wanted Spanish-speaking students out of their English-speaking children's classrooms at Leighton School by providing funds to hire two Spanish-speaking teachers at every grade level. The logic Carol offered was that every student's need would be met with individualized and tailored instruction. When I mentioned this plan also would result in a segregation of students by language and race, I was told that this was the only solution possible because (a) there were limited resources, and (b) school district governing board policy did not allow the transfer of teachers to other schools based on language certification. This happened in 1997. By 1999 Leighton school was a place where Spanish-speaking teachers served classrooms filled beyond student capacity and English-speaking teachers remained committed to the idea that their job was not to work with "those kids who don't speak English." Test scores had plummeted and as the demographics shifted to more second-language learners, it became obvious the teaching configuration was not working, even though it assuaged the conservative, White PTA and the president of the Bells District school board. A dual language acquisition program would be a wonderful lever to desegregate the school and help raise test scores. The school district even won a federal grant that allowed for the funding of a graduate degree or ESL certification for any teacher interested in earning credentials to help teach children who did not speak English. Additionally, the grant gave considerable financial support to schools that had teachers working in teams consisting of one English-speaking teacher and one Spanish-speaking teacher.

There was only one problem: the belief among many White teachers who were primarily English speakers was that they should not be responsible for teaching Spanish speakers because they were not trained as ESL or bilingual instructors. For months I repeatedly spoke with the superintendent about this issue in an effort to advocate for reconfiguring the staff and curriculum to be more inclusive. She responded in the same way each time. She told me that I needed to be more collaborative and that if the staff got angry, it was a reflection on my lack of leadership.

I felt like I was allowing a kind of apartheid on my campus. Like many daughters, I sought out my father's advice about what to do. He gave me the Pensive Athena and asked me to think about pointing my own spear at the truth. We talked about Adolf Eichmann, the Nazi war criminal, whose defense was essentially that he "went along to get along" with the atrocities of Hitler's regime. I recognize that a segregated school is not in the same sphere as the Holocaust. But I also understood the lesson that leadership sometimes mandates thinking beyond career and self-preservation because of the humanitarian obligation to disrupt social structures that harm others. I was afraid I would make my superintendent, the power players in the faculty, the PTA, and the school board president angry. What if I was fired because I no longer fit? This fear sat with me for two months. And then one day I was meeting individually with Juan Costa, one of our bilingual teachers. When he asked about the direction of our school's future, I repeated our superintendent's mantra about collaboration and not making the school board president angry. Juan looked at me at said, "But jefe, this is wrong. Our kids are suffering." There was the spear of truth. It resonated with a power that demanded my attention because this teacher was speaking for his students who did not have a voice. And that moment changed something in me. It gave me a kind of courage that I had not known before because I realized I simply had no choice. I could no longer live with my conscience if I did nothing. And so I began the critical conversations with the staff and the community about equity, race, and the purpose of school in the United States. There were grievances and angry board members. And I was indeed deemed not a fit by my superintendent. I moved on to another job. Eventually a valued community member strategized himself into the presidency of the school board. He called me on the day that the school board fired Carol the superintendent. He called me again when the policies about language and instruction had changed to be more inclusive. The big lessons I learned from this experience are:

- Don't always trust your superior to support you when you engage in the difficult work of confrontation and reform.
- Wrong (or evil) is not always obvious and on a large scale. Often it is a banal and therefore overlooked (Arendt, 1963).
- Never underestimate how important a leader's actions/inactions are to those he or she serves.

Allegory Two: "That's Dr. Dumbass to You"

Eight years after I left Leighton School and become an academic, I found myself a tenured associate professor at a large public university in the Midwestern United States. I was also serving as the educational leadership program coordinator. In the midst of a program meeting focused on our curriculum, a colleague (a full professor) said, "Is this social justice stuff you are talking about really necessary?" I thought carefully about how this man was many years older than I was and enjoyed the only endowed chair position in the college. Then, I thought of Carol, the superintendent, and Athena. I replied, "Yes, I think it is. The national conversations about this are important. I think if we want to stay competitive as a program we need to embrace this line of inquiry. If you read some of the theorists in our field like English, Blount, Brooks, Bogotch, Grogan, and Crow, you will see I am telling you the truth."

While I attempted to support my position that scholars of note were engaged in this work, name-dropping inadvertently implied that my colleague was not current in his studies of the literature in our field. Our program meeting quickly slid into a litany of retorts centered on whose research counted in terms of the preparation of school leaders. The endowed chair referred to me as a "dumbass." I retaliated with, "That's *Dr.* Dumbass to *you.*" This resulted in strained laughter, mouths agog, and an uncomfortable request for a short break.

During the course of the year, our program had eight meetings dedicated to discussions of social justice and curriculum. Eventually our program adopted a social justice focus and hired a scholar who specialized in the area. The endowed chair and I came to a place of détente and framed the exchange as a symptom of organizational growing pains. The big lessons I learned from this experience are:

- Pay attention to how your rank, age, and actions are perceived by others.
- It is nearly impossible to separate the personal from the intellectual in a discussion.
- Disruption of the status quo requires patience and consistency.

Allegory Three: "I Know This Sounds Unethical but I Need This Favor"

Five years after the "Dr. Dumbass" showdown, I moved onward to a the rank of full professor and was the founding director of a high-profile, multi-million-dollar principal preparation center at a flagship institution located in the Southern United States. I directly reported to a supervisor who had a reputation for mishandling conflict, emotional outbursts directed at students and secretaries, and inaccuracies with details. We worked together for three years. When this person yelled at my staff members, I chose to indulge my staff with lunches or team-building exercises and explained that confronting the supervisor was useless because I needed his support in order to run the center. I did my best to take the brunt of the temper tantrums and keep the supervisor away from the staff. Basically, I turned a blind eye to his behavior. How do you hold your own boss accountable? Only when an entire cohort of doctoral students was berated did I ask for advice from the administration of the college. I was told not to rock the boat and that sometimes one has to work around people in a system. This was eerily like the chapter I spent with my former superintendent.

Serving in dysfunctional environments is unpleasant but possible because universities are, essentially, warehouses of independent contractors called academics. It is nearly impossible to fire a tenured employee. And sometimes negotiating fit is accomplished by turning a blind eye. Choices are made to avoid people down the hall in favor of collaborations with colleagues at the national and international level.

For most of my tenure as a center director, I triaged the events that mandated a blind eye in order to give my full energies to the important role of leading the center. Whenever I could, I gave my supervisor face time in order to protect my staff and students so that the diatribes were vented toward me. I did not take it personally and saw this tactic as way to work around the supervisor. And while I continued to share the events with my college administrators, war stories of "dysfunction" failed to carry the gravitas necessary for an intervention in the eyes of the higher ups.

At the beginning of my last year as director, I was asked to provide a passing grade on a nonexistent master's thesis for a student I had never met. This request was in writing and began with, "I know this sounds unethical but I need this favor." Turning the request down was not enough, as I believed that a failure to report this request would result in my own culpability. I worried for several weeks about the ramifications. I expected to be berated in some public forum. I was concerned I would be shunned. Would my travel vouchers still be honored? Would the reimbursement forms I turned in be lost, ignored, or delayed? Would members of my staff endure tantrums because of my actions? I did not know.

I was not looking forward to the consequences of my actions. But I made the choice to interrupt the power structures in my day-to-day life because of the duty owed to our profession of school leadership. How can one serve as a scholar of leadership and yet shy away from moments requiring one to lead? This question haunted others that shared my hallway, and I was not the only person to contribute to the levering of change.

The tangible concerns that were deeper than war stories were addressed this time. And once again opportunity found me in the form of a new role at another university. I believe that the college I left is at a better place than when I arrived, and my career continues on an upward trajectory. However, I would be remiss if I failed to say that the process of leveraging change in this context was difficult, stressful, and anything but a tale of avenging leadership. The big lessons learned from this experience are:

- The choice to fit or disrupt is difficult, not to be glamorized, and everyone has a different tipping point.
- Tipping points toward action can vary with context.
- If you make the decision to leverage change, make sure you understand the kinds of support your have.
- Assess how much support you have and how much you are willing to commit to the work of change before you start the process.

MOTIFS HARMONIZING PARTS 1 AND 2

Discussions about professionalism, obligation, and leadership are rife within academia. However, conversations examining the intersections of politics, career trajectories, and the duty owed to the profession are less prevalent. Leveraging change is a large discursive umbrella that is framed in many ways (as evidenced by the scope of this book). For me, the work is noble and excruciatingly difficult. The fallout from such efforts can be tragic in some instances because the work affects relationships, identities, and lives.

Lessons from this discussion illustrate how working within a group is often about egos and negotiating identity. This demands give and take, reflection on the everyday presentation of self, and a willingness to consider thoughtfully one's world and one's role within it. For example, junior faculty often forget that hallway ethnographies conducted by those who vote on tenure dossiers play a role in a very high-stakes game of career trajectory and job security. This is particularly difficult in the field of educational leadership because many academics are entering the field with a lifetime of experience and yet they are junior to a system.[2] Thus, the quest for tenure (and the professional capital that goes with it) expands from ticking off accomplishments on a vita to include a game of politics.

Navigating the margins between establishing fit and disruption is nuanced work and requires careful consideration. The allegories speak to the identification of the tipping points that motivates one from a position of self preservation to a position of service to others. Sometimes, the obligation to fit is incongruent with the obligation of one's conscience. It is here where the murky questions about leadership and the necessity of professional survival live. I have learned that I do not enjoy confrontation, but that I am not afraid of it. And when issues of integrity and student experience arise in a sea of politics and empty language,[3] this exhausting work is nonnegotiable.

The politics of being a fit and misfit ask if the margins of collegiality and service are still a viable part of our obligations to the professoriate. Such touchstones only reinforce the importance of self-reflection, the engagement of dialog about fit, and the duty owed to our profession. Perhaps that is why Athena is so pensive.

NOTES

1 *Jefe* is the Spanish word for boss. Several of my teachers used this term affectionately when talking with me.

2. Former superintendents and school administrators are notorious for this struggle because academia does not really give one credit for an entire career. It can be quite a culture shock to go from being the center of a school district's power structure to the low man on the totem pole who no longer enjoys the perks of executive leadership (i.e., a personal secretary, a large travel and supply budget).

3. Empty talk (Arendt, 1963) references the ways in which Eichmann responded to direct questions about his choices with sentences that meant nothing. My favorite, most recent example of this is in reference to a colleague who, when pressed as to how he would specifically address specific issues, would say, "You know, it's a knuckleball." Then he would change the subject.

REFERENCES

Arendt, H. (1963). *Eichmann in Jerusalem: A report on the banality of evil.* New York, NY: Penguin Books.

Bruhn, J. G., Zajac, G., Al-Kazemi, A. A., & Prescott, I. D. (2002). Moral positions and academic conduct: Parameters of tolerance for ethics failure. *Journal of Higher Education, 73*(1), 461–493.

Apple, M. (2001). *Educating the "Right" way: Markets, standards, God, and inequality.* New York, NY: Routledge.

Barthes, R. (1968). *Elements of semiology.* New York, NY: Hill and Wang.

Berger, P. L., & Luckmann, T. A. (1966). *Social construction of reality: Treatise in the sociology of knowledge.* London, UK: Allen Lane.

Blackmore, J., & Sachs, J. (2007). *Performing and reforming leaders: Gender, educational restructuring and organizational change.* New York, NY: SUNY Press.

Blount, J. (2005). *Fit to teach: Same sex desire, gender, and school work in the twentieth century.* Albany, NY: State University of New York Press.

Butler, J. (1997). *Excitable speech: A politics of the performative.* New York, NY: Routledge.

Capper, C. A. (1999). (Homo)sexualities, organizations, and administration; Possibilities for in(queery). *Educational Researcher, 28*(5), 4–11.

Charters, W. (1953). Social class and the control of public education. *Harvard Educational Review, 23*, 268–283.

Cherryholmes, C. (1988). *Power and criticism: Post-structural investigations in education.* New York, NY: Teachers College Press.

Curry, B. K. (2000). *Women in power: Pathways to leadership in education.* New York, NY: Teachers College Press.

Derrida, J. (1982). *Of grammatology.* Baltimore, MD: Johns Hopkins University Press.

Edelman, M. (1974). The political language of the helping professions. *Politics and Society, 4*, 295–310.

Edelman, M. (1988) *Constructing the political spectacle.* Chicago, IL: The University of Chicago Press.

Foucault, M. (1975). *Discipline and punish: The birth of a prison.* New York, NY: Vintage Books.

Foucault, M. (1980). *Power/ knowledge: Selected interviews and other writings, 1972–1977.* New York: Pantheon Books.

Foucault, M. (1983). *This is not a pipe* (J. Harkness, Trans.). Berkley, CA: University of California Press.

Fryand, D., & Capper, C. (2003). Do you have any idea who you just hired? A study of open and closeted sexual minority K–12 administrators. *Journal of School Leadership, 13*, 86–125.

Gee, J. P. (1996). *Social linguistics and literacies.* New York, NY: Routledge.

Gergen, K. (1999). *An invitation to social construction.* Thousand Oaks, CA: Sage Publications.

Goffman, E. (1959). *The presentation of self in everyday life.* Garden City, NY: Anchor/Doubleday.

Goffman, E. (1967). *Interaction ritual: Essays on face to face behavior.* Garden City, NY: Anchor/Doubleday.

Gramsci, A. (1971) *Selections from the Prison Notebooks*. London, UK: Lawrence and Wishart Publishing.

hooks, b. (1991). *Yearning, race, gender and cultural politics*. Boston, MA:South End Press.

Jung, E., & Hecht, M. (2004). Elaborating the communication theory of identity: Identity gaps and communication outcomes. *Communication Quarterly, 52*(3), 265–283.

Kroeger, B. (2003). *Passing: When people can't be who they are*. New York: NY: Perseus Book Groups.

Kumashiro, K. K. (2004). *Against common sense: Teaching and learning toward social justice*. New York, NY: Routledge-Falmer.

Laing, R. D. (1966). *Interpersonal perception: A theory and method of research*. London, UK: Tavistock.

Lakoff, R. (2004). *Language and woman's place: Text and commentaries* (M. Vucholtz, Ed., revised and expanded ed.). New York, NY: Oxford Press.

Lather, P. (1991). *Getting smart: Feminist research and pedagogy within the postmodern*. New York, NY: Routledge.

Morkos, H. B. (2003). A constitutive approach to identity. In H. B. Mokros (Ed.), *Identity matters* (pp. 3–28). Creskill, NJ: Hampton Press.

St. Pierre, B., & Pillow, W. (2000) *Working the ruins: Feminist post structuralism*. New York, NY: Routledge.

Scheurich, J. (1997). *Research method in the postmodern*. London, UK: Falmer.

Stryker, S., & Burke, P. (2000). The past, present, and future of identity theory. *Social psychology quarterly, 63*(4) 284–297.

Tooms, A. K., Lugg, C., & Bogotch, I. (2010). School leadership and the politics of fit. *Educational Administration Quarterly, 46*(1), 96–131.

Wittgenstein, L. (1965). *Philosophical investigations*. New York, NY: The Macmillan Company.

EPILOGUE

"Well-Behaved Women Seldom Make History"

Katherine Cumings Mansfield and Whitney Sherman Newcomb

Some history-making is intentional; much of it is accidental. People make history when they scale a mountain, ignite a bomb, or refuse to move to the back of the bus. But they also make history by keeping diaries, writing letters, or embroidering initials on linen sheets. History is a conversation and sometimes a shouting match between present and past, though often the voices we most want to hear are barely audible. People make history by passing on gossip, saving old records, and by naming rivers, mountains, and children. Some people leave only their bones, though bones too make a history when someone notices.

—Laurel Thatcher Ulrich (2007, p. xxxiii)

The purpose of this book was to forefront the voices of women educational scholars who, in their own ordinary and extraordinary ways are interrupting, disrupting, and revolutionizing educational policy and practice. While none of these women (as far as we know) has ever scaled a mountain or ignited a bomb, many have refused to be ignored, left back, or silent, or leave only their bones behind when they leave this side of the ground. Rather, the women in this book (either the authors or the women they have written about or both) have something to say and something to do. Their work is intentional. It is not accidental. These women have plans. These women mean business. And their plans and their business do not include tolerating the status quo or retreating to the soil from whence they came with barely

Women Interrupting, Disrupting, and Revolutionizing Educational Policy and Practice, pages 317–322
Copyright © 2014 by Information Age Publishing
317

a whisper. Via ordinary means such as writing, teaching, serving, creating, speaking, and sometimes shouting, these extraordinary women are making history in their own little corners of the world. Our objective is to give the authors (and the women they write about) a history as well as show how within the "ordinary" one can still be revolutionary.

Laurel Thatcher Ulrich, the woman who coined the phrase, "Well-behaved women seldom make history" is "just" a professor. Contrary to the coffee mugs, posters, and T-shirts that abound, this famous quote did not come from a sexy Hollywood starlet (Marilyn Monroe) or a famous politician (Eleanor Roosevelt). Rather, the phrase first appeared in an article written by Ulrich, a graduate student in history at the time in the 1970s, who published her work on "virtuous women" of the 17th century (Ulrich, 1976). Ulrich's research and teaching agendas focus on the recovery of women's voices to tell the full stories of American History. We believe scholars like Ulrich helped us understand the concept of *herstory*. About 30 years after Ulrich's article appeared in the *American Quarterly*, her book (using the famous phrase as a title) was published (in 2007).

It is interesting to us that while Ulrich, in her book, traces the historical trajectory of feminist thought back to Medieval Europe through what we consider modern feminist thought, many of the themes she notes throughout also coalesce with the themes we noted throughout our authors' chapters. In addition to noticing the (un)intended consequences of making history via the ordinary as embodied through action, record keeping, and remembering, like Ulrich (2007) we see the persistent theme of rebellion in various forms, such as:

1. Committing to recover and remember erased or silenced histories and reiterating where we were, where we are, and where we would like to be
2. Challenging misogynistic norms that insist females must be quiet and compliant, along with the accompanying beliefs that women are inherently overly emotional and nonrational
3. Confronting and disputing Western notions of rationality and science: What counts? Who counts? Whose view is the lens from whence we look at data?
4. Purposefully laboring to empower girls and women to be intelligent, strong, confident, and even audacious enough to be high achievers in their fields
5. Rejecting all assumptions about women's place in the world or what it means to be feminine, including how we gender identify, how we express our gender, or whom we love

The authors in this book (and the women they write about) embody the above themes in a variety of ways. For example, four authors, David,

Gasman, Grogan, and Hermann perform the service of remembering in their historical perspectives, which also serves as a form of record keeping so that we women educators do not forget where we have been, where we are, and where we are going. Boske's artmaking pedagogy is also a type of record keeping in that her students create physical artifacts representing their social justice learning in their educational coursework, documenting their growth and change as educators and social justice agents. Meanwhile, five other chapters, written by Bryant, Mansfield, McNae, Newcomb, and Welton, Brock, and Perry—in concert with the women they write for, with, and about—help craft history through an active agenda that includes mentoring, politicking, advocating, and other dynamic activities.

Authors Grant and Witherspoon-Arnold challenge existing belief systems at the intersection of gender and race. They, along with Welton, Brock, and Perry, shout back to the prevailing norms that work to suppress their voices or label them as "bitch" or "loud Black girls." Bryant presses further to challenge belief systems that include sexual identities. Essential to moving forward in educational leadership research is continuing to challenge behaviors and beliefs that attempt to suppress strong women—especially Black women—to be more calm and accommodating. Women should not be made to feel guilty for rejecting silence when their identities and livelihoods, and those of the next generation, are in jeopardy. Further, challenging misogyny also entails rebellion against heteronormativity, speaking against the notion that the status quo knows best on how we gender identify and whom we love. And, as Bryant points out, sometimes this entails deliberate policy crafting and implementation. In other words, sometimes justice cannot wait for individual women to speak out and speak against continuing the status quo. Sometimes, justice means government and/or organizational intervention—for example, overhauling educator preparation programs.

As far as confronting and disputing Western notions of rationality and science, Mansfield, Welton, and Grogan challenge the notion of supposed gender neutrality of organizational and policy studies to show how research can be made richer by shedding a gender-blind stance. They, in essence, talk back to science by challenging what counts as research evidence and insist that a women's perspective be taken into account in our research efforts. Cyprès also challenges what "counts" when she problematizes "fit" in educational leadership careers. Our field has not only adhered to masculine notions of rationality and science when it comes to research endeavors: These ideas permeate how and whom we hire as school administrators. Even when organizations claim to take a gender-neutral stance in terms of policy and practice, women are still expected to act in particular (male, White, straight) ways.

Three chapters, by Newcomb, Robinson, and Witherspoon-Arnold, share their research on women educational leaders, their strengths, and the challenges they face. Importantly, their research also points to ways that women can be empowered to be audaciously great leaders via building relationships and finding other support systems that strengthen their psyches and build their confidence. Their work also points out how important it is to leverage mentoring to open doors of opportunity. Meanwhile, another three chapters, by Mansfield, McNae, and Welton; Brock; and Perry, inform of us of the importance of starting early: How "girl power" programs have potential to raise up the next generation of intelligent, strong, confident, successful women. As the editors of this book, one of our overarching goals was to provide a current snapshot of what women are doing in leadership education and practice and how they are experiencing their various roles as researchers, teachers, and practitioners. Our intent was not to provide a comprehensive accounting of all work on women or by women or for women in the field of educational leadership and policy, but to provide snapshots or "peeps into the windows" of the work and practice of women we know to be researching and advocating for women and girls. These snapshots indicate that, in many cases, things have not changed. Gender stereotypes still abound, societal expectations for "superwomen" have not waivered, the intersections of multiple identities are under-researched, and voices remain unheard. However, the chapters in the book capture the significance of women moving forward despite societal and workplace stagnation. This is significant in and of itself. Women are moving forward despite difficult circumstances. These authors, and the women they write about, whether they realize it or not, have found a way to torque the flywheel.

Women are continuing to place discrimination and unchanged conditions at the forefront of their conversations and research efforts. However, they are doing this while also highlighting and crafting new knowledge. Women are finding new ways to mentor and push the limits of traditional, didactic mentoring. They are consistent in their efforts to add voices to the literature—voices that are rich and that are the result of multiple identities beyond gender alone. Women are expanding the study of women to girls to grow a pipeline of women capable of sparking and sustaining change. They are implementing new pedagogies that embrace the recognition of leadership as both an art and a science and that celebrate the emotional aspects of leadership. Women are building theories on women's ways of knowing and leading. They are questioning the politics of fit and repainting the image of a leader to be more inclusive. They are making sure that women have a footprint in educational leadership literature, practice, and history. Women are interrupting and disrupting and, in some cases, revolutionizing. They may not be holding signs, staging sit-ins, standing on picket lines, or leading armies into battle, but they are steadfastly taking steps forward.

They are extraordinary despite circumstances that have become and have consistently remained ordinary.

Knowing the work that women in educational leadership are currently engaged in helps us know how to move forward to both continue to feed the flywheel and torque it for pulses of energy. The agenda we put forth here calls for discussion and research aimed at pushing the field forward. It also calls for ideas of action: strategic plans to produce new information, new practices, and new policies. Strategies to move forward might include:

1. Active mentoring of girls and women throughout the P–20 pipeline
2. Active attention to the education of girls and women worldwide to further human rights and increase individual, familial, and community capital
3. Active attention to the new generation of women leaders with a particular focus on how young women are making sense of their roles as leaders and how they make meaning of notions of leadership
4. Active education on the history of women and women's movements so as not to lose momentum that has been gained or lessons learned
5. An increase of case studies of women succeeding as leaders and who push boundaries of traditional notions of leadership and leaders
6. A global look at how women have been (and are) pushing, shaping, and impacting practices and policies in their unique corners of the world
7. An increased effort at understanding intersectionalities
8. Active attention to how women lead in times of crisis
9. Active attention to how women lead despite being surrounded by violence
10. Continued efforts to reveal stagnation, barriers, and binaries
11. Developing new ways to research women's leadership experiences and practices

The list of strategies above is not intended to be exhaustive but, rather, a gathering of some ideas that have potential to serve as torques to the flywheel. Our hope is that both veteran educators and women new to the field will respond to these ideas for change by tackling them one by one and little by little with an unwavering focus on change. We believe it is significant to report and reveal continued stagnation and continue to highlight barriers to both veterans and new women to the field. However, we also believe that while doing this, we must also make efforts to move forward and to continue adding voices and experiences to what we know about leadership and leadership practice.

In closing, one of the most salient points of Ulrich's book reminds us of the cyclical nature of history and how easily movements, people, and efforts toward change can be forgotten. For example, she traced one of the first waves of feminist thought to medieval times in Europe and the precarious nature of women's advancement at the time. She cautions us against letting historical advancements become forgotten or invisible, as many of the most adamant feminists may be oblivious to how far back the roots of the feminist movement can be traced. Ulrich said:

> Waves are inherently cyclical. They move in. They move out. They pound the shore then disappear, often leaving changes too subtle to be observed. If earlier waves of feminist consciousness disappeared, surely the same thing can happen again. A new generation might forget where their freedoms came from, drifting back once again into the sandbar of silence. (Ulrich, 2007, p. 222)

This book, with our collection of scholarship, is our attempt to stem the tide of forgetfulness, forwarding the voices of women scholars attempting to interrupt, disrupt, and revolutionize education policy and practice. Our hope is that these chapters, the authors' gifts to us, will be more than delicate footprints in the sand, susceptible to political deluge—hence leading future generations to robust change that rebuffs ebb tides and consequent disintegration.

REFERENCES

Ulrich, L. T. (1976). Virtuous women found: New England Ministerial literature, 1668–1735. *American Quarterly, 28*(1), xx–xx.

Ulrich, L. T. (2007). *Well-behaved women seldom make history.* New York, NY: Random House.

ABOUT THE CONTRIBUTORS

Noelle Witherspoon Arnold is an associate professor of educational leadership in the Department of Educational Leadership and Policy Analysis at the University of Missouri. Prior to that appointment, she taught elementary school and served as an administrator at the district and state level. Her research interests include religion and spirituality in education, leadership for social justice and advocacy, leadership socialization, womanist and feminist research methodologies, and the intersection of race and gender in educational leadership. Noelle's most recent articles have appeared in the *International Journal of Leadership in Education, International Journal of Qualitative Studies in Education, The Journal of Educational Administration History, Equity and Excellence in Education, The Journal of Negro Education, Teachers College Record*, and the *Journal of Educational Administration.*

Christa Boske is the program coordinator and associate professor in educational administration at Kent State University. She works to encourage school leaders to promote humanity in schools, especially for disenfranchised children and families. Christa's recent work is published in the *Journal of School Leadership, Journal of Research on Leadership Education, Multicultural Education and Technology Journal*, and the *Journal of Curriculum Theorizing*. Her scholarship is informed by work in residential treatment and inner-city schools as a school leader and social worker. She recently edited the book titled *Educational Leadership: Building Bridges Among Ideas, Schools, and Nations* (Information Age Publishing, 2012); co-edited the book with Sarah Diem, *Global Leadership for Social Justice: Taking It from the Field to Practice* (Emerald

Women Interrupting, Disrupting, and Revolutionizing Educational Policy and Practice, pages 323–329
Copyright © 2014 by Information Age Publishing
323

Publishing, 2012); and the book *Bridge Leadership: Connecting Educational Leadership and Social Justice to Improve Schools* with Autumn K. Tooms in 2010 (Information Age Publishing).

Cathy A. R. Brant recently completed her PhD at The Ohio State University from the Department of Teaching and Learning with a specific area of study in multicultural and equity studies in education. Dr. Brant's research interests and expertise include teacher preparation, multicultural education, and social justice teaching and learning, with a particular focus on issues of gender and sexual orientation. Dr. Brant is active in the American Educational Research Association (AERA), serving as graduate student council (GSC) secretary-historian, GSC chair, and membership co-chair for the Queer Studies Special Interest Group. Dr. Brant earned both a BA in sociology and a MEd in elementary education from Rutgers University. An experienced elementary educator, Dr. Brant is interested in pursuing further research studies that explore the relationships between multicultural/social justice teacher education and the effects of that education on teacher practice for both preservice and inservice teachers.

Brooke Brock is recent graduate of Texas A&M University–College Station, where she received her degree in agricultural communications and journalism. Brock has a passion for people and she finds fulfillment in advocating for education and underprivileged youth. Brock believes the greatest stories are those that are told, and her communications and journalism degree helps her express her story. She has interest in public speaking, public relations, social media, and marketing. Brock plans to continue her education in communications, learning how to be a better communicator and advocate.

Autumn Cyprès currently serves as professor and chair of the Department of Educational Leadership at Virginia Commonwealth University in Richmond, Virginia. Her research examines the politics of school leadership and school reform with an area of emphasis on the principalship. Her primary area of interest is centered on building bridges between schools, those who lead schools, and those who prepare aspiring leaders. Dr. Cyprès received her doctorate from Arizona State University in 1996. She began her career as a biology teacher and later served as a school administrator at the elementary, middle, and high school level in Phoenix, Arizona. Her leadership in academia includes service as the 50th president of the University Council for Educational Administration. In addition to her books, Dr. Cyprès' work can be found in tier one journals for scholars and practicing school leaders such as *Educational Administration Quarterly, Kappan,* and *Educational Leadership*.

Miriam E. David, PhD, AcSS, FRSA, is professor emerita of sociology of education and was, until recently, professor (2005–2010) and associate director (higher education) of the ESRC's Teaching & Learning Research Programme (2004–2009) at the Institute of Education University of London. She is a visiting professor in the Centre for Higher Education & Equity Research (CHEER) in the School of Education and Social Work at the University of Sussex. She was formerly a professor at London South Bank (1988–1997), University of the Arts (1997–1999), and Keele University (1999–2005). She has a world-class reputation for her feminist social research on families, gender, social diversity, and inequalities across education. She has published 25 books and reports, and 160 articles or chapters, including an intellectual biography in 2003, *Personal and Political: Feminisms, Sociology and Family Lives* (Stoke-on-Trent: Trentham Books). Her book *Feminism, Gender & Universities: Politics, Passion & Pedagogies* is in press. Marybeth Gasman is a professor of higher education in the Graduate School of Education at the University of Pennsylvania. Her areas of expertise include minority serving institutions, philanthropy and fundraising, and the history of higher education. She is the author of 18 books related to these topics.

Cosette M. Grant is an assistant professor in the educational leadership department at University of Cincinnati and a member of the graduate faculty. She is the director of the Center for the Study of Leadership in Urban Schools and editor of the *International Journal of Educational Leadership (IJUEL)*. Her research focuses on culturally relevant mentoring strategies that might improve the academic and career success for students. Her work also includes emergent work on effective leadership for educational equity in P–12 schools and the inclusion of social justice in leadership development and preparation of educational leaders. Dr. Grant is a former UCEA Jackson Scholar and David L. Clark National Scholar. She currently serves on the advisory board of the UCEA Jackson Scholars Advisory Council.

Margaret Grogan is currently professor of educational leadership and policy in the School of Educational Studies at Claremont Graduate University, California. Originally from Australia, she received a Bachelor of Arts degree in ancient history and Japanese language from the University of Queensland. She taught high school in Australia and was a teacher and an administrator at an international school in Japan, where she lived for 17 years. After graduating from Washington State University with a PhD in educational administration, she taught in principal and superintendent preparation programs at the University of Virginia and at the University of Missouri–Columbia. Among the various leadership positions she has held at her institutions and professional organizations, she served as Dean of the

School of Educational Studies from 2008–2012, Chair of the Department of Educational Leadership and Policy Analysis at the University of Missouri-Columbia, 2002–2008, and she was President of the University Council for Educational Administration in 2003–2004. A frequent keynote speaker, she has also published many articles and chapters and has authored, co-authored or edited six books, including the *Jossey Bass Reader on Educational Leadership*. Her current research focuses on women in leadership, gender and education, the moral and ethical dimensions of leadership, and leadership for social justice.

Mary A. Hermann is an associate professor and chair of the counselor education program at Virginia Commonwealth University. Prior to joining the faculty at VCU, she served as an assistant professor of counseling and women's studies at Mississippi State University. She holds a bachelor's degree in foreign language education and a master's degree and PhD in counselor education from the University of New Orleans. She also earned a law degree from Loyola University New Orleans. Dr. Hermann is a licensed attorney, a licensed professional counselor, a national certified counselor, and a certified school counselor. Her research has focused on legal and ethical issues in counseling, women's development, and social justice. She currently serves as co-chair of the Southern Association for Counselor Education and Supervision (SACES) Women's Interest Network, SACES president-elect, chair of the American Counseling Association Foundation, and a member of the American Counseling Association Ethics Revision Task Force.

Katherine Cumings Mansfield is an assistant professor at Virginia Commonwealth University. She graduated in 2011 from The University of Texas in Austin with a PhD in educational policy and planning and a doctoral portfolio in women's and gender studies. Mansfield's interdisciplinary scholarship draws on critical and interpretive frameworks and qualitative methods to study educational policy with a particular focus on examining political discourse, policy interpretation and implementation, and the impact of policy on underrepresented populations in relation to intersecting dynamics such as history, gender, race, and place. Mansfield is published in a variety of venues including*: Educational Administration Quarterly, Educational Policy Analysis Archives, Journal of Educational Administration, Journal of Research on Leadership Education,* and *Journal of School Leadership.* In 2012, Mansfield was awarded the Leadership for Social Justice Dissertation Award, sponsored by the American Educational Research Association's (AERA) Leadership for Social Justice Special Interest Group (SIG) and the Selma Greenberg Outstanding Dissertation Award, sponsored by AERA's Research on Women and Education SIG. Mansfield is on the editorial board of the Information Age Publishing book series, *New Directions in Educational Leadership:*

Innovations in Scholarship, Teaching, and Service. Mansfield is a first-generation college graduate with 20 years teaching and leadership experience throughout the preschool to PhD pipeline.

Rachel McNae is a senior lecturer and leads the educational leadership sector at the University of Waikato. With a background stemming from her experiences of teaching in high schools, Rachel shifted her focus to tertiary education working with preservice teachers and school leaders. Rachel's research agenda is founded on a firm belief for social justice and utilizes strength-based approaches to assist school leaders to enhance their leadership practices. Generating research that spans the fields of women and leadership, student voice, youth leadership, and leadership curriculum development, Rachel advocates for reshaping leadership learning in order to seek out and interrogate the relational aspects of leadership, so that these experiences are authentic, culturally responsive, relevant, and meaningful. Rachel is a member of International Women Leading in Education and is the Waikato Branch President for the New Zealand Educational Administration and Leadership Society. In 2011 Rachel was awarded the International Emerald-European Foundation for Management and Development Outstanding Research Award for Leadership and Strategy. In 2010 she was the recipient of the New Zealand Education Administration Leadership Society President's Research Award for her PhD work that focused on enhancing young women's leadership development in schools. Married to Darren and blessed with two children, Benjamin (5) and Alexis (2), Rachel is a passionate fisherwoman and volunteers as a trout fishing guide for Casting for Recovery, an international organization providing residential fishing retreats for women faced with the challenges of breast cancer.

Whitney Sherman Newcomb is an associate professor in the Department of Educational Leadership at Virginia Commonwealth University. Her research interests include: leadership preparation and mentoring; women's issues in leadership; and social justice in leadership. Dr. Newcomb's work has been featured in journals including: *Educational Administration Quarterly*, the *Journal of School Leadership*, the *Journal of Educational Administration*, *Educational Policy*, and the *Journal for Research on Leadership Education*. She received the 2011 Distinguished Scholarship Award for VCU's School of Education for her contribution to research and the 2012 Distinguished Teaching Award for excellence in teaching. She serves on the editorial boards of *Educational Administration Quarterly*, the *Journal of School Leadership*, and the *Journal for Research on Leadership Education*. Dr. Newcomb was presented with the Emerald Literati Award for Excellence for the Outstanding Special Issue of 2011 for her work as guest editor of "Globalization: Expanding Horizons in Women's Leadership," a special issue of the *Journal of Educational*

Administration. She also received the 2011 Social Justice Teaching Award from the Leadership for Social Justice SIG of the American Educational Research Association "for work that represents exemplary commitment to teaching that promotes social justice, equity, diversity, and inclusion in the field of educational administration."

Mercedes Perry is a student at Kansas State University. She is pursuing her undergraduate degree in business management with an emphasis in human resources and a minor in American ethnic studies. She is very passionate about helping her peers understand the importance of not only attending college, but completing their degrees and setting high goals for themselves. She invests her time into her peers and helps uplift students of color by being a mentor and campus leader. Perry is involved in the Black Student Union, where she created and spearheads the political action standing committee, McNair Scholars Undergraduate Research Program, and the Multicultural Business Student Association. Perry is also a proud member of Delta Sigma Theta Sorority, Incorporated. Perry plans to continue to be an activist for her community to rid the world of social injustice and inequality for people of color in all aspects of life.

Kerry K. Robinson is an assistant professor at the University of Tennessee Knoxville. She holds a PhD in educational leadership from Virginia Commonwealth University. Prior to her position at UTK, Kerry served as the research director for Project ALL, a United States Department of Education grant funded project, also at VCU. Before entering higher education, Dr. Robinson worked in P–12 education for 16 years as a teacher, assistant principal, instructional specialist, director of instructional administration, and as a director of assessment and data. Her research focuses on the study of the politics of the superintendency in terms of preparation models, gender, and the pipeline of organizational ascension.

Charol Shakeshaft is a professor in the Department of Education Leadership at Virginia Commonwealth University in Richmond, Virginia. She teaches graduate courses in research design, the economics of education, research methods for policy research, gender equity, and technology. Charol is the author of three books and over 200 referred articles and papers, many of which have received national and state awards. Her research focuses on three strands: gender and leadership, sexual abuse of students by adults employed in schools, and the effectiveness of technology for learning, particularly for students of color. She is the author of *Women in Educational Administration* (5th printing), *Women and Educational Leadership* with Margaret Grogan, and *Sexual Abuse in Schools*, scheduled for publication by Jossey Bass in 2014. Other publications have addressed race and sex bias in educational practice and research. Dr. Shakeshaft is the recipient of a \$5.2 million grant to develop state of the art principal preparation to include the first immersive, interactive and web-enabled computer simulation for school administrators. She previously completed a three-year national study of the relationships between a school-based risk prevention program and risk behaviors of 6th to 8th grade students. Dr. Shakeshaft was also the principal investigator on a three-year National Science Foundation project to promote interest in science careers among seventh and eighth grade girls, particularly girls of color from low-income families.

Anjalé D. Welton is an assistant professor in education, policy, organization and leadership at the University of Illinois at Urbana-Champaign. Welton examines how opportunity structures (e.g., issues of stratification, access to college preparation and information) shape connections students of color make to educational resources and matriculate to college. Other research areas include the politics of equity as it pertains to race and diversity in school reform and improvement as well as youth voice in the school improvement process. Welton is published in *Teachers College Record, Journal of School Leadership, Education and Urban Society, Negro Educational Review, Journal of Educational Administration, The Urban Review,* and *Educational Administration Quarterly,* among others. Her professional experiences include being coordinator of a leadership and empowerment program for urban youth, a facilitator of an urban education teacher preparation program, and a teacher in large urban districts. Dr. Welton is also committed to providing professional development for educational leaders on issues of equity and diversity. Dr. Welton received her PhD in educational policy and planning from the University of Texas at Austin.